D1587625

THE THEORY OF THE THEATRE
AND OTHER PRINCIPLES OF
DRAMATIC CRITICISM

THE THEORY OF THE THEATRE

AND OTHER PRINCIPLES OF DRAMATIC CRITICISM

Consolidated Edition Including

THE THEORY OF THE THEATRE
STUDIES IN STAGECRAFT
PROBLEMS OF THE PLAYWRIGHT
SEEN ON THE STAGE

BY

CLAYTON HAMILTON

WITH A FOREWORD BY

BURNS MANTLE

OCTAGON BOOKS

A DIVISION OF FARRAR, STRAUS AND GIROUX

New York   1976

Reprinted 1976
by special arrangement with Holt, Rinehart and Winston, Inc.

OCTAGON BOOKS

A DIVISION OF FARRAR, STRAUS & GIROUX, INC.

19 Union Square West
New York, N.Y. 10003

Library of Congress Cataloging in Publication Data

Hamilton, Clayton Meeker, 1881-1946.
    The theory of the theatre and other principles of dramatic criti-
cism.

    Reprint of the 1939 ed. published by H. Holt, New York.
    1. Theater.   2. Drama—History and criticism.   3. Dramatic
criticism.   I. Title.

PN1631.H385   1976   792   76-39997
ISBN 0-374-93422-3

Manufactured by Braun-Brumfield, Inc.
Ann Arbor, Michigan
Printed in the United States of America

TO

THE MEMORY OF

BRANDER MATTHEWS

WHO FIRST AWAKENED MY CRITICAL INTEREST

IN THE THEORY OF THE THEATRE

PREFACE

INTO this single volume are consolidated most of the chapters which formerly were published in four different books, under the titles of *The Theory of the Theatre* [1910], *Studies in Stagecraft* [1914], *Problems of the Playwright* [1917], and *Seen on the Stage* [1920].

In effecting this consolidation, due respect has been paid (somewhat regretfully) to the tyranny of timeliness. Every chapter whose pertinence appeared to have been diminished by the passage of the years has been discarded; and several other chapters have been submitted to such drastic surgical operations as excision, revision, or amplification, in the hope of endowing them with at least a little longer lease of life.

The order of the remaining chapters has also been rearranged, in the interest of a more logical continuity of exposition.

In preparing this definitive edition, consolidated finally within the compass of a single volume, the author has made an earnest effort to pass down to future commentators the essence of his entire contribution to the theory of the theatre,—based upon an active interest in nearly every aspect of theatric art, which has been maintained unfalteringly through more than forty years.

C. H.

New York City, 1939.

CONTENTS

THE THEORY OF THE THEATRE

OTHER PRINCIPLES OF DRAMATIC CRITICISM

CONTENTS

STUDIES IN STAGECRAFT

PROBLEMS OF THE PLAYWRIGHT

CONTENTS

SEEN ON THE STAGE

FOREWORD
BY
BURNS MANTLE

FOREWORD

ORSON WELLES, a youthful but flaming outpost of the drama in 1937-38, startled a convention of school teachers by announcing in effect that the drama, long dying, had settled finally into a state approaching rigor mortis. Called to account for so sweeping a statement, Mr. Welles laughed merrily and explained that he did not mean exactly what the reporters had credited him with saying. He was, said Mr. Welles, merely sounding a warning. He was advising us, and reminding himself as well, that the theatre had died and could die again.

"The Theatre is in fact so healthy that we of the Theatre can afford the luxury of attacking it," concluded Mr. Welles.

It is always so in the end. No man, nor woman either, has ever been successful in killing the theatre to the point of making it stay dead. Even during that period of suspended animation preceding the Restoration there was a lively kicking beneath the shrouds. The theatre surrenders but never dies. This is the truth.

It is equally true that the fundamentals of the theatre change but little from generation to generation. This includes statements made in such forewords as this. Forms change and styles change in the theatre. We range from the bare stages of the Elizabethans to the bare stages of the Mercury Theatre. We travel from the frank vulgarities of the emboldened dramatists of Continental Europe to the equally frank but it may be more honest vulgarities of our own mice and men. The theatre is still the theatre. The drama is still the drama. Audiences are still dumb (according to the critics), and the critics are even dumber (according to the audiences).

The Theatre of Clayton Hamilton is the Theatre of approximately the last two generations. He approached this theatre with affection and studied it with enthusiasm through the eighteen-nineties. For twenty years extending from 1900 to 1920 he wrote of it appraisingly and critically for many thousands of readers and lectured about it to many hundreds of students at Columbia University, where he served as assistant to that revered commentator and teacher of drama, the late Brander Matthews. For the last fifteen years Mr. Hamilton has continued his observations in writing and lecturing. He knows the whole theatre of our time as few of its observers and critics know it.

If these particular Hamilton years do not represent any notable division of a modern golden age in the theatre, they were at least years of brave and interesting adventure in playgoing and playwriting. They brought to the fullness of their careers most of the actors and actresses, and many of the dramatists, whom we accept to-day as the high representatives of our theatre before it suffered such infiltrations and deletions as a mechanized theatrical art forced upon it. It is, I think, extremely important that the thought as well as the record associated with that theatre should be preserved. Mr. Hamilton, reverting to and reassembling in a proper sequence, his writings of the period, has made an outstanding contribution to this preservation.

In 1910 the first Hamilton book on the theatre was sent to the publisher. It was called *The Theory of the Theatre*. It opened with a chapter captioned "What Is a Play?", ranged through other chapters variously headed "The Psychology of Theatre Audiences," "Economy of Attention in Theatrical Performances," "The Public and the Dramatist," "The Boundaries of Approbation," etc., to a concluding chapter entitled "The Function of Imagination." These were the open-minded observations of an informed enthusiast, if informed enthusiasts are ever capable of a complete open-mindedness, and they present with satisfying vividness a picture of the drama's progress.

Four years later Mr. Hamilton issued a second book, *Studies in Stagecraft*, a companion work to his first book, but one, as he wrote, that dealt chiefly "with principles that seem destined to be bequeathed by the present to the future." Bearing upon and appertaining to this prophecy, *Studies in Stagecraft* was filled with pointed discussion and apt illustration pertaining to the changes then taking place in the theatre. These, in fact, were the changes then forming the foundations of such progress as we note with pride in the theatre of to-day. This volume ranged from "The New Art of Making Plays" through "The Modern Art of Stage Direction," "The Undramatic Drama," "A Plea for a New Type of

Play," etc., to that old, familiar and always interesting item, "The Function of Dramatic Criticism."

Opinions and convictions pressed in upon the drama critic of those active years in a changing theatre. It was only three years this time before the accumulated criticisms, observations, convictions and conclusions of the Hamilton mind demanded a further release. Then a third volume, *Problems of the Playwright*, appeared. Herein we find what I suppose may reasonably be spoken of to-day as the early modern drama represented by such onrushing geniuses of the time as Hauptmann and Maeterlinck, Pinero, Jones and Shaw, Brieux and Reinhardt, Ibsen and Björnson, Craig and D'Annunzio, with an American reflection modestly represented by Fitch and Thomas and a variety of still struggling and uncertain newcomers writing what might be termed *la comédie du jour*.

Finally, in 1920, after three years during which the stage of the world had been occupied with the bloodiest melodrama of our time, came a fourth Hamilton volume entitled *Seen on the Stage*, a collection of reviews of, and comments upon, those performances that had illumined the playwrighting, play-directing, play-acting of the period—a sort of résumé in terms of illustrative examples of what had taken place during twenty years of a significant and important period in our theatre history.

In this volume we come upon such chapters as "Personal Greatness on the Stage," with Sir Harry Lauder an outstanding example; "Hero-Worship in the Drama," with Drinkwater's *Abraham Lincoln* a chief subject; "Acting and Impersonation," to provide a picture of George Arliss' success; "The Laziness of Bernard Shaw," "Understanding the Russians," with evaluations of the drama of Gorki and Tolstoi, etc.

There has been a lapse of eighteen years since the last of the Clayton Hamilton books was issued. These eighteen years belong to still another period of theatre growth and of theatre decline. With them for the moment we have nothing to do, except insofar as they have influenced Mr. Hamilton in the reassembling and re-editing of this single new volume.

Herein the four book titles have been retained, but, in the cause, I assume, of a more logical continuity, the author has grouped under the title of *The Theory of the Theatre* such pieces as deal with general principles that apply to any period; under "Studies in

Stagecraft" such pieces as deal with principles that apply particularly to the present period; under "Problems of the Playwright" such pieces as deal with the technique of playmaking, and under "Seen on the Stage" such pieces as were written in review of certain great achievements.

It is, as I have written, important that a record of both the thought and the achievements of past periods in the theatre should be preserved. This condensation of one critic's writings and observations during a particular twenty years of playgoing and play-study provides a valuable record. It is, I think, fortunate that it should have been written by an able critic sufficiently detached from the rush of daily play reviewing to acquire a sane and balanced perspective.

Mr. Hamilton's work has been done as the conductor of departments of dramatic criticism in a variety of the better class magazines. He never has been called upon to treat the theatre as news, nor to review any of those weakling plays which, rightly or wrongly, suffer a quick extinction. His confessed endeavor to discover merit rather than to find fault has met with the approval of all who hold the theatre in both affection and high esteem. He has, I think, placed all students of the dramatic art, particularly, and all lovers of the theatre, in general, deeply in his debt by this contribution to current theatrical history.

BURNS MANTLE

THE THEORY OF THE THEATRE

1

WHAT IS A PLAY?

A PLAY is a story devised to be presented by actors on a stage before an audience.

This plain statement of fact affords an exceedingly simple definition of the drama,—a definition so simple indeed as to seem at the first glance easily obvious and therefore scarcely worthy of expression. But if we examine the statement thoroughly, phrase by phrase, we shall see that it sums up within itself the entire theory of the theatre, and that from this primary axiom we may deduce the whole practical philosophy of dramatic criticism.

It is unnecessary to linger long over an explanation of the word "story." A story is a representation of a series of events linked together by the law of cause and effect and marching forward toward a predestined culmination,—each event exhibiting imagined characters performing imagined acts in an appropriate imagined setting. This definition applies, of course, to the epic, the ballad, the novel, the short-story, and all other forms of narrative art, as well as to the drama.

But the phrase "devised to be presented" distinguishes the drama sharply from all other forms of narrative. In particular it must be noted that a play is not a story that is written to be read. By no means must the drama be considered primarily as a department of literature,—like the epic or the novel, for example. Rather, from the standpoint of the theatre, should literary method be considered as only one of a multitude of means which the dramatist must employ to convey his story effectively to the audience. The great Greek dramatists needed a sense of sculpture as well as a sense of poetry; and in the contemporary theatre the playwright must manifest the imagination of the painter as well as the imagination of the man of letters. The appeal of a play is primarily visual rather

3

than auditory. On the contemporary stage, characters properly costumed must be exhibited within a carefully designed and painted setting illuminated with appropriate effects of light and shadow; and the art of music is often called upon to render incidental aid to the general impression. The dramatist, therefore, must be endowed not only with the literary sense, but also with a clear eye for the graphic and plastic elements of pictorial effect, a sense of rhythm and of music, and a thorough knowledge of the art of acting. Since the dramatist must, at the same time and in the same work, harness and harmonise the methods of so many of the arts, it would be uncritical to centre studious consideration solely on his dialogue and to praise him or condemn him on the literary ground alone.

It is, of course, true that the very greatest plays have always been great literature as well as great drama. The purely literary element—the final touch of style in dialogue—is the only sure antidote against the opium of time. Now that Æschylus is no longer performed regularly as a playwright, we read him as a poet. But, on the other hand, we should remember that the main reason why he is rarely played to-day is that his dramas do not fit the modern theatre,—an edifice totally different in size and shape and physical appointments from that in which his pieces were devised to be presented. In his own day he was not so much read as a poet as applauded in the theatre as a playwright; and properly to appreciate his dramatic, rather than his literary, appeal, we must reconstruct in our imagination the conditions of the theatre in his day. The point is that his plays, though planned primarily as drama, have since been shifted over, by many generations of critics and literary students, into the adjacent province of poetry; and this shift of the critical point of view, which has insured the immortality of Æschylus, has been made possible only by the literary merit of his dialogue. When a play, owing to altered physical conditions, is tossed out of the theatre, it will find a haven in the closet only if it be greatly written. From this fact we may derive the practical maxim that though a skilful playwright need not write greatly in order to secure the plaudits of his own generation, he must cultivate a literary excellence if he wishes to be remembered by posterity.

This much must be admitted concerning the ultimate importance of the literary element in the drama. But on the other hand it must be granted that many plays that stand very high as drama do not fall within the range of literature. A typical example is the famous melodrama by Dennery entitled *The Two Orphans*. This play has deservedly held the stage for more than half a century, and bids fair still to be applauded after the youngest critic has died. It is undeniably a very good play. It tells a thrilling story in a series of carefully graded theatric situations. It presents nearly a dozen acting parts which, though scarcely real as characters, are yet drawn with sufficient fidelity to fact to allow the performers to produce a striking illusion of reality during the two hours' traffic of the stage. It is, to be sure—especially in the standard English translation—abominably written. One of the two orphans launches wide-eyed upon a soliloquy beginning, "Am I mad? . . . Do I dream?"; and such sentences as the following obtrude themselves upon the astounded ear,—"If you persist in persecuting me in this heartless manner, I shall inform the police." Nothing, surely, could be further from literature. Yet thrill after thrill is conveyed, by visual means, through situations artfully contrived; and in the sheer excitement of the moment, the audience is made incapable of noticing the pompous mediocrity of the lines.

In general, it should be frankly understood by students of the theatre that an audience is not capable of hearing whether the dialogue of a play is well or badly written. Such a critical discrimination would require an extraordinary nicety of ear, and might easily be led astray, in one direction or the other, by the reading of the actors. The rhetoric of Massinger must have sounded like poetry to an Elizabethan audience that had heard the same performers, the afternoon before, speaking lines of Shakespeare's. When Sir Johnston Forbes-Robertson read a poorly-written part, it was hard to hear that the lines were, in themselves, not musical. Literary style is, even for accomplished critics, very difficult to judge in the theatre. Many years ago, Mrs. Fiske presented in New York an English adaptation of Paul Heyse's *Mary of Magdala*. After the first performance—at which I did not happen to be present—I asked several cultivated people who had heard the play whether the English version was written in verse or in prose; and though these people were themselves actors and men of letters, not one of them could tell me. Yet, as appeared later, when the play was published, the English dialogue was written in blank verse by no less accomplished a poet than William Winter. If such an elementary distinction as that between verse and prose was in this case inaudible to cultivated ears, how much harder must it be for the average audience to distinguish between a good phrase and a bad! The fact is that literary style is, for the most part, wasted on an audience. The average auditor is moved mainly by the emotional content of a sentence spoken on the stage, and pays very little attention to the form of words in which the meaning is set forth. At Hamlet's line, "Absent thee from felicity a while" —which Matthew Arnold, with impeccable taste, selected as one of his touchstones of literary style—the thing that really moves the audience in the theatre is not the perfectness of the phrase but the pathos of Hamlet's plea for his best friend to outlive him and explain his motives to a world grown harsh.

That the content rather than the literary turn of dialogue is the thing that counts most in the theatre will be felt emphatically if we compare the mere writing of Molière with that of his successor and imitator, Regnard. Molière is certainly a great writer, in the sense that he expresses clearly and precisely the thing he has to say; his verse, as well as his prose, is admirably lucid and eminently speakable. But assuredly, in the sense in which the word is generally used, Molière is not a poet; and it may fairly be said that, in the usual connotation of the term, he has no style. Regnard, on the other hand, is more nearly a poet, and, from the standpoint of style, writes vastly better verse. He has a lilting fluency that flowers every now and then into a phrase of golden melody. Yet Molière is so immeasurably his superior as a playwright that most critics instinctively set Regnard far below him even as a writer. There can be no question that Edmond Rostand wrote better verse than Emile Augier; but there can be no question, also, that Augier was, on the whole, the greater dramatist. Oscar Wilde probably wrote more clever and witty lines than any other author in the whole history of English comedy; but no one would think of setting him in the class with Congreve and Sheridan.

It is by no means my intention to suggest that great writing is not desirable in the drama; but the point must be emphasised that it is not a necessary element in the immediate merit of a play *as a play*. In fact, excellent plays have often been presented without the use of any words at all. Pantomime has, in every age, been recognised as a legitimate department of the drama. Several years ago, Mme. Charlotte Wiehe acted in New York a one-act play, entitled *La Main*, which held the attention enthralled for forty-five minutes during which no word was spoken. The little piece told a thrilling story with entire clearness and coherence, and exhibited three characters fully and distinctly drawn; and it secured this achievement by visual means alone, with no recourse whatever to the spoken word. Here was a work which by no stretch of terminology could have been included in the category of literature; and yet it was a very good play, and *as drama* was far superior to many a literary masterpiece in dialogue like Browning's *In a Balcony*.

Lest this instance seem too exceptional to be taken as representative, let us remember that throughout an entire important period in the history of the stage, it was customary for the actors to improvise the lines that they spoke before the audience. I refer to the period of the so-called *commedia dell' arte*, which flourished all over Italy throughout the sixteenth century. A synopsis of the play—partly narrative and partly expository—was posted up behind the scenes. This account of what was to happen on the stage was known technically as a *scenario*. The actors consulted this scenario before they made an entrance, and then in the acting of the scene spoke whatever words occurred to them. Harlequin made love to Columbine and quarreled with Pantaloon in new lines every night; and the drama gained both spontaneity and freshness from the fact that it was created anew at each performance. Undoubtedly, if an actor scored with a clever line, he would remember it for use in a subsequent presentation; and in this way the dialogue of a comedy must gradually have become more or less fixed and, in a sense, written. But this secondary task of formulating the dialogue was left to the performers; and the playwright contented himself with the primary task of planning the plot.

The case of the *commedia dell' arte* is, of course, extreme; but it emphasises the fact that the problem of the dramatist is less a task of writing than a task of constructing. His primary concern is so to build a story that it will tell itself to the eye of the audience in a series of shifting pictures. Any really good play can, to a great extent, be appreciated even though it be acted in a foreign language. American students in New York may find in the Yiddish dramas of the East Side an emphatic illustration of how closely a piece may be followed by an auditor who does not understand the words of a single line. *Hamlet*, that masterpiece of meditative poetry, would still be a good play if it were shown in motion pictures. Much, of course, would be sacrificed through the subversion of its literary element; but its essential interest *as a play* would yet remain apparent through the unassisted power of its visual appeal.

There can be no question that, however important may be the dialogue of a drama, the scenario is even more important; and from a full scenario alone, before a line of dialogue is written, it is possible in most cases to determine whether a prospective play is inherently good or bad. Most contemporary dramatists, therefore, postpone the actual writing of their dialogue until they have worked out their scenario in minute detail. They begin by separating and grouping their narrative materials into not more than three or four distinct pigeon-holes of time and place,—thereby dividing their story roughly into acts. They then plan a stage-setting for each act, employing whatever accessories may be necessary for the action. If papers are to be burned, they introduce a fireplace; if somebody is to throw a pistol through a window, they set the window in a convenient and emphatic place; they determine how many chairs and tables and settees are demanded for the narrative; if a piano or a bed is needed, they place it here or there upon the floor-plan of their stage, according to the prominence they wish to give it; and when all such points as these have been determined, they draw a detailed map of the stage-setting for the act. As their next step, most playwrights, with this map before them, and using a set of chess-men or other convenient concrete objects to represent their characters, move the pieces about upon the stage through the successive scenes, determine in detail where every character is to stand or sit at nearly every moment, and note down what he is to think and feel and talk about at the time. Only after the entire play has been planned out thus minutely does the average playwright turn back to the beginning and commence to write his dialogue. He completes his primary task of play-making before he begins his secondary task of play-writing. Many of our established dramatists—like the late Clyde Fitch, for example—sell their plays when the scenario is finished, arrange for the production, select the actors, and afterwards write the dialogue with the chosen actors constantly in mind.

This summary statement of the usual process may seem, perhaps, to cast excessive emphasis on the constructive phase of the playwright's problem; and allowance must of course be made for the divergent mental habits of individual authors. But almost any playwright will tell you that he feels as if his task were practically finished when he arrives at the point when he finds himself prepared to begin the writing of his dialogue. This accounts for the otherwise unaccountable rapidity with which many of the great plays of the world have been written. Dumas *fils* retired to the country and wrote *La Dame aux Camélias*—a four-act play—in eight successive days. But he had previously told the same story in a novel; he knew everything that was to happen in his play; and the mere writing could be done in a single headlong dash. Voltaire's best tragedy, *Zaïre*, was written in three weeks. Victor Hugo composed *Marion Delorme* between June 1 and June 24, 1829; and when the piece was interdicted by the censor, he immediately turned to another subject and wrote *Hernani* in the next three weeks. The fourth act of *Marion Delorme* was written in a single day. Here apparently was a very fever of composition. But again we must remember that both of these plays had been devised before the author began to write them; and when he took his pen in hand he had already been working on them in scenario for probably a year. To write ten acts in Alexandrines, with feminine rhymes alternating with masculine, was still, to be sure, an appalling task; but Hugo was a facile and prolific poet and could write very quickly after he had determined exactly what it was he had to write.

It was with all of the foregoing points in mind that, in the opening sentence of this chapter, I defined a play as a story "devised," rather than a story "written." We may now consider the significance of the next phrase of that definition, which states that a play is devised to be "presented," rather than to be "read."

The only way in which it is possible to study most of the great plays of bygone ages is to read the record of their dialogue; and this necessity has led to the academic fallacy of considering great plays primarily as compositions to be read. In their own age, however, these very plays which we now read in the closet were intended primarily to be presented on the stage. Really to read a play requires a very special and difficult exercise of visual imagination. It is necessary not only to appreciate the dialogue, but also to project before the mind's eye a vivid imagined rendition of the visual aspect of the action. This is the reason why most managers and stage-directors are unable to judge conclusively the merits and defects of a new play from reading it in manuscript. One of our most subtle artists in stage-direction, the late Henry Miller, once confessed to the present writer that he could never decide whether a prospective play was good or bad until he had seen it rehearsed by actors on a stage. Augustus Thomas's unusually successful farce entitled *Mrs. Leffingwell's Boots* was considered a failure by its producing managers until the very last rehearsals, because it depended for its finished effect on many intricate and rapid intermovements of the actors, which until the last moment were understood and realised only in the mind of the playwright. The same author's best and most successful play, *The Witching Hour*, was declined by several managers before it was ultimately accepted for production; and the reason was, presumably, that its extraordinary merits were not manifest from a mere reading of the lines. In 1929 the Pulitzer Prize was won by Elmer Rice, with *Street Scene*, a play so extraordinarily successful that it crowded the theatre every night for nearly an entire year; yet, before this piece was accepted by the veteran William A. Brady, it had been rejected by twenty managers of established reputation, all of whom reported that it was devoid of any "box-office value." If professional producers may go so far astray in their judgment of the merits of a manuscript, how much harder must it be for the layman to judge a play solely from a reading of the dialogue!

This fact should lead the professors and the students in our colleges to adopt a very tentative attitude toward judging the dramatic merits of the plays of other ages. Shakespeare, considered as a poet, is so immeasurably superior to Dryden, that it is difficult for the college student unfamiliar with the theatre to realise that the former's *Antony and Cleopatra* is, considered solely as a play, far inferior to the latter's dramatisation of the same story, entitled *All for Love, or The World Well Lost*. Shakespeare's play upon this subject follows closely the chronology of Plutarch's narrative, and is merely dramatised history; but Dryden's play is reconstructed with a more practical sense of economy and emphasis, and deserves to be regarded as historical drama. *Cymbeline* is, in many passages, so greatly written that it is hard for the closet-student to realise that it is a bad play, even when considered from the standpoint of the Elizabethan theatre,—whereas *Othello* and

Macbeth, for instance, are great plays, not only of their age but for all time. *King Lear* is probably a more sublime poem than *Othello*; and it is only by seeing the two pieces performed equally well in the theatre that we can appreciate by what a wide margin *Othello* is the better play.

This practical point has been felt emphatically by the very greatest dramatists; and this fact offers, of course, an explanation of the otherwise inexplicable negligence of such authors as Shakespeare and Molière in the matter of publishing their plays. These supreme playwrights wanted people to see their pieces in the theatre rather than to read them in the closet. In his own lifetime, Shakespeare, who was very scrupulous about the publication of his sonnets and his narrative poems, printed a carefully edited text of his plays only when he was forced, in self-defense, to do so, by the prior appearance of corrupt and pirated editions; and we owe our present knowledge of several of his dramas merely to the business acumen of two actors who, seven years after his death, conceived the practical idea that they might turn an easy penny by printing and offering for sale the text of several popular plays which the public had already seen performed. Sardou, who, like most French dramatists, began by publishing his plays, carefully withheld from print the master-efforts of his prime; and even such dramatists as habitually print their plays prefer nearly always to have them seen first and read only afterwards.

In elucidation of what might otherwise seem perversity on the part of great dramatic authors like Shakespeare, we must remember that the master-dramatists have nearly always been men of the theatre rather than men of letters, and therefore naturally more avid of immediate success with a contemporary audience than of posthumous success with a posterity of readers. Shakespeare and Molière were actors and theatre-managers, and devised their plays primarily for the patrons of the Globe and the Palais Royal. Ibsen, who is often taken as a type of the literary dramatist, derived his early training mainly from the profession of the theatre and hardly at all from the profession of letters. For half a dozen years, during the formative period of his twenties, he acted as producing manager of the National Theatre in Bergen, and learned the tricks of his trade from studying the masterpieces of contemporary drama, mainly of the French school. In his own work, he began, in such pieces as *Lady Inger of Östrat*, by imitating and applying the formulas of Scribe and the earlier Sardou; and it was only after many years that he marched forward to a technique entirely his own. Both Sir Arthur Wing Pinero and Stephen Phillips began their theatrical careers as actors. On the other hand, men of letters who have written works primarily to be read have almost never succeeded as dramatists. In England, during the nineteenth century, the following great poets all tried their hands at plays—Scott, Southey, Wordsworth, Coleridge, Byron, Shelley, Keats, Browning, Mrs. Browning, Matthew Arnold, Swinburne, and Tennyson —and not one of them produced a work of any considerable value from the standpoint of dramatic criticism. Tennyson, in *Becket*, came nearer to the mark than any of the others; and it is noteworthy that, in this work, he had the advantage of the advice and, in a sense, collaboration of Sir Henry Irving.

The familiar phrase "closet-drama" is a contradiction of terms. The species of literary composition in dialogue that is ordinarily so designated occupies a thoroughly legitimate position in the realm of literature, but no position whatsoever in the realm of dramaturgy. *Atalanta in Calydon* is a great poem; but, from the standpoint of the theory of the theatre, it cannot be considered as a play. Like the lyric poems of the same author, it was written to be read; and it was not devised to be presented by actors on a stage before an audience.

We may now consider the significance of the three concluding phrases of the definition of a play which was offered at the outset of the present chapter. These phrases indicate the immanence of three influences by which the work of the playwright is constantly conditioned.

In the first place, by the fact that the dramatist is devising his story for the use of actors, he is definitely limited both in respect to the kind of characters he may create and in respect to the means he may employ in order to delineate them. In actual life we meet characters of two different classes, which (borrowing a pair of adjectives from the terminology of physics) we may denominate dynamic characters and static characters. But when an actor appears upon the stage, he wants to act; and the dramatist is therefore obliged to confine his attention to dynamic characters, and to exclude static characters almost entirely from the range of his creation. The essential trait of all dynamic characters is the preponderance within them of the element of will; and the persons of a play must therefore be people with active wills and emphatic intentions. When such people are brought into juxtaposition, there necessarily results a clash of contending desires and purposes; and by this fact we are led logically to the conclusion that the proper subject-matter of the drama is a struggle between contrasted human wills. The same conclusion, as we shall notice in the next chapter, may be reached logically by deduction from the natural demands of an assembled audience; and the subject will be discussed more fully during the course of our study of *The Psychology of Theatre Audiences*. At present it is sufficient for us to note that nearly every great play that has ever been devised has presented some phase or other of this single, almost necessary, theme,—a contention of individual human wills. An actor, moreover, is always more effective in scenes of emotion than in scenes of cold logic and calm reason; and the dramatist, therefore, is obliged to select as his leading figures people whose acts are motivated by emotion rather than by intellect. Aristotle, for example, would make a totally uninteresting figure if he were presented faithfully upon the stage. Who could imagine Darwin as the hero of a drama? Othello, on the other hand, is not at all a reasonable being; from first to last his intellect is "perplexed in the extreme." His emotions are the motives for his acts; and in this he may be taken as the type of a dramatic character.

In the means of delineating the characters he has imagined, the dramatist, because he is writing for actors, is more narrowly restricted than the novelist. His people must constantly be doing something, and must therefore reveal themselves mainly through their acts. They may, of course, also be delineated through their way of saying things; but in the theatre the objective action is always more suggestive than the spoken word. We know Sherlock Holmes, in William Gillette's admirable melodrama, solely through the things that we have seen him do; and in this connection we should remember that in the stories by Sir Arthur Conan Doyle from which Mr. Gillette derived his narrative material, Holmes was delineated largely by a very different method,—the method, namely, of expository comment written from the point of view of Doctor Watson. A leading actor seldom wants to sit in his dressing-room while he is being talked about by the other actors on the stage; and therefore the method of drawing character by comment, which is so useful for the novelist, is rarely employed by the playwright except in the waste moments which precede the first entrance of his leading figure. The Chorus Lady, in James Forbes's amusing study of that name, was drawn chiefly through her way of saying things; but though this method of delineation is sometimes very effective for an act or two, it can seldom be sustained without a faltering of interest through a full-grown four-act play. The novelist's expedient of delineating character through mental analysis is of course denied the dramatist, especially in this modern age when the soliloquy (for reasons which will be noted in a subsequent chapter) is usually frowned upon. Sometimes, in the theatre, a character may be exhibited chiefly through his personal effect upon the other people on the stage, and thereby indirectly on the people in the audience. It was in this way, of course, that Manson was delineated in Mr. Charles Rann Kennedy's *The Servant in the House.* But the expedient is a dangerous one for the dramatist to use; because it makes his work immediately dependent on the actor chosen for the leading role, and may in many cases render his play impossible of attaining its full effect except at the hands of a single great performer. In recent years an expedient long familiar in the novel has been transferred to the service of the stage,—the expedient, namely, of suggesting the personality of a character through a visual presentation of his habitual environment. After the curtain had been raised upon the first act of *The Music Master,* and the audience had been given time to look about the room which was represented on the stage, the main traits of the leading character had already been suggested before his first appearance on the scene. The pictures and knick-knacks on his mantelpiece told us, before we ever saw him, what manner of man he was. But such subtle means as this can, after all, be used only to reinforce the one standard method of conveying the sense of character in drama; and this one method, owing to the conditions under which the playwright does his work, must always be the exhibition of objective acts.

In all these general ways the work of the dramatist is affected by the fact that he must devise his story to be presented by actors. The specific influence exerted over the playwright by the individual performer is a subject too extensive to be covered by a mere summary consideration in the present context; and we shall therefore discuss it fully in a later chapter, entitled *The Actor and the Dramatist.*

At present we must pass on to observe that, in the second place, the work of the dramatist is conditioned by the fact that he must plan his plays to fit the sort of theatre that stands ready to receive them. A fundamental and necessary relation has always existed between theatre-building and theatric art. The best plays of any period have been fashioned in accordance with the physical conditions of the best theatres of that period. Therefore, in order fully to appreciate such a play as *Œdipus King*, it is necessary to imagine the theatre of Dionysus; and in order to understand thoroughly the dramaturgy of Shakespeare and Molière, it is necessary to reconstruct in retrospect the altered inn-yard and the converted tennis-court for which they planned their plays. It may seriously be doubted that the works of these earlier masters gain more than they lose from being produced with the elaborate scenic accessories of the modern stage; and, on the other hand, a modern play by Ibsen or Pinero or O'Casey or O'Neill would lose three-fourths of its effect if it were acted in the Elizabethan manner, or produced without scenery (let us say) in the Roman theatre at Orange.

Since, in all ages, the size and shape and physical appointments of the theatre have determined for the playwright the form and structure of his plays, we may always explain the stock conventions of any period of the drama by referring to the physical aspect of the theatre in that period. Let us consider briefly, for purposes of illustration, certain obvious ways in which the art of the great Greek tragic dramatists was affected by the nature of the Attic stage. The theatre of Dionysus was an enormous edifice carved out of a hillside. It was so large that the dramatists were obliged to deal only with subjects that were traditional,—stories which had long been familiar to the entire theatre-going public, including the poorer and less educated spectators who sat farthest from the actors. Since most of the audience was grouped above the stage and at a considerable distance, the actors, in order not to appear dwarfed, were obliged to walk on stilted boots. A performer so accoutred could not move impetuously or enact a scene of violence; and this practical limitation is sufficient to account for the measured and majestic movement of Greek tragedy, and the convention that murders and other violent deeds must always be imagined off the stage and be merely recounted to the audience by messengers. Facial expression could not be seen in so large a theatre; and the actors therefore wore masks, conventionalised to represent the dominant mood of a character during a scene. This limitation forced the performer to depend for his effect mainly on his voice; and Greek tragedy was therefore necessarily more lyrical than later types of drama.

The few points which we have briefly touched upon are usually explained, by academic critics, on literary grounds; but it is surely more sane to explain them on grounds of common sense, in the light of what we know of the conditions of the Attic stage. Similarly, it would be easy to show how Plautus and Calderon, Shakespeare and Molière, adapted the form of their plays to the form of their theatres; but enough has already been said to indicate the principle which underlies this particular phase of the theory of the theatre. The successive changes in the physical aspect of the English theatre during the last three centuries have all tended toward greater naturalness, intimacy, and subtlety, in the drama itself and in the physical aids to its presentment. This progress, with its constant illustration of the interdependence of the drama and the stage, may most conveniently be studied in historical review; and to such a review we shall devote a special chapter, entitled *Stage Conventions in Modern Times.*

We may now observe that, in the third place, the essential nature of the drama is affected greatly by the fact that it is destined to be set before an audience. The dramatist must appeal at once to a heterogeneous multitude of people; and the full effect of this condition will be investigated in a special chapter on *The Psychology of Theatre Audiences.* In an important sense, the audience is a party to the play and collaborates with the actors in the presentation. This fact, which remains often unappreciated by academic critics, is familiar to everyone who has had any practical association with the theatre. It is almost never possible, even for trained dramatic critics, to tell from a final dress-rehearsal in an empty house which scenes of a new play are fully effective and which are not; and the reason why, in America, new plays are tried out on the road is not so much to give the actors practice in their parts, as to determine, from the effect of the piece upon provincial audiences, whether it is worthy of a metropolitan presentation. The point is, as we shall notice in the next chapter, that since a play is devised for a crowd it cannot finally be judged by individuals.

The dependence of the dramatist upon his audience may be

illustrated by the history of many important plays, which, though effective in their own age, have become ineffective for later generations, solely because they were founded on certain general principles of conduct in which the world has subsequently ceased to believe. From the point of view of its own period, *The Maid's Tragedy* of Beaumont and Fletcher is undoubtedly one of the very greatest of Elizabethan plays; but it would be ineffective in the modern theatre, because it presupposes a principle which a contemporary audience would not accept. It was devised for an audience of aristocrats in the reign of James I, and the dramatic struggle is founded upon the doctrine of the divine right of kings. Amintor, in the play, has suffered a profound personal injury at the hands of his sovereign; but he cannot avenge this individual disgrace, because he is a subject of the royal malefactor. The crisis and turning-point of the entire drama is a scene in which Amintor, with the king at his mercy, lowers his sword with the words:—

> But there is
> Divinity about you, that strikes dead
> My rising passions: as you are my king,
> I fall before you, and present my sword
> To cut mine own flesh, if it be your will.

We may imagine the applause of the courtiers of James Stuart, the Presumptuous; but never since the Cromwellian revolution has that scene been really effective on the English stage. In order fully to appreciate a dramatic struggle, an audience must sympathise with the motives that occasion it.

It should now be evident, as was suggested at the outset, that all the leading principles of the theory of the theatre may be deduced logically from the axiom which was stated in the first sentence of this chapter; and that axiom should constantly be borne in mind as the basis of all our subsequent discussions. But in view of several important points which have already come up for consideration, it may be profitable, before relinquishing our initial question, to redefine a play more fully in the following terms:—

A play is a representation, by actors, on a stage, before an audience, of a struggle between individual human wills, motivated by emotion rather than by intellect, and expressed in terms of objective action.

II

THE PSYCHOLOGY OF THEATRE AUDIENCES

I

THE DRAMA is the only art, excepting oratory and certain forms of music, that is designed to appeal to a crowd instead of to an individual. The lyric poet writes for himself, and for such selected persons here and there throughout the world as may be wisely sympathetic enough to understand his musings. The essayist and the novelist write for a reader sitting alone in his library: whether ten such readers or a hundred thousand ultimately read a book, the writer speaks to each of them apart from all the others. It is the same with painting and with sculpture. Though a picture or a statue may be seen by a limitless succession of observers, its appeal is made always to the individual mind. But it is different with a play. Since a drama is, in essence, a story devised to be presented by actors on a stage before an audience, it must necessarily be designed to appeal at once to a multitude of people. We have to be alone in order to appreciate the *Venus of Melos* or the *Sistine Madonna* or the *Ode to a Nightingale* or the *Egoist* or the *Religio Medici;* but who could sit alone in a wide theatre and see *Cyrano de Bergerac* performed? The sympathetic presence of a multitude of people would be as necessary to our appreciation of the play as solitude in all the other cases. And because the drama must be written for a crowd, it must be fashioned differently from the other, and less popular, forms of art.

No writer is really a dramatist unless he recognises this distinction of appeal; and if an author is not accustomed to writing for the crowd, he can hardly hope to make a satisfying play. Tennyson, the perfect poet; Browning, the master of the human mind; Stevenson, the teller of enchanting tales:—each of them failed when

18

he tried to make a drama, because the conditions of his proper art had schooled him long in writing for the individual instead of for the crowd. A literary artist who writes for the individual may produce a great work of literature that is cast in the dramatic form; but the work will not be, in the practical sense, a play. *Samson Agonistes, Faust, Pippa Passes, Peer Gynt,* and the early dream-dramas of Maurice Maeterlinck, are something else than plays. They are not devised to be presented by actors on a stage before an audience. As a work of literature, *A Blot in the 'Scutcheon* is immeasurably greater than *The Two Orphans;* but as a play, it is immeasurably less. For even though, in this particular piece, Browning did try to write for the theatre (at the suggestion of Macready), he employed the same intricately intellectual method of character analysis that has made many of his poems the most solitude-compelling of modern literary works. Properly to appreciate his piece, you must be alone, just as you must be alone to read *A Woman's Last Word.* It is not written for a crowd; *The Two Orphans,* less weighty in wisdom, is. The second is a play.

The mightiest masters of the drama—Sophocles, Shakespeare, and Molière—have recognised the popular character of its appeal and written frankly for the multitude. The crowd, therefore, has exercised a potent influence upon the dramatist in every era of the theatre. One person the lyric poet has to please,—himself; to a single person only, or an unlimited succession of single persons, does the novelist address himself, and he may choose the sort of person he will write for; but the dramatist must always please the many. His themes, his thoughts, his emotions, are circumscribed by the limits of popular appreciation. He writes less freely than any other author; for he cannot pick his auditors. The fastidious Henry James might, if he chose, write novels for the super-civilised; but a crowd is never super-civilised, and therefore characters like those of Henry James could never be successfully presented in the theatre.

In order, therefore, to understand the limitations of the drama as an art and clearly to define its scope, it is necessary to inquire into the psychology of theatre audiences. This subject presents two phases to the student. First, a theatre audience exhibits certain psychological traits that are common to all crowds, of whatever kind,—a political convention, the spectators at a ball-game, or a church congregation, for example. Second, it exhibits certain other traits which distinguish it from other kinds of crowds. These, in turn, will be considered in the present chapter.

II

By the word *crowd*, as it is used in this discussion, is meant a multitude of people whose ideas and feelings have taken a set in a certain single direction, and who, because of this, exhibit a tendency to lose their individual self-consciousness in the general self-consciousness of the multitude. Any gathering of people for a specific purpose—whether of action or of worship or of amusement—tends to become, because of this purpose, a *crowd*, in the scientific sense. Now, a crowd has a mind of its own, apart from that of any of its individual members. The psychology of the crowd was little understood until late in the nineteenth century, when a great deal of attention was turned to it by a group of French philosophers. The subject has been most fully studied by Gustave Le Bon, who devoted some two hundred pages to his *Psychologie des Foules*. According to M. Le Bon, a man, by the mere fact that he forms a factor of a crowd, tends to lose consciousness of those mental qualities in which he differs from his fellows and becomes more keenly conscious of those other mental qualities in which he is at one with them. The mental qualities in which men differ from one another are the acquired qualities of intellect and character; but the qualities in which they are at one are the innate basic passions of the race. A crowd, therefore, is less intellectual and more emotional than the individuals that compose it. It is less reasonable, less judicious, less disinterested, more credulous, more primitive, more partisan; and hence, as M. Le Bon cleverly puts it, a man, by the mere fact that he forms a part of an organised crowd, is likely to descend several rungs on the ladder of civilisation. Even the most cultured and intellectual of men, when he forms an atom of a crowd, tends to lose consciousness of his acquired mental qualities and to revert to his primal simplicity and sensitiveness of mind.

The dramatist, therefore, because he writes for a crowd, writes for a comparatively uncivilised and uncultivated mind, a mind richly human, vehement in approbation, emphatic in disapproval, easily credulous, eagerly enthusiastic, boyishly heroic, and somewhat carelessly unthinking. Now, it has been found in practice that the only thing that will keenly interest a crowd is a struggle of some sort or other. Speaking empirically, Ferdinand Brunetière, in 1893, stated that the drama has dealt always with a struggle between human wills; and his statement, formulated in the catch-phrase, "No struggle, no drama," has since become a common-place of dramatic criticism. But, so far as I know, no one has yet realised the main reason for this, which is, simply, that characters are interesting to a crowd only in those crises of emotion that bring them to the grapple. A single individual, like the reader of an essay or a novel, may be interested intellectually in those gentle influences beneath which a character unfolds itself as mildly as a water-lily; but to what Thackeray called "that savage child, the crowd," a character does not appeal except in moments of conten-tion. There never yet has been a time when the theatre could compete successfully against the amphitheatre. Plautus and Ter-ence complained that the Roman public preferred a gladiatorial combat to their plays; a bear-baiting or a cock-fight used to empty Shakespeare's theatre on the Bankside; and there is not a matinée in town to-day that can hold its own against a foot-ball game. Seventy thousand people gather annually from all quarters of the East to see Yale and Harvard meet upon the field, while such a crowd could not be aggregated from New York to see the great-est play the world has yet produced. For the crowd demands a fight; and where the actual exists, it will scarcely be contented with the semblance.

Hence the drama, to interest at all, must cater to this longing for contention, which is one of the primordial instincts of the crowd. It must present its characters in some struggle of the wills, whether it be flippant, as in the case of Benedick and Beatrice; or delicate, as in that of Viola and Orsino; or terrible, with Macbeth; or piteous, with Lear. The crowd is more partisan than the indi-vidual; and therefore, in following this struggle of the drama, it desires always to take sides. There is no fun in seeing a foot-ball game unless you care about who wins; and there is very little fun in seeing a play unless the dramatist allows you to throw your sympathies on one side or the other of the struggle. Hence, al-though in actual life both parties to a conflict are often partly right and partly wrong and it is hard to choose between them, the dramatist usually simplifies the struggle in his plays by throwing the balance of right strongly on one side. Hence, from the ethical standpoint, the simplicity of theatre characters. Desdemona is all

innocence, Iago all deviltry. Hence also the conventional heroes
and villains of melodrama,—these to be hissed and those to be applauded. Since the crowd is comparatively lacking in the judicial
faculty and cannot look upon a play from a detached and disinterested point of view, it is either all for or all against a character;
and in either case its judgment is frequently in defiance of the
rules of reason. It will hear no word against Camille, though an
individual would judge her to be wrong, and it has no sympathy
with Père Duval. It wants its sympathetic characters, to love; its
antipathetic characters, to hate; and it hates and loves them as un-
reasonably as a savage or a child. The trouble with *Hedda Gabler*
as a play is that it contains not a single personage that the audience
can love. The crowd demands those so-called "sympathetic" parts
that every actor, for this reason, longs to represent. And since the
crowd is partisan, it wants its favored characters to win. Hence
the convention of the "happy ending," insisted on by managers
who feel the pulse of the public. The blind Louise, in *The Two
Orphans*, will get her sight back, never fear. Even the wicked
Oliver, in *As You Like It*, must turn over a new leaf and marry
a pretty girl.

Next to this prime instinct of partisanship in watching a contention, one of the most important traits in the psychology of
crowds is their extreme credulity. A crowd will nearly always believe anything that it sees and almost anything that it is told. An
audience composed entirely of individuals who have no belief in
ghosts will yet accept the Ghost in *Hamlet* as a fact. Bless you,
they have *seen* him! The crowd accepts the disguise of Rosalind,
and never wonders why Orlando does not recognise his love. To
this extreme credulity of the crowd is due the long line of plays
that are founded on mistaken identity,—farces like *The Comedy
of Errors* and melodramas like *The Lyons Mail*, for example. The
crowd, too, will accept without demur any condition precedent
to the story of a play, however impossible it might seem to the
mind of the individual. Œdipus King has been married to his
mother many years before the play begins; but the Greek crowd
forbore to ask why, in so long a period, the enormity had never
been discovered. The central situation of *She Stoops to Conquer*
seems impossible to the individual mind, but is eagerly accepted
by the crowd. Individual critics find fault with Thomas Heywood's lovely old play, *A Woman Killed with Kindness*, on the

ground that though Frankford's noble forgiveness of his erring wife is beautiful to contemplate, Mrs. Frankford's infidelity is not sufficiently motivated, and the whole story, therefore, is untrue. But Heywood, writing for the crowd, said frankly, "If you will grant that Mrs. Frankford was unfaithful, I can tell you a lovely story about her husband, who was a gentleman worth knowing: otherwise there can't be any story"; and the Elizabethan crowd, eager for the story, was willing to oblige the dramatist with the necessary credulity.

There is this to be said about the credulity of an audience, how-ever,—that it will believe what it sees much more readily than what it hears. It might not believe in the ghost of Hamlet's father if the ghost were merely spoken of and did not walk upon the stage. If a dramatist would convince his audience of the generosity or the treachery of one character or another, he should not waste words either praising or blaming the character, but should present him to the eye in the performance of a generous or treacherous action. The audience *hears* wise words from Polonius when he gives his parting admonition to his son; but the same audience *sees* him made a fool of by Prince Hamlet, and will not think him wise.

The fact that a crowd's eyes are more keenly receptive than its ears is the psychologic basis for the maxim that in the theatre action speaks louder than words. It also affords a reason why plays of which the audience does not understand a single word are fre-quently successful. Sarah Bernhardt's thrilling performance of *La Tosca* invariably aroused enthusiasm in London and New York, where the crowd, as a crowd, could not understand the language of the play.

Another primal characteristic of the mind of the crowd is its susceptibility to emotional contagion. A cultivated individual read-ing *The School for Scandal* at home alone will be intelligently ap-preciative of its delicious humor; but it is difficult to imagine him laughing over it aloud. Yet the same individual, when submerged in a theatre crowd, will laugh heartily over this very play, largely because other people near him are laughing too. Laughter, tears, enthusiasm, all the basic human emotions, thrill and tremble through an audience, because each member of the crowd feels that he is surrounded by other people who are experiencing the same emotion as his own. In the sad part of a play it is hard to keep from weeping if the woman next to you is wiping her eyes;

and still harder is it to keep from laughing, even at a sorry jest, if the man on the other side is roaring in vociferous cachinnation. Successful dramatists play upon the susceptibility of a crowd by serving up raw morsels of crude humor and pathos for the unthinking to wheeze and blubber over, knowing that these members of the audience will excite their more phlegmatic neighbors by contagion. The practical dictum that every laugh in the first act is worth money in the box-office is founded on this psychologic truth. Even puns as bad as Israel Zangwill's are of value early in a play to set on some quantity of barren spectators and get the house accustomed to a titter. Scenes like the foot-ball episode in *The College Widow* or the chariot race in *Ben Hur* are nearly always sure to raise the roof; for it is usually sufficient to set everybody on the stage a-cheering in order to make the audience cheer too by sheer contagion. Another and more classical example was the speechless triumph of Henry V's return victorious, in Richard Mansfield's sumptuous production of the play. Here the audience felt that he was every inch a king; for it had caught the fervor of the crowd upon the stage.

This same emotional contagion is, of course, the psychologic basis for the French system of the *claque*, or band of hired applauders seated in the centre of the house. The leader of the *claque* knows his cues as if he were an actor in the piece, and at the psychologic moment the *claqueurs* burst forth with their clatter and start the house applauding. Applause begets applause in the theatre, as laughter begets laughter and tears beget tears.

But not only is the crowd more emotional than the individual; it is also more sensuous. It has the lust of the eye and of the ear,— the savage's love of gaudy color, the child's love of soothing sound. It is fond of flaring flags and blaring trumpets. Hence the rich-costumed processions of the Elizabethan stage, many years before the use of scenery; and hence, in our own day, the success of pieces like *The Miracle* and *The Eternal Road*. Color, light, and music, artistically blended, will hold the crowd better than the most absorbing story. This is the reason for the vogue of musical comedy, with its pretty girls, and gaudy shifts of scenery and lights, and tricksy, tripping melodies and dances.

Both in its sentiments and in its opinions, the crowd is comfortably commonplace. It is, as a crowd, incapable of original thought and of any but inherited emotion. It has no speculation in its eyes.

What it feels was felt before the flood; and what it thinks, its fathers thought before it. The most effective moments in the theatre are those that appeal to basic and commonplace emotions,— love of woman, love of home, love of country, love of right, anger, jealousy, revenge, ambition, lust, and treachery. So great for centuries has been the inherited influence of the Christian religion that any adequate play whose motive is self-sacrifice is almost certain to succeed. Even when the self-sacrifice is unwise and ignoble, as in the first act of *Frou-Frou,* the crowd will give it vehement approval. Countless plays have been made upon the man who unselfishly assumes responsibility for another's guilt. The great tragedies have familiar themes,—ambition in *Macbeth,* jealousy in *Othello,* filial ingratitude in *Lear;* there is nothing in these motives that the most unthinking audience could fail to understand. No crowd can resist the fervor of a patriot who goes down scornful before many spears. Show the audience a flag to die for, or a stalking ghost to be avenged, or a shred of honor to maintain against agonising odds, and it will thrill with an enthusiasm as ancient as the human race. Few are the plays that can succeed without the moving force of love, the most familiar of all emotions. These themes do not require that the audience shall think.

But for the speculative, the original, the new, the crowd evinces little favor. If the dramatist holds ideas of religion, or of politics, or of social theory, that are in advance of his time, he must keep them to himself or else his plays will fail. Nimble wits, like Bernard Shaw, who scorn tradition, can attain a popular success only through the crowd's inherent love of fads; they cannot long succeed when they run counter to inherited ideas. The great successful dramatists, like Molière and Shakespeare, have always thought with the crowd on all essential questions. Their views of religion, of morality, of politics, of law, have been the views of the populace, nothing more. They never raise questions that cannot quickly be answered by the crowd, through the instinct of inherited experience. No mind was ever, in the philosophic sense, more commonplace than that of Shakespeare. He had no new ideas. He was never radical and seldom even progressive. He was a careful money-making business man, fond of food and drink and out-of-doors and laughter, a patriot, a lover, and a gentleman. Greatly did he know things about people; greatly, also, could he write. But he accepted the religion, the politics, and the social ethics of his time, without ever bothering to wonder if these things might be improved.

The great speculative spirits of the world, those who overturn tradition and discover new ideas, have had minds far different from this. They have not written plays. It is to these men,—the philosopher, the essayist, the novelist, the lyric poet,—that each of us turns for what is new in thought. But from the dramatist the crowd desires only the old, old thought. It has no patience for consideration; it will listen only to what it knows already. If, therefore, a great man has a new doctrine to expound, let him set it forth in a book of essays; or, if he needs must sugar-coat it with a story, let him expound it in a novel, whose appeal will be to the individual mind. Not until a doctrine is old enough to have become generally accepted is it ripe for exploitation in the theatre.

On the other hand, one of the surest ways of succeeding in the theatre is to sum up and present dramatically all that the crowd has been thinking for some time concerning any subject of importance. The dramatist should be the catholic collector and wise interpreter of those ideas which the crowd, in its conservatism, feels already to be safely true.

The validity of this point seems to me indisputable. I know that many of the best playwrights of the present day are striving to use the drama as a vehicle for the expression of advanced ideas, especially in regard to social ethics; but in doing this, I think, they are mistaking the scope of the theatre. They are striving to say in the drama what might be said better in the essay or the novel. As the exposition of a theory, Mr. Shaw's *Man and Superman* is not nearly so effective as the writings of Schopenhauer and Nietzsche, from whom the playwright borrowed his ideas. The greatest works of Ibsen can be appreciated only by the cultured individual and not by the uncultured crowd. That is why the breadth of his appeal will never equal that of Shakespeare, in spite of his unfathomable intellect and his perfect mastery of the technique of his art. Only his more commonplace plays—*A Doll's House*, for example— have attained a wide success. And a wide success is a thing to be desired for other than material reasons. Surely it is a good thing for the public that *Hamlet* never fails.

The conservatism of the greatest dramatists asserts itself not only in their thoughts but even in the mere form of their plays. It is the lesser men who invent new tricks of technique and startle the public with innovations. Molière merely perfected the type of Italian comedy that his public long had known. Shakespeare quietly adopted the forms that lesser men had made the crowd familiar with. He imitated Lyly in *Love's Labour's Lost*, Greene in *As You Like It*, Marlowe in *Richard III*, Kyd in *Hamlet*, and Fletcher in *The Tempest*. He did the old thing better than the other men had done it,—that is all.

Yet this is greatly to Shakespeare's credit. He was wise enough to feel that what the crowd wanted, both in matter and in form, was what was needed in the greatest drama. In saying that Shakespeare's mind was commonplace, I meant to tender him the highest praise. In his commonplaceness lies his sanity. He is so greatly *usual* that he can understand all men and sympathise with them. He is above novelty. His wisdom is greater than the wisdom of the few; he is the heir of all the ages, and draws his wisdom from the general mind of man. And it is largely because of this that he represents ever the ideal of the dramatist. He who would write for the theatre must not despise the crowd.

III

All of the above-mentioned characteristics of theatre audiences, their instinct for contention and for partisanship, their credulity, their sensuousness, their susceptibility to emotional contagion, their incapacity for original thought, their conservatism, and their love of the commonplace, appear in every sort of crowd, as Gustave Le Bon has proved with ample illustration. It remains for us to notice certain traits in which theatre audiences differ from other kinds of crowds.

In the first place, a theatre audience is composed of individuals more heterogeneous than those that make up a political, or social, or sporting, or religious convocation. The crowd at a foot-ball game, at a church, at a social or political convention, is by its very purpose selective of its elements: it is made up entirely of college-folk, or Presbyterians, or Prohibitionists, or Republicans, as the case may be. But a theatre audience is composed of all sorts and conditions of men. The same theatre in New York contains the rich and the poor, the literate and the illiterate, the old and the young, the native and the naturalised. The same play, therefore, must appeal to all of these. It follows that the dramatist must be broader in his appeal than any other artist. He cannot confine his message to any single caste of society. In the same single work of art he must incorporate elements that will interest all classes of humankind.

Those promising dramatic movements that have confined their appeal to a certain single stratum of society have failed ever, because of this, to achieve the highest excellence. The trouble with Roman comedy is that it was written for an audience composed chiefly of freedmen and slaves. The patrician caste of Rome walked wide of the theatres. Only the dregs of society gathered to applaud the comedies of Plautus and Terence. Hence the over-simplicity of their prologues, and their tedious repetition of the obvious. Hence, also, their vulgarity, their horse-play, their obscenity. Here was fine dramatic genius led astray, because the time was out of joint. Similarly, the trouble with French tragedy, in the classicist period of Corneille and Racine, is that it was written only for the finest caste of society,—the patrician coterie of a patrician cardinal. Hence its over-niceness, and its appeal to the ear rather than to the eye. Plautus aimed too low and Racine aimed too high. Each of them, therefore, shot wide of the mark; while Molière, who wrote at once for patrician and plebeian, scored a hit.

The really great dramatic movements of the world—that of Spain in the age of Calderon and Lope, that of England in the spacious times of great Elizabeth, that of France from 1830 to 1914 —have broadened their appeal to every class. The queen and the orange-girl joyed together in the healthiness of Rosalind; the king and the gamin laughed together at the rogueries of Scapin. The breadth of Shakespeare's appeal remains one of the most significant facts in the history of the drama. Tell a filthy-faced urchin of the gutter that you know about a play that shows a ghost that stalks and talks at midnight underneath a castle-tower, and a man that makes believe he is out of his head so that he can get the better of a wicked king, and a girl that goes mad and drowns herself, and a play within the play, and a funeral in a churchyard, and a duel with poisoned swords, and a great scene at the end in which nearly every one gets killed: tell him this, and watch his eyes grow wide! I have been to a thirty-cent performance of *Othello* in a middle-western town, and have felt the audience thrill with the headlong hurry of the action. Yet these are the plays that cloistered students study for their wisdom and their style!

And let us not forget, in this connection, that a similar breadth of appeal is neither necessary nor greatly to be desired in those forms of literature that, unlike the drama, are not written for the crowd. The greatest non-dramatic poet and the greatest novelist in English are appreciated only by the few; but this is not in the least to the discredit of Milton and of Meredith. One indication of the greatness of Rudyard Kipling's story, *They,* is that very few have learned to read it.

Victor Hugo, in his preface to *Ruy Blas,* has discussed this entire principle from a slightly different point of view. He divides the theatre audience into three classes—the thinkers, who demand characterisation; the women, who demand passion; and the mob, who demand action—and insists that every great play must appeal to all three classes at once. Certainly *Ruy Blas* itself fulfils this desideratum, and is great in the breadth of its appeal. Yet although all three of the necessary elements appear in the play, it has more action than passion and more passion than characterisation. And this fact leads us to the theory, omitted by Victor Hugo from his preface, that the mob is more important than the women and the women more important than the thinkers, in the average theatre audience. Indeed, a deeper consideration of the subject almost leads us to discard the thinkers as a psychologic force and to obliterate the distinction between the women and the mob. It is to an unthinking and feminine-minded mob that the dramatist must first of all appeal; and this leads us to believe that action with passion for its motive is the prime essential for a play.

For, nowadays at least, it is most essential that the drama should appeal to a crowd of women. Practically speaking, our matinée audiences are composed entirely of women, and our evening audiences are composed chiefly of women and the men that they have brought with them. Very few men go to the theatre unattached; and these few are not important enough, from the theoretic standpoint, to alter the psychologic aspect of the audience. And it is this that constitutes one of the most important differences between a modern theatre audience and other kinds of crowds.

The influence of this fact upon the dramatist is very potent. First of all, as I have said, it forces him to deal chiefly in action with passion for its motive. And this necessity accounts for the preponderance of female characters over male in the large majority of the greatest modern plays. Notice Nora Helmer, Mrs. Alving, Hedda Gabler; notice Magda and Camille; notice Mrs. Tanqueray, Mrs. Ebbsmith, Iris, and Letty,—to cite only a few examples. Furthermore, since women are by nature comparatively inattentive, the femininity of the modern theatre audience forces the dramatist to employ the elementary technical tricks of repetition and parallelism, in order to keep his play clear, though much of it be unattended to. Eugène Scribe, who knew the theatre, used to say that every important statement in the exposition of a play must be made at least three times. This, of course, is seldom necessary in a novel, where things may be said once for all.

The prevailing inattentiveness of a theatre audience at the present day is due also to the fact that it is peculiarly conscious of itself, apart from the play that it has come to see. Many people "go to the theatre," as the phrase is, without caring much whether they see one play or another; what they want chiefly is to immerse themselves in a theatre audience. This is especially true, in New York, of the large percentage of people from out of town who "go to the theatre" merely as one phase of their metropolitan experience. It is true, also, of the many women in the boxes and the orchestra who go less to see than to be seen. It is one of the great difficulties of the dramatist that he must capture and enchain the attention of an audience thus composed. A man does not pick up a novel unless he cares to read it; but many people go to the theatre chiefly for the sense of being there. Certainly, therefore, the problem of the dramatist is, in this respect, more difficult than that of the novelist, for he must make his audience lose consciousness of itself in the consciousness of his play.

One of the most essential differences between a theatre audience and other kinds of crowds lies in the purpose for which it is convened. This purpose is always recreation. A theatre audience is therefore less serious than a church congregation or a political or social convention. It does not come to be edified or educated; it has no desire to be taught: what it wants is to have its emotions played upon. It seeks amusement—in the widest sense of the word—amusement through laughter, sympathy, terror, and tears. And it is amusement of this sort that the great dramatists have ever given it.

The trouble with most of the dreamers who league themselves for the uplifting of the stage is that they consider the theatre with an illogical solemnity. They base their efforts on the proposition that a theatre audience ought to want to be edified. As a matter of fact, no audience ever does. Molière and Shakespeare, who knew the limits of their art, never said a word about uplifting the stage. They wrote plays to please the crowd; and if, through their inherent greatness, they became teachers as well as entertainers, they did so without any tall talk about the solemnity of their mission. Their audiences learned largely, but they did so unawares,—God being with them when they knew it not. The demand for an endowed theatre in America comes chiefly from those who believe that a great play cannot earn its own living. Yet *Hamlet* has made more money than any other play in English; *The School for Scandal* never fails to draw; and in our own day we have seen *Cyrano de Bergerac* coining money all around the world. There were not any endowed theatres in Elizabethan London. Give the crowd the sort of plays it wants, and you will not have to seek beneficence to keep your theatre floating. But, on the other hand, no endowed theatre will ever lure the crowd to listen to the sort of plays it does not want. There is a wise maxim appended to one of Mr. George Ade's *Fables in Slang:* "In uplifting, get underneath." If the theatre in America is weak, what it needs is not endowment: it needs great and popular plays. Give us one great dramatist who understands the crowd, and we shall not have to form societies to propagate his art. Let us cease our prattle of the theatre for the few. Any play that is really great as drama will interest the many.

IV

One point remains to be considered. In any theatre audience there are certain individuals who do not belong to the crowd. They are in it, but not of it; for they fail to merge their individual self-consciousness in the general self-consciousness of the multitude. Such are the professional critics, and other confirmed frequenters of the theatre. It is not for them primarily that plays are written; and any one who has grown individualised through the theatre-going habit cannot help looking back regretfully upon those fresher days when he belonged, unthinking, to the crowd. A first-night audience is anomalous, in that it is composed largely of individuals opposed to self-surrender; and for this reason, a first-night judgment of the merits of a play is rarely final. The dramatist has written for a crowd, and he is judged by individuals. Most dramatic critics will tell you that they long to lose themselves in the crowd, and regret the aloofness from the play that comes of their profession. It is because of this aloofness of the critic that most dramatic criticism fails.

Throughout the present discussion, I have insisted on the point that the great dramatists have always written primarily for the many. Yet now I must add that when once they have fulfilled this prime necessity, they may also write secondarily for the few. And the very greatest have always done so. In so far as he was a dramatist, Shakespeare wrote for the crowd; in so far as he was a lyric poet, he wrote for himself; and in so far as he was a sage and a stylist, he wrote for the individual. In making sure of his appeal to the many, he earned the right to appeal to the few. At the thirty-cent performance of *Othello* that I spoke of, I was probably the only person present who failed to submerge his individuality beneath the common consciousness of the audience. Shakespeare made a play that could appeal to the rabble of that middle-western town; but he wrote it in a verse that none of them could hear:—

> Not poppy, nor mandragora,
> Nor all the drowsy syrups of the world,
> Shall ever medicine thee to that sweet sleep
> Which thou ow'dst yesterday.

The greatest dramatist of all, in writing for the crowd, did not neglect the individual.

III

THE ACTOR AND THE DRAMATIST

WE HAVE already agreed that the dramatist works ever under the sway of three influences which are not felt by exclusively literary artists like the poet and the novelist. The physical conditions of the theatre in any age affect to a great extent the form and structure of the drama; the conscious or unconscious demands of the audience, as we have observed in the preceding chapter, determine for the dramatist the themes he shall portray; and the range or restrictions of his actors have an immediate effect upon the dramatist's great task of character-creation. In fact, so potent is the influence of the actor upon the dramatist that the latter, in creating character, goes to work very differently from his literary fellow-artists,—the novelist, the story-writer, or the poet. Great characters in non-dramatic fiction have often resulted from abstract imagining, without direct reference to any actual person: Don Quixote, Tito Melema, Leatherstocking, sprang full-grown from their creator's minds and struck the world as strange and new. But the greatest characters in the drama have almost always taken on the physical, and to a great extent the mental, characteristics of certain great actors for whom they have been fashioned. Cyrano is not merely Cyrano, but also Coquelin; Mascarille is not merely Mascarille, but also Molière; Hamlet is not merely Hamlet, but also Richard Burbage. Closet-students of the plays of Sophocles may miss a point or two if they fail to consider that the dramatist prepared the part of Œdipus in three successive dramas for a certain star-performer on the stage of Dionysus. The greatest dramatists have built their plays not so much for reading in the closet as for immediate presentation on the stage; they have grown to greatness only after having achieved an initial success that has given them the freedom of the theatre; and their conceptions of character have therefore

33

crystallised around the actors that they have found waiting to present their parts. A novelist may conceive his heroine freely as being tall or short, frail or firmly built; but if a dramatist is making a play for an actress like Maude Adams, an airy, slight physique is imposed upon his heroine in advance.

Shakespeare was, among other things, the director of the Lord Chamberlain's men, who performed in the Globe, upon the Bankside; and his plays are replete with evidences of the influence upon him of the actors whom he had in charge. It is patent, for example, that the same comedian must have created Launce in *Two Gentlemen of Verona* and Launcelot Gobbo in the *Merchant of Venice;* the low comic hit of one production was bodily repeated in the next. It is almost as obvious that the parts of Mercutio and Gratiano must have been intrusted to the same performer; both characters seem made to fit the same histrionic temperament. If Hamlet were the hero of a novel, we should all, I think, conceive of him as slender, and the author would agree with us; yet, in the last scene of the play, the Queen expressly says, "He's fat, and scant of breath." This line has puzzled many commentators, as seeming out of character; but it merely indicates that Richard Burbage was fleshy during the season of 1602.

The Elizabethan expedient of disguising the heroine as a boy, which was invented by John Lyly, made popular by Robert Greene, and eagerly adopted by Shakespeare and Fletcher, seems unconvincing on the modern stage. It is hard for us to imagine how Orlando can fail to recognise his love when he meets her clad as Ganymede in the forest of Arden, or how Bassanio can be blinded to the figure of his wife when she enters the courtroom in the almost feminine robes of a doctor of laws. Clothes cannot make a man out of an actress; and it might seem that Shakespeare was depending over-much upon the proverbial credulity of theatre audiences. But a glance at histrionic conditions in Shakespeare's day will show us immediately why he used this expedient of disguise not only for Portia and Rosalind, but for Viola and Imogen as well. Shakespeare wrote these parts to be played not by women but by boys. Now, when a boy playing a woman disguised himself as a woman playing a boy, the disguise must have seemed baffling, not only to Orlando and Bassanio on the stage, but also to the audience. It was Shakespeare's boy actors, rather than his narrative imagination, that made him recur repeatedly in this case to a dra-

matic expedient which he would certainly discard if he were writing for actresses to-day.

If we turn from the work of Shakespeare to that of Molière, we
shall find many more evidences of the influence of the actor on
the dramatist. In fact, Molière's entire scheme of character-creation
cannot be understood without direct reference to the histrionic
capabilities of the various members of the *Troupe de Monsieur*.
Molière's immediate and practical concern was not so much to
create comic characters for all time as to make effective parts for
La Grange and Du Croisy and Madeleine Béjart, for his wife and
for himself. La Grange seems to have been the Charles Wyndham
of his day,—every inch a gentleman; his part in any of the plays
may be distinguished by its elegant urbanity. In *Les Précieuses
Ridicules* the gentlemanly characters are actually named La Grange
and Du Croisy; the actors walked on and played themselves; it is
as if Eugene O'Neill had called his heroine Pauline Lord, instead
of "Anna Christie." In the early period of Molière's art, before he
broadened as an actor, the parts that he wrote for himself were
often so much alike from play to play that he called them by the
same conventional theatric name of Mascarille or Sganarelle, and
played them, doubtless, with the same costume and make-up. Later
on, when he became more versatile as an actor, he wrote for himself a wider range of parts and individualised them in name as well
as in nature. His growth in depicting the characters of young
women is curiously coincident with the growth of his wife as an
actress for whom to devise such characters. Molière's best woman
—Célimène, in *Le Misanthrope*—was created for Mlle. Molière at
the height of her career, and is endowed with all her physical and
mental traits.

The reason why so many of the Queen Anne dramatists in England wrote comedies setting forth a dandified and foppish gentleman is that Colley Cibber, the foremost actor of the time, could
play the fop better than he could play anything else. The reason
why there is no love scene between Charles Surface and Maria in
The School for Scandal is that Sheridan knew that the actor and
the actress who were cast for these respective roles were incapable
of making love gracefully upon the stage. The reason why Victor
Hugo's *Cromwell* overleaped itself in composition and became impossible for purposes of stage production is that Talma, for whom
the character of Cromwell was designed, died before the piece was

finished, and Hugo, despairing of having the part adequately acted, completed the play for the closet instead of for the stage. But it is unnecessary to cull from the distant past further instances of the direct dependence of the dramatist upon his actors. We have only to look about us in more recent times to see the same influence at work.

For example, the career of one of the very best endowed theatrical composers of the nineteenth century, Victorien Sardou, was molded and restricted for all time by the talents of a single star performer, Mme. Sarah Bernhardt. Under the influence of Eugène Scribe, Sardou began his career at the Théâtre Français with a wide range of well-made plays, varying in scope from the social satire of *Nos Intimes* and the farcical intrigue of *Les Pattes de Mouche* (known to us in English as *The Scrap of Paper*) to the tremendous historic panorama of *Patrie*. When Sarah Bernhardt left the Comédie Française, Sardou followed in her footsteps, and afterwards devoted most of his energy to preparing a series of melodramas to serve successively as vehicles for her. Now, Sarah Bernhardt was an actress of marked abilities, and limitations likewise marked. In sheer perfection of technique she surpasssed all performers of her time. She was the acme of histrionic dexterity; all that she did upon the stage was, in sheer effectiveness, superb. But in her work she had no soul; she lacked the sensitive sweet lure of Duse, the serene and star-lit poetry of Modjeska. Three things she did supremely well. She could be seductive, with a cooing voice; she could be vindictive, with a cawing voice; and, voiceless, she could die. Hence the formula of Sardou's melodramas.

His heroines were almost always Sarah Bernhardts,—luring, tremendous, doomed to die. Fédora, Gismonda, La Tosca, Zoraya, were but a single woman who transmigrated from play to play. We met her in different countries and in different times; but she always lured and fascinated a man, stormed against insuperable circumstance, cooed and cawed, and in the outcome died. One of Sardou's latest efforts, *La Sorcière*, presented the dry bones of the formula without the flesh and blood of life. Zoraya appeared first shimmering in moonlight upon the hills of Spain,—dovelike in voice, serpentining in seductiveness. Next, she was allowed to hypnotise the audience while she was hypnotising the daughter of the governor. She was loved and she was lost. She cursed the high tribunal of the Inquisition,—a dove no longer now. And she died upon cathedral steps, to organ music. *The Sorceress* was but a lifeless piece of mechanism; and when it was performed in English by Mrs. Patrick Campbell, it failed to lure or to thrill. But Sarah Bernhardt, because as an actress she *was* Zoraya, contrived to lift it into life. Justly we may say that, in a certain sense, this was Sarah Bernhardt's drama instead of Victorien Sardou's. With her, it was a play; without her, it was nothing but a formula. The young author of *Patrie* promised better things than this. Had he chosen, he might have climbed to nobler heights. But he chose instead to write, year after year, a vehicle for the Muse of Melodrama, and sold his laurel crown for gate-receipts.

If Sardou suffered through playing the sedulous ape to a histrionic artist, it is no less true that the same practice was advantageous to Edmond Rostand. Rostand wrote shrewdly for the greatest comedian of his period; and Constant Coquelin was the making of him as a dramatist. The poet's early pieces, like *Les Romanesques*, disclosed him as a master of preciosity, exquisitely lyrical, but lacking in the sterner stuff of drama. He seemed a new de Banville—dainty, dallying, and deft—a writer of witty and pretty verses—nothing more. Then it fell to his lot to devise an acting part for Coquelin, which in the compass of a single play should allow that great performer to sweep through the whole wide range of his varied and versatile accomplishment. With the figure of Coquelin before him, Rostand set earnestly to work. The result of his endeavor was the character of Cyrano de Bergerac, which is considered by many critics the richest acting part, save Hamlet, in the history of the theatre.

L'Aiglon was also devised under the immediate influence of the same actor. The genesis of this latter play is, I think, of peculiar interest to students of the drama; and I shall therefore relate it at some length. The facts were told by Coquelin himself to his friend Brander Matthews, who kindly permitted me to state them in this place. One evening, after the extraordinary success of *Cyrano*, Rostand met Coquelin at the Porte St. Martin and said, "You know, Coq, this is not the last part I want to write for you. Can't you give me an idea to get me started—an idea for another character?" The actor thought for a moment, and then answered, "I've always wanted to play a *vieux grognard du premier empire— un grenadier à grandes moustaches*." . . . A grumpy grenadier of Napoleon's army—a grenadier with sweeping moustaches—with this cue the dramatist set to work and gradually imagined the character of Flambeau. He soon saw that if the great Napoleon were to appear in the play he would dominate the action and steal the centre of the stage from the soldier-hero. He therefore decided to set the story after the Emperor's death, in the time of the weak and vacillating Duc de Reichstadt. Flambeau, who had served the eagle, could now transfer his allegiance to the eaglet, and stand dominant with the memory of battles that had been. But after the dramatist had been at work upon the play for some time, he encountered the old difficulty in a new guise. At last he came in despair to Coquelin and said, "It isn't your play, Coq; it can't be; the young duke is running away with it, and I can't stop him; Flambeau is but a secondary figure after all. What shall I do?" And Coquelin, who understood him, answered, "Take it to Sarah; she has just played Hamlet, and wants to do another boy." So Rostand "took it to Sarah," and finished up the duke with her in view, while in the background the figure of Flambeau scowled upon him over *grandes moustaches*—a true *grognard* indeed! Thus it happened that Coquelin never played the part of Flambeau until he came to New York with Sarah Bernhardt in the fall of 1900; and the grenadier conceived in the Porte St. Martin first saw the footlights in the Garden Theatre.

But the recent English-speaking stage furnishes examples just as striking of the influence of the actor on the dramatist. Sir Arthur Wing Pinero's greatest heroine, Paula Tanqueray, has worn since her inception the physical aspect of Mrs. Patrick Campbell. Many of the most effective dramas of Henry Arthur Jones were built around the personality of Sir Charles Wyndham. The Wyndham part in Mr. Jones's plays was always a gentleman of the world, who understood life because he had lived it, and was "wise with the quiet memory of old pain." He was moral because he knew the futility of immorality. He was lonely, lovable, dignified, reliable, and sound. By serene and unobtrusive understanding he straightened out the difficulties in which the other people of the play had wilfully become entangled. He showed them the error of their follies, preached a worldly-wise little sermon to each one, and sent them back to their true places in life, sadder and wiser men and women. In order to give Sir Charles Wyndham an opportunity to display all phases of his experienced gentility in such a character as this, Mr. Jones repeated the part in drama after drama.

Many of the greatest characters of the theatre have been so essentially imbued with the physical and mental personality of the actors who created them that they have died with their performers and been lost forever after from the world of art. In this regard we think at once of Rip Van Winkle. The little play that Joseph Jefferson, with the aid of Dion Boucicault, fashioned out of Washington Irving's story is scarcely worth the reading; and if, a hundred years from now, any student of the drama happens to look it over, he may wonder in vain why it was so beloved, for many, many years, by all America; and there will come no answer, since the actor's art will then be only a tale that is told. So Beau Brummell died with Richard Mansfield; and if our children, who never saw his superb performance, chance in future years to read the lines of this early composition of Clyde Fitch, they will hardly believe us when we tell them that the character of Brummell once was great. With such instances before us, it ought not to be so difficult as many university professors find it to understand the vogue of certain plays of the Elizabethan and Restoration eras which seem to us now, in the reading, lifeless things. When we study the mad dramas of Nat Lee, we should remember Betterton; and properly to appreciate Thomas Otway, we must imagine the aspect and the voice of Elizabeth Barry.

It may truthfully be said that Mrs. Barry created Otway, both as dramatist and poet; for *The Orphan* and *Venice Preserved*, the two most pathetic plays in English, would never have been written but for her. It is often thus within the power of an actor to create a dramatist; and his surest means of immortality is to inspire the composition of plays which may survive his own demise. Now that Duse is dead, poets may read *La Città Morta*, and imagine her. The memory of Coquelin is, in this way, likely to live longer than that of Talma. We can merely guess at Talma's art, because the plays in which he acted are unreadable to-day. But if Rostand's *Cyrano* is read a hundred years from now, it will be possible for students of it to imagine in detail the salient features of the art of Coquelin. It will be evident to them that the actor made love luringly and died effectively, that he was capable of lyric reading and staccato gasconade, that he had a burly humor and that touch of sentiment that trembles into tears. Similarly we know to-day, from the fact that Shakespeare played the Ghost in *Hamlet*, that he must have had a voice that was full and resonant and deep. So from reading the plays of Molière we can imagine the robust figure of Madeleine Béjart, the grace of La Grange, the pretty petulance of the flighty fair Armande.

Some sense of this must have been in the mind of Sir Henry Irving when he strove industriously to create a dramatist who might survive him and immortalise his memory. The facile, uncreative Wills was granted many chances, and in *Charles I* barely lost an opportunity to make a lasting drama. Lord Tennyson came near the mark in *Becket;* but this play, like those of Wills, has not proved sturdy enough to survive the actor who inspired it. For all his striving, Sir Henry left no dramatist as a monument to his art.

STAGE CONVENTIONS IN MODERN TIMES

I

IN 1581 Sir Philip Sidney praised the tragedy of *Gorboduc*, which he had seen acted by the gentlemen of the Inner Temple, because it was "full of stately speeches and well-sounding phrases." A few years later the young poet, Christopher Marlowe, promised the audience of his initial tragedy that they should "hear the Scythian Tamburlaine threatening the world with high astounding terms." These two statements are indicative of the tenor of Elizabethan plays. *Gorboduc*, to be sure, was a ponderous piece, made according to the pseudo-classical fashion that soon went out of favor; while *Tamburlaine the Great* was triumphant with the drums and tramplings of romance. The two plays were diametrically opposed in method; but they had this in common: each was full of stately speeches and of high astounding terms.

Nearly a century later, in 1670, John Dryden added to the second part of his *Conquest of Granada* an epilogue in which he criticised adversely the dramatists of the elder age. Speaking of Ben Jonson and his contemporaries, he said:

> But were they now to write, when critics weigh
> Each line, and every word, throughout a play,
> None of them, no, not Jonson in his height,
> Could pass without allowing grains for weight.

> .   .   .   .   .

> Wit 's now arrived to a more high degree;
> Our native language more refined and free:
> Our ladies and our men now speak more wit
> In conversation than those poets writ.

41

This criticism was characteristic of a new era that was dawning in the English drama, during which a playwright could hope for no greater glory than to be praised for the brilliancy of his dialogue or the smartness of his repartee.

At the present day, if you ask the average theatre-goer about the merits of the play that he has lately witnessed, he will praise it not for its stately speeches nor its clever repartee, but because its presentation was "so natural." In 1934 the Pulitzer Prize was awarded in New York to an unimportant play whose main item of interest was the exactitude with which a well-trained group of actors exhibited every detail of the performance of an emergency operation in a hospital.

These different reactions give evidence of three distinct steps in the evolution of the English drama. During the sixteenth and seventeenth centuries it was essentially a Drama of Rhetoric; throughout the eighteenth century it was mainly a Drama of Conversation; and during the nineteenth and twentieth centuries it has grown to be a Drama of Illusion. During the first period it aimed at poetic power, during the second at brilliancy of dialogue, and during the third at naturalness of representment. Throughout the last three centuries, the gradual perfecting of the physical conditions of the theatre has made possible the Drama of Illusion; the conventions of the actor's art have undergone a similar progression; and at the same time the change in the taste of the theatre-going public has made a well-sustained illusion a condition precedent to success upon the modern stage.

II

A typical Elizabethan play-house, like the Globe or the Blackfriars, stood roofless in the air. The stage was a projecting platform surrounded on three sides by the groundlings who had paid threepence for the privilege of standing in the pit; and around this pit, or yard, were built boxes for the city madams and the gentlemen of means. Often the side edges of the stage itself were lined with young gallants perched on three-legged stools, who twitted the actors when they pleased or disturbed the play by boisterous interruptions. At the back of the platform was hung an arras through which the players entered, and which could be drawn aside to discover a set piece of stage furnishing, like a bed or a banqueting board. Above the arras was built an upper room, which might serve as Juliet's balcony or as the speaking-place of a commandant supposed to stand upon a city's walls. No scenery was employed, except some elaborate properties that might be drawn on and off before the eyes of the spectators, like the trellised arbor in *The Spanish Tragedy* on which the young Horatio was hanged. Since there was no curtain, the actors could never be "discovered" on the stage and were forced to make an exit at the end of every scene. Plays were produced by daylight, under the sun of afternoon; and the stage could not be darkened, even when it was necessary for Macbeth to perpetrate a midnight murder.

In order to succeed in a theatre such as this, the drama was necessarily forced to be a Drama of Rhetoric. From 1576, when James Burbage built the first play-house in London, until 1642, when the theatres were formally closed by act of Parliament, the drama dealt with stately speeches and with high astounding terms. It was played upon a platform, and had to appeal more to the ears of the audience than to their eyes. Spectacular elements it had to some extent,—gaudy, though inappropriate, costumes, and stately processions across the stage; but no careful imitation of the actual facts of life, no illusion of reality in the representment, could possibly be effected.

The absence of scenery forced the dramatists of the time to introduce poetic passages to suggest the atmosphere of their scenes. Lorenzo and Jessica opened the last act of *The Merchant of Venice* with a pretty dialogue descriptive of a moonlit evening, and the banished duke in *As You Like It* discoursed at length upon the pleasures of life in the forest. The stage could not be darkened in *Macbeth;* but the hero was made to say, "Light thickens, and the crow makes wing to the rooky wood." Sometimes, when the scene was supposed to change from one country to another, a Chorus was sent forth, as in *Henry V*, to ask the auditors frankly to transfer their imaginations overseas.

The fact that the stage was surrounded on three sides by standing spectators forced the actor to emulate the platform orator. Set speeches were introduced bodily into the text of a play, although they impeded the progress of the action. Jacques reined a comedy to a standstill while he discoursed at length upon the seven ages of man. Soliloquies were common, and formal dialogues prevailed. By convention, all characters, regardless of their education or station in life, were considered capable of talking not only verse, but poetry. The untutored sea-captain in *Twelfth Night* spoke of "Arion on the dolphin's back," and in another play the sapheads Salanio and Salarino discoursed most eloquent music.

In San Francisco at the present day a singular similarity to Elizabethan conventions may be noted in the Chinese theatres. Here we have a platform drama in all its nakedness. There is no curtain, and the stage is bare of scenery. The musicians sit upon the stage, and the actors enter through an arras at the right or at the left of the rear wall. The costumes are elaborate, and the players frequently parade around the stage. Long speeches and set colloquies are common. Only the crudest properties are used. Two candlesticks and a small image on a table are taken to represent a temple; a man seated upon an overturned chair is supposed to be a general on a charger; and when a character is obliged to cross a river, he walks the length of the stage trailing an oar behind him. The audience does not seem to notice that these conventions are unnatural,—any more than did the 'prentices in the pit, when Burbage, with the sun shining full upon his face, announced that it was then the very witching time of night.

The Drama of Rhetoric which was demanded by the physical conditions of the Elizabethan stage survived the Restoration and did not die until the day of Addison's *Cato*. Imitations of it even struggled on the stage throughout the nineteenth century. The *Virginius* of Sheridan Knowles and the *Richelieu* of Bulwer-Lytton were both framed upon the Elizabethan model, and carried the platform drama down to recent times. But though traces of the platform drama still exist, the period of its pristine vigor terminated with the closing of the theatres in 1642.

When the drama was resumed in 1660, the physical conditions of the theatre underwent a material change. At this time two great play-houses were chartered,—the King's Theatre in Drury Lane, and the Duke of York's Theatre in Lincoln's Inn Fields. Thomas Killigrew, the manager of the Theatre Royal, was the first to introduce women actors on the stage; and parts which formerly had been played by boys were soon performed by actresses as moving as the great Elizabeth Barry. To William Davenant, the manager of the Duke's Theatre, belongs the credit for a still more important innovation. During the eighteen years when public dramatic performances had been prohibited, he had secured permission now and then to produce an opera upon a private stage. For these musi-

cal entertainments he took as a model the masques, or court cele-
brations, which had been the most popular form of private theatricals in the days of Elizabeth and James. It is well known that
masques had been produced with elaborate scenic appointments
even at a time when the professional stage was bare of scenery.
While the theatres had been closed, Davenant had used scenery in
his operas, to keep them out of the forbidden pale of professional
plays; and now in 1660, when he came forth as a regular theatre
manager, he continued to use scenery, and introduced it into the
production of comedies and tragedies.

But the use of scenery was not the only innovation that carried
the Restoration theatre far beyond its Elizabethan prototype. Play-
houses were now regularly roofed; and the stage was artificially
lighted by lamps. The shifting of scenery demanded the use of a
curtain; and it became possible for the first time to disclose actors
upon the stage and to leave them grouped before the audience
at the end of an act.

All of these improvements rendered possible a closer approach
to naturalness of representment than had ever been made before.
Palaces and flowered meads, drawing-rooms and city streets, could
now be suggested by actual scenery instead of by descriptive passages in the text. Costumes became appropriate, and properties
were more nicely chosen to give a flavor of actuality to the scene.
At the same time the platform receded, and the groundlings no
longer stood about it on the sides. The gallants were banished
from the stage, and the greater part of the audience was gathered
directly in front of the actors. Some traces of the former platform
system, however, still remained. In front of the curtain, the stage
projected into a wide "apron," as it was called, lined on either side
by boxes filled with spectators; and the house was so inadequately
lighted that almost all the acting had to be done within the focus
of the footlights. After the curtain rose, the actors advanced into
this projecting "apron" and performed the main business of the act
beyond the range and scenery and furniture.

With the "apron" stage arose a more natural form of play than
had been produced upon the Elizabethan platform. The Drama of
Rhetoric was soon supplanted by the Drama of Conversation. Oratory gradually disappeared, set speeches were abolished, and poetic
lines gave place to rapid repartee. The comedy of conversation
that began with Sir George Etherege in 1664 reached its culmina-

tion with Sheridan in a little more than a hundred years; and during this century the drama became more and more natural as the years progressed. Even in the days of Sheridan, however, the conventions of the theatre were still essentially unreal. An actor entered a room by walking through the walls; stage furniture was formally arranged; and each act terminated with the players grouped in a semicircle and bowing obeisance to applause. The lines in Sheridan's comedies were indiscriminately witty. Every character, regardless of his birth or education, had his clever things to say; and the servant bandied epigrams with the lord.

It was not until the nineteenth century was well under way that a decided improvement was made in the physical conditions of the theatre. When Madame Vestris assumed the management of the Olympic Theatre in London in 1831 she inaugurated a new era in stage conventions. Her husband, Charles James Mathews, says in his autobiography, "There was introduced that reform in all theatrical matters which has since been adopted in every theatre in the kingdom. Drawing-rooms were fitted up like drawing-rooms and furnished with care and taste. Two chairs no longer indicated that two persons were to be seated, the two chairs being removed indicating that the two persons were *not* to be seated." At the first performance of Boucicault's *London Assurance*, in 1841, a further innovation was marked by the introduction of the "box set," as it is called. Instead of representing an interior scene by a series of wings set one behind the other, the scene-shifters now built the side walls of a room solidly from front to rear; and the actors were made to enter, not by walking through the wings, but by opening actual doors that turned upon their hinges. At the same time, instead of the formal stage furniture of former years, appointments were introduced that were carefully designed to suit the actual conditions of the room to be portrayed. From this time stage-settings advanced rapidly to greater and greater degrees of naturalness. Acting, however, was still largely conventional; for the "apron" stage survived, with its semicircle of footlights, and every important piece of stage business had to be done within their focus.

The greatest revolution of modern times in stage conventions owes its origin directly to the invention of the electric light. Now that it is possible to make every corner of the stage clearly visible from all parts of the house, it is no longer necessary for an actor to hold the centre of the scene. The introduction of electric lights abolished the necessity of the "apron" stage and made possible the picture-frame proscenium; and the removal of the "apron" struck the death-blow to the Drama of Conversation and led directly to the Drama of Illusion. As soon as the picture-frame proscenium was adopted, the audience demanded a picture to be placed within the frame. The stage became essentially pictorial, and began to be used to represent faithfully the actual facts of life. Now for the first time was realised the graphic value of the curtain-fall. It became customary to ring the curtain down upon a picture that summed up in itself the entire dramatic accomplishment of the scene, instead of terminating an act with a general exodus of the performers or with a semicircle of bows.

The most extraordinary advances in natural stage-settings have been made within the memory of the present generation of theatre-goers. Sunsets and starlit skies, moonlight rippling over moving waves, fires that really burn, windows of actual glass, fountains plashing with real water,—all of the naturalistic devices of the latter-day Drama of Illusion have been developed in the last half century.

III

Acting in Elizabethan days was a presentative, rather than a representative, art. The actor was always an actor, and absorbed his part in himself rather than submerging himself in his part. Magnificence rather than appropriateness of costume was desired by the platform actor of the Drama of Rhetoric. He wished all eyes to be directed to himself, and never desired to be considered merely as a component part of a general stage picture. Actors at that time were often robustious, periwig-pated fellows who sawed the air with their hands and tore a passion to tatters.

With the rapid development of the theatre after the Restoration, came a movement toward greater naturalness in the conventions of acting. The player in the "apron" of a Queen Anne stage resembled a drawing-room entertainer rather than a platform orator. Fine gentlemen and ladies in the boxes that lined the "apron" applauded the witticisms of Sir Courtly Nice or Sir Fopling Flutter, as if they themselves were partakers in the conversation. Actors like Colley Cibber acquired a great reputation for their natural representment of the manners of polite society.

The Drama of Conversation, therefore, was acted with more natural conventions than the Drama of Rhetoric that had preceded it. And yet we find that Charles Lamb, in criticising the old actors of the eighteenth century, praises them for the essential unreality of their presentations. They carried the spectator far away from the actual world to a region where society was more splendid and careless and brilliant and lax. They did not aim to produce an illusion of naturalness as our actors do to-day. If we compare the old-style acting of *The School for Scandal,* that is described in the essays of Lamb, with the modern performances of *Beaucaire* or *Sweet Kitty Bellairs,* which dealt with the same period, we shall see at once how modern acting has grown less presentative and more representative than it was in the days of Bensley and Bannister.

The Drama of Rhetoric and the Drama of Conversation both struggled on in sporadic survivals throughout the first half of the nineteenth century; and during this period the methods of the platform actor and the parlor actor were consistently maintained. The actor of the "old school," as we are now fond of calling him, was compelled by the physical conditions of the theatre to keep within the focus of the footlights, and therefore in close proximity to the spectators. He could take the audience into his confidence more readily than can the player of the present. Sometimes even now an actor steps out of the picture in order to talk intimately with the audience; but usually at the present day it is customary for actors to seem totally oblivious of the spectators and remain always within the picture on the stage. The actor of the "old school" was fond of the long speeches of the Drama of Rhetoric and the brilliant lines of the Drama of Conversation. It may be remembered that the old actor in *Trelawny of the Wells* condemned a new-style play because it didn't contain "what you could really call a speech." He wanted what the French term a *tirade* to exercise his lungs and split the ears of the groundlings.

But with the growth of the Drama of Illusion, produced within a picture-frame proscenium, actors have come to recognise and apply the maxim, "Actions speak louder than words." What an actor *does* is now considered more important than what he *says.* The most powerful moment in Mrs. Fiske's performance of *Hedda Gabler* was the minute or more in the last act when she remained absolutely silent. This moment was worth a dozen of the "real speeches" that were sighed for by the old actor in *Trelawny.* Few of those who saw James A. Herne in *Shore Acres* will forget the impressive close of the play. The stage represented the living-room of a homely country-house, with a large open fireplace at one side. The night grew late; and one by one the characters retired, until at last old Nathaniel Berry was left alone upon the stage. Slowly he locked the doors and closed the windows and put all things in order for the night. Then he took a candle and went upstairs to bed, leaving the room empty and dark except for the flaming of the fire on the hearth.

Great progress toward naturalness in contemporary acting has been occasioned by the abrogation of the soliloquy and the aside. The relinquishment of these two time-honored expedients has been accomplished only in most recent times. Sir Arthur Pinero's early farces abounded with asides and even lengthy soliloquies; but his later plays were made entirely without them. The present prevalence of objection to both is due largely to the strong influence of Ibsen's rigid dramaturgic structure. Dramatists have become convinced that the soliloquy and the aside are lazy expedients, and that with a little extra labor the most complicated plot may be developed without resort to either. The passing of the aside has had an important effect on naturalness of acting. In speaking a line audible to the audience but supposed to be unheard by the other characters on the stage, an actor was forced by the very nature of the speech to violate the illusion of the stage picture by stepping out of the frame, as it were, in order to take the audience into his confidence. Not until the aside was abolished did it become possible for an actor to follow the modern rule of seeming totally oblivious of his audience.

There is less logical objection to the soliloquy, however; and I am inclined to think that the present avoidance of it is overstrained. Stage soliloquies are of two kinds, which we may call for convenience the constructive and the reflective. By a constructive soliloquy we mean one introduced arbitrarily to explain the progress of the plot, like that at the beginning of the last act of *Lady Windermere's Fan*, in which the heroine frankly tells the audience what she has been thinking and doing between the acts. By a reflective soliloquy we mean one like those of *Hamlet*, in which the audience is given merely a revelation of a train of personal thought or emotion, and in which the dramatist makes no utilitarian reference to the structure of the plot. The constructive soliloquy is as undesirable as the aside, because it forces the actor out of the stage picture in exactly the same way; but a good actor may easily read a reflective soliloquy without seeming in the least unnatural. Certainly Eugene O'Neill, with the artistic triumph of *Strange Interlude*, has rendered a real service to the modern drama by reminding us of the vastitude and depth of those psychologic regions which can be explored only by the expedient of the reflective soliloquy.

Modern methods of lighting, as we have seen, have carried the actor away from the centre of the stage, so that now important business is often done far from the footlights. This tendency has led to further innovations. Actors now frequently turn their backs to the audience,—a thing unheard of before the advent of the Drama of Illusion; and frequently, also, they do their most effective work at moments when they have no lines to speak.

But the present tendency toward naturalness of representment has, to some extent, exaggerated the importance of stage-management even at the expense of acting. A successful play by Clyde Fitch usually owed its popularity, not so much to the excellence of the acting as to the careful attention of the author to the most minute details of the stage picture. Fitch could make an act out of a wedding or a funeral, a Cook's tour or a steamer deck, a bed or an automobile. The extraordinary cleverness and accuracy of his observation of those petty details that make life a thing of shreds and patches were all that distinguished his method from that of the melodramatist who makes a scene out of a buzz-saw or a waterfall, a locomotive or a ferryboat. Oftentimes the contemporary playwright follows the method suggested by Mr. Crummles to Nicholas Nickleby, and builds his piece around "a real pump and two washing-tubs."

This emphasis of stage illusion is fraught with certain dangers to the art of acting. In the modern picture-play the lines themselves are often of such minor importance that the success or failure of the piece depends little on the reading of the words. Many young actors, therefore, cannot get that rigid training in the art of reading which could be secured in the stock companies of the generation past. Poor reading is the one great weakness of contemporary acting. It has become possible, under present conditions, for young actresses ignorant of elocution and unskilled in the first principles of impersonation to be exploited as stars merely because of their personal charm. A beautiful young woman, whether she can act or not, may easily appear "natural" in a play especially written around her; and the public, lured by a pair of eyes or a head of hair, is made as blind as love to the absence of histrionic art.

IV

A comparison of an Elizabethan audience with a theatreful of people at the present day is, in many ways, disadvantageous to the latter. With our forefathers, theatre-going was an exercise in the lovely art of "making-believe." They were told that it was night and they forgot the sunlight; their imaginations swept around England to the trampling of armored kings, or were whisked away at a word to that Bohemia which is a desert country by the sea; and while they looked upon a platform of bare boards, they breathed the sweet air of the Forest of Arden. They needed no scenery by Alma-Tadema to make them think themselves in Rome. "What country, friends, is this?", asked Viola. "This is Illyria, lady." And the boys in the pit scented the keen, salt air and heard the surges crashing on the rocky shore.

Nowadays elaborateness of stage illusion has made spoiled children of us all. We must have a doll with real hair, or else we cannot play at being mothers. We have been pampered with mechanical toys until we have lost the art of playing without them. Where have our imaginations gone, that we must have real rain upon the stage? Shall we clamor for real snow before long, that must be kept in cold storage against the spring season? A longing for concreteness has befogged our fantasy. Even so excellent an actor as Sir Johnston Forbes-Robertson could not read the great speech beginning, "Look here, upon this picture and on this," in which Hamlet obviously refers to two imaginary portraits in his mind's eye, without pointing successively to two absurd caricatures that were daubed upon the scenery.

The theatre has grown older since the days when Burbage recited that same speech upon a bare platform; but I am not entirely sure that it has grown wiser. We theatre-goers have come to manhood and have put away childish things; but there was a sweetness about the naïveté of childhood that we can never quite regain. No longer do we dream ourselves in a garden of springtide blossoms; we can only look upon canvas trees and paper flowers. No longer are we charmed away to that imagined spot where journeys end in lovers' meeting; we can only look upon love in a parlor and notice that the furniture is natural. No longer do we harken to the rich resonance of the Drama of Rhetoric; no longer do our minds kindle with the brilliant epigrams of the Drama of Conversation. Good reading is disappearing from the stage; and in its place we are left the devices of the stage-carpenter.

It would be absurd to deny that modern stagecraft has made possible in the theatre many excellent effects that were not dreamt of in the philosophy of Shakespeare. Sir Arthur Pinero's plays are better made than those of the Elizabethans, and in a narrow sense hold the mirror up to nature more successfully than theirs. But our latter-day fondness for natural representment has afflicted us with one tendency that the Elizabethans were luckily without. In our desire to imitate the actual facts of life, we sometimes become nearsighted and forget the larger truths that underlie them. We give our plays a definite date by founding them on passing fashions; we make them of an age, not for all time. We discuss contemporary social problems on the stage instead of the eternal verities lodged deep in the general heart of man. We have outgrown our pristine simplicity, but we have not yet arrived at the age of wisdom. Perhaps when playgoers have progressed for another century or two, they will willingly discard some of the trappings and the suits of our present drama, and become again like little children.

V

ECONOMY OF ATTENTION IN THEATRICAL PERFORMANCES

ACCORDING to Herbert Spencer, the sole source of force in writing is an ability to economise the attention of the reader. The word should be a window to the thought and should transmit it as transparently as possible. He says, toward the beginning of his *Philosophy of Style:*

A reader or listener has at each moment but a limited amount of mental power available. To recognise and interpret the symbols presented to him requires a part of this power; to arrange and combine the images suggested requires a further part; and only that part which remains can be used for realising the thought conveyed. Hence, the more time and attention it takes to receive and understand each sentence, the less time and attention can be given to the contained idea; and the less vividly will that idea be conveyed.

Spencer drew his illustrations of this principle mainly from the literature of the library; but its application is even more important in the literature of the stage. So many and so diverse are the elements of a theatrical performance that, unless the attention of the spectator is attracted at every moment to the main dramatic purpose of the scene, he will sit wide-eyed, like a child at a three-ring circus, with his mind fluttering from point to point and his interest dispersed and scattered. A perfect theatrical performance must harmonise the work of many men. The dramatist, the actors main and minor, the stage-manager, the scene-painter, the costumer, the leader of the orchestra, must all contribute their separate talents to the production of a single work of art. It follows that a nice adjustment of parts, a discriminating subordination of minor elements to major, is absolutely necessary in order that the attention of the audience may be focused at every moment upon the central meaning of the scene. If the spectator looks at scenery when he should be listening to lines, if his attention is startled by some unexpected device of stage-management at a time when he ought to be looking at an actor's face, or if his mind is kept for a moment uncertain of the most emphatic feature of a scene, the main effect is lost and that part of the performance is a failure.

It may be profitable to notice some of the technical devices by which attention is economised in the theatre and the interest of the audience is thereby centred upon the main business of the moment. In particular it is important to observe how a scattering of attention is avoided; how, when many things are shown at once upon the stage, it is possible to make an audience look at one and not observe the others. We shall consider the subject from the point of view of the dramatist, from that of the actor, and from that of the stage-director.

II

The dramatist, in writing, labors under a disadvantage that is not suffered by the novelist. If a passage in a novel is not perfectly clear at the first glance, the reader may always turn back the pages and read the scene again; but on the stage a line once spoken can never be recalled. When, therefore, an important point is to be set forth, the dramatist cannot afford to risk his clearness upon a single line. This is particularly true in the beginning of a play. When the curtain rises, there is always a fluttering of programs and a buzz of unfinished conversation. Many spectators come in late and hide the stage from those behind them while they are taking off their wraps. Consequently, most dramatists, in the preliminary exposition that must always start a play, contrive to state every important fact at least three times: first, for the attentive; second, for the intelligent; and third, for the large mass that may have missed the first two statements. Of course, the method of presentment must be very deftly varied, in order that the artifice may not appear; but this simple rule of three is almost always practised. It was used with fine effect by Eugène Scribe, who, although he was too clever to be great, contributed more than any other writer of the nineteenth century to the science of making a modern play.

In order that the attention of the audience may not be unduly distracted by any striking effect, the dramatist must always prepare for such an effect in advance, and give the spectators an idea of what they may expect. The extraordinary nose of Cyrano de Bergerac is described at length by Ragueneau before the hero comes upon the stage. If the ugly-visaged poet should enter without this preliminary explanation, the whole effect would be lost. The spectators would nudge each other and whisper half aloud, "Look at his nose! What *is* the matter with his face?", and would be less than half attentive to the lines. Before Lady Macbeth is shown walking in her sleep and wringing her hands that are sullied with the damned spot that all great Neptune's ocean could not wash away, her doctor and her waiting gentlewoman are sent to tell the audience of her "slumbery agitation." Thus, at the proper moment, the attention is focused on the essential point instead of being allowed to lose itself in wonder.

A logical development of this principle leads us to the corollary that a dramatist should never keep a secret from his audience, although this is one of the favorite devices of the novelist. Let us suppose for a moment that the spectators were not let into the secret of Hero's pretty plot, in *Much Ado*, to bring Beatrice and Benedick together. Suppose that, like the heroine and the hero, they were led to believe that each was truly in love with the other. The inevitable revelation of this error would produce a shock of surprise that would utterly scatter their attention; and while they were busy making over their former conception of the situation, they would have no eyes nor ears for what was going on upon the stage. In a novel, the true character of a hypocrite is often hidden until the book is nearly through: then, when the revelation comes, the reader has plenty of time to think back and see how deftly he has been deceived. But in a play, a rogue must be known to be a rogue at his first entrance. The other characters in the play may be kept in the dark until the last act, but the audience must know the secret all the time. In fact, any situation which shows a character suffering from a lack of such knowledge as the audience holds secure always produces a telling effect upon the stage. The spectators are aware of Iago's villainy and know of Desdemona's innocence. The play would not be nearly so strong if, like Othello, they were kept ignorant of the truth.

In order to economise attention, the dramatist must centre his interest in a few vividly drawn characters and give these a marked preponderance over the other parts. Many plays have failed because of over-elaborateness of detail. Ben Jonson's comedy of *Every Man in His Humour* would at present be impossible upon the stage, for the simple reason that *all* the characters are so carefully drawn that the audience would not know in whom to be most interested. The play is all background and no foreground. The dramatist fails to say, "Of all these sixteen characters, you must listen most attentively to some special two or three"; and, in consequence, the piece would require a constant effort of attention that no modern audience would be willing to bestow. Whatever may be said about the disadvantages of the so-called "star system" in the theatre, the fact remains that the greatest plays of the world—*Œdipus King, Hamlet, As You Like It, Tartufe, Cyrano de Bergerac*—have almost always been what are called "star plays." The "star system" has an obvious advantage from the point of view of the dramatist. When Hamlet enters, the spectators know that they must look at him; and their attention never wavers to the minor characters upon the stage. The play is thus an easy one to follow: attention is economised and no effect is lost.

It is a wise plan to use familiar and conventional types to fill in the minor parts of a play. The comic valet, the pretty and witty chambermaid, the *ingénue*, the pathetic old friend of the family, are so well known upon the stage that they spare the mental energy of the spectators and leave them greater vigor of attention to devote to the more original major characters. What is called "comic relief" has a similar value in resting the attention of the audience. After the spectators have been harrowed by Ophelia's madness, they must be diverted by the humor of the grave-diggers in order that their susceptibilities may be made sufficiently fresh for the solemn scene of her funeral.

We have seen that any sudden shock of surprise should be avoided in the theatre, because such a shock must inevitably cause a scattering of attention. It often happens that the strongest scenes of a play require the use of some physical accessory,—a screen in *The School for Scandal*, a horse in *Shenandoah*, a perfumed letter in *Diplomacy*. In all such cases, the spectators must be familiarised beforehand with the accessory object, so that when the climax comes they may devote all of their attention to the action that is accomplished with the object rather than to the object itself. In a quarrel scene, an actor could not suddenly draw a concealed weapon in order to threaten his antagonist. The spectators would stop to ask themselves how he happened to have the weapon by him without their knowing it; and this self-muttered question would deaden the effect of the scene. The *dénouement* of Ibsen's *Hedda Gabler* requires that the two chief characters, Eilert Lövborg and Hedda Tesman, should die of pistol wounds. The pistols that are to be used in the catastrophe are mentioned and shown repeatedly throughout the early and middle scenes of the play; so that when the last act comes, the audience thinks not of pistols, but of murder and suicide. A striking illustration of the same dramaturgic principle was shown in Mrs. Fiske's admirable performance of this play. The climax of the piece comes at the end of the penultimate act, when Hedda casts into the fire the manuscript of the book into which Eilert has put the great work of his life. The stove stands ready at the left of the stage; but when the culminating moment comes, the spectators must be made to forget the stove in their horror at Hedda's wickedness. They must, therefore, be made familiar with the stove in the early part of the act. Ibsen realised this, and arranged that Hedda should call for some wood to be cast upon the fire at the beginning of the scene. In acting this incident, Mrs. Fiske kneeled before the stove in the very attitude that she was to assume later on when she committed the manuscript to the flames. The climax gained greatly in emphasis because of this device to secure economy of attention at the crucial moment.

III

In the *Autobiography of Joseph Jefferson*, that humorous and human and instructive book, there is a passage that illustrates admirably the bearing of this same principle of economy of attention upon the actor's art. In speaking of the joint performances of his half-brother, Charles Burke, and the famous actor-manager, William E. Burton, Jefferson says:

It was a rare treat to see Burton and Burke in the same play: they acted into each other's hands with the most perfect skill; there was no striving to outdo each other. If the scene required that for a time one should be prominent, the other would become the background of the picture, and so strengthen the general effect; by this method they produced a perfectly harmonious work. For instance, Burke would remain in repose, attentively listening while Burton was delivering some humorous speech. This would naturally act as a spell upon the audience, who became by this treatment absorbed in what Burton was saying, and having got the full force of the effect, they would burst forth in laughter or applause; then, by one accord, they became silent, intently listening to Burke's reply, which Burton was now strengthening by the same repose and attention. I have never seen this element in acting carried so far, or accomplished with such admirable results, not even upon the French stage, and I am convinced that the importance of it in reaching the best dramatic effects cannot be too highly estimated. It was this characteristic feature of the acting of these two great artists that always set the audience wondering which was the better. The truth is there was no "better" about the matter. They were not horses running a race, but artists painting a picture; it was not in their minds which should win, but how they could, by their joint efforts, produce a perfect work.

I am afraid that this excellent method of team play is more honored in the breach than in the observance among many of our eminent actors of more recent times. When Richard Mansfield played the part of Brutus, he destroyed the nice balance of the quarrel scene with Cassius by attracting all of the attention of the audience to himself, whereas a right reading of the scene would demand a constant shifting of attention from one hero to the other. When Joseph Haworth spoke the great speech of Cassius beginning, "Come, Antony, and young Octavius, come!", he was shrouded in the shadow of the tent, while the lime-light fell full upon the form of Brutus. This arrangement so distracted the audience from the true dramatic value of the scene that neither Mansfield's heroic carriage, nor his eye like Mars to threaten and command, nor the titanic resonance of his ventriloquial utterance, could atone for the mischief that was done.

In an earlier paragraph, we noticed the way in which the "star system" may be used to advantage by the dramatist to economise the attention of the audience; but it will be observed, on the other hand, that the same system is pernicious in its influence upon the actor. A performer who is accustomed to the centre of the stage often finds it difficult to keep himself in the background at moments when the scene should be dominated by other, and sometimes lesser, actors. Artistic self-denial is one of the rarest of virtues. This is the reason why "all-star" performances are almost always bad. A famous player is cast for a minor part; and in his effort to exploit his talents, he violates the principle of economy of attention by attracting undue notice to a subordinate feature of the performance. That's villainous, and shows a most pitiful ambition, as Hamlet truly says. A rare proof of the genius of the great Coquelin was given by his performances of Père Duval and the Baron Scarpia in support of the Camille and Tosca of Sarah Bernhardt. These parts are both subordinate; and, in playing them, Coquelin so far succeeded in obliterating his own special talents that he never once distracted the attention of the audience from the acting of his fellow star. This was an artistic triumph worthy of ranking with the same actor's sweeping and enthralling performance of Cyrano de Bergerac,—perhaps the richest acting part in the history of the theatre.

A story is told of how Sir Henry Irving, many years ago, played the role of Joseph Surface at a special revival of *The School for Scandal* in which most of the other parts were filled by actors and actresses of the older generation, who attempted to recall for one performance the triumphs of their youth. Joseph Surface is a hypocrite and a villain; but the youthful grace of Henry Irving so charmed a lady in the stalls that she said she "could not bear to see those old unlovely people trying to get the better of that charming young man, Mr. Joseph." Something must have been wrong with the economy of her attention.

The chief reason why mannerisms of walk or gesture or vocal intonation are objectionable in an actor is that they distract the attention of the audience from the effect he is producing to his method of producing that effect. Mansfield's peculiar manner of pumping his voice from his diaphragm and Irving's corresponding system of ejaculating his phrases through his nose gave to the reading of those great artists a rich metallic resonance that was vibrant with effect; but a person hearing either of those actors for the first time was often forced to expend so much of his attention in adjusting his ears to the novel method of voice production that he was unable for many minutes to fix his mind upon the more important business of the play. An actor without mannerisms, like the great Adolf von Sonnenthal, was able to make a more immediate appeal.

IV

At the first night of E. H. Sothern's *Hamlet*, in the fall of 1900, I had just settled back in my chair to listen to the reading of the soliloquy on suicide, when a woman behind me whispered to her neighbor, "Oh, look! There are two fireplaces in the room!" My attention was distracted, and the soliloquy was spoiled; but the fault lay with the stage-manager rather than with the woman who spoke the disconcerting words. If Mr. Sothern was to recite his soliloquy gazing dreamily into a fire in the centre of the room, the stage-manager should have known enough to remove the large fireplace on the right of the stage.

Sarah Bernhardt, when she acted *Hamlet* in London in 1899, introduced a novel and startling effect in the closet scene between the hero and his mother. On the wall, as usual, hung the counterfeit presentments of two brothers; and when the time came for the ghost of buried Denmark to appear, he was suddenly seen standing luminous in the picture-frame which had contained his portrait. The effect was so unexpected that the audience could look at nothing else, and thus Hamlet and the queen failed to get their proper measure of attention.

These two instances show that the necessity of economising the attention of an audience is just as important to the stage-director as it is to the dramatist and the actor. In the main, it may be said that any unexpected innovation, any device of stage-management that is by its nature startling, should be avoided in the crucial situations of a play. Brander Matthews has given an interesting illustration of this principle in his essay on *The Art of the Stage-Manager*, which is included in his volume entitled *Inquiries and Opinions*. He says:

The stage-manager must ever be on his guard against the danger of sacrificing the major to the minor, and of letting some little effect of slight value in itself interfere with the true interest of the play as a whole. At the first performance of Mr. Bronson Howard's *Shenandoah*, the opening act of which ends with the firing of the shot on Sumter, there was a wide window at the back of the set, so that the spectators could see the curving flight of the bomb and its final explosion above the doomed fort. The scenic marvel had cost time and money to devise; but it was never visible after the first performance, because it drew attention to itself, as a mechanical effect, and so took off the minds of the audience from the Northern lover and the Southern girl, the Southern lover and the Northern girl, whose loves were suddenly sundered by the bursting of that fatal shell. At the second performance, the spectators did not see the shot, they only heard the dread report; and they were free to let their sympathy go forth to the young couples.

Nowadays, perhaps, when the theatre-going public is more used to elaborate mechanism on the stage, this effect might be attempted without danger. It was owing to its novelty at the time that the device disrupted the attention of the spectators.

But not only novel and startling stage effects should be avoided in the main dramatic moments of a play. Excessive magnificence and elaborateness of setting are just as distracting to the attention as the shock of a new and strange device. When *The Merchant of Venice* was revived at Daly's Theatre toward the end of the eighteen-nineties, a scenic set of unusual beauty was used for the final act. The gardens of Portia's palace were shadowy with trees and dreamy with the dark of evening. Slowly in the distance a round and yellow moon rose rolling, its beams rippling over the moving waters of a lake. There was a murmur of approbation in the audience; and that murmur was just loud enough to deaden the lyric beauty of the lines in which Lorenzo and Jessica gave expression to the spirit of the night. The audience could not look and listen at the self-same moment; and Shakespeare was sacrificed for a lime-light.

This point suggests a discussion of the advisability of producing Shakespeare without scenery, in the very interesting manner that was advocated for so many years by Sir Philip Ben Greet and was accepted with clamorous applause when *Julius Cæsar* was presented in New York, in 1937, by the Mercury Theatre, under the leadership of Orson Welles and John Houseman. Leaving aside the argument that with a sceneless stage it is possible to perform all the incidents of the play in their original order, and thus give the story a greater narrative continuity, it may also be maintained that with a bare stage there are far fewer chances of dispersing the attention of the audience by attracting it to insignificant details of setting. But, unfortunately, the same argument for economy of attention may work also in the contrary direction. We have been so long used to scenery in our theatres that a sceneless production requires a new adjustment of our minds to accept the unwonted convention; and it may readily be feared that this mental adjustment may disperse more attention than would be scattered by the customary stage effects. On the whole, it would probably be wisest to produce Shakespeare with very simple scenery, in the mood and manner of that admirable artist, Robert Edmond Jones, in order, on the one hand, not to dim the imagination of the spectators by elaborate magnificence of setting, and, on the other, not to distract their minds by the unaccustomed conventions of a sceneless stage.

What has been said of scenery may be applied also to the use of incidental music. So soon as such music becomes obtrusive, it distracts the attention from the business of the play: and it cannot be insisted on too often that in the theatre the play's the thing. But a running accompaniment of music, half-heard, half-guessed, that moves to the mood of the play, now swelling to a climax, now softening to a hush, may do much toward keeping the audience in tune with the emotional significance of the action.

A perfect theatrical performance is the rarest of all works of art. I have seen several perfect statues and perfect pictures; and I have read many perfect poems: but I have never seen a perfect performance in the theatre. I doubt if such a performance has ever been given, except, perhaps, in ancient Greece. But it is easy to imagine what its effect would be. It would rivet the attention throughout upon the essential purport of the play; it would proceed from the beginning to the end without the slightest distraction; and it would convey its message simply and immediately, like the sky at sunrise or the memorable murmur of the sea.

VI

EMPHASIS IN THE DRAMA

B Y APPLYING the negative principle of economy of attention, the dramatist may, as we have noticed, prevent his auditors at any moment from diverting their attention to the subsidiary features of the scene; but it is necessary for him also to apply the positive principle of emphasis in order to force them to focus their attention on the one most important detail of the matter in hand. The principle of emphasis, which is applied in all the arts, is the principle whereby the artist contrives to throw into vivid relief those features of his work which incorporate the essence of the thing he has to say, while at the same time he gathers and groups within a scarcely noticed background those other features which merely contribute in a minor manner to the central purpose of his plan. This principle is, of course, especially important in the acted drama; and it may therefore be profitable to examine in detail some of the methods which dramatists employ to make their points effectively and bring out the salient features of their plays.

It is obviously easy to emphasise by position. The last moments in any act are of necessity emphatic because they are the last. During the intermission, the minds of the spectators will naturally dwell upon the scene that has been presented to them most recently. If they think back toward the beginning of the act, they must first think through the concluding dialogue. This lends to curtain-falls a special importance of which our modern dramatists rarely fail to take advantage.

It is interesting to remember that this simple form of emphasis by position was impossible in the Elizabethan theatre and was quite unknown to Shakespeare. His plays were produced on a platform without a curtain; his actors had to make an exit at the end of every scene; and usually his plays were acted from beginning to end without any intermission. It was therefore impossible for him to bring his acts to an emphatic close by a clever curtain-fall. We have gained this advantage only in recent times because of the improved physical conditions of our theatre.

A few years ago it was customary for dramatists to end every act with a bang that would reverberate in the ears of the audience throughout the *entr'acte*. Recently our playwrights have shown a tendency toward more quiet curtain-falls. The exquisite close of the first act of *The Admirable Crichton* was merely dreamfully suggestive of the past and future of the action; and the second act ended pictorially, without a word. But whether a curtain-fall gains its effect actively or passively, it should, if possible, sum up the entire dramatic accomplishment of the act that it concludes and foreshadow the subsequent progress of the play.

Likewise, the first moments in an act are of necessity emphatic because they are the first. After an intermission, the audience is prepared to watch with renewed eagerness the resumption of the action. The close of the first act of *The Second Mrs. Tanqueray* makes the audience long expectantly for the opening of the second; and whatever the dramatist may do after the raising of the curtain will be emphasised because he does it first. An exception must be made of the opening act of a play. A dramatist seldom sets forth anything of vital importance during the first ten minutes of his piece, because the action is likely to be interrupted by late-comers in the audience and other distractions incident to the early hour. But after an intermission, he is surer of attention, and may thrust important matter into the openings of his acts.

The last position, however, is more potent than the first. It is because of their finality that exit speeches are emphatic. It has become customary in the theatre to applaud a prominent actor nearly every time he leaves the stage; and this custom has made it necessary for the dramatist to precede an exit with some speech or action important enough to justify the interruption. Though Shakespeare and his contemporaries knew nothing of the curtain-fall, they at least understood fully the emphasis of exit speeches. They even tagged them with rhyme to give them greater prominence. An actor likes to take advantage of his last chance to move an audience. When he leaves the stage, he wants at least to be remembered.

In general it may be said that any pause in the action emphasises by position the speech or business that immediately preceded it. This is true not only of the long pause at the end of an act: the point is illustrated just as well by an interruption of the play in mid-career, like Mrs. Fiske's ominous and oppressive minute of silence in the last act of *Hedda Gabler*. The employment of pause as an aid to emphasis is of especial importance in the reading of lines.

It is also customary in the drama to emphasise by proportion. More time is given to significant scenes than to incidents of subsidiary interest. The strongest characters in a play are given most to say and do; and the extent of the lines of the others is proportioned to their importance in the action. Hamlet says more and does more than any other character in the tragedy in which he figures. This is as it should be; but, on the other hand, Polonius, in the same play, seems to receive greater emphasis by proportion than he really deserves. The part is very fully written. Polonius is often on the stage, and talks incessantly whenever he is present; but, after all, he is a man of small importance and fulfils a minor purpose in the plot. He is, therefore, falsely emphasised. That is why the part of Polonius is what French actors call a *faux bon rôle*,—a part that seems better than it is.

In certain special cases, it is advisable to emphasise a character by the ironical expedient of inverse proportion. Tartufe is so imphasised throughout the first two acts of the play that bears his name. Although he is withheld from the stage until the second scene of the third act, so much is said about him that we are made to feel fully his sinister dominance over the household of Orgon; and at his first appearance, we already know him better than we know any of the other characters. In Victor Hugo's *Marion Delorme*, the indomitable will of Cardinal Richelieu is the mainspring of the entire action, and the audience is led to feel that he may at any moment enter upon the stage. But he is withheld until the very final moment of the drama, and even then is merely carried mute across the scene in a sedan-chair. Similarly, in Paul Heyse's *Mary of Magdala*, and again in Maurice Maeterlinck's *Mary Magdalene*, the Supreme Person who guides and controls the souls of all the struggling characters is never introduced upon the scene, but is suggested merely through his effect on Mary, Judas, and the other visible figures in the action.

One of the easiest means of emphasis is the use of repetition; and this is a favorite device with Henrik Ibsen. Certain catch-words, which incorporate a recurrent mood of character or situation, are repeated over and over again throughout the course of his dialogue. The result is often similar to that attained by Wagner, in his music-dramas, through the iteration of a *leit-motiv*. Thus in *Rosmersholm*, whenever the action takes a turn that foreshadows the tragic catastrophe, allusion is made to the weird symbol of "white horses." Similarly, in *Hedda Gabler*—to take another instance—the emphasis of repetition is flung on certain leading phrases,—"Fancy that, Hedda!", "Wavy-haired Thea," "Vine-leaves in his hair," and "People don't do such things!"

Another obvious means of emphasis in the drama is the use of antithesis,—an expedient employed in every art. The design of a play is not so much to expound characters as to contrast them. People of varied views and opposing aims come nobly to the grapple in a struggle that vitally concerns them; and the tensity of the struggle will be augmented if the difference between the characters is marked. The comedies of Ben Jonson, which held the stage for two centuries after their author's death, owed their success largely to the fact that they presented a constant contrast of mutually foiling personalities. But the expedient of antithesis is most effectively employed in the balance of scene against scene. What is known as "comic relief" is introduced in various plays, not only, as the phrase suggests, to rest the sensibilities of the audience, but also to emphasise the solemn scenes that come before and after it. It is for this purpose that Shakespeare, in *Macbeth*, introduces a low-comic soliloquy into the midst of a murder scene. Hamlet's ranting over the grave of Ophelia is made more emphatic by antithesis with the foolish banter that precedes it.

This contrast of mood between scene and scene was unknown in ancient plays and in the imitations of them that flourished in the first great period of the French tragic stage. Although the ancient drama frequently violated the three unities of action, time, and place, it always preserved a fourth unity, which we may call unity of mood. It remained for the Spaniards and the Elizabethan English to grasp the dramatic value of the great antithesis between the humorous and the serious, the grotesque and the sublime, and to pass it on through Victor Hugo to the contemporary theatre.

A further means of emphasis is, of course, the use of climax. This principle is at the basis of the familiar method of working up an entrance. My lady's coach is heard clattering behind the scenes. A servant rushes to the window and tells us that his mistress is alighting. There is a ring at the entrance; we hear the sound of footsteps in the hall. At last the door is thrown open, and my lady enters, greeted by a salvo of applause.

A first entrance unannounced is rarely seen upon the modern stage. Shakespeare's *King John* opens very simply. The stage direction reads, "Enter King John, Queen Elinor, Pembroke, Essex, Salisbury and others, with Chatillon"; and then the king speaks the opening line of the play. Yet when Sir Herbert Beerbohm Tree revived this drama at Her Majesty's Theatre in 1899, he devised an elaborate opening to give a climacteric effect to the entrance of the king. The curtain rose upon a vaulted room of state, impressive in its bare magnificence. A throne was set upon a dais to the left, and several noblemen in splendid costumes were lingering about the room. At the back was a Norman corridor approached by a flight of lofty steps which led upward from the level of the stage. There was a peal of trumpets from without, and soon to a stately music the royal guards marched upon the scene. They were followed by ladies with gorgeous dresses sweeping away in long trains borne by pretty pages, and great lords walking with dignity to the music of the regal measure. At last Mr. Tree appeared and stood for a moment at the top of the steps, every inch a king. Then he strode majestically to the dais, ascended to the throne, and turning about with measured majesty spoke the first line of the play, some minutes after the raising of the curtain.

But not only in the details of a drama is the use of climax necessary. The whole action should sweep upward in intensity until the highest point is reached. In the Shakespearean drama the highest point came somewhat early in the piece, usually only a little more than halfway through the action; but in modern plays the climax is almost always placed at the end of the penultimate act,—the fourth act if there are five, and the third act if there are four. At the close of the nineteenth century, the four-act pattern with a strong climax at the end of the third act was the form most often used. This was the form, for instance, of Ibsen's *Hedda Gabler*, of Henry Arthur Jones's *Mrs. Dane's Defense*, and of Sir Arthur Pinero's *The Second Mrs. Tanqueray*, *The Notorious Mrs. Ebbsmith*, and *The Gay Lord Quex*. Each began with an act of exposition, followed by an act of rising interest. Then the whole action of the play rushed upward toward the curtain-fall of the third act, after which an act was used to bring the play to a terrible or a happy conclusion. In still more recent seasons, the tendency has been to abbreviate the pattern to three acts and to withhold the climax until the latter half of the last act, thus necessitating a sudden, swift catastrophe.

A less familiar means of emphasis is that which owes its origin to surprise. This expedient must be used with great delicacy, because a sudden and startling shock of surprise is likely to diseconomise the attention of the spectators and flurry them out of a comprehensive conception of the scene. But if a moment of surprise has been carefully led up to by anticipatory suggestion, it may be used to throw into sharp and sudden relief an important point in the play. No one knows that Cyrano de Bergerac is on the stage until he rises in the midst of the crowd in the Hôtel de Bourgogne and shakes his cane at Montfleury. When Sir Herbert Tree played D'Artagnan in *The Musketeers*, he emerged suddenly in the midst of a scene from a suit of old armor standing monumental at the back of the stage,—a *deus ex machina* to dominate the situation. American playgoers will remember the disguise of Sherlock Holmes in the last act of William Gillette's admirable melodrama. The appearance of the ghost in the closet scene of *Hamlet* is made emphatic by its unexpectedness.

But perhaps the most effective form of emphasis in the drama is emphasis by suspense. Wilkie Collins, who with all his faults as a critic of life remains the most skilful maker of plots in English fiction, used to say that the secret of holding the attention of one's readers lay in the ability to do three things: "Make 'em laugh; make 'em weep; make 'em wait." There is no use in making the auditors wait, however, unless you first give them an inkling of what they are waiting for. The dramatist must play with his spectators as we play with a kitten when we trail a ball of yarn before its eyes, only to snatch it away just as the kitten leaps for it.

This method of emphasising by suspense gives force to what are known technically as the *scènes à faire* of a drama. A *scène à faire* —the phrase was devised by Francisque Sarcey—is a scene late in a play that is demanded absolutely by the previous progress of the plot. The audience knows that the scene must come sooner or later, and if the element of suspense be ably managed, is made to long for it some time before it comes. In *Hamlet*, for instance, the killing of the king by the hero is of course a *scène à faire*. The audience knows before the first act is over that such a scene is surely coming. When the king is caught praying in his closet and Hamlet stands over him with naked sword, the spectators think at last that the *scène à faire* has arrived; but Shakespeare "makes 'em wait" for two acts more, until the very ending of the play.

In comedy the commonest *scènes à faire* are love scenes that the audience anticipates and longs to see. Perhaps the young folks are frequently on the stage, but the desired scene is prevented by the presence of other characters. Only after many movements are the lovers left alone; and when at last the pretty moment comes, the audience glows with long-awaited enjoyment.

It is always dangerous for a dramatist to omit a *scène à faire*,— to raise in the minds of his audience an expectation that is never satisfied. Sheridan did this in *The School for Scandal* when he failed to introduce a love scene between Charles and Maria, and Henry Arthur Jones did it in *Whitewashing Julia* when he made the audience expect throughout the play a revelation of the truth about the puff-box and then left them disappointed in the end. But these cases are exceptional. In general it may be said that an unsatisfied suspense is no suspense at all.

One of the most effective instances of suspense in the modern drama is offered in the opening of *John Gabriel Borkman*, one of Ibsen's later plays. Many years before the drama opens, the hero has been sent to jail for misusing the funds of a bank of which he was director. After five years of imprisonment, he has been released, eight years before the opening of the play. During these eight years, he has lived alone in the great gallery of his house, never going forth even in the dark of night, and seeing only two people who come to call upon him. One of these, a young girl, sometimes plays for him on the piano while he paces moodily up and down the gallery. These facts are expounded to the audience in a dialogue between Mrs. Borkman and her sister that takes place in a lower room below Borkman's quarters; and all the while, in the pauses of the conversation, the hero is heard walking overhead, pacing incessantly up and down. As the act advances, the audience expects at any moment that the hero will appear. The front door is thrown open; two minor characters enter; and still Borkman is heard walking up and down. There is more talk about him on the stage; the act is far advanced, and soon it seems that he must show himself. From the upper room is heard the music of the Dance of Death that his young girl friend is playing for him. Now to the dismal measures of the dance the dialogue on the stage swells to a climax. Borkman is still heard pacing in the gallery. And the curtain falls. Ten minutes later the raising of the curtain discloses John Gabriel Borkman standing with his hands behind his back, looking at the girl who has been playing for him. The moment is trebly emphatic,—by position at the opening of an act, by surprise, and most of all by suspense. When the hero is at last discovered, the audience looks at him.

Of course there are many minor means of emphasis in the theatre, but most of these are artificial and mechanical. The proverbial lime-light is one of the most effective. The intensity of the dream scene in Sir Henry Irving's performance of *The Bells* was due largely to the way in which the single figure of Mathias was silhouetted by a ray of light against a shadowy and inscrutable background ominous with voices.

In this materialistic age, actors even resort to blandishments of costume to give their parts a special emphasis. Our leading ladies are more richly clad than the minor members of their companies. Even the great Mansfield resorted in his performance of Brutus to the indefensible expedient of changing his costume act by act and dressing always in exquisite and subtle colors, while the other Romans, Cassius included, wore the same togas of unaffected white throughout the play. This was a fault in emphasis.

A novel and interesting device of emphasis in stage-direction was introduced by Sir Johnston Forbes-Robertson in his production of *The Passing of the Third Floor Back*. This dramatic parable by Jerome K. Jerome deals with the moral regeneration of eleven people, who are living in a Bloomsbury boarding-house, through the personal influence of a Passer-by, who is the Spirit of Love incarnate; and this effect is accomplished in a succession of dialogues, in which the Stranger talks at length with one boarder after another. It is necessary, for reasons of reality, that in each of the dialogues the Passer-by and his interlocutor should be seated at their ease. It is also necessary, for reasons of effectiveness in presentation, that the faces of both parties to the conversation should be kept clearly visible to the audience. In actual life, the two people would most naturally sit before a fire; but if a fireplace should be set in either the right or the left wall of the stage and two actors should be seated in front of it, the face of one of them would be obscured from the audience. The producer therefore adopted the expedient of imagining a fireplace in the fourth wall of the room,—the wall that is supposed to stretch across the stage at the line of the footlights. A red-glow from the central lamps of the string of footlights was cast up over a brass railing such as usually bounds a hearth, and behind this, far forward in the direct centre of the stage, two chairs were drawn up for the use of the actors. The right wall showed a window opening on the street, the rear wall a door opening on an entrance hall, and the left wall a door opening on a room adjacent; and in none of these could the fireplace have been logically set. The unusual device of stage-direction, therefore, contributed to the verisimilitude of the set as well as to the convenience of the action. The experiment was successful for the purposes of this particular piece; it did not seem to disrupt the attention of the audience; and the question, therefore, was suggested whether it might not, in many other plays, be advantageous to make imaginary use of the invisible fourth wall.

VII

THE FOUR LEADING TYPES OF DRAMA

I. TRAGEDY AND MELODRAMA

TRAGEDY and melodrama are alike in this,—that each exhibits a set of characters struggling vainly to avert a predetermined doom; but in this essential point they differ,—that whereas the characters in melodrama are drifted to disaster in spite of themselves, the characters in tragedy go down to destruction because of themselves. In tragedy the characters determine and control the plot; in melodrama the plot determines and controls the characters. The writer of melodrama initially imagines a stirring train of incidents, interesting and exciting in themselves, and afterward invents such characters as will readily accept the destiny that he has foreordained for them. The writer of tragedy, on the other hand, initially imagines certain characters inherently predestined to destruction because of what they are, and afterward invents such incidents as will reasonably result from what is wrong within them.

It must be recognised at once that each of these is a legitimate method for planning a serious play, and that by following either the one or the other, it is possible to make a truthful representation of life. For the ruinous events of life itself divide themselves into two classes—the melodramatic and the tragic—according as the element of chance or the element of character shows the upper hand in them. It would be melodramatic for a man to slip by accident into the Whirlpool Rapids and be drowned; but the drowning of Captain Webb in that tossing torrent was tragic, because his ambition for preëminence as a swimmer bore evermore within itself the latent possibility of his failing in an uttermost stupendous effort.

As Stevenson has said, in his *Gossip on Romance*, "The pleasure that we take in life is of two sorts,—the active and the passive.

Now we are conscious of a great command over our destiny; anon we are lifted up by circumstance, as by a breaking wave, and dashed we know not how into the future." A good deal of what happens to us is brought upon us by the fact of what we are; the rest is drifted to us, uninvited, undeserved, upon the tides of chance. When disasters overwhelm us, the fault is sometimes in ourselves, but at other times is merely in our stars. Because so much of life is casual rather than causal, the theatre (whose purpose is to represent life truly) must always rely on melodrama as the most natural and effective type of art for exhibiting some of its most interesting phases. There is therefore no logical reason whatsoever that melodrama should be held in disrepute, even by the most fastidious of critics.

But, on the other hand, it is evident that tragedy is inherently a higher type of art. The melodramatist exhibits merely what may happen; the tragedist exhibits what must happen. All that we ask of the author of melodrama is a momentary plausibility. Provided that his plot be not impossible, no limits are imposed on his invention of mere incident: even his characters will not give him pause, since they themselves have been fashioned to fit the action. But of the author of tragedy we demand an unquestionable inevitability: nothing may happen in his play which is not a logical result of the nature of his characters. Of the melodramatist we require merely the negative virtue that he shall not lie: of the tragedist we require the positive virtue that he shall reveal some phase of the absolute, eternal Truth.

The vast difference between merely saying something that is true and really saying something that gives a glimpse of the august and all-controlling Truth may be suggested by a verbal illustration. Suppose that, upon an evening which at sunset has been threatened with a storm, I observe the sky at midnight to be cloudless, and say, "The stars are shining still." Assuredly I shall be telling something that is true; but I shall not be giving in any way a revelation of the absolute. Consider now the aspect of this very same remark, as it occurs in the fourth act of John Webster's tragedy, *The Duchess of Malfi*. The Duchess, overwhelmed with despair, is talking to Bosola:

Duchess.   I'll go pray;—
    No, I'll go curse.

Bosola   O, fie!
Duchess.   I could curse the stars.
Bosola.   **O,** fearful.
Duchess. And those three smiling seasons of the year
            Into a Russian winter: nay, the world
                To its first chaos.
Bosola.   Look you, the stars shine still.

This brief sentence, which in the former instance was comparatively meaningless, here suddenly flashes on the awed imagination a vista of irrevocable law.

A similar difference exists between the august Truth of tragedy and the less revelatory truthfulness of melodrama. To understand and to expound the laws of life is a loftier task than merely to avoid misrepresenting them. For this reason, though melodrama has always abounded, true tragedy has always been extremely rare. Nearly all the tragic plays in the history of the theatre have descended at certain moments into melodrama. Shakespeare's final version of *Hamlet* stands nearly on the highest level; but here and there it still exhibits traces of that preëxistent melodrama of the school of Thomas Kyd from which it was derived. Sophocles is truly tragic, because he affords a revelation of the absolute; but Euripides is for the most part melodramatic, because he contents himself with imagining and projecting the merely possible. In our own age, Ibsen is the only author who, consistently, from play to play, commands catastrophes which are not only plausible but unavoidable. It is not strange, however, that the entire history of the drama should disclose very few masters of the tragic; for to envisage the inevitable is to look within the very mind of God.

II. COMEDY AND FARCE

If we turn our attention to the merry-mooded drama, we shall discern a similar distinction between comedy and farce. A comedy is a humorous play in which the actors dominate the action; a farce is a humorous play in which the action dominates the actors. Pure comedy is the rarest of all types of drama; because characters strong enough to determine and control a humorous plot almost always insist on fighting out their struggle to a serious issue, and thereby lift the action above the comic level. On the other hand, unless the characters thus stiffen in their purposes, they usually allow the play to lapse to farce. Pure comedies, however, have now and then been fashioned, without admixture either of farce or of serious drama; and of these *Le Misanthrope* of Molière may be taken as a standard example. The work of the same master also affords many examples of pure farce, which never rises into comedy,—for instance, *Le Médecin Malgré Lui.* Shakespeare nearly always associated the two types within the compass of a single humorous play, using comedy for his major plot and farce for his subsidiary incidents. Farce is decidedly the most irresponsible of all the types of drama. The plot exists for its own sake, and the dramatist need fulfil only two requirements in devising it:— first, he must be funny, and second, he must persuade his audience to accept his situations at least for the moment while they are being enacted. Beyond this latter requisite, he suffers no subservience to plausibility. Since he needs to be believed only for the moment, he is not obliged to limit himself to possibilities. But to compose a true comedy is a very serious task; for in comedy the action must be not only possible and plausible, but must be a necessary result of the nature of the characters. This is the reason why *The School for Scandal* is a greater accomplishment than *The Rivals*, though the latter play is fully as funny as the former. The one is comedy, and the other merely farce.

VIII

THE MODERN SOCIAL DRAMA

THE MODERN social drama—or the problem play, as it is popularly called—did not come into existence till the fourth decade of the nineteenth century; but in the last hundred years it has shown itself to be the fittest expression in dramaturgic terms of the spirit of this modern age; and it is therefore being written, to the exclusion of almost every other type, by nearly all the contemporary dramatists of international importance. This type of drama, currently prevailing, is being continually impugned by a certain set of critics, and by another set continually defended. In especial, the morality of the modern social drama has been a theme for bitter conflict; and critics have been so busy calling Ibsen a corrupter of the mind or a great ethical teacher that they have not found leisure to consider the more general and less contentious questions of what the modern social drama really is, and of precisely on what ground its morality should be determined. It may be profitable, therefore, to stand aloof from such discussion for a moment, in order to inquire calmly what it is all about.

I

Although the modern social drama is sometimes comic in its mood—*The Gay Lord Quex*, for instance—its main development has been upon the serious side; and it may be criticised most clearly as a modern type of tragedy. In order, therefore, to understand its essential qualities, we must first consider somewhat carefully the nature of tragedy in general. The theme of all serious drama is, of course, a struggle of human wills; and the special theme of tragic drama is a struggle necessarily foredoomed to failure because the individual human will is pitted against opposing forces stronger than itself. Tragedy presents the spectacle of a human being shattering himself against insuperable obstacles. Thereby it awakens pity, because the hero cannot win, and terror, because the forces arrayed against him cannot lose.

If we rapidly review the history of tragedy, we shall see that three types, and only three, have thus far been devised; and these types are to be distinquished according to the nature of the forces set in opposition to the wills of the characters. In other words, the dramatic imagination of all humanity has thus far been able to conceive only three types of struggle which are necessarily foredoomed to failure,—only three different varieties of forces so strong as to defeat inevitably any individual human being who comes into conflict with them. The first of these types was discovered by Æschylus and perfected by Sophocles; the second was discovered by Christopher Marlowe and perfected by Shakespeare; and the third was discovered by Victor Hugo and perfected by Ibsen.

The first type, which is represented by Greek tragedy, displays the individual in conflict with Fate, an inscrutable power dominating alike the actions of men and of gods. It is the God of the gods, —the destiny of which they are the instruments and ministers. Through irreverence, through vainglory, through disobedience, through weakness, the tragic hero becomes entangled in the meshes that Fate sets for the unwary; he struggles and struggles to get free, but his efforts are necessarily of no avail. He has transgressed the law of laws, and he is therefore doomed to inevitable agony. Because of this superhuman aspect of the tragic struggle, the Greek drama was religious in tone, and stimulated in the spectator the reverent and lofty mood of awe.

The second type of tragedy, which is represented by the great Elizabethan drama, displays the individual foredoomed to failure, no longer because of the preponderant power of destiny, but because of certain defects inherent in his own nature. The Fate of the Greeks has become humanised and made subjective. Christopher Marlowe was the first of the world's dramatists thus to set the God of all the gods within the soul itself of the man who suffers and contends and dies. But he imagined only one phase of the new and epoch-making tragic theme that he discovered. The one thing that he accomplished was to depict the ruin of an heroic nature through an insatiable ambition for supremacy, doomed by its own vastitude to defeat itself,—supremacy of conquest and dominion with Tamburlaine, supremacy of knowledge with Dr.

Faustus, supremacy of wealth with Barabas, the Jew of Malta. Shakespeare, with his wider mind, presented many other phases of this new type of tragic theme. Macbeth is destroyed by vaulting ambition that o'erleaps itself; Hamlet is ruined by irresoluteness and contemplative procrastination. If Othello were not overtrustful, if Lear were not decadent in senility, they would not be doomed to die in the conflict that confronts them. They fall self-ruined, self-destroyed. This second type of tragedy is less lofty and religious than the first; but it is more human, and therefore, to the spectator, more poignant. We learn more about God by watching the annihilation of an individual by Fate; but we learn more about Man by watching the annihilation of an individual by himself. Greek tragedy sends our souls through the invisible; but Elizabethan tragedy answers, "Thou thyself art Heaven and Hell."

The third type of tragedy is represented by the modern social drama. In this the individual is displayed in conflict with his environment; and the drama deals with the mighty war between personal character and social conditions. The Greek hero struggles with the superhuman; the Elizabethan hero struggles with himself; the modern hero struggles with the world. Dr. Stockmann, in Ibsen's *An Enemy of the People*, is perhaps the most definitive example of the type, although the play in which he appears is not, strictly speaking, a tragedy. He says that he is the strongest man on earth because he stands most alone. On the one side are the legions of society; on the other side a man. This is such stuff as modern plays are made of.

Thus, whereas the Greeks religiously ascribed the source of all inevitable doom to divine foreordination, and the Elizabethans poetically ascribed it to the weaknesses the human soul is heir to, the moderns prefer to ascribe it scientifically to the dissidence between the individual and his social environment. With the Greeks the catastrophe of man was decreed by Fate; with the Elizabethans it was decreed by his own soul; with us it is decreed by Mrs. Grundy. Heaven and Hell were once enthroned high above Olympus; then, as with Marlowe's Mephistophilis, they were seated deep in every individual soul; now at last they have been located in the prim parlor of the conventional dame next door. Obviously the modern type of tragedy is inherently less religious than the Greek, since science has as yet induced no dwelling-place for

God. It is also inherently less poetic than the Elizabethan, since sociological discussion demands the mood of prose.

II

Such being in general the theme and the aspect of the modern social drama, we may next consider briefly how it came into being. Like a great deal else in contemporary art, it could not possibly have been engendered before that tumultuous upheaval of human thought which produced in history the French Revolution and in literature the resurgence of romance. During the eighteenth century, both in England and in France, society was considered paramount and the individual subservient. Each man was believed to exist for the sake of the social mechanism of which he formed a part: the chain was the thing,—not its weakest, nor even its strongest, link. But the French Revolution and the cognate romantic revival in the arts unsettled this conservative belief, and made men wonder whether society, after all, did not exist solely for the sake of the individual. Early eighteenth century literature is a polite and polished exaltation of society, and preaches that the majority is always right; early nineteenth century literature is a clamorous pæan of individualism, and preaches that the majority is always wrong. Considering the modern social drama as a phase of history, we see at once that it is based upon the struggle between these two beliefs. It exhibits always a conflict between the individual revolutionist and the communal conservatives, and expresses the growing tendency of these opposing forces to adjust themselves to equilibrium.

Thus considered, the modern social drama is seen to be inherently and necessarily the product and the expression of the nineteenth century. Through no other type of drama could this modern age reveal itself so fully; for the relation between the one and the many, in politics, in religion, in the daily round of life itself, has been, and still remains, the most important topic of our times. The paramount human problem of the last hundred years has been the great, as yet unanswered, question whether the strongest man on earth is he who stands most alone or he who subserves the greatest good of the greatest number. Upon the struggle implicit in this question the modern drama necessarily is based, since the dramatist, in any period when the theatre is really alive, is obliged to tell the people in the audience what they have themselves been thinking. Those critics, therefore, have no ground to stand on who belittle the importance of the modern social drama and regard it as an arbitrary phase of art devised, for business reasons merely, by a handful of clever playwrights.

Although the third and modern type of tragedy has grown to be almost exclusively the property of realistic writers, it is interesting to recall that it was first introduced into the theatre of the world by the king of the romantics. It was Victor Hugo's *Hernani*, produced in 1830, which first exhibited a dramatic struggle between an individual and society at large. The hero is a bandit and an outlaw, and he is doomed to failure because of the superior power of organised society arrayed against him. So many minor victories were won at that famous *première* of *Hernani* that even Hugo's followers were too excited to perceive that he had given the drama a new subject and the theatre a new theme; but this epoch-making fact may now be clearly recognised in retrospect. *Hernani*, and all of Victor Hugo's subsequent dramas, dealt, however, with distant times and lands; and it was left to another great romantic, Alexandre Dumas, *père*, to be the first to give the modern theme a modern setting. In his best play, *Antony*, which exhibits the struggle of a bastard to establish himself in the so-called best society, Dumas brought the discussion home to his own country and his own period. In the hands of that extremely gifted dramatist, Emile Augier, the new type of serious drama passed over into the possession of the realists, and so downward to the latter-day realistic dramatists of France and England, Germany and Scandinavia. The supreme and the most typical creative figure of the entire period is, of course, the Norwegian Henrik Ibsen, who —such is the irony of progress—despised the romantics of 1830, and frequently expressed a bitter scorn for those predecessors who discovered and developed the type of tragedy which he perfected.

III

We are now prepared to inquire more closely into the specific sort of subject which the modern social drama imposes on the dramatist. The existence of any struggle between an individual and the conventions of society presupposes that the individual is unconventional. If the hero were in accord with society, there would be no conflict of contending forces: he must therefore be one of society's outlaws, or else there can be no play. In modern times, therefore, the serious drama has been forced to select as its leading figures men and women outcast and condemned by conventional society. It has dealt with courtesans (*La Dame Aux Camélias*), demi-mondaines (*Le Demi-Monde*), erring wives (*Frou-Frou*), women with a past (*The Second Mrs. Tanqueray*), free lovers (*The Notorious Mrs. Ebbsmith*), bastards (*Antony; Le Fils Naturel*), ex-convicts (*John Gabriel Borkman*), people with ideas in advance of their time (*Ghosts*), and a host of other characters that are usually considered dangerous to society. In order that the dramatic struggle might be tense, the dramatists have been forced to strengthen the cases of their characters so as to suggest that, perhaps, in the special situations cited, the outcasts were right and society was wrong. Of course it would be impossible to base a play upon the thesis that, in a given conflict between the individual and society, society was indisputably right and the individual indubitably wrong; because the essential element of struggle would be absent. Our modern dramatists, therefore, have been forced to deal with *exceptional* outcasts of society,—outcasts with whom the audience might justly sympathise in their conflict with convention. The task of finding such justifiable outcasts has of necessity narrowed the subject-matter of the modern drama. It would be hard, for instance, to make out a good case against society for the robber, the murderer, the anarchist. But it is comparatively easy to make out a good case for a man and a woman involved in some sexual relation which brings upon them the censure of society but which seems in itself its own excuse for being. Our modern serious dramatists have been driven, therefore, in the great majority of cases, to deal almost exclusively with problems of sex.

This necessity has pushed them upon dangerous ground. Man is, after all, a social animal. The necessity of maintaining the solidarity of the family—a necessity (as John Fiske luminously pointed out) due to the long period of infancy in man—has forced mankind to adopt certain social laws to regulate the interrelations of men and women. Any strong attempt to subvert these laws is dangerous not only to that tissue of convention called society but also to the development of the human race. And here we find our dramatists forced—first by the spirit of the times, which gives them their theme, and second by the nature of the dramatic art, which demands a special treatment of that theme—to hold a brief for cer-

tain men and women who have shuffled off the coil of those very
social laws that man has devised, with his best wisdom, for the
preservation of his race. And the question naturally follows: Is a
drama that does this moral or immoral?

But the philosophical basis for this question is usually not understood at all by those critics who presume to answer the question
off-hand in a spasm of polemics. It is interesting, as an evidence
of the shallowness of most dramatic criticism, to read over, in the
course of Mr. Shaw's nimble essay on *The Quintessence of Ibsen-
ism*, the collection which the author has made of the adverse notices of *Ghosts* which appeared in the London newspapers on the
occasion of the first performance of the play in England. Unanimously they commit the fallacy of condemning the piece as immoral because of the subject that it deals with. And, on the other
hand, it must be recognised that most of the critical defenses of
the same piece, and of other modern works of similar nature, have
been based upon the identical fallacy,—that morality or immorality is a question of subject-matter. But either to condemn or to
defend the morality of any work of art because of its material
alone is merely a waste of words. There is no such thing, *per se*,
as an immoral subject for a play: in the treatment of the subject,
and only in the treatment, lies the basis for ethical judgment of
the piece. Critics who condemn *Ghosts* because of its subject-
matter might as well condemn *Othello* because the hero kills his
wife—what a suggestion, look you, to carry into our homes! *Macbeth* is not immoral, though it makes night hideous with murder.
The greatest of all Greek dramas, *Œdipus King*, is in itself sufficient proof that morality is a thing apart from subject-matter; and
Shelley's *The Cenci* is another case in point. The only way in
which a play may be immoral is for it to cloud, in the spectator,
the consciousness of those invariable laws of life which say to man
"Thou shalt not" or "Thou shalt"; and the one thing needful in
order that a drama may be moral is that the author shall maintain
throughout the piece a sane and truthful insight into the soundness or unsoundness of the relations between his characters. He
must know when they are right and know when they are wrong,
and must make clear to the audience the reasons for his judgments.
He cannot be immoral unless he is untrue. To make us pity his
characters when they are vile or love them when they are noxious,
to invent excuses for them in situations where they cannot be

excused—in a single word, to lie about his characters—this is for the dramatist the one unpardonable sin. Consequently, the only sane course for a critic who wishes to maintain the thesis that *Ghosts*, or any other modern play, is immoral, is not to hurl mud at it, but to prove by the sound processes of logic that the play tells lies about life; and the only sane way to defend such a piece is not to prate about the "moral lesson" the critic supposes that it teaches, but to prove logically that it tells the truth.

The same test of truthfulness by which we distinguish good workmanship from bad is the only test by which we may conclusively distinguish immoral art from moral. Yet many of the controversial critics never calm down sufficiently to apply this test. Instead of arguing whether or not Ibsen tells the truth about Hedda Gabler, they quarrel with him or defend him for talking about her at all. It is as if zoölogists who had assembled to determine the truth or falsity of some scientific theory concerning the anatomy of a reptile should waste all their time in contending whether or not the reptile was unclean.

And even when they do apply the test of truthfulness, many critics are troubled by a grave misconception that leads them into error. They make the mistake of applying *generally* to life certain ethical judgments that the dramatist means only to apply *particularly* to the special people in his play. The danger of this fallacy cannot be too strongly emphasised. It is not the business of the dramatist to formulate general laws of conduct; he leaves that to the social scientist, the ethical philosopher, the religious preacher. His business is merely to tell the truth about certain special characters involved in certain special situations. If the characters and the situations be abnormal, the dramatist must recognise that fact in judging them; and it is not just for the critic to apply to ordinary people in the ordinary situations of life a judgment thus conditioned. The question in *La Dame Aux Camélias* is not whether the class of women which Marguerite Gautier represents is generally estimable, but whether a particular woman of that class, set in certain special circumstances, was not worthy of sympathy. The question in *A Doll's House* is not whether any woman should forsake her husband and children when she happens to feel like it, but whether a particular woman, Nora, living under special conditions with a certain kind of husband, Torwald, really did deem herself justified in leaving her doll's home, perhaps forever. The ethics of any play should be determined, not externally, but within the limits of the play itself. And yet our modern social dramatists are persistently misjudged. We hear talk of the moral teaching of Ibsen,—as if, instead of being a maker of plays, he had been a maker of golden rules. But Mr. Shaw came nearer to the truth with his famous paradox that the only golden rule in Ibsen's dramas is that there is no golden rule.

It must, however, be admitted that the dramatists themselves are not entirely guiltless of this current critical misconception. Most of them happen to be realists, and in devising their situations they aim to be narrowly natural as well as broadly true. The result is that the circumstances of their plays have an *ordinary* look which makes them seem simple transcripts of everyday life instead of special studies of life under peculiar conditions. Consequently the audience, and even the critic, is tempted to judge life in terms of the play instead of judging the play in terms of life. Thus falsely judged, *The Wild Duck* (to take an emphatic instance) is outrageously immoral, although it must be judged moral by the philosophic critic who questions only whether or not Ibsen told the truth about the particular people involved in its depressing story. The deeper question remains: Was Ibsen justified in writing a play which was true and therefore moral, but which necessarily would have an immoral effect on nine spectators out of every ten, because they would instinctively make a hasty and false generalisation from the exceptional and very particular ethics implicit in the story?

For it must be bravely recognised that any statement of truth which is so framed as to be falsely understood conveys a lie. If the dramatist says quite truly, "This particular leaf is sere and yellow," and if the audience quite falsely understands him to say, "All leaves are sere and yellow," the gigantic lie has illogically been conveyed that the world is ever windy with autumn, that spring is but a lyric dream, and summer an illusion. The modern social drama, even when it is most truthful within its own limits, is by its very nature liable to just this sort of illogical conveyance of a lie. It sets forth a struggle between a radical exception and a conservative rule; and the audience is likely to forget that the exception is merely an exception, and to infer that it is greater than the rule. Such an inference, being untrue, is immoral; and in so far as a dramatist aids and abets it, he must be judged dangerous to the theatre-going public.

Whenever, then, it becomes important to determine whether a new play of the modern social type is moral or immoral, the critic should decide first whether the author tells lies specifically about any of the people in his story, and second, provided that the playwright passes the first test successfully, whether he allures the audience to generalise falsely in regard to life at large from the specific circumstances of his play. These two questions are the only ones that need to be decided. This is the crux of the whole matter.

IX

A NEW DEFENSE OF MELODRAMA

I

IT is the fate of many amiable words to be debased by vulgar usage until they acquire a derogatory connotation. Thus has the sweet word *homely* been deflowered; so that nowadays to assure a woman that she is homely has ceased to seem a gentle compliment. The adjective *amateur*, which in its original sense exactly defines the quality of such delicate and loving art as that of Austin Dobson or of Kenneth Grahame, has come to connote the daubing of a bungler. Anybody who labors earnestly, though only in a humble way, to fulfil the purpose of criticism—which was defined by Matthew Arnold as "a disinterested endeavor to learn and propagate the best that is known and thought in the world"—must endure the continual discouragement of hearing the word *criticism* bandied about on careless lips as if it signified an interested endeavor to discredit the nobility of art. If one may muse for a moment in the mood of Elia—would it not be a gracious act to erect a monument to fallen words, like *censure, common, cynic, nice, mistress, gentleman,* to remind the present age of what they used to mean before they fell on evil days and evil tongues? . . .

In the vocabulary of theatre-goers, no word has suffered more from this iniquitous degeneration than the adjective *melodramatic*. Careless writers are now accustomed to call a play melodramatic when they wish to indicate that it is bad; whereas they might with equal logic try to damn a play by calling it tragic, or comic, or poetic. There are good tragedies and bad tragedies, good melodramas and bad melodramas; and it is no more sound to assume that all melodramas are bad than to assume that all tragedies are good. But the very word *melodrama* has so fallen into disrepute that nowadays when a man puts forth a melodrama he usually pretends that it is something else and writes in a few extraneous passages to justify his press-agent in advertising it as a social study or a comedy.

Consequently, if we are to converse with any seriousness about the noble art of melodrama, we must agree at the outset to divest the word of all derogatory connotation. Most people consider it pedantic to insist on definitions; and the minority of writers who refuse to use such an adjective as *romantic* without explaining what they mean by it are usually labeled academic—which is supposed to be synonymous with dull. Yet a great deal of the fret and bother of the world would be averted if people in general would only educate themselves to definition. For instance, if only the socialists would agree upon a definition of *socialism* and formulate it in a single paragraph, we should all be able to determine at a glance whether or not we wanted to be socialists; and this procedure would save reformers the expense of printing innumerable pamphlets and spare us a great deal of mouthing and sawing the air.

By *melodrama*—if we use the word nicely—is signified a serious play in which the incidents determine and control the characters. There are, to be sure, a few other abiding features of melodrama that should be accounted for in any final definition of the form, and these we shall consider in due time; but for the present this primary principle will serve to convince us that melodrama not only has an excuse for being but is in reality one of the noblest types of art. In both tragedy and comedy the characters control the plot; in farce, as in melodrama, a train of incidents is foreordained and the characters are subsequently woven into the pattern of destiny that has been predetermined for them; and it is clearly reasonable for us to accept that convention of criticism which regards tragedy and comedy as more heroic than their sister arts. But life itself is more frequently melodramatic than tragic and much more often farcical than comic; in fact, the utter dominance of character over coincidence is so rare in the record of humanity as to call for chapter-headings in our histories; and since the purpose of the drama—like that of all the other arts—is to represent the truth of life, the theatre must always rely on farce and melodrama to complete its comment on humanity. Much of our life—in fact, by far the major share—is casual instead of causal. As Stevenson remarked, in his *Gossip on Romance*, "The pleasure that we take in life is of two sorts—the active and the passive. Now we are conscious of a great command over our destiny; anon we are lifted up by circumstance, as by a breaking wave, and dashed we know not how into the future." It is not granted to many of us to realize with any constancy that boast of Henley's and to regard ourselves as masters of our fate or captains of our soul; for nearly all the good or ill that happens to us is drifted to us, uncommanded, undeserved, upon the tides of chance. It is this immutable truth—the persistency of chance in the serious concerns of life and the inevitable influence of accident on character —that melodrama aims to represent: and to damn melodrama as an inconsiderable type of art is to deny the divinity of Fortune, whom the wisest of all men, in the seventh canto of his *Hell*, exalted "with the other Deities."

II

It is because melodrama casts its emphasis on incident instead of character that it has been in every age the most popular of all the types of drama. Each of us is avid of adventure; and to find ten dollars in the street strikes us as more interesting than to earn ten dollars by accomplishing our share in the established division of labor. Similarly—though in this we are not logical—it strikes us as more interesting to be gagged and bound, and rescued by the provident police, than to quarrel with our wife or husband over the duration of the boiling of an egg and to purchase forgiveness by the gift of a brass bracelet or a box of trust-made but untrustworthy cigars. Though in our waking senses we may contemn that Deity whose name is Fortune, we all worship her in dreams; and in the theatre we bless the happy chance that agreeably rewards the innocent and consigns the villainous to jail.

In our own lives, we remember what has happened to us, by some lucky or unlucky accident, more vividly than we remember what we were: our past selves are clouded with oblivion, but our past adventures float before the eyes of memory as stories instant and alive. So, in our experience of theatre-going, we forget characters—like Hedda Gabler—but we remember incidents—like that moment in *The Two Orphans* when the lost Louise is heard singing in the street and the incarcerated Henriette is stopped at the door by the entering guards while she hears her sister being dragged unwillingly away to a continuance of beggary. Adventure moves us more than character; because adventure is always with us—it is often an adventure to look over the edge of our morning paper at the person seated opposite in the subway—but character is an element of destiny of which we grow aware only in the small minority of incidents which are commanded and controlled.

And there is another point which explains the popularity of melodrama; and that is that, since the characters are not rigidly defined, we experience no difficulty in putting ourselves in the positions of the characters and imagining that what is happening upon the stage is happening to us. We observe the clearly drawn characters of tragedy with a conscious aloofness that is, to some degree, discomforting. Hedda Gabler interests us merely as a specimen; and what happens to her does not in any real sense happen to us. The fact of what she is convinces us that she must ultimately kill herself; but if *we* were flung into the same position, we should crawl out by some easier way. We realize that Othello is doomed to kill his wife, but we understand also that the tragical oblation is absurd: if *we* were in the same position, we should perceive that Desdemona had been maligned by the perversity of evidence. We should not behave like Hedda or Othello, because we are not at all like either of them. Each of them is clearly characterized and convinces us of an essential disparity with ourselves. But in melodrama the heroine and hero are not clearly characterized; they are represented not as particular people, but merely as *anybody* involved in the situation of the moment; and we naturally take the stage, adopt their destiny as our own, and experience in our particular imagination all that is happening to them. Thus, in William Gillette's admirable melodrama entitled *Held by the Enemy*, when the captured Confederate lieutenant confesses to the Union court-martial that he is a spy, and glories in his sinister vocation, inviting with a smile the death that will complete his sense of duty done, it is not so much to him that the incident occurs as to you or me, seated in the audience; for at that moment, in imagination, we take the stage and speak the words of martyrdom ourselves. For it is the special grace of melodrama to represent not what a particular person will do in a given situation, but what *anybody* would do under such a stress of circumstance; and since anybody is easily identifiable with ourself, we imagine the situation as happening to us and adopt it into our particular experience.

This is, of course, the philosophic point which explained the popularity of that special species of melodrama which, in New York, in the early days of Mr. Owen Davis, used to flourish on Third Avenue and Eighth Avenue, before it was driven out of existence by the motion-picture play. The devotees of cheap melodrama were workaday people to whom, in the orderly procession of the days, nothing noteworthy ever happened; and in the theatre they demanded the sort of play in which surprising and startling adventures should happen not only to the people on the stage but to themselves. Therefore the characters on the stage must not be so sharply drawn as to be set apart from any person in the audience; and adventure must be represented for its own sake, regardless of the personality of the people it involved. As Sir Thomas Browne loved to lose himself in a mystery, so the auditors of our ten, twenty, and thirty-cent theatres loved to lose themselves in an irresponsible train of circumstances which conceivably might happen to themselves. In a word, they went to the theatre to enjoy *themselves*—which is to say their own imagined hesitancies and imperilments—and decidedly not to enjoy some totally different and extraneous creature like Hedda Gabler or Othello. The popularity, as a character, of Bertha (the sewing-machine girl) or Nellie (the beautiful cloak-model) was explicable by the fact that neither of them was, in any precise sense, a character at all; and that therefore any woman in the audience could, without the slightest straining of imagination, set herself in the heroine's place and experience vicariously the adventures that befell her.

Let us recapitulate a moment, for the sake of clearness. We have already observed that melodrama epitomizes the major portion of habitual experience, because it emphasizes incident above character as a factor in human destiny; and also, since it leaves the hero and the heroine uncharacterized, that it permits, more easily than tragedy, that the spectator should in imagination take the stage and assume as his own the adventures of the plot. But there is another very important point which must be accounted for in any final definition of the art of melodrama.

This point—perhaps the most important that we have to consider—is that the abiding mood of melodrama is an absolute and dauntless optimism. The world of melodrama is a just and lucky world where all things fall out fitly. We are granted from the outset an assurance that in the end the guilty will be punished and the virtuous attain their due reward. No innocent Ophelia or Cordelia will be dragged down in the maelström of catastrophe. Our cherished characters are flung repeatedly into imminent danger of death, and we feel their pangs and perils as our own; but we know all along—and bless ourselves with knowing—that no one will be killed except the villain. This is the great charm of melodrama—that it deals with charmed lives. Sherlock Holmes will surely escape from the gas-chamber—though *how*, indeed, we cannot possibly foresee. In watching melodrama of a cruder sort, we experience this same sense of a comfortable providence. You may lock the heroine in a lion's cage, throw her down from Brooklyn Bridge, tie her to the subway tracks, and dangle her by a rope from the windy summit of the Singer tower; but we know all along that the kindly gods who look after the destiny of heroines will rescue her from harm and consign her as good as new to the strong arms of the hero. And there is another matter which, in the interests of criticism, it is surely not indelicate to mention; and that is that we derive a world of solid comfort from our certainty that the virtue of the heroine is inviolable. At every moment she is chaperoned by destiny. What Milton expressed supremely in his portrayal of the Lady in *Comus*, our melodramatists repeat with cruder emphasis; namely, that virginity is its own defense and virtue shields itself with spiritual armor. The silly girl of a heroine who has run away from home with a deep-dyed villain with whom she thinks herself in love, is providentially preserved in purity till she may meet and marry the most lovable of heroes. Here is a vision of the world as we would have it. If ever we were erected to the exalted state of Zeus-upon-Olympus, it is thus that we should stage-direct the tremendous drama of humanity. It is true, indeed, that life as it exists is not so ordered: we look about us and it seems that there is neither right nor reason in the inappealable decrees of destiny. But meanwhile the noble art of melodrama stands up scornful before many spears and confronts the iniquity of fate with a laugh "broad as a thousand beeves at pasture."

No art has ever succeeded because of its defects; and the fact that melodrama has been and is perennially popular can be explained only by what is great and noble in it. Melodrama answers one of the most profound of human needs:—it ministers to that motive which philosophers term the will to believe. It looks at life

—as Paul enjoined humanity to look at it—with faith and hope. So, when the toilers in our sweat-shops attend the ten, twenty, and thirty-cent theatres, they escape into a region where faith is not an idle jest and hope is not an irony; and thereafter, when they reassume the heavy and the weary weight of all their unintelligible world, they may yet smile backward in remembrance of that momentary dream-world in which destiny was just and kind and good. A happy face in the street is a gift to the community; and this art that always wears a happy face is a gift to humanity at large.

III

We may now redefine melodrama as a serious play in which the incidents determine and control the characters and in which the auditors are assured from the outset that all will come out as they wish it in the end. Thus defined, melodrama must be admitted to include many of the most important plays in the history of the drama. It must not be supposed that the art began with Victorien Sardou; it is at least as old as Euripides, and was highly honored in the Spain of Calderon and Lope and the England of the spacious times of great Elizabeth. Many of the stirring plays which used to pass for tragedies in our histories of the drama are now seen to be merely melodramas. Tragedy must exhibit an inevitable doom; and the inevitable is nearly as rare in art as it is in life. Life itself is seldom tragic, in any exact and technical sense; and there are very few unquestionable tragedies in the history of art. Victor Hugo, who admitted that his three prose plays were melodramas, thought that his plays in verse were tragedies; but we now perceive that *Hernani* and *Ruy Blas* and all the rest of them are melodramas also—and we like them none the less because of the change of label. Those windy suspirations of forced breath which in mid-Victorian days were esteemed as tragedies, were all melodramas, and melodramas of a rather crude and secondary sort. The *Virginius* of Sheridan Knowles, the *Richelieu* of Bulwer-Lytton, the *Fool's Revenge* of Tom Taylor (an adaptation from Hugo), were melodramas pure and simple, though they wore the literary trappings and the suits of tragedy. It is always disconcerting to find one art masquerading in the dress of another; a melodrama that pretends to be a tragedy afflicts us ultimately with an overwhelming sense that it is ashamed of itself; and the sense of shame is incompatible with the sense of easy enjoyment. Retrospective criticism must therefore finally prefer such frank and gloating melodramas as the *Tour de Nesle* of the elder Dumas, the *Fédora* of Sardou, the *Two Orphans* of Dennery, or those favorites of our fathers, *The Ticket-of-Leave Man* and *Jim the Penman*. *Jim the Penman* thrilled the younger generation when it was revived a few years ago; and *The Two Orphans*, which is always with us, is—if not a thing of beauty—at least a joy forever.

Since melodrama casts its emphasis on action, rather than on character, it calls, far more than tragedy, for an exhibition of the uttermost mechanical equipment of the stage. We turn to the tragedies and comedies of other ages to see the highest development of the drama in those times; but if we wish to acquaint ourselves with the highest development of theatric presentation in any age, we must turn our attention to its melodramas. When David Belasco produced a quiet comedy like *The Concert*, he exhibited less emphatically his skill in stage-direction than when he produced a melodrama like *The Girl of the Golden West*. *The Great Ruby* gave more noticeable evidence of the ability of Augustin Daly as a producer than did *The School for Scandal* or *The Merchant of Venice*. The mechanism of melodrama has been carried to the highest efficiency in London, on the stage of Drury Lane. In *The Whip*, which ran a year at Old Drury, a railroad train was wrecked upon the stage (in pursuance of the villain's plot to kill the hero's race-horse, which was being transported in a box-car); and the sight of the derailed and overturning engine panting and puffing bravely after the intolerable crash thrilled through the thousand-fold assembled audience and evoked a tremor even from the sophisticated critic. In *The Sins of Society*, another Drury Lane melodrama, a battleship went down, with all hands rallied round the flag. It may be finer dramatic art for Mrs. Fiske to sit still and think hard in *Rosmersholm*; but it is more wonderful theatric art to sink a ship upon the stage; and on purely human grounds there are many reasons for regarding a sinking ship as a more pathetic spectacle than a falling woman.

And this suggests a final word that must be said in favor of melodrama:—it gives the actors an opportunity to act. In every scene they have to *do* things; they cannot—like Mrs. Patrick Campbell—turn away from the audience and think with their backs. Thinking with the back may be the most mystical and esoteric performance that is possible to humankind: at least we have, in support of this belief, the high authority of Auguste Rodin, who once told a visitor of his that the secret of his *Penseur* is that he thinks with his back. But on the stage it is surely more thrilling to watch the blind Louise grope her way down the banister of a declining stairway, and then pass inadvertently within six inches of the prostrate form of the fainting Henriette, whom she has sought so long and with so many heartaches, and is not destined to discover until the whirligig of the melodrama brings in its final revenges. Even so—as a matter of mere acting—we would rather watch the Negro servant, in the last act of *Secret Service*, remove the bullets from the stacked guns of the Union guards, than watch the facial play of Hedda Gabler as she sits in silence debating her problem of impending suicide. For in this the theatre differs from life:— that, on the stage, action speaks louder than character, and to *do* is more important than to *be*.

Latterly there has appeared in our theatres a new type of the sort of melodrama that is ashamed of itself—which, while not pretending to be tragedy, pretends to be a serious study of contemporary social problems. Nowadays it is considered an evidence of earnestness to talk about capital and labor, just as in the middle ages it was considered an evidence of earnestness to talk about how many angels could dance on the head of a pin; fashions change in tall talk, while the singing world rolls on; but when a man finds a melodrama made to his hand, why, in the name of art, should he ruin it by trying to turn it into something else? The new melodrama will never rival the glory of the old until it sloughs off all sophistication and disguise, and comes forward frankly as a play of plot supervised by a kindly and ingratiating providence. Mascarille becomes ignoble only when he masquerades as a nobleman; and a lesser art retains its dignity only so long as it refrains from emulation of a greater.

*OTHER PRINCIPLES OF DRAMATIC
CRITICISM*

THE PUBLIC AND THE THEATRE

A STUDY of the public is an indispensable detail of the study of the drama; for the public, in conjunction with the actors and the author, constitutes a corner of that eternal triangle upon which, as a fundamental basis, the edifice of the drama must be reared. If some Mæcenas, endowed with an exacting taste and an all-commanding pocketbook, should desire to enjoy a better drama than is ordinarily offered in the theatre of to-day, he might spend his time and money in the search for finer actors or for nobler authors, but he could accomplish his intention much more easily and quickly by collecting and delivering to the theatre a finer and a nobler audience. It has frequently been stated that the public always gets as good a drama as it deserves, since the managers, in order to make money, must give the public what the public wants; and this somewhat cynical theory is true to this extent,—that the public never gets a better drama than it concertedly requests. To improve the quality of the supply, it is necessary, first of all, to improve the quality of the demand. Though the drama is an art, the theatre is a business; and it does not pay to cast pearls before people who are lacking in intelligence and taste.

One of the main troubles with the theatre in America to-day is that it suffers tragically from a lack of constant patronage by people of intelligence and taste. Our supply of plays is not determined by the demand of our most cultured public, but only by the demand of a public that is by no means representative of the best that is thought and felt in this country at the present time. Any study of this problem must begin and end in the city of New York; for it is an unfortunate fact that our theatre is so constituted that the rest of the country is allowed to see only plays which have previously made money in the metropolis. As conditions stand at present in the professional theatre, a metropolitan verdict is the only one that counts; and an author or an actor, in order to reach the rest of the country, must first secure the privilege of being booked throughout the circuits of the smaller cities by passing a favorable examination in New York. Thus—except for. the admirable work that is being accomplished here and there in little independent theatres—the destiny of the drama in this country is still decided by the people who habitually pay to be amused in the tiny circle that is centered in Times Square. The question, then, becomes of prime importance whether these people are adequately representative of America, either as it is or as it yearns to be: and to this important question the answer is, emphatically, "No."

Any one who makes a practice of attending every play that is exhibited in the metropolis needs only to look about him in the orchestra to see at a glance that the success or failure of an offering is not determined by an audience that is representative of America or even of New York. The audience is recruited mainly from that artificial region that is known, in the language of the theatre, as Broadway,—a region in which real people do not live, and cannot live, because it is lighted only by electric lamps instead of by the sun and moon and stars.

The prospect would be hopeless if the public of Broadway were the only public in New York that the theatre might appeal to; but this is not the case. There are very many people of intelligence and taste—people of the sort who welcome eagerly the best that is thought and said through the medium of any of the arts—who have ceased to attend the theatre in New York because the theatre, for the most part, has ceased to give them the sort of stimulus that they desire. It is easy enough for any student of this problem to meet these people face to face, for their patronage of art is an active and a public exercise. Whenever the *Ninth Symphony* of Beethoven is played by a great orchestra in Carnegie Hall, the enormous auditorium is crowded to the roof by people who would also patronize the theatre if the theatre would afford them a commeasurable exaltation. A cultured and appreciative public pays seven dollars a seat at the Metropolitan Opera House to hear the finest singing in the world. Yet the opera and the orchestra are arts less democratic than the drama—less popular in their appeal—and a more specific culture is required for the due appreciation of them. An afternoon stroll through the galleries of the various art-dealers on Fifth Avenue will also bring the student face to face with still another public composed of people who are quick to welcome the best that can be thought and said in terms of art. These people, who love painting and sculpture, would also love the theatre if the theatre should set out to woo them in the mood of beauty and of truth; and the teeming thousands who annually study the exhibits in the Metropolitan Museum of Art might crowd the galleries of any theatre that should successfully appeal to them.

The tragic fact of the matter seems to be that these thousands and thousands of people, who patronize music and painting and sculpture and dancing and all the other arts, have ceased to patronize the theatre. People of the same class, half a century ago, attended every production at Daly's or the old Lyceum and exercised an active influence on the traffic of the stage; but nowadays, for the most part, they stay at home and permit the destiny of the drama to be determined by a mob of other people who are inferior in intelligence and taste. They behave like educated voters on Election Day who remain away from the polls and allow some vulgar politician to sneak into a great office by default.

The immediate problem at the present time is to find an effective method of convincing the cultured public that ten or a dozen of the round number of two hundred plays that are now produced every season in New York are genuinely worthy of the patronage of people of intelligence and taste. The best public must be won back to the support of the best drama; and this public must be organized and delivered so effectively that once again—as in the distant days of Daly's Theatre—it will become impossible for a really fine production to fail for lack of patronage.

One of the main difficulties of the situation is the decadence of dramatic criticism in New York. Dramatic criticism may be defined—in the terminology of Matthew Arnold—as "a disinterested endeavor to learn and propagate the best that is known and thought in the theatre of the world." This endeavor was at least attempted a generation ago; but, in more recent years, the majority of our most influential newspapers have ceased to treat the drama as an art and have chosen, rather, to regard the theatre merely as a function of Broadway.

Thus the editing of our theatre for an inferior public is fostered by the fact that the dramatic columns in our newspapers are edited for the same public and confine themselves, for the most part, to an utterly uncritical endeavor to estimate in advance the success or failure of an undertaking in the theatre. They print a guess that a certain play will run a year, or else they print a guess that the production will be carted to the storehouse in a week. In other words, they judge the offerings of art according to a standard which is determined merely by the taste of an uncultivated audience.

The point is not that our individual dramatic critics are lacking in discernment. Nearly half a dozen of the writers who are employed at the present time to report the doings of the theatre in New York are endowed sufficiently, in education and in taste, to distinguish a work of art from a product of commercial manufacture; but the general attitude of our public press—considered as a whole—obscures their individual efforts "to learn and propagate the best that is known and thought in the theatre of the world." These writers are required to devote as many columns—or nearly as many—to the consideration of inconsiderable offerings as they are permitted to devote to the ten or twelve productions every year that really count. They are condemned, nine-tenths of the time, to write news about nothing.

That our newspapers, for the most part, have ceased to treat the drama as an art, is a fact that can be easily established by a study of their pages. Whenever a new opera is produced at the Metropolitan Opera House, it is analyzed in detail by an expert who interprets its defects and qualities to an audience of cultured readers; exhibitions of painting or of sculpture are studied carefully by scholars who talk about art in terms that receive respect from an initiated public; but new plays, in the same newspapers, are merely written up amusingly as items in the general doings of the day. The policy of our newspapers toward music and painting and sculpture is scholarly and critical; but, with one or two exceptions, their policy toward the drama is merely reportorial. They treat the theatre mainly from the standpoint of its value as a fountainhead of news. By editing their dramatic columns for the uncultivated public of Broadway, instead of for that finer public that desires to learn and to enjoy the best that is known and thought in the world and is eager to patronize any exercise of art where art may be discerned, our newspapers make it very difficult for people of refinement to keep actively in touch with the best that is being done in the theatre of America.

The decadence of dramatic criticism is all the more dangerous at a time when the theatre is required to endure the insidious assaults of a system of mendacious puffery. It would scarcely be an exaggeration to state that the greatest foe of the contemporary drama is the contemporary press-agent. This functionary is employed to beat a big drum in front of every theatre and to tell the public that every play presented is a masterpiece. The weakness of the press-agent arises from the fact that, in the nature of things, he can't fool all the people all the time; but the tragedy of his position arises from the fact that, by fooling some of the people some of the time, he prevents nearly everybody from believing him, on some subsequent occasion, when he happens to come forward with the truth.

A perusal, at any time, of the advertising pages in the Sunday newspapers might lead to the impression that each of the forty plays then current in New York was the greatest play of the twentieth century; but this impression would be speedily corrected by a visit to the plays themselves. The trouble of the matter is that it would cost a cultured theatre-goer no less than two hundred and fifty dollars, and forty evenings of priceless time, to find out for himself that all these advertisements were nothing but mere lies; and, after this expensive experience, he might feel indisposed to risk another six dollars and another evening to see a masterpiece. The efforts of many press-agents to lure him to attend inferior productions are more than likely, in the long run, to result in keeping him away from a production which he would be very glad to patronize.

II

ORGANIZING AN AUDIENCE

I

ART THRIVES upon appreciation; and the most vital and human art has been produced in those periods when the love of art has been widespread throughout a great community. The general public of Periclean Athens loved architecture, sculpture, and the drama with a love like that for food and drink; and Phidias and Sophocles were hailed as heroes by adoring boys. If you had cast a casual stone in fourteenth-century Florence, you would have hit some lover of Madonnas. When Cimabue had completed his *Virgin Enthroned,* the entire town turned out for a holiday, and bore the picture—*their* picture—triumphantly along the Street of the Beautiful Ladies, to set it up in the south transept of Santa Maria Novella. And if in Elizabethan London you had mingled with the jostling throng that swarmed over London Bridge, you might have been sure that any one who trod upon your toes had applauded the acting of Burbage and hearkened to the hallowed line, "The rest is silence." So, in the great age of Gothic architecture, the entire populace of Amiens, from the highest noble to the lowest peasant, toiled and saved and sacrificed, and poured their life's substance and their heart's desire into that supreme cathedral, which stands not as the monument of a single architect, nor even of a group of architects, but as a monument of civic aspiration and communistic joy.

Art is misconceived by those *dilettanti* who regard it merely as the personal expression of some select and lonely soul. Art, at its highest, is neither lonely nor select, but public and general in its appeal and its importance; and a great work of art, once fashioned, ceases to belong personally to the man who made it, but belongs instead to his nation and his age. The fact that great artists appear not singly but in groups, and always at such times and places when

102

the general public recognizes their utterance as the expression of its own unuttered ecstasy of life, indicates that art should be regarded not as a function of the individual, but as a function of the populace. It follows that the best way to evoke great art is to educate the public to a great appreciation. Give the plant the proper soil, and it will thrive and flower. What the people really want they assuredly shall have; and when they want great art, great artists will emerge to give it to them. If we want great statues for our city, our primary concern is not to educate a sculptor to fashion them, for the sculptor can educate himself; our concern is, rather, to educate our citizens to desire them. It is not so much our painters that we need to send to Rome and Paris; but if—in a spiritual sense—we could send our whole community to the capitals of art, we should surely have our painting. For history teaches us that great men arise, as if by miracle, to fulfil a great and public need: there has rarely been a revolution without its Washington, there has seldom been a civil war without its Lincoln. Gather a great community all eager for listening, and Art shall speak to it with a great voice. When all Italy wants a Michelangelo, all Italy shall surely have him; and when all Elizabethan London loves the drama, some Shakespeare shall certainly arise.

But if all this applies to art in general, it applies with a particular emphasis to that most democratic of the arts—the drama. In a special and immediate sense, the drama is a function of the populace. The reality of an acted play is evoked by a collaboration between those whose minds are active behind the footlights and those whose minds are active in the auditorium; and the phenomenon will fail unless the minds of the artists and the minds of the auditors answer each to each with sympathy and appreciation. It is no longer necessary, in these pages, to insist that the dramatist is dependent on his audience—that his themes, his thoughts, and his emotions, must fall within the mental range of the multitude that he is writing for. Without an appreciative audience a play cannot endure: empty your auditorium, and your work of art ceases to exist: and in the theatre the general and democratic public tells emphatically, by its patronage, what it is the public wants. The power to save or damn a play is vested neither in the author nor the actor nor the critic nor the manager; it is vested solely in the audience. It follows, with irrefutable logic, that to support a worthy drama you must have a worthy public, and that a noble dramatist can arise and do his work only when he is assured of the appreciation of a noble audience.

Here, then, we strike at the heart of the fallacy of most of those dreamers who endeavor to uplift the stage. They begin upon the wrong side of the footlights. They try to uplift the author or the actor or the manager; whereas, to attain any real result, they ought first to uplift the audience. They complain because the managers are commercial; but there is no solid ground for this complaint. Every art must be fostered by a business; the dramatic art must be exploited by the theatre business; and the manager must be a business man. A business man would be a fool unless he regulated his business in accordance with the primary economic principle of supply and demand. Shakespeare and Molière, who were managers, as well as actors and dramatists, conducted their business upon this economic principle and were just as commercial as Mr. Shubert or Mr. Brady. Also, when a dramatist has written one sort of play that the public likes, it is futile to berate him and demand that he shall write another sort of play that his public does not like; and it is silly to ask an actress who plays a chorus-lady well to play Lady Macbeth badly, in the fancied interests of art. The only movement for uplifting the stage which can have any practical and good result must be a movement for uplifting the audience. The way to improve the author, the actor, and the manager leads through the box-office. Pay them better to produce and exploit the best dramatic art, and they will not fob you off with art that is inferior; they will not be able to afford to do so.

These considerations are immediate and practical; but, in a larger and more idealistic outlook, it is clear that we cannot expect great art in our theatre until our audience is ready for it. So long as the public remains contented with inferiority, our drama will remain inferior. One of the things that the American theatre of to-day stands most in need of is a sane, persistent movement to educate the public taste in drama and improve the mental tenor of the average audience.

II

But, in present-day America, the problem of educating the theatre-going public, and the further problem of holding it together after it is educated, are both extremely difficult. In reviewing the history of the theatre, we perceive that in every great age of dramatic art the audience has heretofore been concentrated in a single city. Sophocles in Athens, Shakespeare in London, Molière in Paris, could look their auditors in the eyes. The entire state was centered in a city; and the whole theatre-going population of that city was under the immediate observation of the great theatric artists. They were not troubled by any doubt as to where their public was to be found or who the people were who made it up. The theatre-going population of Athens, London, or Paris was not, according to our modern notions, very large; but it was so concentrated that it could easily and eagerly support a whole great group of dramatists. In America, at the present day, there must actually be more people who are able to appreciate the best dramatic art than there ever were in the Athens of Sophocles, the London of Shakespeare, or the Paris of Molière; there must, indeed, be many times the number, for our population is enormous and the standards of our public education are higher than those of Elizabethan London or the Paris of the *Grand Monarque*. But our problem is to find out who these people are and where they are. They are not concentrated in a single city. They are scattered over a widespread continent; and they are intermingled with a hundred million other people who do not care about dramatic art at all. No dramatist can look them in the eyes; and when a play is produced that makes a special appeal to the best minds, the manager does not know where to send it.

Our problem, therefore, is not only to improve our audience but also to organize it. We need to discover what people constitute already our best theatre-going public; we want their names and their addresses; we need to estimate their numerical strength and to study their geographic distribution. If they will come forward publicly, in a solid organization, and will demand good drama, the managers will have to find it for them, and will be forced, by that same principle of supply and demand, to cry out to the creators for good art until they get it.

III

THE POSITION OF THE DRAMATIST

N
O OTHER artist is so little appreciated by the public that enjoys his work, or is granted so little studious consideration from the critically minded, as the dramatist. Other artists, like the novelist, the painter, the sculptor, or the actor, appeal directly to the public and the critics; nothing stands between their finished work and the minds that contemplate it. A person reading a novel, or looking at a statue or a picture, may see exactly what the artist has done and what he has not, and may appreciate his work accordingly. But when the dramatist has completed his play, he does not deliver it directly to the public; he delivers it only indirectly, through the medial interpretation of many other artists,—the actor, the stage-director, the scene-painter, and still others of whom the public seldom hears. If any of these other and medial artists fails to convey the message that the dramatist intended, the dramatist will fail of his intention, though the fault is not his own. None of the general public, and few of the critics, will discern what the dramatist had in mind, so completely may his creative thought be clouded by inadequate interpretation.

The dramatist is obviously at the mercy of his actors. His most delicate love scene may be spoiled irrevocably by an actor incapable of profound emotion daintily expressed; his most imaginative creation of a hard and cruel character may be rendered unappreciable by an actor of too persuasive charm. And, on the other hand, the puppets of a dramatist with very little gift for characterisation may sometimes be lifted into life by gifted actors and produce upon the public a greater impression than the characters of a better dramatist less skilfully portrayed. It is, therefore, very difficult to determine whether the dramatist has imagined more or less than the particular semblance of humanity exhibited by the actor on the stage. Othello, as portrayed by Ermete Novelli, was a man devoid of dignity and majesty, a creature intensely animal and nervously impulsive; and if we had never read the play, or seen other performances of it, we should probably deny to Shakespeare the credit due for one of his most grand conceptions. On the other hand, when we witnessed David Warfield's beautiful and truthful performance of *The Music Master*, we were tempted not to notice that the play itself was faulty in structure, untrue in character, and obnoxiously sentimental in tone. Because Mr. Warfield, by the sheer power of his histrionic genius, had lifted sentimentality into sentiment and conventional theatricism into living truth, we were tempted to give to Charles Klein the credit for having written a very good play instead of a very bad one.

An occasion is remembered in theatric circles when, at the tensest moment in the first-night presentation of a play, the leading actress, entering down a stairway, tripped and fell sprawling. Thus a moment which the dramatist intended to be hushed and breathless with suspense was made overwhelmingly ridiculous. A cat once caused the failure of a play by appearing unexpectedly upon the stage during the most important scene and walking foolishly about. A dramatist who has spent many months devising a melodrama which is dependent for its effect at certain moments on the way in which the stage is lighted may have his play sent suddenly to failure at any of those moments if the stage-electrician turns the lights incongruously high or low. These instances are merely trivial, but they serve to emphasise the point that so much stands between the dramatist and the audience that it is sometimes difficult even for a careful critic to appreciate exactly what the dramatist intended.

And the general public, at least in present-day America, never makes the effort to distinguish the intention of the dramatist from the interpretation it receives from the actors and (to a less extent) the stage-director. The people who support the theatre see and estimate the work of the interpretative artists only; they do not see in itself and estimate for its own sake the work of the creative artist whose imaginings are being represented well or badly. The public in America goes to see actors; it seldom goes to see a play. If the average theatre-goer has liked a leading actor in one piece, he will go to see that actor in the next piece in which he is advertised to appear. But very, very rarely will he go to see a new play by a certain author merely because he has liked the last play by the same author. Indeed, the chances are that he will not even know that the two plays have been written by the same dramatist. Bronson Howard, who was by far the most celebrated and successful of the first generation of American dramatists, once told me that he was very sure that not more than one person in ten out of all the people who had seen *Shenandoah* knew who wrote the play. How many people who remember vividly Sir Henry Irving's performance of *The Story of Waterloo* could tell you who wrote the little piece? If you should ask them who wrote the Sherlock Holmes detective stories, they would answer you at once. Yet *The Story of Waterloo* was written by the author of those same detective stories.

The general public seldom knows, and almost never cares, who wrote a play. What it knows, and what it cares about primarily, is who is acting in it. The extraordinary success of *The Master Builder*, when it was presented in New York by Mme. Nazimova several years ago, was an evidence of this. The public that filled the coffers of the old Bijou Theatre was paying its money not so much to see a play by the author of *A Doll's House* and *Hedda Gabler* as to see a performance by a clever and tricky actress of alluring personality, who was better advertised and, to the average theatre-goer, better known than Henrik Ibsen.

Since the public at large is much more interested in actors than it is in dramatists, and since the first-night critics of the daily newspapers write necessarily for the public at large, they usually devote most of their attention to criticising actors rather than to criticising dramatists. Hence the general theatre-goer is seldom aided, even by the professional interpreters of theatric art, to arrive at an understanding and appreciation, for its own sake, of that share in the entire artistic production which belongs to the dramatist and the dramatist alone.

For, in present-day America at least, production in the theatre is the dramatist's only adequate means of publication, his only medium for conveying to the public those truths of life he wishes to express. Only a few plays are printed nowadays, and those few are rarely read: seldom, therefore, do they receive as careful critical consideration as even third-class novels. Since, therefore, speaking broadly, the dramatist can publish his work only through production, it is only through attending plays and studying what lies beneath the acting and behind the presentation that even the most well-intentioned critic of contemporary drama can discover what our dramatists are driving at.

The great misfortune of this condition of affairs is that the failure of a play as a business proposition cuts off suddenly and finally the dramatist's sole opportunity for publishing his thought, even though the failure may be due to any one of many causes other than incompetence on the part of the dramatist. A very good play may fail because of bad acting or crude production, or merely because it has been brought out at the wrong time of the year or has opened in the wrong sort of city. Sheridan's *Rivals*, as everybody knows, failed when it was first presented. But when once a play has failed at the present day, it is almost impossible for the dramatist to persuade any manager to undertake a second presentation of it. Whether good or bad, the play is killed, and the unfortunate dramatist is silenced until his next play is granted a hearing.

IV

DRAMATIC ART AND THE THEATRE
BUSINESS

A RT MAKES things which need to be distributed; business dis-
tributes things which have been made: and each of the
arts is therefore necessarily accompanied by a business,
whose special purpose is to distribute the products of
that art. Thus, a very necessary relation exists between the painter
and the picture-dealer, or between the writer and the publisher
of books. In either case, the business man earns his living by ex-
ploiting the products of the artist, and the artist earns his living
by bringing his goods to the market which has been opened by
the industry of the business man. The relation between the two
is one of mutual assistance; yet the spheres of their labors are quite
distinct, and each must work in accordance with a set of laws
which have no immediate bearing upon the activities of the other.
The artist must obey the laws of his art, as they are revealed by
his own impulses and interpreted by constructive criticism; but of
these laws the business man may, without prejudice to his efficiency, be largely ignorant. On the other hand, the business man
must do his work in accordance with the laws of economics,—a
science of which artists ordinarily know very little. Business is,
of necessity, controlled by the great economic law of supply and
demand. Of the practical workings of this law the business man is
in a position to know much more than the artist; and the latter
must always be greatly influenced by the former in deciding as to
what he shall make and how he shall make it. This influence of the
publisher, the dealer, the business manager, is nearly always bene-
ficial, because it helps the artist to avoid a waste of work and to
conserve and concentrate his energies; yet frequently the mind
of the maker desires to escape from it, and there is scarcely an
artist worth his salt who has not at some moments, with the zest
of truant joy, made things which were not for sale. In nearly all

110

the arts it is possible to secede at will from all allegiance to the business which is based upon them; and Raphael may write a century of sonnets, or Dante paint a picture of an angel, without considering the publisher or picture-dealer. But there is one of the arts—the art of the drama—which can never be disassociated from its concomitant business—the business of the theatre. It is impossible to imagine a man making anything which might justly be called a play merely to please himself and with no thought whatever of pleasing also an audience of others by presenting it before them with actors on a stage. But the mere existence of a theatre, a company of actors, an audience assembled, necessitates an economic organisation and presupposes a business manager; and this business manager, who sets the play before the public and attracts the public to the play, must necessarily exert a potent influence over the playwright. The only way in which a dramatist may free himself from this influence is by managing his own company, like Molière, or by conducting his own theatre, like Shakespeare. Only by assuming himself the functions of the manager can the dramatist escape from him. In all ages, therefore, the dramatist has been forced to confront two sets of problems rather than one. He has been obliged to study and to follow not only the technical laws of the dramatic art but also the commercial laws of the theatre business. And whereas, in the case of the other arts, the student may consider the painter and ignore the picture-dealer, or analyse the mind of the novelist without analysing that of his publisher, the student of the drama in any age must always take account of the manager, and cannot avoid consideration of the economic organisation of the theatre in that age. Those who are most familiar with the dramatic and poetic art of Christopher Marlowe and the histrionic art of Edward Alleyn are the least likely to underestimate the important influence which was exerted on the early Elizabethan drama by the illiterate but crafty and enterprising manager of these great artists, Philip Henslowe. Students of the Queen Anne period may read the comedies of Congreve, but they must also read the autobiography of Colley Cibber, the actor-manager of the Theatre Royal. And the critic who considers the drama of to-day must often turn from problems of art to problems of economics, and seek for the root of certain evils not in the technical methods of the dramatists but in the business methods of the managers.

V

THE HAPPY ENDING IN THE THEATRE

THE QUESTION whether or not a given play should have a so-called happy ending is one that requires more thorough consideration than is usually accorded to it. It is nearly always discussed from one point of view, and one only,—that of the box-office; but the experience of ages goes to show that it cannot rightly be decided, even as a matter of business expediency, without being considered also from two other points of view,—that of art, and that of human interest. For in the long run, the plays that pay the best are those in which a self-respecting art is employed to satisfy the human longing of the audience.

When we look at the matter from the point of view of art, we notice first of all that in any question of an ending, whether happy or unhappy, art is doomed to satisfy itself and is denied the recourse of an appeal to nature. Life itself presents a continuous sequence of causation, stretching on; and nature abhors an ending as it abhors a vacuum. If experience teaches us anything at all, it teaches us that nothing in life is terminal, nothing is conclusive. Marriage is not an end, as we presume in books; but rather a beginning. Not even death is final. We find our graves not in the ground but in the hearts of our survivors, and our slightest actions vibrate in ever-widening circles through incalculable time. Any end, therefore, to a novel or a play, must be in the nature of an artifice; and an ending must be planned not in accordance with life, which is lawless and illogical, but in accordance with art, whose soul is harmony. It must be a strictly logical result of all that has preceded it. Having begun with a certain intention, the true artist must complete his pattern, in accordance with laws more rigid than those of life; and he must not disrupt his design by an illogical intervention of the long arm of coincidence. Stevenson stated this point in a letter to Sidney Colvin: "Make another end to it? Ah, yes, but that's not the way I write; the whole tale is implied; I never use an effect when I can help it, unless it prepares the effects that are to follow; that's what a story consists in. To make another end, that is to make the beginning all wrong." In this passage the whole question is considered *merely* from the point of view of art. It is the only point of view which is valid for the novelist; for him the question is comparatively simple, and Stevenson's answer, emphatic as it is, may be accepted as final. But the dramatist has yet another factor to consider,—the factor of his audience.

The drama is a more popular art than the novel, in the sense that it makes its appeal not to the individual but to the populace. It sets a contest of human wills before a multitude gathered together for the purpose of witnessing the struggle; and it must rely for its interest largely upon the crowd's instinctive sense of partisanship. As Marlowe said, in *Hero and Leander,*—

> When two are stripped, long e'er the course begin,
> We wish that one should lose, the other win.

The audience takes sides with certain characters against certain others; and in most cases it is better pleased if the play ends in a victory for the characters it favors. The question therefore arises whether the dramatist is not justified in cogging the dice of chance and intervening arbitrarily to insure a happy outcome to the action, even though that outcome violate the rigid logic of the art of narrative. This is a very important question; and it must not be answered dogmatically. It is safest, without arguing *ex cathedra,* to accept the answer of the very greatest dramatists. Their practice goes to show that such a violation of the strict logic of art is justifiable in comedy, but is not justifiable in what we may broadly call the serious drama. Molière, for instance, nearly always gave an arbitrary happy ending to his comedies. Frequently, in the last act, he introduced a long lost uncle, who arrived upon the scene just in time to endow the hero and heroine with a fortune and to say "Bless you, my children!" as the curtain fell. Molière evidently took the attitude that since any ending whatsoever must be in the nature of an artifice, and contrary to the laws of life, he might as well falsify upon the pleasant side and send his auditors happy to their homes. Shakespeare took the same attitude in many comedies, of which *As You Like It* may be chosen as an illustration. The sudden reform of Oliver and the tardy repentance of the usurping duke are both untrue to life and illogical as art; but Shakespeare decided to throw probability and logic to the winds in order to close his comedy with a general feeling of good-will. But this easy answer to the question cannot be accepted in the case of the serious drama; for—and this is a point that is very often missed —in proportion as the dramatic struggle becomes more vital and momentous, the audience demands more and more that it shall be fought out fairly, and that even the characters it favors shall receive no undeserved assistance from the dramatist. This instinct of the crowd—the instinct by which its demand for fairness is proportioned to the importance of the struggle—may be studied by any follower of professional base-ball. The spectators at a ball-game are violently partisan and always want the home team to win. In any unimportant game—if the opposing teams, for instance, have no chance to win the pennant—the crowd is glad of any questionable decision by the umpires that favors the home team. But in any game in which the pennant is at stake, a false or bad decision, even though it be rendered in favor of the home team, will be received with hoots of disapproval. The crowd feels, in such a case, that it cannot fully enjoy the sense of victory unless the victory be fairly won. For the same reason, when any important play which sets out to end unhappily is given a sudden twist which brings about an arbitrary happy ending, the audience is likely to be displeased. And there is yet another reason for this displeasure. An audience may enjoy both farce and comedy without believing them; but it cannot fully enjoy a serious play unless it believes the story. In the serious drama, an ending, to be enjoyable, must be credible; in other words, it must, for the sake of human interest, satisfy the strict logic of art. We arrive, therefore, at the paradox that although, in the final act, the comic dramatist may achieve popularity by renouncing the laws of art, the serious dramatist can achieve popularity only by adhering rigidly to a pattern of artistic truth.

This is a point that is rarely understood by people who look at the general question from the point of view of the box-office; they seldom appreciate the fact that a serious play which logically demands an unhappy ending will make more money if it is planned in accordance with the sternest laws of art than if it is given an arbitrary happy ending in which the audience cannot easily believe. The public wants to be pleased, but it wants even more to be satisfied. In the early eighteenth century both *King Lear* and *Romeo and Juliet* were played with fabricated happy endings; but the history of these plays, before and after, proves that the alteration, considered solely from the business standpoint, was an error. And yet, after all these centuries of experience, our modern managers still remain afraid of serious plays which lead logically to unhappy terminations, and, because of the power of their position, exercise an influence over writers for the stage which is detrimental to art and even contrary to the demands of human interest.

VI

THE BOUNDARIES OF APPROBATION

WHEN Hamlet warned the strolling players against making the judicious grieve, and when he lamented that a certain play had proved caviare to the general, he fixed for the dramatic critic the lower and the upper bound for catholicity of approbation. But between these outer boundaries lie many different precincts of appeal. *The Two Orphans* of Dennery and *The Misanthrope* of Molière aim to interest two different types of audience. To say that *The Two Orphans* is a bad play because its appeal is not so intellectual as that of *The Misanthrope* would be no less a solecism than to say that *The Misanthrope* is a bad play because its appeal is not so emotional as that of *The Two Orphans*. The truth is that both stand within the boundaries of approbation. The one makes a primitive appeal to the emotions, without, however, grieving the judicious; and the other makes a refined appeal to the intelligence, without, however, subtly bewildering the mind of the general spectator.

Since success is to a play the breath of life, it is necessary that the dramatist should please his public; but in admitting this, we must remember that in a city so vast and varied as New York there are many different publics, which are willing to be pleased in many different ways. The dramatist with a new theme in his head may, before he sets about the task of building and writing his play, determine imaginatively the degree of emotional and intellectual equipment necessary to the sort of audience best fitted to appreciate that theme. Thereafter, if he build and write for that audience and that alone, and if he do his work sufficiently well, he may be almost certain that his play will attract the sort of audience he has demanded; for any good play can create its own public by the natural process of selecting from the whole vast theatre-going population the kind of auditors it needs. That problem of the dramatist to please his public reduces itself, therefore, to two very simple phases: first, to choose the sort cf public that he wants to please, and second, to direct his appeal to the mental make-up of the audience which he himself has chosen. This task, instead of hampering the dramatist, should serve really to assist him, because it requires a certain concentration of purpose and consistency of mood throughout his work.

This concentration and consistency of purpose and of mood may be symbolised by the figure of aiming straight at a predetermined target. In the years when firearms were less perfected than they are at present, it was necessary, in shooting with a rifle, to aim lower than the mark, in order to allow for an upward kick at the discharge; and, on the other hand, it was necessary, in shooting with heavy ordnance, to aim higher than the mark, in order to allow for a parabolic droop of the cannon-ball in transit. Many dramatists, in their endeavor to score a hit, still employ these compromising tricks of marksmanship: some aim lower than the judgment of their auditors, others aim higher than their taste. But, in view of the fact that under present metropolitan conditions the dramatist may pick his own auditors, this aiming below them or above them seems (to quote Sir Thomas Browne) "a vanity out of date and superannuated piece of folly." While granting the dramatist entire liberty to select the level of his mark, the critic may justly demand that he shall aim directly at it, without allowing his hand ever to droop down or flutter upward. That he should not aim below it is self-evident: there can be no possible excuse for making the judicious grieve. But that he should not aim above it is a proposition less likely to be accepted off-hand by the fastidious: Hamlet spoke with a regretful fondness of that particular play which had proved caviare to the general. It is, of course, nobler to shoot over the mark than to shoot under it; but it is nobler still to shoot directly at it. Surely there lies a simple truth beneath this paradox of words:—it is a higher aim to aim straight than to aim too high.

If a play be so constituted as to please its consciously selected auditors, neither grieving their judgment by striking lower than their level of appreciation, nor leaving them unsatisfied by snobbishly feeding them caviare when they have asked for bread, it must be judged a good play for its purpose. The one thing needful is that it shall neither insult their intelligence nor trifle with their taste. In view of the many different theatre-going publics and their various demands, the critic, in order to be just, must be endowed with a sympathetic versatility of approbation. He should take as his motto those judicious sentences with which the Autocrat of the Breakfast-Table prefaced his remarks upon the seashore and the mountains:—"No, I am not going to say which is best. The one where your place is is the best for you."

VII

STRATEGY AND TACTICS

_____

IN HIS very valuable lecture on *Robert Louis Stevenson: The Dramatist*, Sir Arthur Pinero has drawn a distinction between what he calls the "strategy" and the "tactics" of play-making. He defines *strategy* as "the general laying out of a play" and *tactics* as "the art of getting the characters on and off the stage, of conveying information to the audience, and so forth." Though this definition is by no means complete, it is sufficiently suggestive to afford a convenient addition to the terminology of dramatic criticism. The distinction between strategy and tactics is a distinction between large and little, between the general and the particular; and while to strategy it seems appropriate to apply the adjective "dramatic," it appears more logical to link the adjective "theatrical" with tactics.

It is easily evident that a genius for strategy and a talent for tactics do not necessarily go hand in hand. Every great dramatist must be a great strategist,—a master, as Sir Arthur says, of "the general laying out of a play"; but the utmost cleverness in tactics is usually attained by dramatists who hover, at their best, a little lower than the greatest. A mind that is capable of imagining the large is often neglectful of the little. Thus, the general laying out of the later acts of *Romeo and Juliet* is masterly and massive; but the particular turn in tactics because of which Romeo fails to receive the message from Friar Laurence is merely accidental, and must be regarded, therefore, as a fault in art. A secondary playwright, less obsessed with the grandeur of the general conception, would probably have been more careful of this dangerous detail; for minor men, who deal with minor themes, have more attention left to be devoted to theatrical perfections.

Ibsen also, though supreme in strategy, is often faulty in his tactics. Consider, for example, the last act of *Hedda Gabler*. The general laying out of this act is unexceptionable; for all that is exhibited would, sooner or later, inevitably happen. But the tactics are defective; for, yielding to the irretardable impulsion that seemed hurrying the play to its catastrophe, the author has permitted Mrs. Elvsted and Professor Tesman to begin their calm work of collaboration in piecing together Eilert Lövborg's posthumous book while the body of their ironically martyred friend is still lying unburied in a hospital. This is a mistake in tactics that a lesser playwright would have caught at once and remedied; for a lesser playwright would have known himself unable to afford the risk of lying about life at the culminating moment of a drama.

We admire Alexandre Dumas, *fils*, for his mastery of strategy,—particularly in the laying out of first acts and in the command of memorable curtain-falls; but, in the minor point of tactics, even so great an artist was excelled by so clever a craftsman as Victorien Sardou. Sardou was seldom a great strategist, for he loved the theatre more than life and preferred invention to imagination; but, precisely because of this restriction of his talent, he attained an eminence as a theatrical tactician which, thus far, has never been surpassed.

If we turn to a consideration of our own American drama in the light of this distinction, we shall see at once that the majority of our native playwrights are weak in strategy but strong in tactics. The life-work of Clyde Fitch was clearly illustrative of this assumption. Fitch was almost inordinately clever in his tactics. He could always expound a play with ease and interest by the aid of some original and dexterous invention. He seemed supremely clever in delineating minor characters, and in inventing means by which these minor characters should seem to have a finger in determining the destiny he had to deal with. But, at the same time, he nearly always failed in the general laying out of his play. He could not draw a leading character consistently throughout a logical succession of four acts. Even in his highest efforts, like *The Truth*, he permitted his tactics to override his strategy and allowed a big dramatic scheme to shatter itself into a myriad of minor clevernesses.

The same merits in tactics and defects in strategy remain apparent in the most typical products of the American drama of to-day. So long as we continue to fix our eyes upon the theatre instead of allowing them to wander over the unlimited domain of life, so long as we continue to value invention more dearly than imagination, so long as we continue to worship immediate expediency in preference to untimely and eternal truth, we shall continue to advance in tactics and to retrograde in strategy; we shall continue to improve the technique of the theatre, but we shall contribute nothing to the technique of the drama.

VIII

MIDDLE CLASS OPINION

I N THEIR mental attitude toward any subject, all people may be
divided into three classes, which may be called most conveniently by those terms so dear to sociologists and snobs,—
a lower class, a middle class, and an upper class. The lower
class is composed of those people who know nothing at all about
the subject in question; the middle class is composed of those
people who know a little about the subject, but not much; and
the upper class is composed of those people who know a great deal
about it. Any single individual may hold a lower class opinion on
one subject, a middle class opinion on another, and an upper class
opinion on a third. Thus, the same man might know nothing about
poetry, a little about politics, and a great deal about plumbing.
Again, a person with an upper class opinion about dogs may hold
a lower class opinion about dogmas. Nearly everybody is an expert in his line and an ignoramus in certain other lines; but, toward a considerable number of intervening matters, nearly everybody holds a middle class opinion,—the opinion of one who knows
a little, but not much.

Every work of art appeals for the approbation of all three
classes of observers—those who know nothing about the art that is
being exercised, those who know a little about it, and those who
know a great deal about it. Every professional dancer, for example,
must be judged by people who dance well, by people who dance a
little, and by people who do not dance at all. If, like Mordkin or
Nijinsky, he can capture the approbation of all three classes of
observers, his reputation is assured; but such an absolute and un-
disputed triumph is very rare in the history of art.

In the history of art, it frequently happens that the opinion of
the lower class is supported and affirmed by the opinion of the
upper class. The adage about the meeting of extremes is curiously

122

sustained by this phenomenon. But, in such cases, it nearly always happens that the middle class dissents sharply from the united and preponderant opinion of those who know less and those who know more. Indeed, the statement may be ventured that the mental middle class is nearly always a class of dissenters.

Let us consider how this formula works out when applied to concrete instances. People who know nothing about painting regard the efforts of the cubists as absurd; people who know a great deal about painting regard them, also, as absurd. These efforts are considered seriously only by people who know a little about painting, but not much. "A little knowledge"—as the most common-sensible of English poets stated—"is a dangerous thing." Here we have an instance of the sharp dissent of middle class opinion from the united opinion of the lower and the upper class. The extremes meet; but the middle term refuses to conjoin.

Again, let us consider, in this regard, the reputation of Tennyson as a writer. Among the lower class—the class of people who know nothing whatsoever about the art of writing—Tennyson is the most popular of all British poets. Among the upper class—a class composed, in this instance, of the thirty people in England and the twenty people in America who know how to write the English language—Tennyson is revered as the finest technical craftsman (with the certain exception of Milton and the possible exception of Keats) in the entire history of English verse. In this case, again, the few experts agree with the multitudinous proletariat. But among the middle class—the class of people who know a little about writing, but not much—the perfect art of Tennyson is sneered at and spoken of with scorn. Representatives of middle class opinion always prefer the artistry of Browning—or say that they do. In saying so, and thus dissenting from the opinion of the lower class, they think they are asserting their superiority. Little do they realize that, at the same time, they are emphasizing their inferiority to those who know much more than they do about the art of writing.

Browning is a great poet—a greater poet, it is possible, than Tennyson—but the point to be noted in the present context is that he has been taken up by the middle class of readers not because of his merits as a poet, but because of his defects as a writer. Browning is praised by the middle class not because he is admired by the upper class but because he is not admired by the lower class. The cult of Browning is essentially a snobbish cult,—a cult just as snobbish as that undervaluation of the art of Tennyson which has arisen merely from an ineradicable spirit of dissent.

Unfortunate is any artist—even though he be so great a man as Browning—if he endures the danger of being praised by middle class opinion. Such a man is always praised for his defects,—the faults that make him seem both different and queer. The mind of the middle class is incapable of criticism. The lower class—to quote a common formula of words—may not know anything about art, but it knows what it likes and what it doesn't like; and this knowledge is basically human and essentially sincere. The upper class is capable of criticism on a higher plane. Any man who has ever written a good sentence [such men are very rare] knows that Tennyson can write, because he knows that Tennyson can beat him at a difficult endeavor that, in Dante's phrase, has kept him lean for twenty years. But people of the middle class pride themselves mainly on liking things that other people do not like. Their favorite adjective is "different." They flatter themselves by propagating fads.

This analysis will help us to define the position of Mr. Bernard Shaw in the modern English-speaking theatre. Both lower class and upper class opinion have set him lower than Sir Arthur Pinero and Henry Arthur Jones; but he is set much higher than either of these rivals in the opinion of the middle class. [It should, perhaps, be noted in parenthesis that Sir James Barrie is exempted from this comparison because it has been his fortune to secure the equal approbation of all three classes of opinion.] People who know nothing about the drama have always preferred Pinero and Jones to Shaw; people who know a great deal about the drama still prefer Pinero and Jones to Shaw; but people who know a little about the drama, but not much, always prefer—or say that they prefer—Shaw to Pinero and Jones. The sort of people who organize Browning Circles never study *The Second Mrs. Tanqueray* or *The Liars;* they always read *Getting Married,* and pride themselves on "being different."

The man who knows a great deal is never made bashful by agreeing with the man who knows nothing at all. It is only the man who knows a little, but not much, who feels uncomfortable in conformity. Mr. Shaw is lauded as the foremost English playwright of his generation only by people who are conscious that they are disagreeing with the lower class but are utterly unconscious that they are also disagreeing with the upper class.

It has been the misfortune of Mr. Shaw to assemble and to concentrate the admiration of a special public,—a public that is composed almost entirely of people of the mental middle class. This fact is a misfortune, because—to repeat a previous statement—the mind of the middle class is incapable of criticism. When Pinero and Jones wrote bad plays, like *A Wife Without a Smile* or *Lydia Gilmore*, these plays were rejected by the lower class and condemned by the upper class; but when Shaw wrote a bad play, like *Misalliance*, it was praised by his special public in precisely the same terms that had been applied to his good plays, like *Man and Superman*. No middle class person would dare to say that a bad play by Mr. Shaw was a bad play; because, by doing so, he would relinquish his assumption of superiority over the lower class.

The thing called "fashion" is always a function of the middle class. A workman wears a flannel shirt when he wants to; an aristocrat wears a flannel shirt when he wants to; but a middle class person does not dare appear in public without a linen collar. To assert his social superiority to the workman he is obliged to confess his social inferiority to the aristocrat. It is the same in matters of opinion regarding art. A middle class person prides himself on disagreeing with the lower class when he asserts that *Candida* is more "intellectual," more "literary," more "paradoxical," more heaven-knows-what, than *The Second Mrs. Tanqueray*. Meanwhile, the greater play is valued more highly, not only by the many whom this middle class dissenter prides himself on looking down upon, but also by the few who, without pride and without protest, look down upon him with an unobserved, indulgent smile.

To say that it is fashionable to praise Mr. Shaw is, therefore, only another way of saying that his plays are commonly regarded as exempt from criticism. The middle class assumes that, like a king, Mr. Shaw can do no wrong. The lower class, knowing nothing of kings, still knows that they are not infallible; the upper class, knowing kings particularly well, also knows that they are not infallible; no king is a hero to his valet—or his queen: but the middle class plumps itself upon its knees and tries to persuade itself that a king must always be immune from criticism. Mr. Shaw has made himself a king in the imagination of the middle class of theatre-goers. It is the danger of kings that they may come to look upon themselves through the eyes of their admirers,—that they may come to regard themselves with a middle class opinion. It is evident from the prefaces of Mr. Shaw that he has latterly assumed a middle class opinion of himself. This has been bad for his art. In his estimation of his own work, a man should be influenced by the opinion of people who know nothing; he should also be influenced by the opinion of people who know a great deal: but when he accepts the opinion of people who know a little, but not much, his work must suffer. In such a case, there is a loss to him; but, alas!, there is a greater loss to humanity at large.

IX

IMITATION AND SUGGESTION
IN THE DRAMA

THERE is an old saying that it takes two to make a bargain or a quarrel; and, similarly, it takes two groups of people to make a play,—those whose minds are active behind the footlights, and those whose minds are active in the auditorium. We go to the theatre to enjoy ourselves, rather than to enjoy the actors or the author; and though we may be deluded into thinking that we are interested mainly by the ideas of the dramatist or the imagined emotions of the people on the stage, we really derive our chief enjoyment from such ideas and emotions of our own as are called into being by the observance of the mimic strife behind the footlights. The only thing in life that is really enjoyable is what takes place within ourselves; it is our own experience, of thought or of emotion, that constitutes for us the only fixed and memorable reality amid the shifting shadows of the years; and the experience of anybody else, either actual or imaginary, touches us as true and permanent only when it calls forth an answering imagination of our own. Each of us, in going to the theatre, carries with him, in his own mind, the real stage on which the two hours' traffic is to be enacted; and what passes behind the footlights is efficient only in so far as it calls into activity that immanent potential clash of feelings and ideas within our brain. It is the proof of a bad play that it permits us to regard it with no awakening of mind; we sit and stare over the footlights with a brain that remains blank and unpopulated; we do not create within our souls that real play for which the actual is only the occasion; and since we remain empty of imagination, we find it impossible to enjoy *ourselves*. Our feeling in regard to a bad play might be phrased in the familiar sentence,—"This is all very well; but what is it *to me?*" The piece leaves us unresponsive and aloof; we miss

127

that answering and *tallying* of mind—to use Whitman's word—which is the soul of all experience of worthy art. But a good play helps us to enjoy ourselves by making us aware of ourselves; it forces us to think and feel. We may think differently from the dramatist, or feel emotions quite dissimilar from those of the imagined people of the story; but, at any rate, our minds are consciously aroused, and the period of our attendance at the play becomes for us a period of real experience. The only thing, then, that counts in theatre-going is not what the play can give us, but what we can give the play. The enjoyment of the drama is subjective, and the province of the dramatist is merely to appeal to the subtle sense of life that is latent in ourselves.

There are, in the main, two ways in which this appeal may be made effectively. The first is by imitation of what we have already seen around us; and the second is by suggestion of what we have already experienced within us. We have seen people who were like Hedda Gabler; we have been people who were like Hamlet. The drama of facts stimulates us like our daily intercourse with the environing world; the drama of ideas stimulates us like our mystic midnight hours of solitary musing. Of the drama of imitation we demand that it shall remain appreciably within the limits of our own actual observation; it must deal with our own country and our own time, and must remind us of our daily inference from the affairs we see busy all about us. The drama of facts cannot be transplanted; it cannot be made in France or Germany and remade in America; it is localised in place and time, and has no potency beyond the bounds of its locality. But the drama of suggestion is unlimited in its possibilities of appeal; ideas are without date, and burst the bonds of locality and language. In the eighteen nineties, Americans in Paris could see the ancient Greek drama of *Œdipus King* played in modern French by the incomparable Mounet-Sully, and could experience thereby that inner overwhelming sense of the sublime which is more real than the recognition of any simulated actuality.

The distinction between the two sources of appeal in drama may be made a little more clear by an illustration from the analogous art of literature. When Whitman, in his poem on *Crossing Brooklyn Ferry*, writes, "Crowds of men and women attired in the usual costumes!", he reminds us of the environment of our daily existence, and may or may not call forth within us some recollection of experience. In the latter event, his utterance is a failure; in the former, he has succeeded in stimulating activity of mind by the process of setting before us a reminiscence of the actual. But when, in the *Song of Myself*, he writes, "We found our own, O my Soul, in the calm and cool of the daybreak," he sets before us no imitation of habituated externality, but in a flash reminds us by suggestion of so much, that to recount the full experience thereof would necessitate a volume. That second sentence may well keep us busy for an evening, alive in recollection of uncounted hours of calm wherein the soul has ascended to recognition of its universe; the first sentence we may dismiss at once, because it does not make anything important happen in our consciousness.

It must be confessed that the majority of the plays now shown in our theatres do not stimulate us to any responsive activity of mind, and therefore do not permit us, in any real sense, to enjoy ourselves. But those that, in a measure, do succeed in this prime endeavor of dramatic art may readily be grouped into two classes, according as their basis of appeal is imitation or suggestion.

X

HOLDING THE MIRROR UP TO NATURE

D OUBTLESS no one would dissent from Hamlet's dictum that the purpose of playing is "to hold, as 't were, the mirror up to nature"; but this statement is so exceedingly simple that it is rather difficult to understand. What special kind of mirror did that wise dramatic critic have in mind when he coined this memorable phrase? Surely he could not have intended the sort of flat and clear reflector by the aid of which we comb our hair; for a mirror such as this would represent life with such sedulous exactitude that we should gain no advantage from looking at the reflection rather than at the life itself which was reflected. If I wish to see the tobacco jar upon my writing table, I look at the tobacco jar: I do not set a mirror up behind it and look into the mirror. But suppose I had a magic mirror which would reflect that jar in such a way as to show me not only its outside but also the amount of tobacco shut within it. In this latter case, a glance at the represented image would spare me a more laborious examination of the actual object.

Now Hamlet must have had in mind some magic mirror such as this, which, by its manner of reflecting life, would render life more intelligible. Goethe once remarked that the sole excuse for the existence of works of art is that they are different from the works of nature. If the theatre showed us only what we see in life itself, there would be no sense at all in going to the theatre. Assuredly it must show us more than that; and it is an interesting paradox that in order to show us more it has to show us less. The magic mirror must refuse to reflect the irrelevant and non-essential, and must thereby concentrate attention on the pertinent and essential phases of nature. That mirror is the best that reflects the least which does not matter, and, as a consequence, reflects most clearly that which does. In actual life, truth is buried beneath a bewilderment of facts. Most of us seek it vainly, as we might seek a needle in a haystack. In this proverbial search we should derive no assistance from looking at a reflection of the haystack in an ordinary mirror. But imagine a glass so endowed with a selective magic that it would not reflect hay but would reflect steel. Then, assuredly, there would be a valid and practical reason for holding the mirror up to nature.

The only real triumph for an artist is not to show us a haystack, but to make us see the needle buried in it,—not to reflect the trappings and the suits of life, but to suggest a sense of that within which passeth show. To praise a play for its exactitude in representing facts would be a fallacy of criticism. The important question is not how nearly the play reflects the look of life, but how much it helps the audience to understand life's meaning. The sceneless stage of the Elizabethan *As You Like It* revealed more meanings than our modern scenic forests empty of Rosalind and Orlando. There is no virtue in reflection unless there be some magic in the mirror. Certain enterprising modern managers permit their press-agents to pat them on the back because they have set, say, a locomotive on the stage; but why should we pay three dollars to see a locomotive in the theatre when we may see a dozen locomotives in the Grand Central Station without paying anything? Why, indeed!—unless the dramatist contrives to reveal an imaginable human mystery throbbing in the palpitant heart—no, not of the locomotive, but of the locomotive-engineer. That is something that we could not see at all in the Grand Central Station, unless we were endowed with eyes as penetrant as those of the dramatist himself.

But not only must the drama render life more comprehensible by discarding the irrelevant and attracting attention to the essential; it must also render us the service of bringing to a focus that phase of life it represents. The mirror which the dramatist holds up to nature should be a concave mirror, which concentrates the rays impinging on it to a luminous focal image. Hamlet was too much a metaphysician to busy his mind about the simpler science of physics; but surely this figure of the concave mirror, with its phenomenon of concentration, represents most suggestively his belief concerning the purpose of playing and of plays. The trouble with most of our dramas is that they render scattered and incoherent images of life; they tell us many unimportant things, instead of telling us one important thing in many ways. They reveal but little, because they reproduce too much. But it is only by bringing all life to a focus in a single luminous idea that it is possible, in the two hours' traffic of the stage, "to show virtue her own feature, scorn her own image, and the very age and body of the time his form and pressure."

An interesting instance of how a dramatist, by holding, as it were, a concave mirror up to nature, may concentrate all life to a focus in a single luminous idea is afforded by that justly celebrated drama entitled *El Gran Galeoto,* by José Echegaray. This play was first produced at the Teatro Español on March 19, 1881, and achieved a triumph that soon diffused the fame of its author, which till then had been but local, beyond the Pyrenees. It is now generally recognised as one of the standard monuments of the modern social drama. It owes its eminence mainly to the unflinching emphasis which it casts upon a single great idea. This idea is suggested in its title.

In the old French romance of Launcelot of the Lake, it was Gallehault who first prevailed on Queen Guinevere to give a kiss to Launcelot: he was thus the means of making actual their potential guilty love. His name thereafter, like that of Pandarus of Troy, became a symbol to designate a go-between, inciting to illicit love. In the fifth canto of the *Inferno,* Francesca da Rimini narrates to Dante how she and Paolo read one day, all unsuspecting, the romance of Launcelot; and after telling how her lover, allured by the suggestion of the story, kissed her on the mouth all trembling, she adds,   Galeotto fu'l libro e chi lo scrisse,

which may be translated, "The book and the author of it performed for us the service of Gallehault." Now Echegaray, desiring to retell in modern terms the old familiar story of a man and a woman who, at first innocent in their relationship, are allured by unappreciable degrees to the sudden realisation of a great passion for each other, asked himself what force it was, in modern life, which would perform for them most tragically the sinful service of Gallehault. Then it struck him that the great Gallehault of modern life—*El Gran Galeoto*—was the impalpable power of gossip, the suggestive force of whispered opinion, the prurient allurement of evil tongues. Set all society to glancing slyly at a man and a woman whose relation to each other is really innocent, start the wicked tongue a-babbling, and you will stir up a whirlwind which will blow them giddily into each other's arms. Thus the old theme might be recast for the purposes of modern tragedy. Echegaray himself, in the critical prose prologue which he prefixed to his play, comments upon the fact that the chief character and main motive force of the entire drama can never appear upon the stage, except in hints and indirections; because the great Gallehault of his story is not any particular person, but rather all slanderous society at large. As he expresses it, the villain-hero of his drama is *todo el mundo,*—everybody, or all the world.

This, obviously, is a great idea for a modern social drama, because it concentrates within itself many of the most important phases of the perennial struggle between the individual and society; and this great idea is embodied with direct, unwavering simplicity in the story of the play. Don Julián, a rich merchant about forty years of age, is ideally married to Teodora, a beautiful woman in her early twenties, who adores him. He is a generous and kindly man; and upon the death of an old and honored friend, to whose assistance in the past he owes his present fortune, he adopts into his household the son of this friend, Ernesto. Ernesto is twenty-six years old; he reads poems and writes plays, and is a thoroughly fine fellow. He feels an almost filial affection for Don Julián and a wholesome brotherly friendship for Teodora. They, in turn, are beautifully fond of him. Naturally, he accompanies them everywhere in the social world of Madrid; he sits in their box at the opera, acting as Teodora's escort when her husband is detained by business; and he goes walking with Teodora of an afternoon. Society, with sinister imagination, begins to look askance at the triangulated household; tongues begin to wag; and gossip grows. Tidings of the evil talk about town are brought to Don Julián by his brother, Don Severo, who advises that Ernesto had better be requested to live in quarters of his own. Don Julián nobly repels this suggestion as insulting; but Don Severo persists that only by such a course may the family name be rendered unimpeachable upon the public tongue.

Ernesto, himself, to still the evil rumors, goes to live in a studio alone. This simple move on his part suggests to everybody—*todo el mundo*—that he must have had a real motive for making it. Gossip increases, instead of diminishing; and the emotions of Teodora, Don Julián, and himself are stirred to the point of nervous tensity. Don Julián, in spite of his own sweet reasonableness, begins subtly to wonder if there could be, by any possibility, any basis for his brother's vehemence. Don Severo's wife, Doña Mercedes, repeats the talk of the town to Teodora, and turns her imagination inward, till it falters in self-questionings. Similarly the great Gallehault,—which is the word of all the world,—whispers unthinkable and tragic possibilities to the poetic and self-searching mind of Ernesto. He resolves to seek release in Argentina. But before he can sail away, he overhears, in a fashionable café, a remark which casts a slur on Teodora, and strikes the speaker of the insult in the face. A duel is forthwith arranged, to take place in a vacant studio adjacent to Ernesto's. When Don Julián learns about it, he is troubled by the idea that another man should be fighting for his wife, and rushes forthwith to wreak vengeance himself on the traducer. Teodora hears the news; and in order to prevent both her husband and Ernesto from endangering their lives, she rushes to Ernesto's rooms to urge him to forestall hostilities. Meanwhile her husband encounters the slanderer, and is severely wounded. He is carried to Ernesto's studio. Hearing people coming, Teodora hides herself in Ernesto's bedroom, where she is discovered by her husband's attendants. Don Julián, wounded and enfevered, now at last believes the worst.

Ernesto seeks and slays Don Julián's assailant. But now the whole world credits what the whole world has been whispering. In vain Ernesto and Teodora protest their innocence to Don Severo and to Doña Mercedes. In vain they plead with the kindly and noble man they both revere and love. Don Julián curses them, and dies believing in their guilt. Then at last, when they find themselves cast forth by the entire world, their common tragic loneliness draws them to each other. They are given to each other by the world. The insidious purpose of the great Gallehault has been accomplished; and Ernesto takes Teodora for his own.

XI

DRAMATIC LITERATURE AND THEATRIC JOURNALISM

O NE REASON why journalism is a lesser thing than literature is that it subserves the tyranny of timeliness. It narrates the events of the day and discusses the topics of the hour, for the sole reason that they happen for the moment to float uppermost upon the current of human experience. The flotsam of this current may occasionally have dived up from the depths and may give a glimpse of some underlying secret of the sea; but most often it merely drifts upon the surface, indicative of nothing except which way the wind lies. Whatever topic is the most timely to-day is doomed to be the most untimely to-morrow. Where are the journals of yester-year? Dig them out of dusty files, and all that they say will seem wearisomely old, for the very reason that when it was written it seemed spiritedly new. Whatever wears a date upon its forehead will soon be out of date. The main interest of news is newness; and nothing slips so soon behind the times as novelty.

With timeliness, as an incentive, literature has absolutely no concern. Its purpose is to reveal what was and is and evermore shall be. It can never grow old, for the reason that it has never attempted to be new. Early in the nineteenth century, the gentle Elia revolted from the tyranny of timeliness. "Hang the present age!", said he, "I'll write for antiquity." The timely utterances of his contemporaries have passed away with the times that called them forth: his essays live perennially new. In the dateless realm of revelation, antiquity joins hands with futurity. There can be nothing either new or old in any utterance which is really true or beautiful or right.

In considering a given subject, journalism seeks to discover what there is in it that belongs to the moment, and literature seeks to reveal what there is in it that belongs to eternity. To journalism facts are important because they are facts; to literature they are important only in so far as they are representative of recurrent truths. Literature speaks because it has something to say: journalism speaks because the public wants to be talked to. Literature is an emanation from an inward impulse: but the motive of journalism is external; it is fashioned to supply a demand outside itself. It is frequently said, and is sometimes believed, that the province of journalism is to mold public opinion; but a consideration of actual conditions indicates rather that its province is to find out what the opinion of some section of the public is, and then to formulate it and express it. The successful journalist tells his readers what they want to be told. He becomes their prophet by making clear to them what they themselves are thinking. He influences people by agreeing with them. In doing this he may be entirely sincere, for his readers may be right and may demand from him the statement of his own most serious convictions; but the fact remains that his motive for expression is centred in them instead of in himself. It is not thus that literature is motivated. Literature is not a formulation of public opinion, but an expression of personal and particular belief. For this reason it is more likely to be true. Public opinion is seldom so important as private opinion. Socrates was right and Athens wrong. Very frequently the multitude at the foot of the mountain are worshiping a golden calf, while the prophet, lonely and aloof upon the summit, is hearkening to the very voice of God.

The journalist is limited by the necessity of catering to majorities; he can never experience the felicity of Dr. Stockmann, who felt himself the strongest man on earth because he stood most alone. It may sometimes happen that the majority is right; but in that case the agreement of the journalist is an unnecessary utterance. The truth was known before he spoke, and his speaking is superfluous. What is popularly said about the educative force of journalism is, for the most part, baseless. Education occurs when a man is confronted with something true and beautiful and good which stimulates to active life that "bright effluence of bright essence increate" which dwells within him. The real ministers of education must be, in Emerson's phrase, "lonely, original, and pure." But journalism is popular instead of lonely, timely rather than original, and expedient instead of pure. Even at its best, journalism remains an enterprise; but literature at its best becomes no less than a religion.

These considerations are of service in studying what is written for the theatre. In all periods, certain contributions to the drama have been journalistic in motive and intention, while certain others have been literary. There is a good deal of journalism in the comedies of Aristophanes. He often chooses topics mainly for their timeliness, and gathers and says what happens to be in the air. Many of the Elizabethan dramatists, like Dekker and Heywood and Middleton for example, looked at life with the journalistic eye. They collected and disseminated news. They were, in their own time, much more "up to date" than Shakespeare, who chose for his material old stories that nearly every one had read. Ben Jonson's *Bartholomew Fair* is glorified journalism. It brims over with contemporary gossip and timely witticisms. Therefore it is out of date to-day, and is read only by people who wish to find out certain facts of London life in Jonson's time. *Hamlet* in 1602 was not a novelty; but it is still read and seen by people who wish to find out certain truths of life in general.

At the present day, a very large proportion of the contributions to the theatre must be classed and judged as journalism. Many of our most popular American plays are nothing more or less than dramatised newspapers. A piece of this sort, however effective it may be at the moment, must soon suffer the fate of all things timely and slip behind the times. Whenever an author selects a subject because he thinks the public wants him to talk about it, instead of because he knows he wants to talk about it to the public, his motive is journalistic rather than literary. A timely topic may, however, be used to embody a truly literary intention. In *Winterset*, for example, although it was suggested by an actual murder case in Massachusetts, journalism was lifted into literature by the sincerity of Mr. Maxwell Anderson's conviction that he had something real and significant to say. The play became important because there was a man behind it. Individual personality is perhaps the most dateless of all phenomena. The fact of any great individuality once accomplished and achieved becomes contemporary with the human race and sloughs off the usual limits of past and future.

Whatever Sir James Barrie has written is literature, because he dwelt isolate amidst the world in a wise minority of one. The things that he says are of importance because nobody else could have said them. He achieved individuality, and thereby passed out of hearing of the ticking of clocks into an ever-ever land where dates are not and consequently epitaphs can never be. What he utters is of interest to the public, because his motive for speaking is private and personal. Instead of telling people what they think that they are thinking, he tells them what they have always known but think they have forgotten. He performs, for an oblivious generation, the service of a great reminder. He lures us from the strident and factitious world of which we read daily in the first pages of the newspapers, back to the serene eternal world of little, nameless, unremembered acts of kindness and of love. He educates the many, not by any crass endeavor to formulate or even to mold the opinion of the public, but by setting simply before them thoughts which do often lie too deep for tears.

The distinguishing trait of Barrie's genius is that he looks upon life with the simplicity of a child and sees it with the wisdom of a woman. He has a woman's subtlety of insight, a child's concreteness of imagination. He is endowed (to reverse a famous phrase of Matthew Arnold's) with a sweet unreasonableness. He understands life not with his intellect but with his sensibilities. As a consequence, he is familiar with all the tremulous, delicate intimacies of human nature that every woman knows, but that most men glimpse only in moments of exalted sympathy with some wise woman whom they love. His insight has that absoluteness which is beyond the reach of intellect alone. He knows things for the unutterable woman's reason,—"because . . ."

But with this feminine, intuitive understanding of humanity, Barrie combines the distinctively masculine trait of being able to communicate the things that his emotions know. The greatest poets would, of course, be women, were it not for the fact that women are in general incapable of revealing through the medium of articulate art the very things they know most deeply. Most of the women who have written have said only the lesser phases of themselves; they have unwittingly withheld their deepest and most poignant wisdom because of a native reticence of speech. Many a time they reach a heaven of understanding shut to men; but when they come back, they cannot tell the world. The rare artists among women, like Sappho and Mrs. Browning and Christina Rossetti and Laurence Hope, in their several different ways, have managed to express themselves only through a sublime and glorious unashamedness. As Hawthorne once remarked very wisely, women have achieved art only when they have stood naked in the market-place. But men in general are not withheld by a similar hesitance from saying what they feel most deeply. No woman could have written Sir James Barrie's biography of his mother; but for a man like him there was a sort of sacredness in revealing emotion so private as to be expressible only in the purest speech. Barrie was apparently born into the world of men to tell us what our mothers and our wives would have told us if they could,—what in deep moments they have tried to tell us, trembling exquisitely upon the verge of words. The theme of his best work has always been "what every woman knows." In expressing this, he has added to the permanent recorded knowledge of humanity; and he has thereby lifted his plays above the level of theatric journalism to the level of true dramatic literature.

XII

THE INTENTION OF PERMANENCE

I

A T CONEY ISLAND and Atlantic City and many other seaside resorts whither the multitude drifts to drink oblivion of a day, an artist may be watched at work modeling images in the sand. These he fashions deftly, to entice the immediate pennies of the crowd; but when his wage is earned, he leaves his statues to be washed away by the next high surging of the tide. The sand-man is often a good artist; let us suppose he were a better one. Let us imagine him endowed with a brain and a hand on a par with those of Praxiteles. None the less we should set his seashore images upon a lower plane of art than the monuments Praxiteles himself hewed out of marble. This we should do instinctively, with no recourse to critical theory; and that man in the multitude who knew the least about art would express this judgment most emphatically. The simple reason would be that the art of the sand-man is lacking in the Intention of Permanence.

The Intention of Permanence, whether it be conscious or subconscious with the artist, is a necessary factor of the noblest art. Some of us remember the Court of Honor at the World's Columbian Exposition at Chicago nearly half a century ago. The sculpture was good and the architecture better. In chasteness and symmetry of general design, in spaciousness fittingly restrained, in simplicity more decorative than deliberate decoration, those white buildings blooming into gold and mirrored in a calm lagoon dazzled the eye and delighted the æsthetic sense. And yet, merely because they lacked the Intention of Permanence, they failed to awaken that solemn happy heartache that we feel in looking upon the tumbled ruins of some ancient temple. We could never quite forget that the buildings of the Court of Honor were fabrics of frame and stucco sprayed with whitewash, and that the statues

140

were kneaded out of plaster: they were set there for a year, not for all time. But there is at Pæstum a crumbled Doric temple to Poseidon, built in ancient days to remind the reverent of that incalculable vastness that tosses men we know not whither. It stands forlorn in a malarious marsh, yet eternally within hearing of the unsubservient surge. Many of its massive stones have tottered to the earth; and irrelevant little birds sing in nests among the capitals and mock the solemn silence that the Greeks ordained. But the sacred Intention of Permanence that filled and thrilled the souls of those old builders stands triumphant over time; and if only a single devastated column stood to mark their meaning, it would yet be a greater thing than the entire Court of Honor, built only to commemorate the passing of a year.

In all the arts except the acted drama, it is easy even for the layman to distinguish work which is immediate and momentary from work which is permanent and real. It was the turbulent untutored crowd that clamored loudest in demanding that the Dewey Arch, in celebration of our victory over Spain, should be rendered permanent in marble: it was only the artists and the art-critics who were satisfied by the monument in its ephemeral state of frame and plaster. But in the drama, the layman often finds it difficult to distinguish between a piece intended merely for immediate entertainment and a piece that incorporates the Intention of Permanence. In particular he almost always fails to distinguish between what is really a character and what is merely an acting part. When a dramatist really creates a character, he imagines and projects a human being so truly conceived and so clearly presented that any average man would receive the impression of a living person if he were to read in manuscript the bare lines of the play. But when a playwright merely devises an acting part, he does nothing more than indicate to a capable actor the possibility of so comporting himself upon the stage as to convince his audience of humanity in his performance. From the standpoint of criticism, the main difficulty is that the actor's art may frequently obscure the dramatist's lack of art, and *vice versa*, so that a mere acting part may seem, in the hands of a capable actor, a real character, whereas a real character may seem, in the hands of an incapable actor, an indifferent acting part. Rip Van Winkle, for example, was a wonderful acting part for Joseph Jefferson; but it was, from the standpoint of the dramatist, scarcely a character at all, as any one may see who takes the trouble to read the play. Beau Brummell, also, was an acting part rather than a character. And yet the layman, under the immediate spell of the actor's representative art, is tempted in such cases to ignore that the dramatist has merely modeled an image in the sand.

Likewise, on a larger scale, the layman habitually fails to distinguish between a mere theatric entertainment and a genuine drama. A genuine drama always reveals through its imagined struggle of contesting wills some eternal truth of human life, and illuminates some real phases of human character. But a theatric entertainment may present merely a deftly fabricated struggle between puppets, wherein the art of the actor is given momentary exercise. To return to our comparison, a genuine drama is carved out of marble, and incorporates, consciously or not, the Intention of Permanence; whereas a mere theatric entertainment may be likened to a group of figures sculptured in the sand.

Those of us who ask much of the contemporary theatre may be saddened to observe that most of the current dramatists seem more akin to the sand-man than to Praxiteles. They have built Courts of Honor for forty weeks, rather than temples to Poseidon for eternity. Yet it is futile to condemn an artist who does a lesser thing quite well because he has not attempted to do a greater thing which, very probably, he could not do at all. Criticism, in order to render any practical service, must be tuned in accordance with the intention of the artist. The important point for the critic of the sand-man at Coney Island is not to complain because he is not so enduring an artist as Praxiteles, but to determine why he is, or is not, as the case may be, a better artist than the sand-man at Atlantic City.

II

Whatever is worth doing at all is worth doing well: and this is the only answer that is necessary to critics who question the importance of technical accomplishment in art. In that decadent period which suddenly ceased to be in August, 1914, a hare-brained handful of young anarchs in all the nations that had gone to seed asserted, very noisily, that art was merely a matter of impulse and was not dependent upon craftsmanship. The first duty of the painter,—we were told,—was not to learn to paint; the first duty of the writer was not to learn to write; the first duty of the musical composer was not to learn the laws of harmony and counterpoint. The cubists, the futurists, the imagists, the vorticists,—one can't remember any longer the interminable list of "ists,"—proclaimed that crudity was a proof of genius and that the aim of art was to be emphatically inartistic. This disease attacked the drama; and the heresy was held that the one thing that a playwright should avoid was any effort or ambition to produce a well-made play. The very phrase—"a well-made play"—was bandied about by anarchistic critics as if it were a badge of scorn. We were asked to admire *The Madras House* of Mr. Granville Barker —an appallingly unpopular play—for the reason that it was inchoate and helter-skelter, like a London suburb, instead of planned and patterned, like that Lantern of the World, the high Acropolis. Even Mr. Bernard Shaw, who had made great plays and made them well—consider *Candida*, for instance—caught the fever, and allowed himself—in *Getting Married* and in *Misalliance*—to make two plays as badly as he could, in order to prove himself a "genius."

The criticism of that now-forgotten period was marked by a jaunty impudence toward any craftsman who had ever taken pains to learn his craft. Stevenson was sneered at, because of his picked and polished prose; Raphael was ridiculed, because he knew how to draw; Tennyson was insulted, because of his unfaltering and faultless eloquence; Pinero was patted scornfully upon the head because he happened to be a master of his craft. It was assumed that, if a man had taken time and pains to learn to say things well, he could not possibly have anything to say. A respect for the traditions of the past was airily dismissed as "mid-Victorian." It was considered merely "scholarly" and "dull" for any person to remember the almost religious reverence of such a master-craftsman as Velasquez for the very tools of his trade. Poor Velasquez!—he had never learned to paint carelessly and badly:—he was, therefore, not a "genius," after all!

That anarchistic period is past. The world is done with mental drunkenness and with the lassitude that comes of over-leisure. The change came when the earth was rocked with war, and nothing any more was heard except the clarion that called to battle "the army of unalterable law." Rheims was bombarded: Venice was endangered: and men who loved both Rheims and Venice learned to die for those ideals that erring little creatures used to laugh at, a little—such a little—while before.

Thoughts fade and die; ideas are transitory; opinions pass like little ripples on the surface of an utterly immeasurable sea. Even the seeming certainties of science crumble and decay, like rocks beneath the beating of repeated rain. What survives? . . . Let Austin Dobson answer, with these lines:—

> All passes. Art alone
>   Enduring stays to us.
> The Bust out-lasts the Throne,—
>   The Coin, Tiberius.

Only,—the bust must be beautiful, and the coin must be cunningly designed; for, in the league-long history of art, there is no antidote against the opium of time except that Workmanship which is won only by good and faithful servants.

Much has been said about the "message" of the artist; but, to any great artist, his material seems less important than his method. Thoughts, opinions, and ideas may be controverted within that winking of an eye that mortals call a century; but Time itself can cast no dust upon a piece of work that has been done supremely well. The world no longer seriously ponders the abstract contributions made to philosophic thought by Thomas De Quincey; but such a pattern of alliteration as, "Sweet funeral bells from some incalculable distance, wailing over the dead that die before the dawn," will never be forgotten, so long as living men have ears to hear. This man knew how to write. That is his epitaph; and it is also the token of his immortality. World-conquering religions, after centuries, dissolve themselves into discarded myths: but eloquence lives on. Artistry—or to call it by that other and more ugly name, Technique—is not a matter to be laughed at, after all: for technique is the sole preservative of art against corruption and decay.

XIII

THE QUALITY OF NEW ENDEAVOR

M<small>ANY</small> critics seem to be of the opinion that the work of a new and unknown author deserves and requires less serious consideration than the work of an author of established reputation. There is, however, an important sense in which the very contrary is true. The function of the critic is to help the public to discern and to appreciate what is worthy. The fact of an established reputation affords evidence that the author who enjoys it has already achieved the appreciation of the public and no longer stands in need of the intermediary service of the critic. But every new author advances as an applicant for admission into the ranks of the recognised; and the critic must, whenever possible, assist the public to determine whether the newcomer seems destined by inherent right to enter among the good and faithful servants, or whether he is essentially an outsider seeking to creep or intrude or climb into the fold.

Since everybody knows already the reputation of Eugene O'Neill and what may be expected of him, the only question for the critic, in considering a new play from his practiced pen, is whether or not the author has succeeded in advancing or maintaining the standard of his earlier and remembered efforts. If, as in *Dynamo*, he falls far below that standard, the critic may condemn the play, and let the matter go at that. Although the new piece may be discredited, the author's reputation will suffer no abiding injury from the deep damnation of its taking off; for the public will continue to remember *Anna Christie*, and will remain assured that O'Neill is worth while. But when a play by a new author comes up for consideration, the public needs to be told not only whether the work itself has been well or badly done, but also whether or not the unknown author seems to be inherently a person of importance, from whom more worthy works may be

145

expected in the future. The critic must not only make clear the playwright's present actual accomplishment, but must also estimate his promise. An author's first or second play is important mainly— to use Whitman's phrase—as "an encloser of things to be." The question is not so much what the author has already done as what he is likely to do if he is given further hearings. It is in this sense that the work of an unknown playwright requires and deserves more serious consideration than the work of an acknowledged master. Accomplishment is comparatively easy to appraise, but to appreciate promise requires forward-looking and far-seeing eyes.

In the real sense, it matters very little whether an author's early plays succeed or fail. The one point that does matter is whether, in either case, the merits and defects are of such a nature as to indicate that the man behind the work is inherently a man worth while. In either failure or success, the sole significant thing is the quality of the endeavor. A young author may fail for the shallow reason that he is insincere; but he may fail even more decisively for the sublime reason that as yet his reach exceeds his grasp. He may succeed because through earnest effort he has done almost well something eminently worth the doing; or he may succeed merely because he has essayed an unimportant and an easy task. Often more hope for an author's future may be founded upon an initial failure than upon an initial success. It is better for a young man to fail in a large and noble effort than to succeed in an effort insignificant and mean. For in labor, as in life, Stevenson's maxim is very often pertinent:—to travel hopefully is a better thing than to arrive.

And in estimating the work of new and unknown authors, it is not nearly so important for the critic to consider their present technical accomplishment as it is for him to consider the sincerity with which they have endeavored to tell the truth about some important phase of human life. Dramatic criticism of an academic cast is of little value either to those who write plays or to those who see them. The man who buys his ticket to the theatre knows little and cares less about the technique of play-making; and for the dramatist himself there are no ten commandments. I have been gradually growing to believe that there is only one commandment for the dramatist,—that he shall tell the truth; and only one fault of which a play is capable,—that, as a whole or in details, it tells a lie. A play is irretrievably bad only when the average theatre-

goer—a man, I mean, with no special knowledge of dramatic art—
viewing what is done upon the stage and hearing what is said, re-
volts instinctively against it with a feeling that I may best express
in that famous sentence of Judge Brack's, "People don't do such
things." A play that is truthful at all points will never evoke this
instinctive disapproval; a play that tells lies at certain points will
lose attention by jangling those who know.

The test of truthfulness is the final test of excellence in drama.
In saying this, of course, I do not mean that the best plays are
realistic in method, naturalistic in setting, or close to actuality in
subject-matter. *The Tempest* is just as true as *The Merry Wives
of Windsor*, and *Peter Pan* is just as true as *Ghosts*. I mean merely
that the people whom the dramatist has conceived must act and
speak at all points consistently with the laws of their imagined
existence, and that these laws must be in harmony with the laws
of actual life. Whenever people on the stage fail of this consistency with law, a normal theatre-goer will feel instinctively, "Oh,
no, he did *not* do that," or, "Those are *not* the words she said." It
may safely be predicated that a play is really bad only when the
audience does not believe it; for a dramatist is not capable of a
single fault, either technical or otherwise, that may not be viewed
as one phase or another of untruthfulness.

XIV

THE EFFECT OF PLAYS UPON
THE PUBLIC

I N THE course of his glorious *Song of the Open Road*, Walt
Whitman said, "I and mine do not convince by arguments,
similes, rhymes; we convince by our presence"; and it has
always seemed to me that this remark is peculiarly applicable
to dramatists and dramas. The primary purpose of a play is to give
a gathered multitude a larger sense of life by stimulating its emotions to a consciousness of terror and pity, laughter and love. Its
purpose is not primarily to rouse the intellect to thought or call
the will to action. In so far as the drama uplifts and edifies the
audience, it does so, not by precept or by syllogism, but by emotional suggestion. It teaches not by what it says, but rather by
what it deeply and mysteriously is. It convinces not by its arguments, but by its presence.

It follows that those who think about the drama in relation to
society at large, and consider as a matter of serious importance the
effect of the theatre on the ticket-buying public, should devote
profound consideration to that subtle quality of plays which I may
call their *tone*. Since the drama convinces less by its arguments
than by its presence, less by its intellectual substance than by its
emotional suggestion, we have a right to demand that it shall be
not only moral but also healthful and inspiriting.

After witnessing the admirable performance of Mrs. Fiske and
the members of her skilfully selected company in Henrik Ibsen's
dreary and depressing *Rosmersholm*, I went home and sought
solace from a reperusal of an old play, by the buoyant and healthy
Thomas Heywood, which is sweetly named *The Fair Maid of the
West*. *Rosmersholm* is of all the social plays of Ibsen the least interesting to witness on the stage, because the spectator is left entirely in the dark concerning the character and the motives of

148

Rebecca West until her confession at the close of the third act, and can therefore understand the play only on a second seeing. But except for this important structural defect the drama is a masterpiece of art; and it is surely unnecessary to dwell upon its many merits. On the other hand, *The Fair Maid of the West* is very far from being masterly in art. In structure it is loose and careless; in characterisation it is inconsistent and frequently untrue; in style it is uneven and without distinction. Ibsen, in sheer mastery of dramaturgic means, stands fourth in rank among the world's great dramatists. Heywood was merely an actor with a gift for telling stories, who flung together upward of two hundred and twenty plays during the course of his casual career. And yet *The Fair Maid of the West* seemed to me that evening, and seems to me evermore in retrospect, a nobler work than *Rosmersholm;* for the Norwegian drama gives a doleful exhibition of unnecessary misery, while the Elizabethan play is fresh and wholesome, and fragrant with the breath of joy.

Of two plays equally true in content and in treatment, equally accomplished in structure, in characterisation, and in style, that one is finally the better which evokes from the audience the healthiest and hopefulest emotional response. This is the reason why *Œdipus King* is a better play than *Ghosts.* The two pieces are not dissimilar in subject and are strikingly alike in art. Each is a terrible presentment of a revolting theme; each, like an avalanche, crashes to foredoomed catastrophe. But the Greek tragedy is nobler in tone, because it leaves us a lofty reverence for the gods, whereas its modern counterpart disgusts us with the inexorable laws of life,—which are only the old gods divested of imagined personality.

Slowly but surely we are growing very tired of dramatists who look upon life with a wry face instead of with a brave and bracing countenance. In due time, when we have become again like little children, we shall realise that plays like *As You Like It* are better than all the *Magdas* and the *Hedda Gablers* of the modern stage. We shall realise that the way to heal old sores is to let them alone, rather than to rip them open, in the interest (as we vainly fancy) of medical science. We shall remember that the way to help the public is to set before it images of faith and hope and love, rather than images of doubt, despair, and infidelity.

The queer thing about the morbid-minded specialists in fabricated woe is that they believe themselves to be telling the whole truth of human life instead of telling only the worser half of it. They expunge from their records of humanity the very emotions that make life worth the living, and then announce momentously, "Behold reality at last; for this is Life." It is as if, in the midnoon of a god-given day of golden spring, they should hug a black umbrella down about their heads and cry aloud, "Behold, there is no sun!" Shakespeare did that only once,—in *Measure for Measure*. In the deepest of his tragedies, he voiced a grandeur even in obliquity, and hymned the greatness and the glory of the life of man.

Suppose that what looks white in a landscape painting be actually bluish gray. Perhaps it would be best to tell us so; but failing that, it would certainly be better to tell us that it is white than to tell us that it is black. If our dramatists must idealise at all in representing life, let them idealise upon the positive rather than upon the negative side. It is nobler to tell us that life is better than it actually is than to tell us that it is worse. It is nobler to remind us of the joy of living than to remind us of the weariness. "For to miss the joy is to miss all," as Stevenson remarked; and if the drama is to be of benefit to the public, it should, by its very presence, convey conviction of the truth thus nobly phrased by Matthew Arnold:

> Yet the will is free:
> Strong is the Soul, and wise, and beautiful:
> The seeds of godlike power are in us still:
> Gods are we, Bards, Saints, Heroes, if we will.—
> Dumb judges, answer, truth or mockery?

XV

PLEASANT AND UNPLEASANT PLAYS

T HE CLEVER title, *Plays Pleasant and Unpleasant,* which Bernard Shaw selected for the earliest issue of his dramatic writings, suggests a theme of criticism that Mr. Shaw, in his lengthy prefaces, might profitably have considered if he had not preferred to devote his entire space to a discussion of his own abilities. In explanation of his title, the author stated only that he labeled his first three plays Unpleasant for the reason that "their dramatic power is used to force the spectator to face unpleasant facts." This sentence, of course, is not a definition, since it merely repeats the word to be explained; and therefore, if we wish to find out whether or not an unpleasant play is of any real service in the theatre, we shall have to do some thinking of our own.

It is an axiom that all things in the universe are interesting. The word *interesting* means *capable of awakening some activity of human mind;* and there is no imaginable topic, whether pleasant or unpleasant, which is not, in one way, or another, capable of this effect. But the activities of the human mind are various, and there are therefore several different sorts of interest. The activity of mind awakened by music over waters is very different from that awakened by the binomial theorem. Some things interest the intellect, others the emotions; and it is only things of prime importance that interest them both in equal measure. Now if we compare the interest of pleasant and unpleasant topics, we shall see at once that the activity of mind awakened by the former is more complete than that awakened by the latter. A pleasant topic not only interests the intellect but also elicits a positive response from the emotions; but most unpleasant topics are positively interesting to the intellect alone. In so far as the emotions respond at all to an unpleasant topic, they respond usually with a negative activity.

Regarding a thing which is unpleasant, the healthy mind will feel aversion—which is a negative emotion—or else will merely think about it with no feeling whatsoever. But regarding a thing which is pleasant, the mind may be stirred through the entire gamut of positive emotions, rising ultimately to that supreme activity which is Love. This is, of course, the philosophic reason why the thinkers of pleasant thoughts and dreamers of beautiful dreams stand higher in history than those who have thought unpleasantness and have imagined woe.

Returning now to that clever title of Mr. Shaw's, we may define an unpleasant play as one which interests the intellect without at the same time awakening a positive response from the emotions; and we may define a pleasant play as one which not only stimulates thought but also elicits sympathy. To any one who has thoroughly considered the conditions governing theatric art, it should be evident *a priori* that pleasant plays are better suited for service in the theatre than unpleasant plays. This truth is clearly illustrated by the facts of Mr. Shaw's career. As a matter of history, it will be remembered that his vogue in our theatres has been confined almost entirely to his pleasant plays.

Mrs. Warren's Profession is just as interesting to the thoughtful reader as *Candida*. It is built with the same technical efficiency, and written with the same agility and wit; it is just as sound and true, and therefore just as moral; and as a criticism, not so much of life as of society, it is indubitably more important. Why, then, is *Candida* a better work? The reason is that the unpleasant play is interesting merely to the intellect and leaves the audience cold, whereas the pleasant play is interesting also to the emotions and stirs the audience to sympathy. It is possible for the public to feel sorry for Morell; it is even possible for them to feel sorry for Marchbanks: but it is absolutely impossible for them to feel sorry for Mrs. Warren. The multitude instinctively demands an opportunity to sympathise with the characters presented in the theatre. Since the drama is a democratic art, and the dramatist is not the monarch but the servant of the public, the voice of the people should, in this matter of pleasant and unpleasant plays, be considered the voice of the gods. This thesis seems to me axiomatic and unsusceptible of argument. Yet since it is continually denied by the professed "uplifters" of the stage, who persist in looking down upon the public and decrying the wisdom of the many, it may be necessary to explain the eternal principle upon which it is based.

The truth must be self-evident that theatre-goers are endowed with a certain inalienable right—namely, the pursuit of happiness. The pursuit of happiness is the most important thing in the world; because it is nothing less than an endeavor to understand and to appreciate the true, the beautiful, and the good. Happiness comes of loving things which are worthy; a man is happy in proportion to the number of things which he has learned to love; and he, of all men, is most happy who loveth best all things both great and small. For happiness is the feeling of harmony between a man and his surroundings, the sense of being at home in the universe and brotherly toward all worthy things that are. The pursuit of happiness is simply a continual endeavor to discover new things that are worthy, to the end that they may waken love within us and thereby lure us loftier toward an ultimate absolute awareness of truth and beauty. It is in this simple, sane pursuit that people go to the theatre. The important thing about the public is that it has a large and longing heart. That heart demands that sympathy be awakened in it, and will not be satisfied with merely intellectual discussion of unsympathetic things. It is therefore the duty, as well as the privilege, of the dramatist to set before the public incidents which may awaken sympathy and characters which may be loved. He is the most important artist in the theatre who gives the public most to care about. This is the reason why Joseph Jefferson's *Rip Van Winkle* must always be rated as one of the greatest creations of the American stage. The play was shabby as a work of art, and there was nothing even in the character to think about; but every performance of the part left thousands happier, because their lives had been enriched with a new memory that made their hearts grow warm with sympathy and large with love.

XVI

THEMES AND STORIES ON THE STAGE

I

As the final curtain falls upon the majority of the plays that somehow get themselves presented in the theatres of New York, the critical observer feels tempted to ask the playwright that simple question of young Peterkin in Robert Southey's ballad, *After Blenheim,*—"Now tell us what 't was all about"; and he suffers an uncomfortable feeling that the playwright will be obliged to answer in the words of old Kaspar, "Why, that I cannot tell." The critic has viewed a semblance of a dramatic struggle between puppets on the stage; but what they fought each other for he cannot well make out. And it is evident, in the majority of cases, that the playwright could not tell him if he would, for the reason that the playwright does not know. Not even the author can know what a play is all about when the play isn't about anything. And this, it must be admitted, is precisely what is wrong with the majority of the plays that are shown in our theatres, especially with plays written by American authors. They are not about anything; or, to say the matter more technically, they haven't any theme.

By a theme is meant some eternal principle, or truth, of human life—such a truth as might be stated by a man of philosophic mind in an abstract and general proposition—which the dramatist contrives to convey to his auditors concretely by embodying it in the particular details of his play. These details must be so selected as to represent at every point some phase of the central and informing truth, and no incidents or characters must be shown which are not directly or indirectly representative of the one thing which, in that particular piece, the author has to say. The great plays of the world have all grown endogenously from a single, central idea; or, to vary the figure, they have been spun like spider-webs, filament after filament, out of a central living source. But most of our native playwrights seem seldom to experience this necessary process of the imagination which creates. Instead of working from the inside out, they work from the outside in. They gather up a haphazard handful of theatric situations and try to string them together into a story; they congregate an ill-assorted company of characters and try to achieve a play by letting them talk to each other. Many of our playwrights are endowed with a sense of situation; several of them have a gift for characterisation, or at least for caricature; and most of them can write easy and natural dialogue, especially in slang. But very few of them start out with something to say, as William Vaughn Moody started out in *The Great Divide* and Augustus Thomas in *The Witching Hour* and Eugene O'Neill in *Beyond the Horizon*.

When a play is really about something, it is always possible for the critic to state the theme of it in a single sentence. Thus, the theme of *The Witching Hour* is that every thought is in itself an act, and that therefore thinking has the virtue, and to some extent the power, of action. Every character in the piece was invented to embody some phase of this central proposition, and every incident was devised to represent this abstract truth concretely. Similarly, it would be easy to state in a single sentence the theme of *Le Tartufe*, or of *Othello*, or of *Ghosts*. But who, after seeing four out of five of the American plays that are produced upon Broadway, could possibly tell in a single sentence what they were about?

The only sort of play that permits itself to be remembered is a play that presents a distinct theme to the mind of the observer. It is thirty years since I have seen *Le Tartufe* and twenty years since last I read it; and yet, since the theme is unforgettable, I could at any moment easily reconstruct the piece by retrospective imagination and summarise the action clearly in a paragraph. But on the other hand, I should at any time find it impossible to recall, with sufficient clearness to summarise them, any of a dozen American plays of the usual type which I had seen within the preceding six months. Details of incident or of character or of dialogue slip the mind and melt away like smoke into the air. To have seen a play without a theme is the same, a month or two later, as not to have seen a play at all. But a piece like *The Second Mrs. Tanqueray*, once seen, can never be forgotten; because the mind clings to the central proposition which the play was built in order to reveal, and from this ineradicable recollection may at any moment proceed by psychologic association to recall the salient concrete features of the action. To develop a play from a central theme is therefore the sole means by which a dramatist may insure his work against the iniquity of oblivion. In order that people may afterward remember what he has said, it is necessary for him to show them clearly and emphatically at the outset why he has undertaken to talk and precisely what he means to talk about.

Most of our American playwrights, like Juliet in the balcony scene, speak, yet they say nothing. They represent facts, but fail to reveal truths. What they lack is purpose. They collect, instead of meditating; they invent, instead of wondering; they are clever, instead of being real. They are avid of details: they regard the part as greater than the whole. They deal with outsides and surfaces, not with centralities and profundities. They value acts more than they value the meanings of acts; they forget that it is in the motive rather than in the deed that Life is to be looked for. For Life is a matter of thinking and of feeling; all act is merely Living, and is significant only is so far as it reveals the Life that prompted it. Give us less of Living, more of Life, must ever be the cry of earnest criticism. Enough of these mutitudinous, multifarious facts: tell us single, simple truths. Give us more themes, and fewer fabrics of shreds and patches.

II

In olden fairy-tales we read of many honorable souls condemned to dwell in cramped and crooked bodies, and we also read of many goodly bodies that walk the world untenanted by any soul. These fables lay a finger on one of the monstrous ironies of life. It would seem to our finite minds that if the creative spirit of the universe were at all reasonable in its workings it would clothe a fine soul with a fair body and use a foul body as the tenement of an evil soul; but this harmony is seldom to be seen in actual creation. The irresponsible Mary Stuart looks the loveliest of women; the serene, sagacious Socrates wears a funny face; and very few people enjoy, like John Keats, the privilege of looking like themselves. Seldom does the soul fit the body, or the body fit the soul; and this might almost be imagined as a reason for that disassociation known as death.

What is true of human beings is also true of works of art; for any genuine work of art, because it is a living thing, may be imagined to have a body and a soul. Sometimes, as in the case of the poems of Walt Whitman or the paintings of El Greco, the soul is finer than the body; sometimes, as in the case of the paintings of Andrea del Sarto or the poems of Poe, the body is fairer than the soul; but very rarely are the two of equal beauty, as in the supreme poem of Dante and the supreme painting of Leonardo.

The soul of a play is its theme, and the body of a play is its story. A play may have a great theme and an inadequate story, or an interesting story and scarcely any theme at all: it may be a noble-minded hunch-back or a shallow-pated Prince Charming; but only a few great plays reveal profound, important themes beneath the lineaments of engaging and enthralling stories.

By the theme of a play is meant some principle, or truth, of human life—such a truth as might be formulated critically in an abstract and general proposition—which the dramatist contrives to convey concretely to his auditors through the particular medium of his story. Thus, the theme of *Ghosts* is that the sins of the fathers are visited on the children, and the theme of *The Pigeon* is that the wild spirits and the tame spirits of the world can never understand each other. Granted a good theme, a playwright may invent a dozen or a hundred stories to embody it; but the final merit of his work will depend largely on whether or not he has succeeded in selecting a story that is at all points worthy of his theme.

As an instance of the desired harmony between the two we may point to *A Doll's House*, which succeeds in illustrating Whitman's maxim that "the soul is not more than the body" and "the body is not more than the soul." The theme of this modern tragedy was thus formulated by Ibsen in a note penciled on the back of an envelope in Rome on October 19, 1878: "There are two kinds of spiritual law, two kinds of conscience—one in man, and another, altogether different, in woman. They do not understand each other; but in practical life the woman is judged by man's law, as though she were not a woman but a man. . . . A woman cannot be herself in the society of the present day, which is an exclusively masculine society, with laws framed by men and with a judicial system that judges feminine conduct from a masculine point of view." This thesis is the soul of *A Doll's House:* its body is merely a story setting forth an instance of the commonplace crime of forgery. Yet this instance is so skilfully selected that the story develops naturally and inevitably to that astounding final dialogue which incorporates the essence of the theme and seems not of an age but for all time. Here is a story that is eminently adequate to the occasion that called it forth; and yet it is conceivable that Ibsen might have invented an entirely different narrative to carry and deliver the message of his drama.

The broad scope of the playwright's range of possible invention is indicated by the fact that the same theme has often served as the basis of several great plays, by different authors, whose stories have shown no obvious resemblance to each other. Thus, the theme of *Macbeth* is that vaulting ambition which o'erleaps itself will fall on the other side; and this is also the theme of *The Master Builder*, which tells a very different story. Likewise *Hamlet* and *L'Aiglon*, which are unlike in narrative details, are identical in theme—the essential basis of each being the failure of a youth of poetic and reflective temperament to cope with circumstances that demand a man of action.

In view of the wide range of possible invention, it is surprising that so many of our playwrights fail to devise stories that are worthy to incorporate their themes. No other source of failure in the theatre comes more often to the fore. An instance of this inadequacy is offered by the celebrated play called *Milestones*, by Messrs. Arnold Bennett and Edward Knoblock. The soul of this piece is a great theme—namely, that "crabbèd age and youth cannot live together," because youth is always radical and forward-looking and age is always backward-looking and conservative; but its body is merely a sedentary, unimportant story that deals with such a minor problem as whether ships should be built of wood or iron or steel, and such an ordinary question as who shall ultimately marry whom. And because of the inadequacy of its narrative, the critic who envisages the theme of *Milestones* must regard the finished fabric as less impressive than the authors should have made it.

Sometimes, but more rarely, the contrary fault may be exhibited in the theatre. There is a type of play that commands attention by its cleverness of plot and its deft manipulation of suspense and of surprise, without revealing any central and essential theme or conveying any general truth of life for the auditor to add to his experience. Such a play may succeed for the moment, but it is not likely to live in after years. For (to return to our former statement) a work of art is like a human being; and nothing can survive of either but the soul. As Browning remarked, with sardonic truthfulness—"The soul, doubtless, is immortal—where a soul can be discerned." Generations breathe and eat and laugh and love and die; but only those few men remain immortal who leave their souls behind them. If a man shall say, not merely with his breath but with the entire mood and meaning of his living, "Beauty is truth, truth beauty" or "Thou shalt love thy neighbor as thyself," the world must evermore remember the life of which this message was the theme; but it easily forgets the million men whose inexpressive dust returns to dust. So it is with plays. Those that succeed in saying something have earned an opportunity to live; but those that say nothing must suffer, sooner or later, the iniquity of oblivion. A good story is necessary in order that a play may attain an immediate success; but a great theme is necessary in order that it may require the attention of posterity.

III

It would not be possible for anybody to devise an utterly new story for a play. The dramatic material in life is limited. According to certain critics, the number of different dramatic situations is a little more than thirty; according to others, it is a little less than twenty; but all are agreed that the number is extremely small. Novelty in the drama can therefore be attained not by the discovery of new materials, but only by the invention of new combinations of materials that are as old as man.

Yet the invention of new combinations affords ample scope for the exercise of ingenuity. The range of imaginable numbers is not limited by the fact that all may be recorded with the ten digits of the Arabic notation; nor does the world in springtime look monotonous in color because every apparent tint may be regarded as exhibiting a permutation of red and blue and yellow. The twenty or thirty standard situations may be shuffled and dealt into innumerable plots, each of which is new though all of its component parts are old.

A play appeals in two ways to an audience. In so far as its component situations are traditional, it calls forth the response of recognition, and in so far as its compounded plot is novel it stimulates the reaction of surprise. In considering these two appeals, we must remember always that the emotion of recognition is more profound, and therefore more enjoyable, than the titillation of surprise. The best part of our enjoyment in the theatre arises not from vainly wondering what will happen, but from eagerly wanting some specific thing to happen and having our want fulfilled. A noticeable novelty, even in the combination of materials that in themselves are thoroughly familiar, is therefore not always to be praised as a merit in a play, but may often be regarded as a fault.

But if originality of subject-matter is impossible, and if originality of arrangement is often undesirable, why should we care to see new plays instead of old? Why should we see *The Liars*, which treats the same theme as *Le Misanthrope?* The answer seems a paradox; but undeniably our enjoyment arises from the fact that the very antiquity of the author's materials emphasizes his originality of mind.

Any club-member can bear witness that the same anecdote may seem dull if told by one narrator and highly humorous if recounted by another. In the theatre, the ultimate significance of any story is proportioned to the importance of the mind through which it passes to the audience. The trial of Shylock, and the subterfuge by which Portia confutes him, would seem silly stuff indeed if it were told us by a child of ten; but it does not seem silly as told to us by Shakespeare. It is the author's attitude of mind toward his material, the intelligence with which he regards it, the mood that it awakens in him, that renders his work distinct from that of any other author who has used the same material, and stamps it an original creation.

It is a significant fact that the three greatest dramatists of the world—Sophocles, Shakespeare, and Molière—eschewed the invention of new narrative and exercised their high originality of mind in the treatment of stories with which their public had been long familiar. The critic, therefore, should never condemn a playwright because his story is old; but he may reasonably expect the author to illuminate the narrative with ideas and moods that shall be new because they are essentially his own. "I take my own where I find it," said Molière; and whatever he took he made his own by the divine right of thinking more deeply about it than the man from whom he took it. Sir Arthur Pinero, in *The Thunderbolt*, employed the stale old story of the stolen will; but he set it forth with a soundness of sense and a poignancy of sensibility that made it seem original and new.

Any dramatic story belongs ultimately, not to the man who used it first, nor even to the man who used it last, but to the man who has used it best. In reviewing new plays with old stories, the critic should inquire whether or not the author has afforded new illumination to the ancient drift of narrative. If so, he has really made the traditional material his own; but otherwise he has merely wasted attention by a meaningless repetition.

XVII

THE FUNCTION OF IMAGINATION

WHENEVER the spring comes round and everything beneath the sun looks wonderful and new, the habitual theatre-goer, who has attended every legitimate performance throughout the winter season in New York, is moved to lament that there is nothing new behind the footlights. Week after week he has seen the same old puppets pulled mechanically through the same old situations, doing conventional deeds and repeating conventional lines, until at last, as he watches the performance of yet another play, he feels like saying to the author, "But, my dear sir, I have seen and heard all this so many, many times already!" For this spring-weariness of the frequenter of the theatre, the common run of our contemporary playwrights must be held responsible. The main trouble seems to be that, instead of telling us what they think life is like, they tell us what they think a play is like. Their fault is not—to use Hamlet's phrase—that they "imitate humanity so abominably": it is, rather, that they do not imitate humanity at all. Most of our playwrights, especially the newcomers to the craft, imitate each other. They make plays for the sake of making plays, instead of for the sake of representing life. They draw their inspiration from the little mimic world behind the footlights, rather than from the roaring and tremendous world which takes no thought of the theatre. Their art fails to interpret life, because they care less about life than they care about their art. They are interested in what they are doing, instead of being interested in why they are doing it. "Go to!", they say to themselves, "I will write a play"; and the weary auditor is tempted to murmur the sentence of the cynic Frenchman: *"Je n'en vois pas la nécessité."*

But now, lest we be led into misapprehension, let us understand clearly that what we desire in the theatre is not new material, but rather a fresh and vital treatment of such material as the play-wright finds made to his hand. It is a curious paradox of criticism that for new plays old material is best. This statement is supported historically by the fact that all the great Greek dramatists, nearly all of the Elizabethans, Corneille, Racine, Molière, and, to a great extent, the leaders of the drama in the nineteenth century, made their plays deliberately out of narrative materials already familiar to the theatre-going public of their times. The drama, by its very nature, is an art traditional in form and resumptive in its subject-matter. It would be futile, therefore, for us to ask contemporary playwrights to invent new narrative materials. Their fault is not that they deal with what is old, but that they fail to make out of it anything which is new. If, in the long run, they weary us, the reason is not that they are lacking in invention, but that they are lacking in imagination.

That invention and imagination are two very different faculties, that the second is much higher than the first, that invention has seldom been displayed by the very greatest authors, whereas im-agination has always been an indispensable characteristic of their work,—these points have all been made clear in a very suggestive essay by Brander Matthews, which is included in his volume en-titled *Inquiries and Opinions*. It remains for us to consider some-what closely what the nature of imagination is. Imagination is nothing more or less than the faculty for *realisation*,—the faculty by which the mind makes real unto itself such materials as are pre-sented to it. The full significance of this definition may be made clear by a simple illustration.

Suppose that some morning at breakfast you pick up a news-paper and read that a great earthquake has overwhelmed Messina or Tokio, killing countless thousands and rendering an entire province desolate. You say, "How very terrible!"—after which you go blithely about your business, untroubled, undisturbed. But suppose that your little girl's pet pussy-cat happens to fall out of the fourth-story window. If you chance to be an author and have an article to write that morning, you will find the task of com-position heavy. Now, the reason why the death of a single pussy-cat affects you more than the death of a hundred thousand human beings is merely that you realise the one and do not realise the other. You do not, by the action of imagination, make real unto yourself the disaster at Tokio or Messina; but when you see your little daughter's face, you at once and easily imagine woe. Similarly, on the largest scale, we go through life realising only a very little part of all that is presented to our minds. Yet, finally, we know of life only so much as we have realised. To use the other word for the same idea,—we know of life only so much as we have imagined. Now, whatever of life we make real unto ourselves by the action of imagination is for us fresh and instant and, in a deep sense, new,—even though the same materials have been realised by millions of human beings before us. It is new because we have made it, and we are different from all our predecessors. Landor imagined Italy, realised it, made it instant and afresh. In the subjective sense, he created Italy, an Italy that had never existed before,—Landor's Italy. Later Browning came, with a new imagination, a new realisation, a new creation,—Browning's Italy. The materials had existed through immemorable centuries; Landor, by imagination, made of them something real; Browning imagined them again and made of them something new. But a Cook's tourist hurrying through Italy is likely, through deficiency of imagination, not to realise an Italy at all. He reviews the same materials that were presented to Landor and to Browning, but he makes nothing out of them. Italy for him is tedious, like a twice-told tale. The trouble is not that the materials are old, but that he lacks the faculty for realising them and thereby making of them something new.

A great many of our contemporary playwrights travel like Cook's tourists through the traditional subject-matter of the theatre. They stop off here and there, at this or that eternal situation; but they do not, by imagination, make it real. Thereby they miss the proper function of the dramatist, which is to imagine some aspect of the perennial struggle between human wills so forcibly as to make us realise it, in the full sense of the word,—realise it as we daily fail to realise the countless struggles we ourselves engage in. The theatre, rightly considered, is not a place in which to escape from the realities of life, but a place in which to seek refuge from the unrealities of actual living in the contemplation of life realised,—life made real by imagination.

The trouble with most ineffective plays is that the fabricated life they set before us is less real than such similar phases of actual life as we have previously realised for ourselves. We are wearied because we have already unconsciously imagined more than the playwright professionally imagines for us. With a great play our experience is the reverse of this. Incidents, characters, motives which we ourselves have never made completely real by imagination are realised for us by the dramatist. Intimations of humanity which in our own minds have lain jumbled fragmentary, like the multitudinous pieces of a shuffled picture-puzzle, are there set orderly before us, so that we see at last the perfect picture. We escape out of chaos into life.

This is the secret of originality: this it is that we desire in the theatre:—not new material, for the old is still the best; but familiar material rendered new by an imagination that informs it with significance and makes it real.

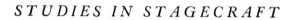

STUDIES IN STAGECRAFT

1

THE NEW ART OF MAKING PLAYS

T HE GREAT Spanish dramatist, Lope de Vega, once wrote a didactic poem entitled *The New Art of Making Plays;* and this title seems particularly applicable to the art of the drama at the present time. We are living in a progressive period, when the methods of all our practical and theoretical activities are undergoing a rapid revolution; and it is therefore not surprising that we should find the technique of the drama changing year by year before our very eyes.

A few years ago, the late President Eliot of Harvard University made the somewhat startling statement that civilization had progressed faster and further in the last hundred years than in all of the preceding twenty centuries, and that the conditions of life at the close of the eighteenth century differed more from the conditions at the present day than they differed from those which appertained to ancient Rome. Similarly, it may be asserted that the art of the theatre has progressed faster and further in the last fifty years than in all of the preceding centuries that have intervened since Æschylus, and that we find ourselves confronted at the present time with an utterly new art of making plays. In this connection it should be confessed at once that progress is not necessarily amelioration, and that there is always a possibility that a step forward may be a step away from the ideal. In some respects the general life of ancient Athens was better than our general life to-day, for all its practical advantages of telephones and motor-cars; and in many respects the drama of Sophocles and Shakepeare was better than the drama of Eugene O'Neill, in spite of all our present perfectness of craftsmanship. But the student of any art should dally little with such absolute and final questions as that of what is better and what is worse; and he may spend his time more profitably in the modest endeavor of defining differences.

The differences between the drama of to-day and the drama of all preceding periods have not as yet been clearly and emphatically defined to the theatre-going public; and this is the reason why many of the best artistic efforts of our current theatre remain misunderstood and are denied their proper measure of appreciation. In the evolution of any art, creation always precedes criticism, since criticism is merely an analysis of what has been created; and the main difficulty that is encountered by the best practitioners of the new art of making plays is the fact that our current dramatic criticism has not as yet caught up with them. Their new efforts are judged by old standards; and *The Thunderbolt*, or *The Pigeon*, or *The Blue Bird*, or *What Every Woman Knows*, or *Strange Interlude*, or *Within the Gates*, are still considered to be something less than masterpieces, because, in both materials and methods, they differ markedly from *As You Like It* or *Tartufe*. It is therefore desirable that we should endeavor to enumerate at least a few of the definitive features of the new art of making plays; and this purpose may be most easily fulfilled by setting forth several of the most noticeable differences between the drama of the present and the drama of the past.

In the first place, we should note that, whereas the drama of other days was compounded of only two elements of narrative—namely, character and action—the drama of to-day is compounded of three elements—namely, action, character, and setting. Dramatic incidents which used to be conceived as happening anywhere and anywhen are now conceived as happening at a particular time and in a particular place.

This localization of incidents in place and time may be noted, in all the narrative arts, as the one feature that distinguishes modern work from that of all preceding periods. In his essay on Victor Hugo's romances, Robert Louis Stevenson pointed out that the one new note introduced into the novel at the outset of the nineteenth century was the insistence on environment as a formative influence on character and a determining motive toward action. But the drama could not cope with this modern philosophical conception of the importance of environment until the great wave of mechanical invention which swept over the world during the middle of the nineteenth century had equipped the theatre with those appurtenances which were necessary to enable it to project the element of setting adequately to the eye.

But this epoch-making revolution in the physical equipment of the stage occasioned an alteration in the very essence of the drama. In all former ages the drama had made its appeal primarily to the ear, like the arts of poetry and music; but now for the first time it was enabled to make its appeal directly to the eye, like the arts of painting and sculpture. In our own days the art of the drama has ceased to be essentially an auditory art and has ranked itself for the first time in history as a visual art; and this point must be clearly understood if we are to appreciate properly the new art of making plays.

For this revolution in the basis of dramatic appeal occasioned a necessary evolution in the art of acting. Whereas acting had formerly been a presentative art, it now became a representative art. The actor had formerly attracted attention to himself, like an orator upon a platform, and always in his work had presupposed an audience; but he was now required to comport himself as if no audience were present, and to treat his particular personality as only a component part of a general stage-picture.

And this alteration in the art of acting required an alteration in the art of writing for the stage. For the presentative actor it was necessary to write rotund, rhetorical speeches which should give him ample opportunity for elocution and the use of sweeping gesture; but for the representative actor it is necessary to write in the terms of common conversation. Any speech that is at all rhetorical will pull the modern actor out of the picture and will shatter that illusion of actuality which is the ultimate aim of the contemporary stage.

From this consideration we derive the precept that the highest exhibition of literary tact that may be achieved by the contemporary playwright is to persuade his audience that he is not employing any trick of literary style. Formerly plays were written in verse or polished prose; nowadays they must be written for the most part in casual, drifting colloquialisms. People do not actually talk in verse; neither do they talk in formal prose; and it has therefore become the leading literary merit of our latter-day drama to present its dialogue divested of all "literary" turns of phrase.

Actions speak louder than words. This proverb has become an axiom of our new art of making plays. No less an authority than Augustus Thomas has asserted that every good play of the contemporary type must merely add the element of dialogue to a pantomime that is already good. The modern playwright must rely more upon his visual imagination than upon his literary skill, and must be able to conceive his narrative primarily as a drift of moving pictures.

In this requirement he may be aided greatly by the collaboration of that new and very interesting functionary of the modern theatre, the stage-director of his play. It is the business of the stage-director to coördinate the contributions of the author, the actors, the designer of the scenery and costumes, and the manipulator of the lights, into an harmonious work of art. The stage-director is often, in the contemporary theatre, the dominant artist of the drama; and in any critical consideration of a play that has passed through his hands, it is frequently more necessary to devote attention to his artistry than to that of either the actors or the author. Any play, for instance, that was produced by David Belasco had always to be studied as a Belasco play, regardless of who wrote it or of who the actors were.

These alterations in the materials and methods of the drama have required, in recent years, a corresponding change in the construction of our theatres. So long as the drama remained an auditory art projected by a presentative actor, it could be housed effectively in an ample auditorium; but when it became a visual art exhibited by an unobtrusive actor, it called for a theatre that should gather a selected audience into intimate proximity with the stage. Hence, throughout the last half century, our theatres have progressively been diminished in size, until the prevailing type at present is no larger than the Empire Theatre in New York. It is a matter of history that the promising project of the New Theatre [1910-1912] failed mainly because the edifice which housed the institution was too large to permit of the effective presentation of the prevailing type of contemporary drama. Very recently an exaggeration of the present tendency in theatrical construction has been evidenced by the advent of the Little Theatre, which is surely more diminutive than necessary. But this current aspect of the craft of theatre-building is one of the points that must be taken into consideration in any critical judgment of our new art of making plays.

It should be evident from these brief enumerations that it is impossible to measure the contemporary drama by the same critical standards that have been applied to the dramatic art of other ages.

The very merits of the Elizabethan drama become defects when we observe them from the point of view of the contemporary theatre; and the faults of other-minded periods have been erected into the virtues of our own.

A new art of criticism is required to interpret our new art of making plays. As yet our contemporary creation in the drama is more noble than the interpretation that it has received. This is the reason, doubtless, why so many well-meaning societies are organized for the "uplifting" of the modern stage, and why so few endeavors are instituted for the appreciation of the theatre of to-day. But any age of the drama that is illustrated by the achievements of Pinero and Brieux and Sudermann and Maeterlinck and Shaw and Hauptmann and Hervieu and Galsworthy and Sean O'Casey and Eugene O'Neill is undeniably a great age; and it is therefore the responsible and humble duty of our dramatic critics to teach the general public to estimate it at its worth.

THE PICTORIAL STAGE

THE ELEVATION of the element of setting to an importance coördinate with that of the elements of character and action, which has rendered the contemporary drama more visual in its appeal than the drama of any earlier period, was occasioned by the combination of two causes, one of which was artistic and the other scientific, yet both of which tended toward that end which is the aim of every epoch-making revolution—namely, a return to nature.

The first, or artistic, cause of the revolution in the drama had already been at work for a long time in the other arts to which the drama is allied. If we review the history of any of the arts which represent human beings, we shall notice that the one feature which distinguishes most clearly their ancient from their modern manifestations is the growing importance which has been bestowed in modern times upon the element of setting. Ancient art projects its figures abstractly, out of place, out of time; modern art projects them concretely, in a particular place, at a particular time. Even in imagination we cannot localize the *Venus of Melos;* we are forced to look upon her with no sense of where or when. But we know that Saint-Gaudens's *Farragut* is standing on the bridge of a ship and peering forward into the wind to direct the course of its progress; and we know that his *Lincoln* in Chicago has just risen from a chair upon the platform at a public assembly and is about to address the audience before him.

The same distinction may be noted between ancient and modern painting. There is no background at all to the figures in Pompeiian frescoes; we see a dozen Cupids dancing, but we derive no idea whether they are dancing on the greensward or on a marble floor. Even in the great age of Italian painting the background is developed for a merely decorative purpose and is not brought into actual relation with the figures in the foreground. Leonardo's in-scrutable background of jagged rocks and undetermined sky does not help us to decide whether Monna Lisa is actually indoors or out of doors; wherever she is, she is certainly not wandering through that lonely and unhabitable vale. I doubt if any of the Italians ever painted a greater landscape than that which decorates the distance in the Castelfranco *Madonna* of Giorgione; but, in the actual and literal sense, that landscape has absolutely nothing to do with the Madonna herself or either of her two attendant saints. But the Dutch, who in this regard are the first of modern painters, chose to display their human figures in living relation to the landscape or comfortably at home in an interior belonging to them. In such a typical modern painting as the *Angelus* of Millet, the people would lose all meaning if they were taken out of the landscape and the landscape would lose all meaning if it were divested of the people; the sense of a definite time and a definite place, which ancient art suppresses, are here as necessary to the picture as the people themselves or the act of devotion in which they are engaged.

A similar revolution has been accomplished gradually in the art of literary narrative. The earliest tales in the literature of every nation happen "once upon a time,"—it does not matter when, it hardly matters where. Medieval stories like the *novelle* of Boccac-cio happen either out of doors in a conventional landscape or in-doors in a conventional palace; but all palaces look alike, and every landscape is more decorative than habitable. It was only toward the end of the eighteenth century that novelists began to develop their settings in harmony with their action and their characters; and it was not until the nineteenth century that they began to insist that certain people can accomplish certain deeds only in a certain place and at a certain time. Such a story, for example, as Rudyard Kipling's *An Habitation Enforced*, in which the setting is the prime motive and (as it were) the hero of the tale, is ex-clusively characteristic of the present age of narrative and could never have been conceived in any former period.

It was inevitable that this growing sense of the importance of the element of setting as a necessary factor in human life, and there-fore as an essential detail of art, should overtake the drama; but its conquest of the drama was deferred until the present age, be-cause at no earlier period was the theatre adequately equipped to cope with the demands that it imposed. The second, or scientific, cause of the revolution in the drama was the great wave of practical invention which swept over the nineteenth century and made the modern theatre possible. The introduction in quick succession of gas lamps, the calcium light, and electrical illumination, the consequent abolition of the "apron" stage, the invention of the "box-set," the new conception of the proscenium as a picture-frame and the stage itself as a picture placed within it, the growing zest for actuality in the appointments and the furniture of the stage—these practical improvements in the theatre had to be accomplished before the drama could follow the lead of all the other narrative arts in exhibiting characters in action with precise attention to particularities of time and place.

We derive from a typical Greek tragedy no more definite sense of place and time than we derive from looking at the *Venus of Melos*. The action simply happens—we care not when or where. In most Elizabethan plays the action is exhibited merely as happening on the bare platform of the stage. When an actor walks upon the stage he walks into the story; when he leaves the stage he leaves the story, and we never ask where he has gone. A few of the Elizabethans—and this is particularly true of Shakespeare—exhibit a truly modern feeling for setting as an influence on character and action; but since their theatre was not equipped to represent setting to the eye, they were forced to suggest it to the imagination in passages of descriptive poetry. Whenever we need to know the exact place or the exact hour of a scene, Shakespeare has to tell us in his lines. He does it wonderfully—"How sweet the moonlight sleeps upon this bank," or " 'Tis now the very witching time of night"; but on the modern stage we do all this with scenery and lighting, and make the same effect directly, by pictorial, rather than indirectly, by literary, means. The tragedies of Corneille and Racine could all be played in a single stage-set—the conventional hall of a conventional palace. Molière, in his entire series of comedies and farces, used only three distinct stage-sets— one the public square of old Italian comedy in which are situated all the houses of all the leading characters, another conceived vaguely out of doors in the country, and the third representing a room in a house. When the action happens in a room, as in *Le Tartufe*, the set is not designed particularly to represent the personality of the man who owns the house nor the habits of the people who live in it. Furthermore, it is the only room in the whole house that is imagined to exist; and when a character leaves the stage he does not go into an adjacent room but walks bodily out of the story.

But for every act of every play in the contemporary theatre we imagine a particular set that is entirely new and is devised especially to fit the action and to complement the characters. We know exactly what is beyond every door and every window; and when an actor passes through a door we know where he is going. We select and arrange the furniture for the insight it will give into the habits and the taste of the person to whom the room belongs. We keep a most careful accounting of time, and indicate its passage by minute gradations in the lighting. We convey as much as we possibly can by visual means, and we rely upon the lines only when the appeal to the eye has reached its limit.

It is an axiom of art that a new opportunity imposes a new obligation; and the artist in the modern theatre is obliged to make his setting tell as much of his story as it can be made to tell. No better illustration of this point has been afforded in recent times than the novel and charming set devised by Louis N. Parker for his pleasant little comedy of happiness, *Pomander Walk*. The stage exhibited five little Queen Anne houses arrayed in a crescent beside the loitering Thames and inhabited by a dozen or more delectable people wearing the picturesque old costumes of 1805; and the narrative was woven out of the humorous and sentimental threads of their several life-stories. Divested of its setting, this exquisite little piece could not possibly be presented; the play would lose all its meaning if it should lose its scenery.

In the modern theatre we have learned to convey abstract ideas by visual "business," as Augustus Thomas conveyed his ideas about nervous and hysterical disease by the "business" of the cat's-eye jewel in the last act of *The Witching Hour*, or as he explained his theory of the influence of colors on the human temperament in the third act of *The Harvest Moon*. We have learned to draw character completely to the eye, without the use of words, as Sir James Barrie, at the opening of *What Every Woman Knows*, made us fully acquainted with the personal traits of all three of Maggie's men folk in the three or four minutes that elapsed before the first line of the play was spoken. In Herman Bahr's *The Concert*, the theme and the entire story of the play were summed up and uttered eloquently to the eye in a period of protracted silence which culminated at the second curtain-fall.

Whereas the poetry of the drama was formerly expressed exclusively in the lines, it is now expressed mainly through the pictorial appurtenances of the stage. It is by no means true that the drama has lost its capacity for expressing poetry; it has merely altered its means of expressing it. David Belasco's original one-act version of *Madam Butterfly* was fully as poetic as the Elizabethan plays of Fletcher, whose verse still haunts our ears with melody as it echoes through the silence of three centuries. Poetry, in a large and general sense, may be defined as that solemn, tremulous happiness that overcomes us when we become surprisedly and poignantly aware of the existence and the presence of the beautiful. Poetry, thus conceived, may be expressed through the medium of any art; and Raphael is assuredly no less a poet though he may never have written that fabled century of sonnets. And poetry may be conveyed as fittingly through our new art of making plays as through the rich and resonant medium of Elizabethan verse. In my entire experience of play-going I remember no more poetic moment in the theatre than that moment in the first act of Maeterlinck's *Sister Beatrice*, as produced at the New Theatre in New York, when the Prince Bellidor appeared to Beatrice through the opened doorway, and the audience looked afar through a tracery of half-imagined trees to a sky of blue awakening to gray and palpitant with a single throbbing star.

In Elizabethan times it was necessary that every playwright should be able to express himself in verse. Nowadays a different equipment is required for the task of making plays. The contemporary theatre demands a vividness of visual imagination which has never in any other age been demanded of the dramatist. As the drama has reduced its reliance on the purely literary, it has increased its reliance on the purely pictorial; if it demands less of the imagination of the writer, it demands more of the imagination of the painter.

But this state of affairs has arisen only within the memory of the present generation of playgoers; and the art of designing stage scenery may, therefore, fairly be denominated the youngest of all the arts. This art is still so young, and is being developed so rapidly year by year, that it is as yet extremely difficult to codify its leading principles. But three of these, at least, seem certain to subsist through any future unfolding of the art; and these three may safely be formulated at the present time.

First of all, the scenic artist must always plan his set to meet the narrative exigencies of the action. This fact imposes on him many limitations to which the usual painter of landscapes or interiors is not submitted; but, as a compensation, it offers to him many suggestions at the outset of his work which may prove stimulating to his instinct of invention. If a pistol is to be thrown through a window, as at the climax of *The City*, the window must be set in a convenient and emphatic place. If an important letter is to be written, a desk must be set in such a situation as to reveal the facial expression of the actor who is to write it. The number and the place of the doors to a room are conditioned by the narrative nature of the entrances; and the arrangement of trees and rocks in a landscape must conform to the needs of the actors in the traffic of the stage. The late Clyde Fitch, who always planned his own scenery, was exceedingly deft in devising settings that would aid the business of his narrative. In his last play, *The City*, he contrived a set for the first act that made it possible for him to conduct an extended and important scene with no actors on the stage. He slanted a room so that two walls only were exhibited to the audience, one of which was pierced with sliding doors opening on a hallway which disclosed a flight of stairs leading to an upper story. The elder Rand, in the play, made an exit into the hallway, after which he was heard to drop heavily to the floor; and subsequently a hurried passing-by of many people in the hall, with sentences half-interjected through the opened doors, revealed to the audience that Rand had died suddenly of heart failure. On the other hand, in the production of *The School for Scandal* at the New Theatre, the setting of the screen scene was faulty because it hampered the business of the play. A staircase was devised elaborately to lead upward into the apartment of Joseph Surface from an outer door imagined under the stage; and this staircase was so arranged that every actor at his exit was obliged to turn his back to the audience and launch his final line over his shoulder. Thereby the sharp wit of Sheridan's exit speeches was impaired. Even if the stairway had been turned about, the entrance speeches of the actors would have been discounted similarly by the concealment of their faces. The only logical conclusion is that the staircase, which is clearly implied in Sheridan's lines, should have been imagined off the stage, as it was in Sheridan's own day at Drury Lane, beyond an entrance door in the set itself.

The second duty, or opportunity, of the scenic artist—according as we view the case—is to make his set so conform to the mood of the play that it will reveal immediately, through its visual appeal to the audience, as much as possible of the essential nature of the action. Contemporary dramatists depend upon their scenery to localize their plays in place and time, and to suggest the emotional spirit in which the story must be viewed. The duality of mood which dominated the whole play of *The Witch*, which was presented at the New Theatre, was indicated at the outset by the stage-set of the first act. This set exhibited a forlorn and barren landscape punctuated in the foreground by an apple-tree in full blossom; and the aspect of the setting suggested at once the general atmosphere of grave and gray New England which permeated the play, relieved only by the single florid figure of the young, impassioned heroine.

The third, and perhaps the most important, preoccupation of the modern scenic artist is to devise a set within which the natural grouping of the actors at every moment of the play will arrange itself in conformity with the laws of pictorial composition. The leading lines of the stage-picture should converge on certain points which may be utilized in the most important business of the act. In this exigency, which is similar to that which is submitted to by every master of graphic composition, the scenic artist is aided greatly by his ability to effect a mechanical focus of light upon any selected detail of his stage-picture. Except in scenes imagined to progress in the full, unchanging light of noon, he may emphasize one section or another of the stage by the deft employment of electric lights. But, whenever this recourse to mechanics is denied him, he may accomplish his effect of emphasis by the graphic expedient of converging lines.

It should be evident from these notes that the new art of designing stage scenery is very intricate and difficult, but that it offers possibilities for pictorial appeal which as yet have hardly been completely realized. The advantages of being permitted to render a picture in three dimensions instead of one, and of being allowed to alter the lighting of the picture almost at will, afford the followers of the new art obvious opportunities which are denied the ordinary painter; but the attendant difficulties of the art are great, because of the threefold limitation to which the scenic artist must evermore submit.

III

THE DECORATIVE DRAMA

BOTH in painting and in sculpture, the decorative artist labors under limitations more precisely technical than those which are imposed upon his freer fellow-craftsmen. A decorative painting must fit the room that it is destined to adorn; and, to this end, its mere patterning of lines and colors becomes more important than the subject it sets forth. A decorative bit of sculpture must be molded in reference to the general architectural design of which it is a mere detail; and it cannot be judged by the same standards that we apply to the appreciation of a statue modeled by and for itself.

In the exercise of every art there are two steps,—first, a selection of details from nature, and second, an arrangement of the details selected, in accordance with a pattern. To the ordinary painter, the ordinary sculptor, the first of these steps is the more important of the two; and his work will interest us mainly on account of the details he has decided to select from nature. But to the decorative artist, the pattern is of prime importance: it scarcely matters what details he chooses to exhibit, so long as he arranges them in accordance with a satisfying scheme.

The ordinary painting must tell us something about life: if it be a portrait, it must exhibit the painter's appreciation of a person; if it be a landscape, it must exhibit his appreciation of some phase of out-of-doors; but the decorative painting may deal with either cabbages or kings, without expressing any sympathy with either, provided that the motive be developed in a composition that shall be harmonious in itself and appropriate in line and color to the room that it completes. The same distinction holds in sculpture. If any single figure in that serried rank of kings that is strung across the façade of Notre Dame de Paris were taken down from its niche and set up on a pedestal, it would look abnormally tall and slender, and curiously cramped; because, like any ordinary statue, it would then be set in competition with nature. But, in its proper place, the figure is not intended to compete with nature: it is intended merely to continue, and not disrupt, a pattern that covers the face of an entire building.

It will be seen that the art of decoration is, of all the arts, the most removed from nature. It is the one art in which the subject-matter is of very small account and the technical presentment is of overwhelming importance. An egg is not an interesting object, and neither is a dart; but the egg-and-dart molding that the Greeks developed is so superbly decorative that it has held its own, against all attempts at innovation, throughout immemorable centuries. In decoration, art is exercised solely for the sake of art. The decorative painter values lines and colors, the decorative sculptor values forms and shadows, utterly for their own sakes, without particular reference to the objects which happen to furnish them to his hand. But the ordinary painter, the ordinary sculptor, works with his eye upon the object: the object interests him in and for itself, and he marshals technical details merely to minister to his purpose to render the thing as he sees it.

A good painting, a good statue, awakens us to a realization of life; but a good decoration relieves us from such a realization. Paintings and statues assert the importance of nature; but decorations assert the importance of art. The painter and the sculptor ask us to admire a subject; but the decorator asks us to admire a pattern.

If, with this distinction in our minds, we compare the contributions of Puvis de Chavannes and Edwin A. Abbey to the walls of the Boston Public Library, we shall see that the Frenchman excels from the decorative standpoint and that the American excels from the pictorial standpoint. It is the merit of the panels of Puvis that they melt into the surrounding marble and refuse to arrest the transitory eye by reminding it of life. The mild and misty colors, the conventional and uninsistent outlines, abstain from capturing attention to the subjects that are touched upon; and the wanderer comes away, remembering that he has climbed a lovely stairway but forgetting that he has paused to look at pictures. But Abbey's Tennysonian narrative of the legend of Sir Galahad attracts attention to itself, reminds the loiterer of life, and makes him utterly forget that he is in a building. It disrupts the room that it was meant to decorate, by rendering the observer impatient of a roof. From the technical standpoint, it spoils the room by sweeping it away.

Readers of these pages do not need to be again reminded that the drama, in this modern age, has tended to become more visual than auditory in its medium of appeal, and has allied itself, in recent years, more with the art of painting than with the art of literature. Ever since the adoption of the picture-frame proscenium, the prevalent and customary play has been pictorial. But very recently it has occurred to certain producers to go a step further and to handle the drama not merely as a series of pictures, but, finally, as a series of decorations. That interesting, inconsistent theorist, Sir Edward Gordon Craig, was one of the leaders of this movement; but its most successful practical exponent has been Professor Max Reinhardt.

Professor Reinhardt at the present time [he began his career in conformity with other theories] frequently conceives an acted play as a bit of decoration. He does not desire that a drama should offer a judgment or a criticism of life: he desires, rather, that it should offer a continuously seductive pattern of lines and colors, forms and shadows, to the eye. In his present view, the drama should not, like a picture, compete with nature by awakening the spectator to a realization of life: it should, rather, like a decoration, satisfy the spectator by an utterly esthetic patterning of visual details. Whereas, in recent years, the majority of our theatric artists have been striving to return to nature, Professor Reinhardt is now endeavoring to get away from it. He does not ask us to be interested primarily in life: he asks us to be interested primarily in art.

This consideration should be borne in mind in any criticism of the memorable pantomime of *Sumurûn*. This production of Professor Reinhardt's may be taken as a type of the Decorative Drama; and it should, properly, be appreciated by some critic of the decorative arts instead of by a critic of the theatre. By divesting the drama of the spoken word, Professor Reinhardt has removed it from the realm of literature and bereaved it of any reference to actuality: he has conceived it, rather, as a continuous frieze of flitting, ever fluctuating, decorations.

A glance at any scene in *Sumurûn* indicated that this Oriental panorama should be judged less as drama than as painting, and less as painting than as decoration. The stage-pictures were rendered in that particular style of secessionistic artistry that was popularly known in Germany as the *Jugend-Stil*. It gets its name from the fact that, although the original inspiration came from Paris, it became most popular in Germany through the work of a clever group of artists illustrating the satirical magazines, *Jugend* and *Simplicissimus*. They made it an effective fashion for all decorative purposes. They found that flat backgrounds, utterly lacking in perspective, that striking outlines and solid blocks of color [they favored Egyptian angles for the rendering of figures], served particularly well for poster and cartoon work,—for work, in other words, in which an idea had to be impressed in an instant on the spectator, even in the most careless glance, so emphatically that it should remain for some time in his memory. This method—a method devised, in the first instance, for the adornment of magazine covers—Professor Reinhardt has adopted for the uses of the Decorative Drama.

He divests his backgrounds of perspective lines, and renders them in monochrome. In consequence, they stop the eye, and fling into vivid relief the costumes of the actors. These costumes are designed not as dresses, in reference to life, but as blocks of color, in reference to art; and the colors are simple in themselves and harmonious with one another. The method of the entire decoration is impressionistic. It proceeds by the suppression of details, and by the arrangement of the very few details selected, in accordance with a pattern of conventional simplicity. The lighting of the stage is emphatically simple. In the scene of the Sheik's bedchamber, which may be taken as typical, there are only two light-values,—a lantern at the head of the stairway, and a streaming light cast down funnel-wise over the bed of the Sheik. The most impressive scene of the entire play is a mere procession of all the characters across the stage, before a blank wall of unobtrusive gray, above which is seen a black palace, drawn, without perspective, upon a sky of slate.

The drama thus exhibited as decoration tells in pantomime two distinct but intricately intertangled stories, accompanied by interpretative music patterned, in post-Wagnerian fashion, out of the intermingling of appropriate "leading motives." It is unnecessary, in this consideration, to summarize either of these narratives. Both of them are inevitably violent, since they must tell themselves immediately to the eye without the aid of words. The passion of love must express itself in lust, the passion of revenge must express itself in murder, the mood of humor must express itself in physical buffoonery, in a narrative that is conceived as decoration.

In America, the subject-matter of *Sumurûn* astounded a certain section of the public [and even a certain number of the newspaper reviewers] by its absolute divorce from all morality. It is, of course, unimaginable that a decoration should be either moral or immoral. A mere pattern of lines and colors suggests no logical association with life; and it is only in the sphere of life that a distinction between morality and immorality can have any pertinence. In life, for instance, murder is indubitably an immoral occupation; but if a decorative artist, desiring merely a splash of red to complete a color-composition, should choose to represent a murdered man dripping the harmless necessary pool of blood, it would be illogical to accuse him of immorality. Such an art as decoration, which has nothing to do with life, must not be judged in terms of life; and *Sumurûn*, though lust and murder run rampant through its decorative narrative, is no more immoral than the egg-and-dart molding that adorns the buildings of the world. To conceive such decoration as immoral is to confess a lack of culture.

IV

THE DRAMA OF ILLUSION

IT IS proverbial that the average person will believe the evidence of his eyes more readily than the evidence of his ears. Beneath that sage and cogent phrase of current slang, "You'll have to show me," there lurks indeed a psychologic law. A man may doubt what you have merely told him; but he is much less likely to doubt what he himself has seen. For this reason, those arts which make their appeal to the eye, like painting and sculpture, are more convincing to the average person than those which make their appeal to the ear, like poetry and music. If I say, in terms of the ungraphic art of prose, "I have seen the most beautiful woman in the world; she is, indeed, the perfect woman,"— even if I ascend upon the wings of words and call her, with the eloquence of Alfred Noyes, the "white culmination of the dreams of earth,"—I shall leave the average reader cold; but if I could lead the reader to that tiny room in Paris where the armless, radiant wonder leans a little backward through the air, and looks forth, illimitably serene, over the heads of the noisy and nervous visitors that swarm around, all impotent to interrupt her utter and divine quiescence, the reader would indeed believe me,—conquered beyond question by the evidence of his eyes.

The drama is a compound art, in that it appeals simultaneously to the eye and to the ear: it is at once an auditory art, like poetry and music, and a visual art, like painting and sculpture. But, in different ages of the drama, the proportion to each other of these two appeals—the auditory and the visual—has been adjusted variously. If we review, with a single sudden sweep of mind, the whole history of the dramatic art, we shall see that the drama began by being principally auditory, and that it has grown more and more visual from age to age, until to-day, for the first time, it makes its appeal mainly to the eye. Beneath this evolution we shall notice, as

187

its motive, a constant and continual striving of the drama for more absolute, unquestionable credence. Æschylus was striving to make you credit what he told you: our contemporary realists are striving to make you credit what you see. The latter task, as we already have observed, is psychologically simpler; and therefore it is evident that the drama has gained conviction by the change.

There is a certain profit in speculating as to whether, in attending the performance of a typical play of any chosen epoch, it would have been more or less disadvantageous to be blind or to be deaf. For instance, it becomes evident that a blind person would have lost comparatively little in the theatre of Dionysus but would have lost comparatively much in the Belasco Theatre; whereas a deaf person would have been able to follow the performance of *The Return of Peter Grimm*, but would not have been able to follow the performance of *Œdipus King*. Owing to the conditions of its representment, the Greek drama was required to rely principally on its appeal to the ear. In a theatre so open and so spacious there could be no facial expression, no intimate and delicate gesticulation. The movements of the three actors were necessarily conventional and sculpturesque; the evolutions of the chorus were necessarily formal and measured. Conviction had to be conveyed by eloquence of speech, in poetry large and luminous and overwhelming; and an author, to succeed as a dramatist, had to be a master of sea-surgings in the medium of verse. The great Elizabethan drama, as represented to us in the works of Shakespeare, thrilled and trembled at the parting of the ways. It was a drama devoid of any particularity of visual appeal, set without scenery on a bare platform, and played by actors surrounded on three sides by a public practised more in listening than in looking. Yet it is evident that Shakespeare, more than any of his fellows, felt keenly the influence of time and place on character and action; for, unlike the Greeks, he strove continually to make his auditors *see*—with that subtle sense that Hamlet called the "mind's eye"—the particular environment of place and time in which his action was imagined to occur. Since his theatre was not equipped to present this environment directly to the eye, he was required to force his auditors to imagine it by hurling into their ears descriptive passages so potent in visual suggestion as to require them to seem to see what, actually, they had only heard. What Shakespeare chiefly stood in need of—if we consider him, for the moment, solely as what we now call a "producer" of plays—was a direct, unmeta-phorical medium for the expression of his visual imagination.

Such a medium is offered by the modern stage; and the invention of this medium has had, thus far, two different results.

Late in the nineteenth century, the newly devised equipment of the theatre to represent the look of actuality contributed, for the moment, to the spread of realism in the drama. Realism had already long been rampant in the other arts of narrative, and now it was at last enabled to broaden its dominion to include the stage. The drama was immediately dominated by a zest for imitating actuality: it strove to represent the very look of life, and to force the spectator to induce that desirable and necessary sense of truth which is the end of art, from the contemplation of a selected and arranged assortment of familiar facts. But very recently the drama, weary at last of imitating actuality, has begun to strive to use the modern mechanical medium of concreteness to convey ideas essentially abstract, and is trying at last to employ the modern mastery of visual suggestion to convey a sense of the invisible. Twenty or thirty years ago, our playwrights strove only to make their spectators believe what they saw before them on the stage: but now our playwrights strive, by visual suggestion, to make their spectators imagine much more than what they actually see. Paradoxical as it might seem to a merely aloof and theoretic contemplation, the mechanical and concrete particularity of the contemporary stage has begun to minister to the rise of a new mysticism in the drama, —a mysticism which, thus far, has found its fullest expression in the elusive and imaginative Maeterlinck. In *Sister Beatrice*, for instance, M. Maeterlinck relied frankly on the harmonious collaboration of the designer of scenery and costumes, the stage-director, and (most of all) the electrician of the theatre, for the complete conveyance of his imagined and designed effect: but, by means of all these marshaled media for visual suggestion, he contrived to lure the spectator airily aloft to a region where he winged his way among invisibilities.

We may regard it as the ultimate and utter triumph of the Drama of Illusion that, precisely because its medium of expression is more concrete, it is better endowed than the drama of any other age to symbolize ideas that are essentially abstract. By mastering the means of visual represention, the drama has learned at last to embody, vividly and convincingly, a sense of the invisible. This

is an artistic triumph that was difficult for Sophocles and Shakespeare, but which—owing to the physical evolution of the theatre
—was comparatively easy for M. Maeterlinck. Granted the great
advantage of the mechanical equipment of the modern stage, a
man of comparatively small imagination may make the public
see more, and in consequence believe more, than many a giant of
imagination in an age of the merely auditory drama. No one, for
example, would believe the story of *The Return of Peter Grimm*
if you merely told it to him, even if you told it in language as
eloquent as that of Sophocles or Shakespeare; but the late David
Belasco easily compelled from his spectators an artistic credence
of his play—during the brief period, at least, while they were
watching it—by the mechanical, but none the less enthralling, expedient of forcing them to believe the evidence of their eyes.

Considered as a literary composition, *The Return of Peter
Grimm* did not offer any notable elucidation of life, nor did it even
embody an especially imaginative searching of the mystery of
death; but considered as a fabric for the theatre, it offered a very
remarkable instance of the technical triumph of the Drama of
Illusion,—one of the most remarkable, in fact, that has been set
before our eyes in recent years. It conveyed with absolute concreteness an idea that was essentially abstract; and it succeeded,
by a mastery of visualization, in convincing the spectator that he
was seeing the invisible.

The play was designed to embody that spiritistic theory of the
persistence of personal energy after death which, in recent years,
has been deemed worthy of thorough scientific investigation by
the Society for Psychical Research. According to this theory, the
liberated soul retains its human individuality, and, hovering regretfully about the scenes of its foregone activities on earth, strives
to communicate, through the entranced minds of spiritistic me-
diums, with its former relatives and friends. The accumulated scientific evidence in support of this hypothesis, in spite of its vasty
bulk, is utterly unsatisfactory; and looked at *a priori*, the theory
seems extremely unimaginative. The maintenance of human individuality after bodily death has never yet been proved in all the
centuries of searching, even though it has been assumed as an
axiom in many of the great religions of the world; but even if we
accept it as a fact, it would be pitifully unimaginative to assume
that a soul set free by death to range the boundless universe should

still be tethered to that twirling inconsiderable grain of dust we call our world,—that a soul at last enfranchised to illimitable possibilities of experience should find no loftier application for its energies than to try to talk in human terms, about temporal trivialities, with souls still body-bound and anchored to the earth.

This is neither the time nor the place for a detailed philosophic argument against the spiritistic theory; and my present purpose is merely to indicate that the thesis which David Belasco selected as the basis of his play,—though it seems to appeal to many minds and is often popularly dallied with,—is by no means easy to believe. All the more remarkable, therefore, as a technical triumph of the Drama of Illusion, was the fact that Mr. Belasco succeeded in compelling an artistic acceptance of the thesis throughout the presentation of his play. And there is no denying that he did succeed. Mainly by his mastery of the subtle art of lighting, he laid siege to the emotions of the spectator and conquered credence for his story. The eye was captivated by an overwhelming visual illusion. At no previous period in the history of the drama could such a play have been successfully produced; and it deserves to be remembered as a signal triumph of the modern visual art of stage-direction.

V

THE MODERN ART OF STAGE-DIRECTION

I

THE ACTED drama is a compound work of art, exhibiting a coördination of the labors of several different artists, each of whom employs his own distinct medium of expression. Thus, in this multifarious modern age, a single acted play may call into conjunction the diverse arts of writing, acting, dancing, painting, sculpture, decoration, music, and illustrative illumination; and the artist who supplies any of these separate elements to the general and finished fabric may be ignorant of the methods of his fellow-laborers. No one man, unaided, can accomplish the entire work; and yet, if the final product is to be worthy of the name of art, some individual among these many and diverse collaborators must be singled out and made finally responsible for the appeal of the acted drama as a whole.

The drama has altered its complexion from age to age, according as one or another of these associated artists has been set in supreme command, to the subordination of his fellow-craftsmen. Until the present age, the captaincy has always fallen either to the author or to the actor, and the other artists have always been subservient to these. In reviewing the history of the drama from the earliest times until our own, we might easily divide it into literary periods and histrionic periods, according as the author or the actor has, for the moment, assumed dominion over it. A curious and interesting point is that the periods of great authors and the periods of great actors have never coincided. Whenever the artist of one type has been supreme, the artist of the other type has been (necessarily, it would seem in retrospect) merely a contributory functionary.

History, which has engraved on granite the names of the authors of the great Greek tragedies, has told us next to nothing of their actors. The two actors employed by Æschylus, the three employed by Sophocles, were granted very little opportunity for the exploitation of themselves. Their masks robbed them of the personal appeal of facial expression; their stilted boots inhibited any movements except those which were conventionally plastic; and all that was left to them was to give voice to the commentary of the poet on a national and familiar fable. The evolutions of the chorus must have offered scope for the contributions of a master of the allied arts of sculpture and the dance; but the primary and all-important appeal of the drama was invested in the lines. If the verse were spoken audibly and read with dignity, the play would have its chance; and its success or failure depended almost solely on the prowess of the author. Sophocles and Euripides could win prizes by themselves, without any indispensable assistance from a collaborating actor.

Again, in the Elizabethan period, the appeal of the acted drama depended mainly on the author. History has recorded reverently the names of innumerable writers of that spacious age, but has deleted from recollection the names of all but the very foremost actors. Alleyn and Burbage are remembered; but, with the fullest data bequeathed to us by contemporary commentators, it is impossible for us to publish the entire cast of any play of Shakespeare's. The reason is that, in the Elizabethan period, the lines themselves were immeasurably more important than any speaker of them, and the actor was regarded only as a secondary, and comparatively unimportant, artist.

But when, a little later in history, we turn our attention to the records of great actors, we perceive (with a little wonderment at first) that they have flourished only in periods when dramatic authorship has been at a very low ebb. Betterton is the first great tragic actor of whom we read in the records of the English stage; and he ruled the theatre at a time when (if we except the two masterpieces of Otway) the authorship of tragedy had sunk beneath contempt. Garrick, the greatest actor that the English stage remembers, flourished in an age when tragedy was absolutely sterile and when comedy had paused to catch its breath in mid-transition between Congreve and Sheridan. He played *King Lear* with a fabricated happy ending, and made his last appearance on the stage in a comedy by the now forgotten Mrs. Centlivre. Later, when Sheridan begins to write, we hear a great deal of him and very little of his actors; and still later, in the early nineteenth century, when dramatic authorship dived downward to the lowest point that it has ever touched in England, we observe (in reminiscence) a great galaxy of actors,—Kean, and the Kembles, and Mrs. Siddons, and Macready.

The obvious deduction from this summary historical review appears to be that the theatre-going public will pay its money for only one thing at a time,—either to hear what an author has to say, or to see an actor act; and that it has never supported the theatre to receive both of these distinct impressions simultaneously and equally. Thus, in a retrospective view of history, we perceive a subsistent antagonism between the author and the actor which has always been contrary to the highest theory of the acted drama.

This unfortunate antagonism may be observed, at nearer view, in the records of the nineteenth century. Throughout the first three-quarters of that most recent of completed cycles, the actor reigned supreme; but (somewhat suddenly) in the last quarter, he resigned his supremacy to some other of his collaborative artists. The period that William Winter remembered with such pathetic eloquence in his backward-looking books was a period of memorable actors; and this (according to our logic) is only another way of saying that, at that time, there were no authors of any consequence. The public was equally interested in the art of Edwin Booth, whether he was presenting a supreme play like *Othello* or a rhetorical and imitative play like *Richelieu*, whether he was acting a great part like Hamlet or an artificial part like Bertuccio. Shakespeare, Bulwer-Lytton, Tom Taylor, looked alike to the admirers of this matchless actor. But, in studying a later and more literary age, we reread *The Second Mrs. Tanqueray* without regard for Mrs. Patrick Campbell, and we perceive that *Mrs. Dane's Defence* is a very well-made play without recalling that Miss Lena Ashwell was an artificial actress.

The most recent shift of emphasis from the drama of the actor to the drama of the author has occurred within the recollection of theatre-goers only fifty years of age; and the greatest British actor and the greatest American actor of recent times belonged to the age that now is past and finished, instead of to the age that now seems blossoming around us. There can scarcely be a doubt that Sir Henry Irving and Richard Mansfield were the greatest actors of recent times in England and America; and yet neither of them did anything at all to further what Henry Arthur Jones has aptly termed the "Renascence of the English Drama" in our days. They made their great successes, for the most part, in inconsiderable plays, like *The Bells* and *Dr. Jekyll and Mr. Hyde.* Irving never presented a play by Pinero or Jones,—the foremost authors among his contemporary countrymen; and Mansfield never presented a play by any considerable American author,—if we except *Beau Brummell,* by the youthful Clyde Fitch, a piece in which its author's special gifts could scarcely be made manifest. Irving rejected *Michael and His Lost Angel,* although it contained two admirable parts precisely suited to himself and to Miss Terry,—for the reason, apparently, that he could endure, in his immediate vicinity, no playwright who really counted as an author. Mansfield followed out a similar career,—giving great performances in bad plays by secondary writers, and centering attention always on himself.

But, most recently of all, the drama has taken a new turning, as a result of which the prime responsibility is shouldered no longer either on the actor or on the author, but on a new and very interesting functionary,—the stage-director. This functionary, who has appeared only lately in the history of the theatre, has already, in many instances, assumed dominion over both the author and the actor, and bids fair, in the age that is immediately to come, to be the supreme leader of the acted drama. To this new artist—the stage-director—and to his special art, we must therefore devote particular attention in the present context.

II

The importance of the stage-director in the drama of to-day is rarely appreciated by the uninitiated theatre-goer. The actor appeals immediately to the eyes of the public, the author appeals immediately to their ears; but the stage-director, whose work has been completed in the period of rehearsal, is never seen in the theatre, and seldom even talked about, after his finished fabric has been offered to the audience. Yet nearly all that is shown upon the stage is the result of his selection and arrangement, and the credit for a satisfactory performance is often due less to the actors than to him.

It is the function of the stage-director to coördinate the work of the author, the actors, the pictorial artists who design the scenery and costumes, the electrician, the musicians, into a single and self-consistent whole. He decides upon the setting and the lighting of each act, selects and arranges the furniture and properties, and works out what is called the "business" of the play. He rehearses the associated actors, and patterns their individual contributions into a balanced and harmonious performance.

His work is analogous to that of the conductor of a modern orchestra,—who, although he plays no instrument himself, coordinates the contributions of a hundred individual performers into an artistic whole, regulating the *tempo* and commanding every variation in the emphasis. Or perhaps we may call attention to a still closer analogy that exists between the stage-director and the manager of a professional baseball team. It is a well-known fact that baseball pennants are won not so much because of the prowess of individual players as because of the crafty handling of a team by the directing manager.

In some instances the manager of a baseball team may be himself one of the participants in the game; in other instances he may be an ex-player, who has retired from actual exercise; or he may be a student of the game who was never noted as a player on his own account. To return to our analogy—the stage-director may be the author of the play, as in the case of Mr. Bernard Shaw or Mr. Marc Connelly; he may be the leading actor, as in the case of Sir Henry Irving or Mrs. Fiske; he may be both of these, as in the case of Mr. Granville Barker; he may be a retired actor, like the late Henry Miller when he produced a piece in which he played no part; or he may be some student of the stage who is not known to the public as an individual performer, like Mr. Guthrie McClintic. The ideal situation is indubitably that in which the functions of author, leading actor, and stage-director are combined in one person, as in the classic case of Molière or in the modern instance of William Gillette; for the greater the measure of the compound imagining that is concentrated in a single mind, the greater the likelihood of a harmonious result. But in cases where the labor is divided among different people, the final and supreme responsibility, in the contemporary theatre, is vested in the stage-director. At the present time, the actor and the author can escape the domination of the stage-director only by assuming his special functions in addition to their own.

Thus, though in reviewing the history of former ages we may divide it into periods of the author's dominance and periods of the actor's dominance, we must define the present age as a period of the dominance of the stage-director. This all-important functionary has only recently been evolved, to cope with the complexity of our modern Drama of Illusion. We are told by historians of music that in the seventeenth century there was no such thing as a conductor for an orchestra: one of the associated players, while performing on an instrument himself, merely set the *tempo* for his fellow-artists. Similarly, in the early history of baseball, the conduct of games depended almost entirely on the physical skill of individual contestants: it was only later in the evolution of the sport that such managerial expedients as the sacrifice hit, the hit and run, the squeeze play, and the double steal, came to be ordered, by hidden signals, from the bench. The problem of the contemporary theatre, for the first time in the history of the drama, is a problem of team-play, in which the contributions of the individual artists must be studiously subordinated to the directing will of a manager, or conductor, of the stage.

In their own periods people went to hear Shakespeare or went to see Garrick; and neither at the Globe Theatre nor at Drury Lane was a stage-director thought of. But, at the present day, people often flock to the theatre, not so much to listen to the author or to observe the actors, as to enjoy the stage-direction of Max Reinhardt,—who rarely writes any of his plays and never acts in them.

III

It is not surprising that the history of stage-direction in the last half century has been the history of a return to nature. Never before has the theatre approached our present-day success in holding up the mirror to contemporary life. The plays of Mr. Granville Barker, who stage-directs his own productions as author and as actor, reflect the very look of daily life; and it seems safe to assert that the modern art of stage-direction has carried realism to its ultimate achievement in the art of drama.

Let us admit this as the special triumph of the last fifty years of the theatre. But the very merits of our realistic stage-direction at its best carry with them certain concomitant defects. Our pursuit of actuality has lured us aloof from that eternal race wherein the greatest athletes among artists pass onward, in relays, the torch of truth. Our eagerness to record the temporary fact has blinded us a little to the vision of the perennial, recurrent generality. We set forth plays that have the very look of here and now, instead of revealing intimations of immortality.

The most obvious errors of the realistic art of stage-direction (and each of these, of course, is closely related to a merit and a triumph) are three in number. First, by its insistence on details, it disperses and distracts the attention of the audience; secondly, it imposes an unnecessary and unfortunate expense upon the business-manager of the production; and thirdly, it is, in the highest sense, inartistic, because it is unimaginative.

The most enjoyable experience in life is the easy exercise of one's own mind; and the spectators in the theatre will enjoy themselves in proportion as their minds are called easily into activity by the spectacle that is presented to them. The stage-director should therefore study not so much how he may accomplish the creative work himself as how he may contrive to make the audience accomplish it during the two hours' traffic of the stage. There is no advantage in setting half of Rome upon the boards to listen to Marc Antony's oration, if, with a mere handful of supernumeraries, the stage-director can make the audience imagine that half of Rome is present. We have carried the photographic method to its uttermost development: a change is obviously needed: and it is apparent that the next turn that the art of the theatre must take is a turn toward more imaginative stage-direction.

IV

The stage-direction of the immediate future has already cast its light before it. Even before the disruptive outbreak of the World War, three thoroughly practicable remedies had been suggested for the three evils that have been enumerated. Professor Max Reinhardt had shown us how we might obtain relief from the insistence on details; the Irish Players had shown us how to save money wisely in the preparation of productions; and Sir Edward Gordon Craig had shown us in his practice (and endeavored, somewhat vainly, to teach us in his theory) how we might turn the theatre to more imaginative uses.

It is instructive now to look backward a few years, in order to compare the memorable production of *Kismet*—which was put on, according to the customary photographic method, by one of our best American stage-directors, Mr. Harrison Grey Fiske—with Professor Reinhardt's production of *Sumurûn*. Both of these plays told fantastic Oriental stories imitated from the *Arabian Nights;* but the methods of production were diametrically dissimilar. *Kismet* was made beautiful by the elaboration of details; but *Sumurûn* was made beautiful by the suppression of details. Mr. Fiske's method was to multiply effects; but Professor Reinhardt's method was to simplify them. Much of his scenery was deliberately crude. There was, for instance, a pink palace with wabbly little windows that looked as if a child had painted it playfully in a picturebook. *Kismet* was localized, with archæological accuracy, in the Baghdad of a thousand years ago, and was consistently Arabian; but *Sumurûn* displayed a careful lack of localization in either place or time. Some of the costumes suggested Turkey, others Persia or Arabia, others China or Japan; and there was no possible means of guessing at any definite date for the story. The architecture belonged to no country and to no age; it was merely fantastically Oriental. Throughout the whole production the truth was impressed upon the eye that the Orient of *Sumurûn* was an Orient of dream; and the setting had no anchorage in actuality.

The second problem—the problem of expense—has been coped with practically by the Irish Players. These associated lovers of the drama carry with them an extensive repertory, and they cannot afford to spend any considerable sum of money on the investiture of any of their plays; but they have successfully surmounted this economic difficulty by casting emphasis, not on the scenery and properties, but on the reading of the lines and on the lighting of the stage. When they present a play of Synge's or Sean O'Casey's, they let the author do the work, by reading with undisrupted fluency the long roll of his rhythm. At other times they contrive to decorate a scarcely furnished stage by a deft manipulation of their lighting. *Birthright*, by T. C. Murray, for example, is set in a homely cottage, with only a few necessary bits of furniture and scarcely any properties. There is a fireplace [left forward], and a staircase leading off-stage to the right. The set is very shallow. The back discloses a blank, bare wall, interrupted only by a window and a door. Not a single picture is hung upon this surface of dingy plaster. But the footlights are suppressed. The stage is lighted only by the firelight, a candle on the table, and some unindicated illumination in the flies. The result is that the actors, as they move about, cast huge and varying shadows over the bare surface of the wall and decorate it continuously with fluctuating and impressive designs. Again, in *The Rising of the Moon*, by Lady Gregory, the footlights are suppressed, and the stage is lighted only by two streams of apparent moonlight which come to a focus at a large barrel in the centre, on which the two most important actors seat themselves, while the wharf and the water in the background are merely imagined in a darkness that is inscrutable and alluringly mysterious. In these two instances, the Irish Players contrived to set their stage with rare imaginative effectiveness, without any expenditure of money whatsoever.

V

One of the foremost leaders of the movement toward a more imaginative handling of the stage has always been Sir Edward Gordon Craig. He has toiled throughout his lifetime as a designer of costumes, scenery, and properties; he has tried innumerable experiments in the delicate art of lighting the stage; and he has made a few productions, in various European capitals, which have been very favorably received. He has been regarded by many critics as a salutary idealist, and has been hailed by a few as the prophet of a new era in the theatre. Meanwhile, he has exhibited his designs—all of which are odd and many of which are interesting—and has talked a great deal, in those rapt, ecstatic, and indecipherable terms that excessively impress the uninitiated.

Gordon Craig refuses to regard the drama either as a department of literature or as a department of pictorial art. He regards it as a distinct and independent artistic evocation, of which the elements are action, words, line, color, and rhythm. He considers the stage-director as inevitably the ultimate, supreme commander of the collaboration required by this compound art. All of this is sane enough; but he then proceeds to deify the stage-director. He even goes so far as to express a desire to abolish both the author and the actor in order that the stage-director may not be hampered by any intermediary artists in the expression of his imaginative ideas. Craig would supplant the actor by a perfect, but involuntary, puppet, which he calls by the hybrid and horrific term of *Über-Marionette;* and by a company of these puppets he would have the drama acted without words. Thereby he would cast preponderant emphasis upon the scenery and lighting, and would make the drama only an exercise in stage-direction. It is hardly necessary to remark that this idea is mad.

But when Craig made a production of *Hamlet* in the Art Theatre of Moscow a short time before the War, the accounts of this production were much more worthy of studious consideration than any of his abstract theories. Let us consider the following passage from a report in the *London Times* for January 12, 1912:

Every scene in the *Hamlet* has for its foundation an arrangement of screens which rise to the full height of the proscenium, and consist of plain panels devoid of any decoration. Only two colors are used—a neutral cream shade and gold. A complete change of scene is created simply by the rearrangement of these screens, whose value lies, of course, not so much in themselves, as in their formation and the lighting. Mr. Craig has the singular power of carrying the spiritual significance of words and dramatic situations beyond the actor to the scene in which he moves. By the simplest of means he is able, in some mysterious way, to evoke almost any sensation of time or space, the scenes even in themselves suggesting variation of human emotion.

Take, for example, the Queen's chamber in the Castle of Elsinore. Like all the other scenes, it is simply an arrangement of the screens already mentioned. There is nothing which definitely represents a castle, still less the locality or period; and yet no one would hesitate as to its significance—and why? Because it is the spiritual symbol of such a room. A symbol, moreover, whose form is wholly dependent upon the action which it surrounds; every line, every space of light and shadow, going directly to heighten and amplify the significance of that action, and becoming thereby something more than its mere setting— a vital and component part no longer separable from the whole.

All of this was extremely interesting—though we might have wished that the correspondent of the *Times* had been a little more explicit in elucidating precisely how Craig's arrangement of monochromatic screens became the "spiritual symbol of a room." One point was clear, however: and that is that Craig had apparently succeeded in suppressing all superfluous details, in diminishing considerably the expenditure of the producing manager, and in forcing the audience to create in imagination the most telling features of the investiture of the play. In doing this he pointed the way toward a new manipulation of the exercise of stage-direction, which was more laudatory than the manifestations of this difficult art that are commonly current in the theatre of to-day.

VI

THE NEW STAGECRAFT

I N THE movement known as "the new stagecraft" there is really
nothing new. The apparent innovations of this movement arise
merely from the resumption of many conventions as old as
the theatre itself, which were injudiciously discarded half a
century ago. The purpose of "the new stagecraft" is to effect a
working compromise between the methods of the platform stage
and the methods of the picture-frame stage, so that the merits of
both shall survive and their defects be nullified. The intention of
the leaders of this movement is not to erect a new ideal; it is merely
to reconcile two different ideals, each of which has shown itself
to be of service in the past. Shakespeare could write his plays only
for a platform theatre; Ibsen could write his plays only for a picture-frame theatre; but, if the advocates of "the new stagecraft"
can effect the compromise that constitutes their program, the playwright of to-morrow will be allowed to write his plays for either
type of theatre, or for a combination of the two.

To appreciate this compromise, we must first consider separately
the different merits and defects of both factors to the intended
reconciliation. The drama was produced upon a platform stage
from the days of Æschylus until the second half of the nineteenth
century. Though the theatres of Sophocles, Plautus, Shakespeare,
Calderon, Molière, and Sheridan differed greatly in detail, they
remained alike in their essential features. In each of these theatres
a full half of the stage was employed as a bare platform surrounded
on three sides by spectators. For this projecting platform it is
most convenient to employ the term "apron," by which it was
denominated in the eighteenth century. Any scene in any play
which did not have to be precisely localized in place and time was
always acted in the apron. Within this universal ground, certain
characters accomplished certain acts, immune from any question-

ing of "where" or "when." The actor in the apron was accepted frankly as an actor; his presence presupposed the presence of an audience; and he could address himself directly to the spectators who surrounded him on three sides. At the same time, each of these theatres provided also a "back stage"—distinguished from the "apron"—in which it was possible to localize events in place and time by some summary arrangement of scenery or properties. The background of this secondary stage might be merely architectural, as in the theatre of Sophocles; or it might be decorated with a painted back-drop and wings, as in the theatre of Sheridan. In any case, as in the theatre of Shakespeare, it could be employed for the exhibition of any set-piece of stage-furniture necessitated by the narrative. Withdrawn to the "back stage," the actors reduced themselves to component parts of a general stage-picture; they were no longer surrounded by spectators on three sides; and, to address the audience directly, they had to step out of the picture and advance into the "apron." The convention of the inner and outer stage, however, permitted the dramatist to alternate at will between eternity and time, between somewhere and anywhere, and between the employment of the actor as an orator or merely as a movable detail in a decorative composition.

The development of the picture-frame proscenium in the latter half of the nineteenth century signalized the advent of a different conception of the drama. The "apron" was abolished; and what had formerly been the "back stage" was brought forward and expanded to include the entire domain available for acting. The whole was framed in a proscenium that gave it the aspect of a picture hung upon a wall. For the first time in its history of more than twenty centuries, the drama was conceived as a drift of moving pictures, assiduously localized in place and time. An inviolable boundary was drawn between the auditorium and the stage; and theatrical performances, which formerly had been projected, so to speak, in three dimensions, were now reduced to two. The drama became a thing at which the public looked, instead of a thing in the midst of which the public lived. The time-honored convention which had permitted the actor in the "apron" to address the audience frankly as an actor was swept away with the platform stage that had rendered this convention simple and natural; and, as a consequence of this revolution, the soliloquy and the aside were discarded. For the first time the drama became primarily a visual, instead of an auditory, art. Conviction was carried to the eye, by an arrangement of actual details behind the picture-frame proscenium, instead of to the ear, by the literary appeal of lines delivered from the "apron." The gardens of Portia's Belmont were no longer suggested by the poet's eloquence; they were rendered to the eye, and not the ear, by an artist other than the author. The drama, in other words, became essentially a special sort of painting instead of a special sort of literature.

This new concept of a play as a thing to be seen instead of a thing to be listened to was developed at a time when realism happened to be rampant in all the arts. Whatever traditional conventions of the theatre were anti-realistic were, in consequence, summarily discarded. The actor was no longer permitted to presuppose the presence of an audience; he was required to comport himself as if he were living in life instead of acting in a play. He could never address a public imagined to be non-existent: hence he could never utter a soliloquy or an aside. He was required at all moments to "see himself" (as actors say) as a component part of a picture, instead of addressing a gathered audience with ears to hear.

The "eavesdropping convention," as it was happily labelled by Henry Arthur Jones, rendered an unprecedented service to the realistic drama; for realism is the art of inducing an apprehension of truth from an imitation of facts. For imitating facts, for localizing a story both in place and in time, for reproducing the very look of actuality, the picture-frame theatre was so superior to the platform theatre that, in a single generation, it drove its predecessor out of usage. But, while this sudden, overwhelming triumph of the pictorial, non-literary concept of the drama made easier the composition and production of realistic plays, it set unprecedented difficulties in the path of writers of romantic plays,—the sort of plays that refuse to be confined within set limits of place and time, and depend for their effect more upon the imaginative suggestion of their lines than upon the imitation of actuality in their investiture. Though a precise and accurate scenic setting behind a picture-frame proscenium was an aid to Ibsen, who wrote realistic plays, it was only an encumbrance to Shakespeare, who wrote romantic plays intended for a platform stage.

It occurred, therefore, to the advocates of that latest movement we are now examining that some compromise should be effected which, while rendering to the realists the manifest advantages of picture-frame production, should also reassert for the romantics the no less manifest advantages of production on a platform stage. They decided to readopt the "apron," with all the free conventions that depend upon its use; and, at the same time, to embellish the "back stage" with decorations sufficiently pictorial to satisfy the eye of a public grown accustomed to the visual appeal of the realistic drama.

In the English-speaking theatre, one of the earliest and most notable exponents of "the new stagecraft" was Mr. Granville Barker; and, for a further elucidation of this movement, we need only examine in detail the method of Mr. Barker's productions of the plays of Shakespeare. For these productions, Mr. Barker has constructed a new type of inner and outer stage. An "apron," several feet in depth, projects before the curtain, and descends in terraced steps to the floor of the auditorium. This platform is accessible from either side, by entrances made available by the suppression of the two stage-boxes of the theatre. Upon this "apron," in frank and utter intimacy with the audience, are enacted all scenes that are not precisely localized in place or time, or that do not demand the employment of set-pieces of stage-furniture. Such other scenes as require a pictorial environment are enacted on the "back stage," or on a full stage constituted by an imaginary obliteration of the boundary that separates this "back stage" from the "apron." The "back stage," disclosed behind the curtain, is framed in a rectilinear proscenium of gold. Whatever scenery is used is set within this frame, at the extreme rear of the stage. Mr. Barker's scenery is summary rather than precise, decorative rather than pictorial. It attains its effect not by imitation of the actual but by suggestion of the real. It is so simple that it can be shifted in a few seconds; and, by virtue of this fact, the decorative aspect of the "back stage" can be altered at any moment without interrupting the continuance of the dramatic narrative. No footlights are employed on Mr. Barker's platform: the stage is illuminated from above by artificial light, just as, in the Elizabethan theatre, it was illuminated from above by natural light. His performances seem to be rendered not in two dimensions but in three; and a person seated in the orchestra is made to feel more like a participant in the business of the play than a mere spectator of what is going on.

VII

A PLEA FOR A NEW TYPE OF PLAY

I

THE MIND of the artist has often been defined as a magic glass through which we look at nature—a sort of lens which brings a chosen phase of life clearly to a focus within a definitely bounded field of vision. With this definition in mind, I should like to ask the reader, at the outset of the present chapter, to lay the book aside in order to perform a simple experiment in optics. Let him step to the nearest window and look for a moment steadily at the house across the street. He will see this house at a certain distance and in a certain degree of detail; and, without turning his head, he will also see, though less distinctly, the three or four houses on either side of the one which he is looking at directly. His field of vision is not definitely bounded but fades off on all sides into a gradually growing dimness; and the aspect of the one house on which his eyes are fixed is entirely natural and not particularly interesting.

Let the reader now procure an ordinary pair of opera glasses and bring them to a focus on a single window of the house across the street. This window will look much nearer and much larger than before; it will be seen with greater intimacy of detail; and it will appear within a definitely bounded field of vision—composed, as painters say, within a circle, that stops the eye from wandering. These three advantages have been derived from looking through a pair of lenses; but it should be noted also that the observer has suffered an attendant disadvantage—namely, that he can no longer look at the entire house, but can merely imagine its total aspect by inference from the appearance of that single little circle which has been so marvelously magnified.

Lastly, let the reader turn the opera glasses about and look at the house through what we are accustomed to call the wrong end of the instrument. Again he will observe a field of vision that is definitely bounded by a circle; but this field of vision will embrace immeasurably more than that which was disclosed by the previous experiment. Instead of seeing only a single window, he will now see the entire house and a segment of each of the adjacent houses; and, because of the clearness of the picture, he will seem to see even more than he noticed with the naked eye. These points must be counted as advantages; but, on the other hand, the house will look much farther away and will be seen with less distinctness of detail.

This experiment may help us to an understanding of the processes of art. Looking at the house with the naked eye was like observing life without any intermediary aid; but looking at the house through either end of the opera glasses was like observing life through the medium of the artist's mind. In both cases the artificial, or artistic, vision was more interesting than the natural, or actual; and in either case the reason was the same—namely, that the picture was composed and framed within limits that required the absolute attention of the eye, by forbidding it, for the moment, to glance at anything excluded from the field of vision.

But a very different sort of interest was added to the aspect of the house, according as the observer looked through one end or the other of the opera glasses; and this difference offers us a basis for distinguishing between the two great processes of art. Employed in the more ordinary way, the glasses afforded a nearer view of a smaller field of vision; and turned about in the less ordinary way, they afforded a more distant view of a larger field of vision. Similarly, there is a sort of art that brings us more intimately into touch with life but shows us less of it at a time; and there is another sort of art that removes life to a greater remoteness but shows us more of it at a time. The first type we may call intensive and the second extensive. Intensive art proceeds by amplifying the little, and extensive art proceeds by imagining the large. The one magnifies details, the other minifies them.

Neither of these processes is absolutely more efficient than the other. Intensive art achieves a finer intimacy of representation, but extensive art achieves a greater range and sweep of treatment. In Venetian painting, for example, the two types may be distinguished in the very different aims and methods of Carpaccio and Tintoretto. Carpaccio is forever asking us to look at some detail

of life through a magnifying glass. He is one of the most insinuat-
ingly intimate of artists. He obtrudes a pretty flower or a funny
little animal or some wistful fleeting vision of a face to be taken
to the heart and loved as, for the moment, the most poignantly
interesting object in the world. But Tintoretto has no patience for
details. In his great picture of the *Last Judgment*, in the Madonna
dell' Orto, he swirls us headlong through the roaring and illimitable
vastitudes of space. Appalled amid immensity, we have no use for
any magnifying glass: we cry out, rather, for a minifying glass,
to render more remote that awful whirring of eternal wings.
Carpaccio paints with camel's hair and Tintoretto with a comet's
tail. Which is, finally, the better art? . . . The answer depends
on what it is that you are looking for.

The terms "intensive" and "extensive," as applied to art, are
comparatively unfamiliar; but they seem to me more useful for
the purposes of criticism than such more familiar terms as "realistic" and "romantic," or "prosaic" and "poetic." In nomenclature,
as in life, familiarity seems to breed contempt or, at the least, a
lack of understanding. A coin too often passed loses the clear
image of its minting. Such words as "realistic" and "romantic"
have been so often and so loosely used that they have lost all
definite significance to the majority of minds. But the new terms
"intensive" and "extensive" point to a dichotomy which should be
definite and clear, and offer us a sure divining-rod for distinguishing the two great processes of art.

In the light of this distinction, let us consider the present status
of the great art of the drama. We shall observe at once that the
theatre, in this present period, is given over almost utterly to the
practice of intensive art; although, in all preceding periods, it had
been assumed without question that the proper province of the
theatre was the exhibition of extensive art. The discovery of this
essential difference leads us at once to a central point of view,
from which we may reasonably investigate the special merits and
defects of the drama of to-day, in comparison with the dramatic
art of other ages.

To make this comparison concrete, let us set one of the best
plays of this microscopic modern age beside a couple of the best
plays of the spacious age of great Elizabeth. Let us compare the
structural method pursued by Sir Arthur Pinero in *The Thunderbolt* with that pursued by Shakespeare in *Hamlet* and *Antony and*

Cleopatra. The whole story of *The Thunderbolt* is set forth in three rooms; and, except for the lapse of one month between the first act and the second, the action is entirely continuous. In other words, the narrative is arranged in three distinct pigeon-holes of place and two distinct pigeon-holes of time. But, in setting forth the narrative of *Hamlet*, Shakespeare employed twenty different pigeon-holes of time and place; and, to produce the panoramic effect of *Antony and Cleopatra*, he allowed himself no less than forty-two narrative units, or, as we call them, scenes. The effect of the modern instance is to magnify details; the effect of the Elizabethan is to minify and merge them into a general sense of the drums and tramplings of a world-engirdling empire. The modern work diminishes the natural distance between life and the observer, but constricts the limits of the field of vision; whereas the work of Shakespeare enlarges the limits of the field of vision, but removes life to a more than natural remoteness from the eye of the observer. The merit of either method is the defect of the other. Both Shakespeare and Pinero were asked to cover, in the two hours' traffic of the stage, the same extent of canvas; but the latter filled the picture by amplifying the little and the near, and the former by imagining the large and the remote.

II

It is difficult to estimate the ultimate importance of any big historical development so long as one is living in the midst of it; but it seems safe to assert that, by the historians of future ages, the last fifty years of the development of the drama will be pointed out as especially important because of the unprecedented triumph, in so brief a period, of the methods of intensive art. This development was defined very clearly by Henry Arthur Jones in the illuminative preface to his published play entitled *The Divine Gift*. This essay is so valuable that I shall quote the following sentences at length: "For a long generation our realistic drama of modern life has practised an ever-increasing and more severe economy of scene, and action, and dialogue. It tends to deny itself all trappings and effects but those of ordinary everyday life. It has become an eavesdropping and photographic reporter, taking snapshots and shorthand notes. We may, without intending to depreciate it, call our present convention the eavesdropping convention—the convention which charges playgoers half-a-crown or half-a-guinea for pretending to remove the fourth wall, and pretending to give them an opportunity of spying upon actual life, and seeing everything just as it happens."

Under what Jones thus happily defined as the "eavesdropping convention," we have brought nature nearer to the eye than ever before and have vastly magnified the observation of details of daily life; but, at the same time, we should not neglect to notice that, in doing so, we have narrowed the field of vision and have sacrificed that feeling of remoteness which is inseparable from any contemplation of the vast. To offset the gain that is derivable from intimate particularity of observation, we have lost, as Jones remarked in another passage of the same essay, "the crowded and varied bustle of Shakespeare, the busy hum that comes from his universal workshop, the drums and tramplings of his hundred legions, the long resounding march of assembled humanity as it troops across his boards."

Though we may feel that the welfare of the human race requires that some people should be thin and others should be stout, it would be unreasonable for us to ask an individual to grow both thin and stout at the same time. Similarly, it would be unreasonable for us to expect, within a single period, an equally remarkable development of intensive and extensive artistry. It has taken fifty years for the drama to develop its present high efficiency of intensive art. It would be unwise to undervalue this development, which has resulted in the production of many plays which exhibit an extremely high order of intelligence; and we should not be surprised to note the inevitable corollary, that during the same period the excluded method of extensive art has shown no development of any great importance.

But the drama is a democratic art, whose destinies are guided by an almost universal suffrage; and we learn from the history of all democracies that, after a single party has long remained in power, the public is certain, sooner or later, to elect the opposition party into office, in order to give it a chance to show what it can do. The drama cannot remain forever in the hands of the great intensive artists of the present age. Sooner or later the public will demand, if only for the sake of change, a return to the methods of extensive art.

The moment for such a revolution is the moment when the party in power has finally achieved the utmost of which it has been capable. When one method has attained its climax, the only hope of progress lies in changing to another method. There are many indications that the intensive drama of the present period has already reached its zenith and has thereby destroyed its possibilities of future service. For half a century, as the eavesdropping convention has been more and more improved, the drama has brought us nearer and nearer to actuality, with a constantly increasing magnifying of details and consequent limitation of the field of vision. This development can go no further. Such plays as *The Madras House* and *Hindle Wakes* and *Rutherford and Son* have brought the observer so close to actuality that any further development along the same lines would result in an annihilation of the difference that separates art from life. But this annihilation would be a *reductio ad absurdum*. The drama would retain no reason for existence if it should sacrifice its license of being different from life. In the face of such a danger, there is only one thing to be done. We must at once increase the field of vision by removing the drama to a greater remoteness from actuality.

When the realists threaten to cut their own throats, it is time for us to turn the government over to the romantics. When prose has done its best, it is time for us to call for poetry. And when the intensive drama can proceed no further with its program without destroying its own excuse for being, the time has come to use the theatre once again for the expression of extensive art.

III

But romance and poetry have been so long excluded from the drama that it will be necessary to invent a new type of play in order to domesticate them in the theatre once again. If Shakespeare were alive to-day, he would find the intensive formula of Pinero unsuited to the exhibition of his own extensive art. The eavesdropping convention has admirably served the purpose of our realistic and prosaic writers; but we cannot impose this convention forever on the writers of a newer age.

What must be the formula for the drama of to-morrow? What Ibsen called "the law of change" indicates that this new drama will be extensive in method, romantic in mood, and poetic in tone; but in what particulars must we revise the technique of the present in order to prepare the theatre for this inevitable change?

First of all, it is obvious that the next generation of dramatic artists will require a freer handling of the categories of time and place than is usual in the contemporary drama. To the intensive playwright it is clearly an advantage to crowd his narrative into no more than two or three or four distinct pigeon-holes of place and time; but, even in a period when intensive art is dominant, it is manifestly unfair to impose the same formula upon playwrights whose natural tendency is toward a more extensive exercise of art. It would have been unfair to ask the poetic and romantic Maurice Maeterlinck to cut his plays according to a pattern that had deliberately been developed to suit the very different requirements of the prosaic and realistic Maxim Gorki. We need a new dramatic pattern, which shall afford a freer scope to the beating of the large and luminous wings of the extensive artist.

If Shakespeare could arrange his narrative in twenty, or even forty, scenes (instead of two or three), why is it impossible for us to do so at the present day? The answer is not theoretical but practical. The Elizabethans used no scenery, in the modern sense; and they could therefore change their time and place by the simple expedient of emptying the stage and repeopling it with other actors. This expedient is denied us by the incubus of modern scenery. We must never for a moment allow ourselves to forget that the development of modern scenery is the one scientific factor which has made possible the recent wonderful development and impressive triumph of intensive drama; but we must notice, on the other hand, that this same remarkable invention is the sole factor that impedes us from employing the more extensive narrative convention of the Elizabethan stage and exhibiting "the long resounding march of assembled humanity as it troops across the boards."

A person who, although his youth was poor, has learned to live on twenty thousand dollars a year can never easily return to an expenditure of only two thousand dollars a year. Our public has grown so used to the trappings and the suits of scenery that we could scarcely now expect it to accept the sceneless stage of Shakespeare, even for the purpose of allowing to a poet a less impeded flow of narrative. But the use of such scenery as is commonly employed at present entirely prevents the playwright from adopting the remote and easy attitude toward time and place which was accorded to Elizabethan authors.

This attitude is prevented by two practical considerations. In the first place, it takes so long to set and change a modern scene that a narrative in twenty units would require at least four hours for its presentation, with lapses between the units so protracted that the audience would wander away from the mood of the story; and, in the second place, the expense of twenty modern stage-sets would ruin the manager of any play. When the development of art is prevented by such practical impediments as these, there is only one thing for the artist to do—he must demand new practical inventions, to remove the obstacles that have been set athwart his path.

Obviously, the two inventions that are needed, in order that the way may be cleared for a new development of extensive drama, are, first, a means of shifting scenery in a few seconds and, second, a means of manufacturing scenery at a very small expense. Until these two inventions are perfected, romance and poetry must continue to endure a fruitless exile from the modern stage.

But, fortunately, both of these inventions have been already made and are being rapidly perfected in the futuristic theatres of the world.

The first problem has been solved by the simple and practical invention of the revolving stage. By this invention, a revolving circle is inscribed within the square platform that is disclosed by the proscenium. This circle will accommodate three settings at the same time. After the first set has been used, the stage may be revolved in a few seconds, to disclose the second set; and while this is being employed by the actors, a new scene may be erected in place of the one that has been discarded.

The second problem—the problem of expense—has also been successfully attacked by such inventors as Sir Edward Gordon Craig and Professor Max Reinhardt. It is necessary to build solid and expensive scenery for the exhibition of realistic and intensive plays; but this necessity need no longer be imposed upon the authors of extensive and poetic dramas. For the purpose of impressionistic art, impressionistic scenery is adequate. If the scene be imagined in some forest of Arden, an artistic hanging of green curtains will mean more to the imagination than any rotund and heavy forestry of canvas trees; and a subtler atmosphere may be suggested by the deft manipulation of electric lights than by the definite delineation of a myriad details.

IV

In view of such inventions as these, the critic cannot be accused of a lack of scientific basis in asking for a new type of play to relieve the monotony of the contemporary theatre. It is no longer unpractical to plead with our poetic and romantic authors to construct their narratives in twenty scenes, instead of two or three, in the endeavor to recapture "the busy hum of Shakespeare's universal workshop." Our public has been trained so long to look at life only through the small end of its opera glasses that it has grown to neglect the interest that is derivable from looking through the other and the larger end. In fifty years, the new intensive artistry has been developed to such perfection in the theatre that the public has almost forgotten the foregone delights of the extensive drama. But a younger and a freer generation is forever knocking at the door. The intensive drama has already done its best, and the time has come for a return to the methods of extensive art.

The drama of the present is so excellent, according to its method, that the drama of the future must be different. The new type of play must be not analytic but synthetic. It will not narrow the field of vision to set life apparently under the nose, but will remove life to an enchantment of remoteness in order to enlarge the field of vision. It will not content itself with the analysis of character within constricted bounds of time and place, but will attempt to represent the logical development of character in many places and through many times. It will not be realistic but impressionistic, not prosaic but poetic. It will exhibit more the martial march of Marlowe than the minute and mincing gait of Mr. Philip Barry.

This new type of play will assuredly be written by the poets of the rising generation. How long—one wonders—will the public have to wait until it achieves a conquest of the theatre?

VIII

THE PERIOD OF PRAGMATISM

THERE have been many periods in the history of the drama
—the periods, for instance, of Sophocles, Calderon, Shakespeare, Molière, Racine, and Sheridan—during which
every tragedy or comedy of any excellence has been constructed in accordance with a single formula, a formula in each
case invented by a group of minor artists and developed to its
fullest fruition by the dominant dramatic genius of the age. In
these periods there has been no appreciable disagreement among
playwrights as to how to build a play. The question of form has
been regarded, for the time, as settled, and the scope for individual
innovation has been restricted to the content of the drama. One
dramatist might differ from another in the mood and message of
his plays, but both authors would employ the same methods of
technical attack.

In dealing with such periods as these, it has always been comparatively easy for dramatic critics to determine certain fixed
standards by which to measure the technical merit of any play
of the period. All that Aristotle had to do was to explain inductively the structural principles which had been employed by
Sophocles, and his treatise became at once a text-book for all subsequent authors of Greek tragedy. When Regnard determined
to write comedies, he never thought of asking questions as to how
to build a play. There was but one way, to his mind—the way,
of course, of Molière; and Regnard made his comedies according
to the methods of his master.

But these conditions of creation and of criticism do not obtain
in the present period of the drama. We are, as Tennyson remarked,
"the heirs of all the ages"; and we have taught ourselves, by study
of the past and experiment in the present, a myriad different ways
of making plays. *Ghosts* is a great drama, and so is *The Blue Bird;*

Strife is a good play, and so is *Sumurûn;* but how is the critic to determine inductively, from the study of such dissimilar instances as these, any fixed and serviceable standard by which to measure the technical merit of any other drama of the present period? He might, indeed, determine after a thorough study of *The Second Mrs. Tanqueray* that Pinero's method is the best for making modern plays; but in that case what could he allow himself to say concerning *Cyrano de Bergerac* or *The Playboy of the Western World?*

It was chiefly with this modern age in his mind that William Archer began his manual of craftsmanship entitled *Play-Making* with the sagacious statement that "there are no rules for writing plays." He might have added as a corollary that there can be, in consequence, no rules for judging them. In this eclectic age of composition the critic must fall back upon that attitude of mind known to philosophers as "pragmatism." The pragmatists, despairing of the discovery of any absolute, unalterable Truth—and being tempted even, at times, to doubt of its existence—rely, for the immediate purposes of thinking, upon any theory that seems for the moment to fit the facts, and, whenever this theory is controverted by a more catholic experience, relinquish it cheerfully in favor of some other hypothesis which is adequate to serve its turn. They do not ask for the utter truth, they ask only for a theory that shall seem to serve; and by this modesty they insure their philosophy against any disaster from disproof.

Pragmatism can exist only in an age that is able, without discomfort, to disbelieve in dogma. We live in such a period of the dramatic art. Our contemporary playwrights imagine no necessity to agree upon a creed of making plays. Any method will serve—provided only that it shall prove itself of service. This is the spirit of the present age, an age adventurous and youthful, a period, as the phrase is, "alive and kicking," and therefore one indisputably great. And since criticism must ever follow, and not lead, creation, since the critic must always report the artist like a Boswell instead of teaching him like a Mentor, it follows that the critic of the contemporary drama must maintain an open mind toward any sort of effort and must judge it not in reference to any predetermined rule, but solely in reference to the particular intention of the author. The critic of the modern drama must enjoy *The Thunder-bolt* and must also appreciate *The Yellow Jacket*, though the peculiar merits of either composition would have been transmuted to defects if they had been incorporated in the other. There is no one way of making plays at present; and the duty of the critic is not to argue in favor of any method against any other, but merely to explain in any given case the particular formula that the playwright has chosen to employ.

The one thing that makes the function of the open-minded commentator unfalteringly pleasurable at the present time is that, every year or so, he is required by some new playwright to alter his entire definition of the drama. He may have decided, after long study, that something must always happen in a play; and then suddenly he will be swept from his anchorage by the London performance of Elizabeth Baker's *Chains*, of which the whole point is that nothing, by any possibility, can happen to the characters. He may have stated, time and time again, that the method of our modern drama is more visual than auditory, that at present the scenario is more important than the dialogue and that (as Augustus Thomas stated) every good contemporary play must employ as its basis an interesting pantomime; and suddenly, without forewarning, he will find himself applauding such a piece as *Hindle Wakes*, which reverses all these propositions and builds its merits on their opposites. Any drama that can do this to the critic is undeniably alive; and unless the critic can respond with equal avidity to these incongruous impressions, he is unsuited to this present age of pragmatism.

But even the pragmatists must yearn occasionally for some vision, however fleeting, of that absolute, unalterable Truth, of which they question the existence; and even the most open-minded dramatic critic must sometimes desire to establish some certain standard of judgment by which he may measure the merit of plays so utterly different in intention and in method as *Little Eyolf* and *Peter Pan*. This desire is akin to that which, in all ages, has moved the high and immemorial dreamers of our human lineage to seek some single God to supplant, in the imagination of mankind, the more convenient and pragmatic gods that were assumed by our forefathers as the rulers of the world. The human mind seeks always for some supreme and single thought, and abhors plurality and heterogeneity as nature abhors a vacuum. Therefore—if we may descend suddenly from the general to the particular—the critic of any art desires always some single and indisputable stand-

ard by which to estimate the most divergent and incongruous examples of that art. He feels the necessity of some axiom sufficiently
catholic to cover and to justify his instinctive homage to two
statues so divergent, for example, as the *Venus of Melos* and the
Thinker of Auguste Rodin. In intention and in method these works
are obviously different; but what is the essence of that mystery
that tells us intuitively that both of them are great?

This question is not difficult to answer. Any work of art is
good if it forces the spectator to imagine and to realize some
truth of life; and any effort of art is bad if its fails of this endeavor.
Here is the final test of efficiency, and it should be noted that in
this test there is no question of technique. Any play, regardless of
the method of the author, is a good play if it awakens the audience
to a realization of some aspect of the infinitely various assertions
of the human will. It must impose upon the spectator the educative illusion of reality; it must, by this means, increase vicariously
his experience of life; and, by adding to his understanding of mankind, it must broaden his potential range of sympathy with human
beings both similar and dissimilar to himself. It must exhibit some
picture of the particular, so tactfully selected and displayed that it
shall suggest a momentary vision of the absolute. It must lead the
public out of living into life.

By a standard so essential and so catholic as this, the critic may
equitably estimate the merit of innumerable plays, of any period,
however divergent they may be in method. It does not ultimately
matter whether a play is realistic or romantic, visual or auditory,
tightly or loosely constructed, whether it casts its emphasis on
character or incident, on scenario or dialogue:—it is required only
that it command the spectator to pause for a moment in his drift
of living and to envisage that reality of life which is perennial and
absolute. This is a requirement that is fulfilled by plays so different
in technical details as *Tanqueray* and *Cyrano*, *Ghosts* and *Sumurûn*, *The Green Pastures* and *The Plough and the Stars*. To accomplish this effect, any method will serve, so long as it shall
prove itself of service.

The first thing to be considered in estimating the merit of a new
play is, therefore, the sincerity of the author's purpose. Has he
honestly and earnestly endeavored to say something that is new
and true, or has he merely effected a new combination of old
theatrical materials with the expectation of producing a series of

transitory thrills? In the latter case, although his play may run a year, it cannot be considered an addition to dramatic literature; but in the former case, although the piece may fail, the critic must proclaim it worthy. For, as Stevenson has said, "A spirit goes out of the man who means execution. . . . All who have meant good work with their whole hearts, have done good work. . . . Every heart that has beat strong and cheerfully has left a hopeful impulse behind it in the world, and bettered the tradition of mankind."

But a determination to tell the truth—though it is, indeed, the most important item—is not the only asset of excellence in the drama. Art would be a very simple exercise if telling the truth were, in Hamlet's phrase, "as easy as lying"; but it is often very hard to tell the truth and nothing but the truth. Any telling of the truth implies the collaboration of two parties—the party of the first part, who does the speaking, and the party of the second part, who does the listening. A dramatist must not only represent his truth in a manner that is satisfying to his own mind, but must also express it in a manner that shall be convincing to his audience. To achieve this delicate endeavor, a high degree of technical accomplishment is necessary, in terms of the particular method that the dramatist has chosen.

In the drama, as in every other art, technique is not an end in itself, but only a means to the great end of telling the truth. In the estimation of the critic, technical dexterity should be considered always a secondary, not a primary, concern. Any method must be adjudged a good method unless it betrays the playwright into compromise or falsification; but clever workmanship that is exercised in the display of trivial material is not admirable in itself.

It is difficult to estimate the comparative importance of several dramas, each of which, in its own way, unfalteringly tells the truth; but it is easy enough to determine if a play is bad. Either because of technical inefficiency, or because of a conscious and responsible surrender of his own apprehension of the truth, the playwright will report his characters as doing certain things, or saying certain things, which those people, in those situations, could not possibly have said and done; and the critical auditor will revolt from the representation with a subconscious sense that he knows better than to believe the fable that is being set before him.

IX

THE UNDRAMATIC DRAMA

I

THERE are many indications that the time has come for a revision of those traditional definitions of the drama which we have inherited from a long line of critics stretching all the way from Aristotle down to Brunetière. A critical formula can never be fixed and final like a proposition in geometry. The critic derives a principle inductively, from the analysis of many works of art which exhibit a family relation to one another. This principle may subsequently be applied, in a logical process of deduction, to the measurement of other works of art created in imitation, or in emulation, of those from which the formula was originally inferred. But any attempt to impose this principle upon another group of works of art, created in expression of a totally different impulse, would be illogical and, as a consequence, uncritical. Thus, a critic of the tragedies of Shakespeare would properly infer the principle that the chief incidents in a tragic story should be acted on the stage; but a critic of the tragedies of Racine would be required to infer the contrary principle that the chief incidents in a tragic story should be imagined off the stage.

Such fluctuating principles as these have been altered, easily and unreluctantly, from age to age; but there are a few formulas which have been repeated, with apparent soundness, for so many centuries that they appear as obstacles in the path of critics with whom pragmatism is not a native and instinctive mood of mind. One of these is Aristotle's dictum that action is the prime essential of a play. This ancient critic stated that the method of the drama is to exhibit character in action. So far as I recall, no subsequent critic has ever ventured to argue against this assertion; and yet, if we accept it as a dogma, what are we to do with such a play as

220

Stanley Houghton's *Hindle Wakes?* This work is undeniably a masterpiece according to its kind, because it reminds us vividly of life and tells us something that is new and true; yet it is almost utterly devoid of action. Its method is not to exhibit character in action but to reveal character through dialogue. What—to repeat —shall be done with such a play? It would surely be a cowardly recourse to beg this question by labeling this interesting and admirable work with such an adjective as "undramatic."

Another statement of Aristotle's that has always been accepted without argument is that the plot of a play should exhibit a beginning, a middle, and an end. Yet, if we regard this statement as a dogma, what are we to do with such a play as Mr. Granville Barker's *The Madras House?* This piece reveals no definite beginning; and the author has deliberately planned it in such a way that it shall show no end. Structurally, this work is, so to speak, a succession of four middles. The final stage-direction reads, "She doesn't finish, for really there is no end to the subject"; and then the curtain falls, to cut us off from our momentary participation in a dozen lives which are considered to be as undetermined as our own. Shall we dare to dismiss such a fabric as "unstructural," after it has entertained us for two hours with the activity of one of the keenest intellects of the recent English theatre?

Less than a hundred years ago, the successful German playwright Gustav Freytag wrote a book on *The Technique of the Drama*, in which he asserted that a dramatic plot may be divided into five successive sections,—namely, the Exposition, the Rise, the Climax, the Fall, and the Catastrophe. He induced this principle mainly from a study of the plays of Shakespeare,—a study in which he was hampered by the assumption, which has subsequently been disproved, that Shakespeare planned his plays in five acts instead of in an uncounted series of scenes. This formula of Freytag's has attained a popular currency that is astonishingly wide; and yet, if we should attempt to support it as a dogma, what could we do with such a play as John Galsworthy's *The Pigeon?* This piece, from the outset to the end, is merely an Exposition of a problem of society: it reveals no Rise, no Climax, no Fall, and no Catastrophe: yet it is a very interesting play and has been accepted by the most intelligent citizens of London and New York as one of the most moving dramas of recent years.

It was less than half a century ago that Ferdinand Brunetière announced his famous principle that the essential element of drama is a struggle between human wills. This statement was at once accepted as an axiom. It has been repeated from mouth to mouth so many thousand times, especially in such popular phrases as "dramatic conflict," that very few people realize at present that this formula is not at least as old as Aristotle. Until very recently there have been none so bold to do this principle irreverence, and the formula, "no struggle, no drama," has been accepted as a commonplace of dramatic criticism. Yet, if we receive this statement as a dogma, what are we to do with such a play as *Chains*, by Elizabeth Baker? This piece exhibits not an assertion, but a negation, of human wills. It presents, at most, a struggle of wills with a minus sign in front of them. The entire point of the play is that nothing can happen to the characters. Their wills are paralyzed by an environment which renders them incapable of self-assertion. Yet few plays of recent years have stirred an audience so deeply to a realization of life.

In his manual of craftsmanship entitled *Play-Making*, that bold and pioneering critic, William Archer, devoted a very interesting chapter to a discussion of the intrinsic meaning of the terms "Dramatic and Undramatic." He bravely rejected the formula of Brunetière as inapplicable to many famous instances. Discarding "conflict" as essential to the drama, Archer suggested, in its stead, the element of "crisis." In this point, he seemed to follow Robert Louis Stevenson, who referred to the drama as dealing with "those great, passionate *cruses* of existence where duty and inclination come nobly to the grapple." Yet I did not find it difficult to convince so open-minded a critic as William Archer that the element of "crisis" was no more indispensable to a genuinely interesting drama than the element of "conflict." Where, for instance, was there any crisis in *The Madras House*, which Archer much admired? Where was the element of crisis in *The Pigeon?* And where, after the very first minute of the action, was there any crisis in Arnold Bennett's *The Great Adventure?*

In the face of these negations of even the most modest effort to advance a dogma, it would seem that the only course for the critic is to retreat to the position thus admirably put by Archer, —"The only really valid definition of the dramatic is: Any representation of imaginary personages which is capable of interesting an average audience assembled in a theatre. . . . Any further attempt to limit the content of the term 'dramatic' is simply the expression of an opinion that such-and-such forms of representation will not be found to interest an audience; and this opinion may always be rebutted by experiment."

The fact that, in recent years, every attempt to limit the content of the term "dramatic" has been rebutted by experiment must be accepted as an evidence that we are living in a very vigorous period of dramatic art. No playwright is so indisputably a creative artist as one who can send the critics back to their studies to revise their definitions of the drama. The attitude of such an artist may be phrased familiarly as follows: "You tell me that such-and-such a process has never yet been followed in the drama: very well,—I will show you that it can be followed, with both artistic and popular success." If, after this assumed assertion, the creative artist fails in his endeavor, his failure may be taken as an evidence of the inviolability of the principle he has assaulted; but, if he succeeds, there can be no other recourse for the critic than to discard the ancient formula and to induce a new one.

But this necessity is repugnant to the type of critic who hates to change his mind. In the epilogue to *Fanny's First Play*, Mr. Bernard Shaw has introduced a critic of this type, in the figure of the ultra-Aristotelian Mr. Trotter. Of the later works of Mr. Shaw and many of his emulators, Mr. Trotter simply and definitely says: "They are not plays." He is willing to consider them as essays, as discussions, or as conversations; but he will not consider them as plays, since Aristotle never saw the like of them. But this view of Mr. Trotter's seems unnecessarily narrow. Surely—as Archer has stated—any story presented by actors on a stage, which interests an audience, cannot be denied the name of drama: one might as logically look a lion in the eyes and tell him he was not a lion. And if only an action that is motivated by a struggle of the wills can be labeled with the adjective "dramatic," let us, by all means, hasten to admit that there is such a thing as "undramatic drama."

This playful contradiction in terms affords the critic a convenient label to apply to many modern works which, while violating at several points the traditional canons of dramatic criticism, have evoked an enthusiastic response from audiences of more than usual intelligence. If we smilingly apply to these works the paradoxical adjective "undramatic," this pleasant exercise of whimsicality should be taken as a tribute to the authors' skill in stretching the traditional limitations of the drama to force them to encompass something strange and new.

II

An effort to achieve a new type of "undramatic drama" has made itself apparent in the works of several of our younger realistic writers. It is apparently their purpose to carry the drama more nearly into accord with actuality than it has ever been before, by the expedient of ignoring the tradition of the well-made play. They do not build their stories to a climax at the close of the penultimate act; for they disdain the easy emphasis of curtain-falls and desire to avoid any artificial heightening of a single favored incident. They seem to disagree with the immemorial axiom of Aristotle that a play should have a beginning, a middle, and an end; for they admit only that the drama must exhibit the middle of an action. Their plays begin almost anywhere, and often do not end at all. We feel—and the authors desire us to feel—that they might have stopped an act sooner or written ten acts more. By deliberately avoiding a conclusion, and by starting the story at a point which presupposes innumerable antecedent causes, these authors seek to imitate the drift of life itself,—which exhibits no beginnings and no endings, but only an appalling continuity.

Nature is neither selective of events nor logical in the arrangement of them; but without selection and arrangement it is impossible to make a plot. In this dilemma, the apostles of the "undramatic drama" prefer to side with nature, and are willing, whenever necessary, to get along without a plot. In order to remove attention from the element of plot, they cast entire emphasis upon the element of character. Character is all they care about; and provided that their imaginary people are representative and real, they do not deem it indispensable that these characters shall reveal themselves in terms of action. They even undertake to extend the province of the drama by including in their plays such unassertive characters as have always been regarded hitherto as undramatic. They refuse to restrict the drama to an exhibition of a struggle between human wills resulting necessarily in action, and often

choose instead to exhibit a deadlock between human wills that results in the negation of action.

Such characters as these, when exhibited upon the stage, must
reveal themselves mainly through the medium of dialogue. What
they think and what they feel must express itself more through
what they are heard to say than through what they are seen to do.
The plays of the new realists are therefore less visual, and more
auditory, in their appeal than the majority of our contemporary
dramas. It appears that these young authors might have taken
for their motto that striking phrase of Stevenson's, in a letter to
Henry James—"Death to the optic nerve." By their reliance upon
dialogue as the essential factor of their plays, they seem to be
seeking what may be called a return to literature. Their dialogue
is masterly: it has to be; for their plays appeal so little to the eye
that the audience is required to listen closely to the spoken words.

What, now, shall be said concerning these departures from the
practice of the greatest playwrights of the elder generation?
Much, upon the one hand, may be said against them. The endeavor
of the new realists is based upon the assumption that life itself is
more dramatic than any theatrical selection and arrangement of
events. They therefore exercise their artistry in an effort to con-
ceal the fact that the drama is different from nature. But if this
effort were ever perfectly successful, the drama would cease to
have a reason for existence, and the only logical consequence
would be an abolition of the theatre. It would seem, as a matter
of principle, that there can scarcely be a fruitful future for a movement which, if extended to the utmost, would result in a *reductio
ad absurdum*.

But, on the other hand, if we judge the apostles of the new
realism less by their ultimate aims than by their present achievements, we must admit that they are rendering a very useful service
by holding the mirror up to many interesting contrasts between
human characters which have hitherto been ignored in the theatre
merely because they would not fit neatly into the pattern of the
well-made play. And in presenting their unconventional material,
these young authors have succeeded in producing an astonishing
impression of reality. By suggesting the potential intensity of a
static situation, they often achieve an effect that is more profoundly moving than if they had made the stage noisy with

alarums and excursions. Even a critic who might disagree with their theories could not fail to recognize and to admire the extraordinary talents of many of these authors. Because of the sincerity of their respect for life and the seriousness of their endeavor to represent it faithfully, they have earned a high rank upon the roster of contemporary dramatists.

X

CONTRAST IN THE DRAMA

I N THIS time of the tottering of definitions, it is still desirable that the dramatic critic, in the interest of future playwrights, should seek some certain element of narrative that may be accepted as essential to success upon the stage. In view of the fact that several of our younger realistic writers have successfully evaded the famous assertion of Ferdinand Brunetière that the essential element of drama is a struggle between human wills, it appears to be necessary to agree with William Archer that the Brunetière formula can no longer be accepted as a definition of the drama.

The potency of this attack upon a theory which for twenty years had been regarded as an axiom must not be over-estimated. Not even Arnold Bennett, the author of *The Great Adventure*— from which any positive assertion of the human will was carefully excluded—would have denied that the narrative pattern praised in unexceptionable terms by Brunetière is the one pattern which is most likely to interest an audience assembled in a theatre, or that at least nine-tenths of all the acknowledged masterpieces of the drama, both in the past and in the present, will be found upon examination to incorporate some conflict between human wills. Exceptions—according to the Latin proverb—*test* a rule; but they do not necessarily prove that, as a rule, it has lost its validity. In shifting our critical position, we are merely admitting that the element of conflict is not *essential* to the drama; it is far from our intention to suggest that, in the vast majority of cases, this element is not desirable.

But even to admit that an element which was formerly considered as essential can now be regarded only as advantageous is to feel ourselves somewhat in the position of mariners whose ship has sunk beneath them. This position is pertinently indicated by the familiar phrase "at sea." It is always disconcerting to renounce a seeming certainty; and the normal mind seeks ever to erect some other image to replace an idol that is overthrown. There is a world of meaning in the traditional announcement, "The king is dead; long live the king!" When definitions die, we must immediately seek new definitions to succeed them.

This necessity was felt by William Archer when he dealt his gentle death-blow to the theory that conflict is essential to the drama. He proceeded at once to present a new pretender to the vacant throne:—"What, then, is the essence of drama, if conflict be not it? What is the common quality of themes, scenes, and incidents, which we recognize as specifically dramatic? Perhaps we shall scarcely come nearer to a helpful definition than if we say that the essence of drama is *crisis*. A play is a more or less rapidly-developing crisis in destiny or circumstance, and a dramatic scene is a crisis within a crisis, clearly furthering the ultimate event. The drama may be called the art of crises, as fiction is the art of gradual developments."

This theory of Archer's affords us at least a floating spar to cling to, in the midst of the sea of uncertainty into which we have disturbingly been dropped. It is undeniable that the drama tends to treat life more crisply and succinctly than the novel, both because of the physical limitations of the theatre and because of the psychological demands of the actors and the audience. One way of attaining this crispness and succinctness is to catch life at a crisis and to exhibit the culminating points—or, as Archer said in a later passage, "the interesting culminations"—of the destinies of the characters concerned. But is this the only way? No one would venture to deny that Archer's formula applies to at least nine-tenths of all the acknowledged masterpieces of the drama; but so did the formula of Brunetière. It is obviously advantageous for the drama to catch life at a crisis; but is it absolutely necessary? If we can find as many exceptions to Archer's rule as Archer found to Brunetière's, we shall be compelled to decide that the element of crisis is no more *essential* to the drama than the element of conflict.

Let us now ask if any one can find any crisis in Lady Gregory's one-act comedy entitled *The Workhouse Ward?* This dialogue between two beggars lying in adjacent beds attains that crispness and succinctness which is advocated by the critic, without exhibiting a crisis in either of their lives. The whole point of the play is that we leave the beggars precisely in the same position in which we found them. Yet this comedy is undeniably dramatic. It has been acted successfully in Ireland and England and America, and has proved itself, in all three countries, one of the most popular pieces in the repertory of the Abbey Theatre Players. Would Archer have maintained that *The Great Adventure* exhibits "a more or less rapidly-developing crisis in destiny or circumstance," or that any of the eight scenes of this comedy, except the very first, can be regarded as "a crisis within a crisis, clearly furthering the ultimate event"? Is there any crisis in *The Madras House* or in *The Pigeon?* Or, to go back to Shakespeare, would Archer have attempted to define as "a crisis within a crisis" such a passage as Act V, Scene 1, of *The Merchant of Venice*, in which Lorenzo and Jessica discourse most eloquent music underneath the moon? Is there any crisis in the scenes between Orlando and Rosalind in the Forest of Arden?

To defend the element of crisis as essential in such instances as these would necessitate the same sort of verbal jugglery that would be required to establish the element of conflict. It would seem, therefore, that Archer has not led us any nearer to a certainty than we were before. The friendly spar is floated from our desperate grasp and we find ourselves once more floundering in the sea.

Is there, after all, such a thing as an *essential* element of drama? Is there a single narrative element without which a dramatic scene cannot succeed? I think that there is; but I am willing to revoke this decision so soon as any critic shall show me an exception to the rule. It seems to me at present that the one indispensable element to success upon the stage is the element of *contrast*, and that a play becomes more and more dramatic in proportion to the multiplicity of contrasts that it contains within itself.

The sole reason why *The Workhouse Ward* produces a dramatic effect is that the two beggars are emphatically different from each other. The moonlight scene in *The Merchant of Venice* is interesting on the stage because of the contrast between the contributions of the two lovers to their lyrical duet. Both *The Pigeon* and *The Madras House* derive their value from the fact that they exhibit a series of contrasts between characters. *The Great Adventure* is dramatic because the drifting hero is wonderfully contrasted with the practical and sensible heroine and every scene of the play reveals some minor contrast between antithetic minds. What is the dramatic element in the soliloquies of Hamlet? Do they not derive their theatrical effectiveness from the fact that they present a constant contrast between very different human qualities which, in this case, happen to have been incorporated in a single person? Such a play as *Every Man in His Humour* stands outside the formula of Brunetière, because it exhibits no struggle of contending wills; it also stands outside the formula of Archer, because it exhibits neither a crisis nor a series of crises; but it is a great comedy, because it exhibits an unintermitted series of contrasts between mutually foiling personalities.

One of the most amusing comedies of recent years affords us an emphatic illustration of the principle of contrast. This is *General John Regan*, by Canon Hannay, of St. Patrick's, Dublin,—a genial Irish gentleman who had previously published several novels signed with the utterly English and very solemn pen-name of "George A. Birmingham." *General John Regan* is merely an amplified anecdote. It exhibits no conflict of contending wills; neither does it disclose a crisis in the life of any of the characters; but it is dramatically interesting because it sets forth a series of delightful contrasts between a dozen very different people. This composition is very rich in characterization and unusually humorous in dialogue. Canon Hannay thoroughly knows his Ireland, and he writes with that imaginative glibness which is always evident in Irish humor. His play successfully defies those definitions of the drama which till very recently were held as axioms, and it seems to prove that the sole essential to success in comedy is a sufficiently interesting contrast between characters.

XI

THE VALUE OF STAGE CONVENTIONS

I N HIS *Carol of Occupations* Walt Whitman said, "All architecture is what you do to it when you look upon it; . . . all music is what awakes from you when you are reminded by the instruments." It is particularly true of the drama that the only finally effective scenes are those that happen not so much upon the stage as in the mind of the spectator. The purpose of a play is not to reproduce the actual but to suggest the real, and this suggestion must be made through the medium of many theatrical conventions which, though in themselves unnatural, are competent to stimulate the audience to the imagining of nature.

The conventions of the theatre have differed widely in different times and lands, and the acceptance of any particular set of conventions is merely a matter of public custom. To the theatre-going public of any period the conventions of their own stage always seem simple and natural because they are accustomed to them, whereas the conventions of any other period appear unnatural and forced. To our public at the present time it would seem funny if the actors in a tragedy should wear cardboard masks and walk on stilted boots, yet this convention seemed simple and natural to the Athenians who listened to the tragedies of Sophocles. It would seem unnatural to-day if an ancient Roman emperor should appear upon the stage in the costume of Louis XIV of France, yet this convention was employed without disadvantage in the tragedies of Racine. We should think it odd if an orator on a bare platform out of doors, with the afternoon sun striking full upon his face, should suddenly remark, " 'Tis now the very witching time of night," but Shakespeare's audience in 1602 never thought of laughing when Burbage read this line in *Hamlet*. We should regard it as unusual if an actor should enter a room by walking through the walls, but this convention never bothered the

231

original spectators of *The School for Scandal*. Through such expedients as these, Sophocles and Shakespeare and Racine and Sheridan stimulated in their audiences a keener sense of truth than is ever suggested by our own minute and timorous imitation of the actual.

Because of the influence of custom, the public of to-day pays no attention to many artifices of our own theatre which are fully as unnatural as the conventions that have just been noticed. It is not natural, for instance, that a room should have three walls instead of four, and that nearly all the furniture should be turned to face the invisible fourth wall. In actual life people talk for two hours without moving from a chair; but on our stage they get up at the end of every two or three minutes and cross over to another chair on the opposite side of the room. Furthermore, our actors keep their faces turned nine-tenths of the time in a single, certain direction, and whisper their most intimate concerns in a voice that is easily audible to a thousand people. In our modern theatre people eat an elaborate dinner of a dozen courses in ten minutes or less; they rarely write a letter without reading it aloud as they compose it; and if they light a single lamp, they increase by several hundred candle-power the illumination of the room. An actor who has just dropped dead upon the stage gets up a moment afterwards to smile and make a speech. Two hours elapse in ten minutes, and when an actor fingers a piano the music comes from off the stage. These conventions, viewed from an external and unsympathetic point of view, are just as ridiculous as those which were employed by Sophocles and Shakespeare; and the only reason why we do not laugh at them to-day is that we are accustomed to accept them.

The drama can never be natural, for the ultimate and lofty reason that if ever it should succeed in this endeavor it would annihilate its own excuse for being. Art would be unnecessary unless it were different from nature. In the light of this truth, the present prevailing endeavor of our stage to hold, in a precise and literal sense, the mirror up to nature must be regarded as a waste of energy. Often in our modern theatre we prevent the audience from imagining the real by setting before it too literal an imitation of the actual. It is therefore desirable, for the esthetic education of our contemporary theatre-goers, that they should be reminded now and then of the freer and less literal conventions that have been easily accepted in the drama of other times and lands. From the cultural and critical standpoint this is the main advantage of such exhibitions of the stage conventions of other periods as were offered in that memorable series of historical matinées that marked the closing weeks of the New Theatre in 1912. It is good for us to be reminded now and then that the dramatic method of Shakespeare was, with all its crudities, more stimulating to the imagination than the dramatic method of David Belasco; but to accomplish this, it is necessary to produce Shakespeare in the Elizabethan manner instead of in the manner of to-day. This principle was emphatically proved by the great success, in 1937, of the sceneless production of *Julius Cæsar* by the Mercury Theatre in New York.

Looked upon in the light of such considerations as these, the unforgettable production of *The Yellow Jacket* must be regarded as one of the most educative offerings which have been presented in New York in recent times. *The Yellow Jacket* is an imaginary Chinese play, presented in accordance with the conventions of the Chinese theatre. It was devised and written by J. Harry Benrimo and George C. Hazleton, Jr. The scene represents the stage of the old Jackson Street Theatre in San Francisco, and upon this stage a typical Chinese story is enacted in the Chinese manner.

The conventions of the Chinese stage are curiously similar to those of the Elizabethan theatre, and the story of *The Yellow Jacket* is therefore unfolded in accordance with a narrative method that is almost identical with Shakespeare's. As in the Globe Theatre on the Bankside, the stage is a platform devoid of scenery, but decorated by furniture and properties that are shifted, from dialogue to dialogue, to accommodate the exigencies of the action. Again, as at the Globe, there is a door at either side of the rear of the stage—one for entrances and one for exits. Between these two doors there is an alcove, or recess, which was used by Shakespeare as part of the imagined scene, but is employed in the Chinese theatre to house the orchestra that accompanies the dialogue with incidental music. Over this alcove there is, in both theatres, a balcony, or upper stage, which may be used at any moment in the presentation of the story. The scene is imagined to be wherever the actors say that it is, and the place of the action may be shifted by the simple expedient of emptying the stage through the exit door and bringing on new actors through the entrance door. There is a Chorus, as in Shakespeare's *Henry V*, to ask the audience to imagine the locality of the scene about to be presented; and, from dialogue to dialogue, the furniture is shifted by a property-man, who is dressed in black and is supposed to be invisible.

These Chinese conventions, which are identical at nearly every point with those of Shakespeare, are only in a small degree less natural than those of our American stage to-day; but because our public is not used to them, they seem to us ridiculous. Of this necessary reaction of the occidental audience the authors of *The Yellow Jacket* have carefully made capital. They have invited the American public to laugh at the conventions of the Chinese theatre and have thereby enriched their play with comedy. But, by doing this, they have also accomplished a more difficult achievement. They seem to have reasoned that their auditors, by the mere exercise of laughing their fill at these outlandish artifices, would become so accustomed to them that in time these very conventions would cease to seem ridiculous and might securely be employed for the suggestion of lofty poetry and poignant pathos. This subtle triumph has been successfully achieved.

It would be superfluous to summarize the story of this play, since no enumeration of its ever-fluctuating flow of incidents could suggest the whimsical and subtle art with which the story is unfolded. The black-robed property-man (who is supposed to be invisible) piles a few chairs together in the middle of the stage, smoking all the while a careless cigarette and looking ludicrously bored at the performance. A young man and a young woman climb upon the chairs, and tell you that they are reclining in a flower-boat that is drifting slowly down a river. Two attendants (imagined to be boatmen) stand behind the chairs and pole rhythmically at the unresisting air with slender bamboo-rods (imagined to be oars), while a musician (in full view of the audience) scrapes two pieces of sand-paper together to imitate the swish of water along the bilge of a boat; and lo!, in spite of (or perhaps because of) the crudity of these conventions, the auditor finds himself really and truly (because imaginatively) drifting in a boat, banked with flowers and lyrical with song and redolent of youth and love. To achieve such an eloquent effect as this by means so primitive and childish is a scarcely precedented triumph of theatric art.

The story drifts through many different moods, satiric, tragic, lyric, pathetic; and all these moods are rendered easily through media of utterance at which the audience has laughed heartily only a moment before. The lines are beautifully written, and the action appeals so poignantly to the imagination that we realize a life-revealing vision, of which no literal transcription has been presented on the stage.

XII

THE SUPERNATURAL DRAMA

THERE is a predisposition on the part of the populace (and also of most of the reviewers) to regard any play which employs the supernatural as especially imaginative. Such a work is considered particularly difficult to accomplish; and the result is commonly labeled "literary," in the laudatory connotation of the term. It is considered difficult to invent a devil with horns and a tail, and comparatively easy to create an Iago devoid of those unusual appendages. It is considered especially "literary" to set forth a five o'clock tea given by a guinea-hen, whereas (presumably) it would not be "literary" to exhibit an afternoon tea given by a society woman. To the popular mind, it seems highly imaginative to invent a faun through whose body you may shoot a bullet without hurting him; but it would not (apparently) be imaginative to create a man whose viscera would be disturbed by such a transit. It is considered poetic to invent a piper whom children follow because of some magic in his music; presumably it would not be poetic to create a man whom children would follow because they liked to play with him.

Any *a priori* judgment is uncritical, because it denies the possibility that a new work may prove an exception to the rule on which the judgment has been based. But if the popular mind *must* presume an *a priori* judgment of these exhibitions of the supernatural, it might more safely presume them to be less difficult, less imaginative, less (in the real sense) literary, than plays which reproduce the natural. In the infancy of the human race, as in the infancy of every individual (for the mental history of each of us repeats the mental history of mankind), all stories were supernatural—the reason being that the supernatural is immeasurably easier, both to fabricate and to appreciate, than is the natural. And the supernatural is easier to invent and to understand because it

236

requires less maturity of imagination. Imagination is the faculty
for realization. Contrary to the common belief, children are, as a
rule, incapable of imagination. They tell themselves stories of
ghosts and goblins and fairies because they are unable to realize
men and women and children; they invent exceptions to the laws
of life because they cannot understand the laws; they wonder at
a dog that talks because they have not learned to wonder at a dog
that merely barks. So, in its infancy, the human race told itself
stories of miracles and considered the exceptional divine; it has
required a more matured imagination to perceive that divinity is
evidenced not in "some scission in the continuity of man's experience, some wilful illegality of nature," but in law itself, majestic
and immutable. The function of imagination is to discover truth;
the function of art is to tell it. Myths and fables are of service only
as an easy and a shorthand means of indicating simple truths. The
unusual is of value in art only in so far as it calls attention to the
usual in life; exceptions are important only as they indicate the
rule. To prefer miracles to laws, to dally with the exception rather
than to delve for the rule, is to exercise not the imagination but
the fancy. As the wisest of American critics, W. C. Brownell,
remarked, "Imagination and fancy differ in that, both transcend-
ing experience, one observes and the other transgresses law." Now,
of course, a supernatural fable may be faithful to the laws of life,
may (in other words) embody an imaginative vision; but in practice, in this present age of ours, a reversion to the infancy of art
more often indicates an irresponsibility of fancy, an unwilling-
ness on the part of the artist to undertake and carry through the
lofty task of transmuting the actual to the real. The fancy is a
dangerous faculty, because its exercise is easy and is invariably
attended by great good fun, whereas to exercise imagination is
laborious and cannot be accomplished (to speak figuratively) without fasting and prayer. All that Edmond Rostand had to say in
Chantecler might have been said more profoundly if he had realized his characters as men and women. The piece becomes imaginative only in those passages in which it becomes human; at all
other moments it is merely fanciful—the *jeu d'esprit* of a mind that
dallies instead of the great task of a mind that toils. Since beauty
is synonymous with truth, as Keats has taught us, it is only by
imagination that beauty can be created; all that fancy can contrive
is prettiness. It is usually an artist with a dainty fancy who chooses

to tell us tales of skipping fauns and magic pipes; but it requires an august imagination to reveal to us the beauty inherent in the common life of every day. Sir James Barrie displayed a pretty fancy in *Peter Pan;* but in *What Every Woman Knows* he revealed a beautiful imagination. Of these two plays by the same author, the natural is immeasurably more imaginative than the supernatural.

But if it is a fallacy to prejudge that a supernatural play must be more imaginative, it is no less a fallacy to accord it *a priori* a higher literary rank, than a play of ordinary life. A play deserves to be laureled as dramatic literature only when it expresses, in terms of the technique of the theatre of its age, some truth of human life that is important to humanity. Fine writing does not make dramatic literature. Verbal felicity in dialogue is a beauty that is only skin-deep; the real literary value of a play depends upon the symmetry and strength of its skeleton and the vitality of its flesh and blood. *The Thunderbolt* is a greater work of dramatic literature than *Chantecler*, because it is more profoundly and consistently imagined—in other words, more real; yet in *The Thunderbolt* there is not a single line that is quotable for verbal beauty, while in *Chantecler* there are pages and pages that are marvels of the wizardry of words. The best written speech in Josephine Preston Peabody's *The Piper*—the address to the wayside image—is, dramatically, an error; it is written charmingly, but a master of dramatic literature would not have written it at all. Supernatural plays afford their authors opportunities for verbal flights of fancy which are denied to authors who aim to paraphrase the speech of ordinary men and women; but the task of the latter is no less a feat of literary art. A greater literary imagination is displayed in these bare, undecorative lines of the first act of *The Thunderbolt*—"Ah, Heath, the dining room—!" "Yes, Mr. Elkin, that's over, sir"—lines through which, as they come to us in their context, the full pathos of death looks out upon us with dim, unweeping eyes, than in such a line as Rostand's, *"Que des Coqs rococos pour ce Coq plus cocasse,"* of which the only ground is an astounding rebound of sound.

In one particular respect, supernatural material is especially hazardous for the dramatic artist. The corner-stone of the dramatic art is the freedom of the will. No conflict of wills can afford a true dramatic interest unless the wills of the participants are absolutely free. Now, if, in a story, certain characters are endowed with supernatural powers, while the others are not, no truly dramatic conflict can be possible between the one side and the other. We are asked to watch a game in which we know the dice are loaded. In the last act of *The Faun*, by Mr. Edward Knoblock, the other characters are merely puppets whose wires are pulled by the supernatural hero; and in *The Piper* the people of Hamelin are at all times powerless against the magic of the mountebank. These conceptions abnegate the very possibility of drama. If, then, a playwright is to use the supernatural at all, it is surely wiser for him not to adulterate it with the natural, but to conceive *all* his characters in accordance with a common convention. This is what Edmond Rostand has done in *Chantecler*. His characters all have a fair chance, because all are equally super-actual. He has displayed consummate tact in entirely excluding human beings from his story—a tact which expresses itself very cleverly in the concluding line, "*Chut! Baissez le rideau, vite!— Voilà les hommes!*"

XIII

THE PERSONALITY OF THE PLAYWRIGHT

I N ALL the arts a distinction may be drawn between works which are objective and impersonal and works which are personal and subjective. Creations of the former type seem to have sprung full-grown from their creators' minds, like Athena from the forehead of Zeus, and to exist thereafter as independent entities; whereas creations of the latter type come trailing clouds of glory from the minds that made them. It is the merit of certain works of art that they tell us nothing of their makers; but it is no less the merit of others that they tell us a great deal. It would surely be uncatholic to exalt one type above the other; and no comparison between them should be made for any purpose less disinterested than that of definition.

All art that is inefficient is impersonal, either because the artist has no personality to reveal or because he lacks the power to reveal what personality he has; so that the distinction made above becomes valid only between the worthy works of worthy men. Only when art has risen to the level of efficiency can the question arise whether the artist shall strive to keep himself out of his work or to put himself into it. Of these two endeavors, the former is the more admirable from the technical standpoint, but the latter is the more engaging from the standpoint of humanity.

There is no denying that the supreme and perfect works of art belong to the impersonal, objective type. We do not know who made the *Venus of Melos*, and assuredly we do not care. The nameless sculptor may have been young or middle-aged; he may have been athletic and sociable or ascetic and morose; he may have loved drink, or he may even have been a vegetarian; the *Venus* does not tell us and we do not want to know. We read the *Iliad* and the *Odyssey* without really caring whether Homer was a man or a syndicate of balladists. The perfect works of architecture—

like the Doric temple at Pæstum, the Roman Corinthian jewel-box
at Nîmes, the Sainte Chapelle at Paris or the King's College Chapel
at Cambridge—are entirely impersonal: they tell us a great deal
about the epochs that inspired them, but nothing about the architects who designed them. In modern fiction, the most accomplished artists have worked impersonally. Jane Austen keeps herself out of her novels; and the short-stories of Guy de Maupassant
are utterly objective. What sort of man wrote *La Parure?* We may
answer, "A great artist"; but that is all. So, in the drama, we find
that *Œdipus King* tells us nothing about Sophocles; and though
the keenest of English critics, Walter Bagehot, tried to induce a
sense of Shakespeare's personality from a study of his plays, and
later critics with less sound and more inventive minds have pursued this method to extravagant extremes, we notice that that one
of all his plays which is the finest technical achievement—I mean,
of course, *Othello*—tells us next to nothing about Shakespeare.

But if art at its most perfect is impersonal, we must admit that
the obtrusion of the artist's personality in works that rank only a
little lower than the highest is often an amiable imperfection.
When Ulysses is discovered by the maidens of Nausicaä, it would
trouble us if we had to think of the author as a blind old man;
but—to take an instance of the other type—unless we do think of
the author as a blind old man, we shall lose most of the poignancy
and pathos of the opening of the third book of *Paradise Lost.* We
prefer Chaucer to Spenser not because he is a finer artist, for he is
not so fine, but because he reveals to us a more affable and human
personality. Artistry, after all, is less appealing than humanity; and
Addison, who is an artist, interests us less than Pepys, who is a
man. If artistry were everything, there would be no excuse for
preferring the work of Giotto, who cannot draw hands and feet
and whose perspective goes awry, to the work of Guido Reni,
who is a practised and accomplished painter; but Giotto makes us
love him so much that we overlook his inequalities of craftsmanship, and Guido bores us to such an extent by his conventional
and vulgar mind that we are almost tempted to resent his skill in
draughtsmanship. William Dean Howells, who was himself an objective artist and therefore an apostle of impersonality, commented
adversely on Thackeray's tendency "to stand about in his scene,
talking it over with his hands in his pockets, interrupting the
action, and spoiling the illusion in which alone the truth of art

resides" and condemned him as "a writer who had so little artistic sensibility, that he never hesitated on any occasion, great or small, to make a foray among his characters, and catch them up to show them to the reader and tell him how beautiful or ugly they were; and cry out over their amazing properties." This statement explains readily enough the grounds on which Thackeray must be regarded as a less accomplished artist than Jane Austen, or than Howells himself; but it fails to explain why most of us would rather read Thackeray. We return to *The Newcomes* again and again, not so much for the pleasure of seeing London high society in the early nineteenth century as for the pleasure of seeing Thackeray see it; and it is precisely in those moments of amiable imperfection which Howells has stigmatized that we find ourselves nearest to Thackeray and therefore nearest to our source of pleasure. When William Crary Brownell, in his marvelous destructive criticism of the short-stories of Hawthorne, laid bare their weaknesses as works of art, he lost sight of the fact that our real reason for liking them is not because they are works of art, but because they are written by Hawthorne, and that to reveal the weaknesses of a man we love will only make us love him more. It is in this way that imperfect artists with engaging personalities get around the critics.

In our recent drama we have been confronted by artists of the one type and the other, and it is difficult to choose between them. For instance, we were shown a great example of objective art in *The Thunderbolt* and a great example of subjective art in *Alice Sit-by-the-Fire*; and all that may be said by the critic who would judge between them is that, although Sir Arthur Pinero was incontestably the greatest craftsman among recent English-writing dramatists, Sir James Barrie was nevertheless the best-beloved among them. The wonderful thing about Pinero's characters is their apparent independence of their creator; but the wonderful thing about Barrie's characters is the sense they give us at all moments that they are creatures of his amiable mind. If we adopt for a moment the familiar definition of art as "life seen through a temperament," we shall notice that Pinero emphasizes the life we are looking at and that Barrie emphasizes the temperament we are looking through. All that Pinero values is the relations of his characters with each other; but Barrie values more intensely the relations of his characters with himself. Barrie appears not only as the author of his plays but also as the chief of all the auditors; he sits beside us during the performance, and nudges us or takes our hand at this moment and at that to make sure that we share his own delight at the unfolding of his comedy. But while we are looking at a play by Pinero, we feel that the author has gone home to bed and forgotten all about it. Of course Barrie's habit of taking us into his confidence would annoy us as much as William Dean Howells was annoyed by Thackeray—unless we were fond of Barrie; but as it is, we feel it a personal favor that he should come to the performance with us and let us see it through his eyes. We like Barrie; and that is the sole and all-important reason why we like to see his plays. He may make a good play, like *The Admirable Crichton;* he may make a bad play, like *Little Mary;* but we enjoy them almost equally, because he enjoys them and has won us to enjoy what he enjoys. But in the case of an impersonal artist like Pinero, we lose interest unless he has fashioned for us an admirable work of art. He keeps himself out of his plays, because, as an artist, he does not regard himself as a factor in them. Pinero once told me in conversation that he personally loved the characters in *Mid-Channel* and *The Thunderbolt;* but he has carefully concealed from his public the fact that he loved them. To the average audience those twisted and exacerbated people seem unlovable; and the audience infers that, if anything, the author must have disapproved of them. But, on the other hand, Barrie parades his fondness for his characters; so that sometimes we feel his fondness more clearly than we see the characters, as in looking at Andrea del Sarto's paintings of Lucrezia we see his wife less vividly than we see the haze of sentiment with which he haloed her. In actual experience, all canons of art or lack of art fall down before the potency of personality. After years of technical analysis have convinced us that Burke writes great prose and Lamb writes imperfect prose, we find ourselves returning again and again to the *Dissertation on Roast Pig* (although we have no interest in the origin of cookery) and to *Mrs. Battle's Opinions on Whist* (although in these days of Contract Bridge we have lost interest in the simpler game), merely because Charles Lamb is stammering and chortling through them and—we love Charles Lamb. The appeal of personality is unreasonable, and therefore as irresistible as the love of woman; and criticism, in dealing with personal, subjective works, must therefore cast reason to the winds and estimate only the affection they evoke.

PROBLEMS OF THE PLAYWRIGHT

1

PLAUSIBILITY IN PLAYS

A PLAY can scarcely succeed in the theatre unless, during the two hours' traffic of the stage, the particular audience it appeals to believes the story that it tells; and no piece can be considered an important contribution to dramatic literature unless, upon a critical examination, it proves itself to have been conceived and conducted in accordance with the admitted laws of life. The first question that must be asked of any play that appeals for popularity is, "Is it plausible?": and the only and all-inclusive question that must be asked of any play that bids for more than passing commendation is the question, "Is it true?"

There are innumerable plays that pass the first test successfully and then falter before the second. So long as an audience is gathered in the theatre, it offers to the playwright the advantage of a crowd's credulity; and the actors, by sincerity of art, may charitably cover up a multitude of sins upon the author's part. It is only afterward, when the crowd has disintegrated into its individual components, and these individuals have escaped from the immediate influence of the actors' personal appeal, that, in many cases, it becomes possible to perceive, in retrospect, that the dramatist has trifled with the laws of life; and, as a gambling chance, the playwright is warranted in figuring that very few people will analyze his effort intellectually after they have left the theatre. Not ultimate truth, but only immediate plausibility, is all he needs to master if his ambition is set only on success.

But momentary plausibility is no antidote against the opium of time; and the world will consent to remember the plays of yesteryear only when they have told unfalteringly some truth of human life which was eminently worth the telling. For Truth is the talisman we all are seeking in that running toward the rainbow's foot

247

which is our little life upon this planet; and we are very busy in the running, and cannot pause for long to listen to tales that are not true. Even plausibility itself we are willing to discard, if the unplausible may symbolize for us some nearer revelation of reality. *The Blue Bird* is not a plausible representation of experience; yet it is eternally, immortally true. To tell the truth is a very difficult and delicate task, far heavier than moving mountains; and truth often may be told more lucidly by some dreamful alteration of the unrevelatory terms of actuality. Often we are voyaging in search of some treasure island buried beyond our actual horizon; and to see it we need the mystic aid of a mirage. The poetic drama is a telescope, through which we may look at truths so high that, without its aiding intervention, they would remain invisible; and for that imaginative searching of the skies there are cryptic astronomic principles which transcend the ordinary rules of criticism.

At present, in considering only the need for plausibility in the ordinary play, we must make a certain reservation in favor of the dramatist. We must permit him to begin with almost any premise, and we must allow him to end as he conveniently can; provided that, during the course of his narrative itself, he does not impose any undue tax on our credulity. Any work of art is a conventional patterning of certain selected details of nature; and the convention must be most apparent in the beginning of the work and in the end. For life itself is a continuous sequence of causation: it shows no absolute beginnings and no utter ends. Nothing in life is initiatory, nothing is conclusive. Not even birth is a beginning; for the shadowy and disconcerting science of heredity teaches us to regard it as only an incident in the progress of the race. Not even death is final; for no monumental tombstone can hold an influence quiescent, and our slightest actions vibrate in ever-widening circles through incalculable time. But a play, by the conditions of its representment, must have a beginning and an end. It derives its possibility of existence from an initial and a terminal falsification of the admitted facts of nature. Hence we must pardon the playwright for any necessary cutting of the Gordian knot of his structure at the close; and we may pardon him also for starting his narrative with a posture of circumstances that is scarcely plausible. The one thing that we may not pardon is a violation of plausibility during the progress of the action from the conventional starting-point to the conventional termination. We will grant him his own conditions at the outset, provided that he shall remain faithful to the legitimate requirements of those conditions until the time comes for him to empty the theatre and send us home. He may end his play with a wedding, and delude us with the amiable fiction that marriage is an end instead of a beginning, provided that he has led up to the marriage through a logical development of motives; and he may begin with a staggering impossibility, as Sophocles began in *Œdipus King* or Goldsmith began in *She Stoops to Conquer* (to mention two great plays as far apart as possible in mood), provided that thereafter, when we have granted the conditions precedent to the action, he shall rigorously tell the truth that is necessitated by those conventional conditions. In other words, it may be formulated as a practical rule that a playwright should gather whatever impossibilities may lie latent in his story into that section of the entire narrative that is conceived to have occurred before the play begins. We are willing to accept an antecedent unplausibility, because it is merely stated to us in conventional expository lines; but we refuse to accept a subsequent unplausibility, because we have to watch it being acted out before our very eyes upon the stage. A playwright may begin by asking us to concede (for the sake of the entertainment he is about to offer us) that two is equal to four; but he must afterward adhere logically to the inference that four is equal to eight and eight is equal to sixteen. If he subsequently tells us that four is equal to nine, we shall immediately revolt from the convention of credulity and reject his narrative as unbelievable.

INFIRMITY OF PURPOSE

MANY modern plays which set forth interesting subject-matter and contain several admirable scenes fail of their totality of artistic effect because of an apparent infirmity in the author's purpose. Unless the writer knows at every moment precisely what sort of effect he desires to produce, and can communicate by contagion a clear sense of this precision of purpose, he will muddle the auditor's mind in its endeavor to follow him. If, in the course of a single composition, he mixes up his types, his moods, his styles, in a discordant manner, he will disperse the attention of the auditor and perplex the latter's faculty for unperturbed enjoyment. It is true, of course, that the modern playwright need not always be actuated by a single aim—his play, perhaps, will be all the better if he is not—but there should always be apparent in his purpose what may be called a harmony of aims. But very few of the plays that get themselves produced are harmonious from the outset to the end. Nearly all of them obtrude some jarring note, some discord in the pattern. The reason for this may be undoubtedly referred to an infirmity in the author's faculty of attention on the business in hand. The hardest task on earth is to fix one's mind on anything and hold it fixed; and perhaps our playwrights should be pardoned, therefore, for a little wavering.

This infirmity of purpose may show itself in any of three ways: —first, in a mixture of types; second, in a mixture of moods; or third, in a mixture of styles. These three defects we may discuss in order.

A playwright should always know pretty definitely whether he means to write a farce, a comedy, a melodrama, or a tragedy. Furthermore, he should communicate his purpose early to the audience, and should cling to it throughout the traffic of the stage.

This assertion is not offered *a priori*, as an academic axiom; but it is derivable from a study of the practice of the surest artists. The entire tone of a dramatic composition must result from the author's sense of the type of task that he is dealing with; and unless this sense be definite, the tone will be disrupted into discords. It is, of course, possible, and desirable, to effect certain combinations of types in the course of a single composition; but the number of possible combinations is limited. It is, for instance, natural for farce to stiffen into melodrama, since in both of these types the plot controls the characters; but it is not natural for farce to mellow into emotion or deepen into tragedy. Comedy can quite naturally flower into the poetry of sentiment, but it cannot attain the thrill of melodrama without sacrificing the autonomy of its characters. Tragedy will not mix with farce, though it may accentuate itself with comedy; and it disrobes itself of all its sacred vestments when it descends to melodrama. As principles, these abstract statements (and other corollaries of them which we need not take the time to analyze) seem sufficiently self-evident; and yet the critic often finds them violated by our playwrights, and always to the detriment of the artistic fabric.

It is much more difficult to determine to what extent an author may successfully attempt a mixture of moods; for this problem unlike the problem of a mixture of types—is not based upon an abstract logic, but solely on the author's sense of the degree to which he may depend upon his audience to follow him. Since the normal audience has differed in different ages of the drama, we may best appreciate this problem if we look upon it in historical review.

The ancients very simply solved the problem of a mixture of moods by dodging it entirely. The Greeks were (at any chosen moment) a single-mooded people; and the Romans, who emulated them, were assiduous to imitate their singleness of mood. In the ancient drama we note always a sharp and clear distinction between the serious and the comic, with no admission of a possible commingling of the two. Any ancient play strikes at the very outset the note of that sole mood in which it is conceived, and thereafter concerns itself singly with the broadening and deeping of this invariable mood. If we are given the first few speeches of an Attic tragedy or a Roman comedy, we shall perceive at once what may be called the humour of the entire play. The ancients seem to have felt one way at one time and another at another; but the art that they have left us affords no indication that they allowed themselves to feel two different ways at once.

But this latter complexity of mood seems to have become the dominant and definitive feature of the medieval mind. The contrast may be observed at a glance if we compare the architecture of the Greeks with the architecture of the Goths. Any Greek temple exhibits the serene unfolding of a single mood; but any Gothic cathedral exhibits an antithetic unfolding of a dual mood, at the same time solemn and hilarious. Gargoyles grin at placid saints on the façades of Gothic churches; and sanctity looks back on blasphemy with no dismay. It was this sharp antithesis of mood that Calderon and Shakespeare, who were writing for auditors of medieval mind, strove to attain in the glorious age of Spanish, and the spacious age of English, drama. Even in a solemnly religious play, like *The Devotion of the Cross*, Calderon carries on the action with the aid of a *gracioso*, or clown; and the Elizabethan habit of commingling the funny and the grim is too familiar to require comment.

When, at last, in 1830 (owing to a curious concatenation of historic circumstances) the future destiny of the dramatic art was placed for the moment in the hands of Victor Hugo, this giant had before him, on the one hand, the example of Corneille and Racine, who had imitated the ancients in their singleness of mood, and, on the other hand, the example of Shakespeare, who had agreed with the medieval desire for a commingling of contrasted moods. In the *Preface to Cromwell*, Hugo cast his lot with Shakespeare; and thereafter, in his preachment and his practice, he pleaded for a representation of that vast and meaningful antithesis between the grotesque and the sublime which he regarded as the greatest mood of drama.

But the problem has become more delicate since the days of Victor Hugo. If the note of ancient life was singleness of mood, and the note of medieval life was a contrast of two moods, the note of our modern life has become an intricacy of many moods. Our existence is the most complex that has ever yet emerged in the history of mankind; and, quite naturally and indeed inevitably, our art (whose purpose is to represent our life) is more complex than that of any earlier age. We no longer write plays which exhibit either the gradual intensification of a single mood or a sharp and vivid contrast of two antithetic moods: our purpose is, rather, to exhibit a multiplicity of moods, through the medium of an artistry that is more intricate than that of any former period.

This imposes on our modern playwrights an extraordinary task of orchestration. They may deal with any number and variety of moods, provided that they can modulate them into harmony: but the very freedom of this orchestration makes it the more difficult for them to avoid disrupting discords.

What moods will mix harmoniously and what will not is a question that each playwright must determine for himself. Whether or not his play will strike a discord must depend upon the temper of his audience; and he must therefore be very sure, before attempting an airy shift from one mood to another, that his audience will follow him without effort. Our storehouses are packed with the scenery of plays which have failed merely because of an impossible or injudicious mixture of moods. In this regard, therefore, it behooves our playwrights to attack their tasks with an artistic purpose that shall remain unfalteringly firm.

A more obvious error is a mixture of styles during the course of a single composition. Having hit a certain key of writing at the outset of his dialogue, the author should maintain this to the end. An instance of the violation of this principle which will be readily remembered occurred in the course of James Forbes's interesting study of *The Chorus Lady*. The first two acts of that diverting drama were written in a delectable slang; but the curtain-fall of the third act (at which the innocent heroine was discovered at midnight in the villain's rooms) was written in the conventional rhetoric of melodrama. Slang and rhetoric will not associate on friendly terms; and a play that is written in two styles will not produce upon the auditor an impression of happiness and peace. Stevenson, in several letters written during the composition of *The Beach of Falesá*, has commented on the difficulty of clinging to a certain tone of style and never writing off the key; and this difficulty may be regarded as one of the surest tests of a playwright's firmness of purpose.

III

WHERE TO BEGIN A PLAY

I F WE look at a procession in the street, we can see easily, at any
moment, only three blocks of it, though we may remember
what has gone before and may imagine what is to come after.
And if we were commissioned to take one photograph, and
only one, of the parade, we should have to select that single brief
period of its passage which was at the same time most interesting
in itself, most reminiscent of all that had preceded, and most suggestive of all that was to follow.

Any story of human life that is worth telling in a novel or a
play must concern itself with a procession of events that in reality
is limitless; but the novelist, restricted to a few hundred pages, or
the dramatist, restricted still more rigidly to the two or three
hours' traffic of the stage, can exhibit only a brief and bounded
picture of the eternal sequence of causation and result. To state
the problem more simply,—a novel or a play must assume a beginning and an end; but life itself knows neither. Any actual event
is, in the inspired phrase of Whitman, "an acme of things accomplished and an encloser of things to be": it is at once the result of
innumerable antecedent causes and the motive of innumerable subsequent results: and to dream our way backward or forward over
the procession of events of which it is a momentary incident must
lead us soon to lose our minds in mystery, before the dawn or later
than the dusk of imaginable time. With this eternal panorama of
experience, our concrete art can cope only by halting the procession at some particularly interesting moment and catching a sudden picture that shall look a little beyond, in both directions, the
single incident on which the camera is focused.

Just as different pictures of the same procession in the street may
be chosen by photographers who snap their cameras at different
moments, so various stories might be selected from the same pro-

254

cession of events by novelists or playwrights who should pick out different moments to begin and end their narratives. Any story, to attract and to enthrall attention, must exhibit the crisis, or climax, of a series of events; but the individual artist is left at liberty to determine how far before this crisis he shall set the initiation of his narrative and how far beyond it he shall set the end. If he is interested mainly in causes, he will choose to depict in detail the events that lead up to his climax; and if he is interested mainly in effects, he will prefer to devote the major share of his attention to those subsequent events that are occasioned by his crisis. Thus we discover in practice two types of narratives,—in one of which the main events look forward and are interesting chiefly as causes, and in the other of which the main events look backward and are interesting chiefly as results.

We may select for purposes of illustration the subject-matter of *The Scarlet Letter*. The crisis, or climax, of this imaginary train of incidents is the adultery of Hester Prynne and Arthur Dimmesdale. Hawthorne has chosen to start his story at a moment subsequent to the occurrence of this crisis and to devote his attention entirely to a study of the after-effects of the committed sin on the souls of the three characters concerned; but it is conceivable that another novelist—George Eliot, for instance—might have begun the story many years before and might have chosen to deal mainly with the causes that culminated in the crisis that Hawthorne has assumed as a condition precedent to his narrative. Thus we see that two stories wholly different in plot might be derived from the same procession of events, according as the novelist should choose to begin his narrative late or early in the sequence of causation.

Undoubtedly—in the single instance we have glanced at—Hawthorne began his narrative after the crisis because *The Scarlet Letter* was his first novel and he had been writing short-stories for over twenty years. Naturally enough, he constructed this novel as if it were a short-story. The writer of short-stories is so strictly limited to economy of means that he must deal mainly with results and must ask the reader to assume the antecedent causes; but the novelist, with his ampler scope of narrative, may deal with causes in detail and may presume in hasty summary the subsequent results. The handling of the story of *The Scarlet Letter* which we have assigned theoretically to George Eliot is more typical of the method of the novelist than the short-story structure which was imposed upon the subject-matter by the man who gave the story to the world.

In different periods of its development, the drama has oscillated between these two extremes of treatment, and has approached either the strictness of structure that is characteristic of the short-story or the more easy amplitude of narrative that is customary in the novel. In certain periods it has concerned itself mainly with causes, and in others chiefly with results.

The structure of Greek tragedy was singularly similar to the structure of the modern short-story. There are many obvious reasons for this analogy. In the first place, the physical conditions of the Greek theatre made it most convenient for the playwright to restrict his exhibition to a single place and to confine his action within a single revolution of the sun; and in the second place, the fact that the Greek playwright dealt only with traditional materials permitted him to presuppose, on the part of his audience, a knowledge of his entire story that should warrant him in assuming any number of incidents as having happened in imagination before the play began. Thus, at the performance of *Œdipus King*, the audience merely waited breathless while the hero discovered that appalling inheritance of the accumulated past, of which the audience was thoroughly aware before the play began. The tragedy dealt wholly with results, and not at all with causes.

The other extreme of structure is exhibited in the Elizabethan drama. In studying the plays of Shakespeare, we should remember always that nearly all of them were dramatized novels and that the conventions of the Elizabethan theatre encouraged what we now call a "novelistic" treatment of stories on the stage. Although it was only with apparent difficulty that the Greek playwright could alter the time or place of his action, the Elizabethan playwright could denote a lapse of years, or a shift of scene from one country to another, by the simple expedient of emptying his stage and bringing other actors on to state the new conditions. Using the term "act" with its modern technical meaning, it may be said that a Greek tragedy was constructed in a single act; but a typical Elizabethan play—like *Antony and Cleopatra*—was not conceived in acts, but in an ample and uncounted sequence of half a hundred "scenes." Hence, it is not surprising that Shakespeare, like a nineteenth-century novelist, devoted more of his attention to the development of causes leading up to his crisis than to the analysis of subsequent results.

But the modern drama, reduced by its investiture of scenery to the arrangement of a story in not more than three or four distinct pigeon-holes of time and place, has returned more nearly to the Greek method of exhibiting a story in a single act than to the Elizabethan method of stretching a story out through fifty scenes. The exigencies of the modern stage apparently demand that the dramatist shall start his story at a time as late as possible in his procession of events and shall assume the necessary antecedent incidents in passages of backward-looking exposition. Thus, Ibsen's *Ghosts*, which—from the technical standpoint—is one of the very greatest of modern plays, is constructed according to the method of Sophocles instead of the method of Shakespeare. The entire narrative that is recounted covers nearly thirty years; and yet the actual experience that is exhibited is constricted within the compass of a few hours. And a month after we have seen the play, we remember with equal vividness those events which were disclosed upon the stage and those other events which were merely narrated in passages of retrospective exposition.

Since the average audience in any period expects the dramaturgic method to which it is habituated, it follows that the playwright looking for success should begin his story late or early in his general procession of events, according to the fashion of his time. At present it is undeniably the custom of the most highly accredited playwrights to catch a story at its climax and to build a play more out of the results than out of the causes of the crisis of the narrative. For instance,—Aubrey Tanqueray decides to marry Paula; and Pinero's play exhibits not the causes leading up to this decision but the tragic series of events resultant from it.

From these general considerations it should be evident that a playwright, in any period, may spoil a good story by beginning his play at the wrong moment and exhibiting an ill-selected section of his entire drift of incident. Ibsen—for example—spoiled the story of *Rosmersholm* by beginning his play at a point too far along in the general procession of events; and many other plays have been spoiled by playwrights who have started their stories too far before the crisis of the narrative.

IV

CONTINUITY OF STRUCTURE

O NE OF the most difficult problems of the modern dramatist is to map out what may be called the "time-scheme"
of his play. In two hours and a half of actual acting
time, he must exhibit an imaginary series of events that
in reality would occupy several hours or days, or even, in some
cases, many months or years; and, in presenting these events, he
must contrive to suggest the impression of an uninterrupted continuity of narrative. He is aided in this task by two traditions of
the drama. The first of these is the immemorial convention which
allows him to assume a compression of time during the progress
of an act; and the second is the more modern convention which
permits him to summarize very briefly whatever may have happened in an *entr'acte*. But an injudicious application of these two
conventions may lead to an apparent improbability that will violate the psychologic truth of the entire narrative; and it is therefore necessary that the modern dramatist should account very
carefully for the lapse of time that is imagined between the outset
of his drama and the end.

This careful accounting of time was not demanded in the drama
of any period before the present. The authors of Greek tragedy,
for instance, were not obliged to plan their plays with an eye upon
the clock. Greek tragedy exhibited merely the accumulated effects
of an antecedent series of causes stretching back through many
years; and, expounding their stories retrospectively, it was not
difficult for the Attic authors to confine the time-scheme of their
tragedies to a single revolution of the sun. A Greek play was presented without intermission and occupied about two hours of
actual acting time; but the audience was quite willing that these
actual two hours should be regarded as representative of twenty
hours. In other words, the Greek audience accepted the conven-

tion of a condensation of time in the ratio of ten to one. Early in the course of *Œdipus King*, a certain shepherd is sent for, and he appears upon the scene not more than half an hour afterward, although in actuality he could scarcely have been found in less than half a day; but this compression of time, in a narrative that was logically continuous, did not insult the imagination of the ancient audience.

The Elizabethan drama did not even attempt to restrict itself to a ten to one ratio in dealing with the element of time. In fact, the majority of the extant Elizabethan plays exhibit no conscious time-scheme whatsoever. The compositions of this period were probably acted without any intermission; and they were constructed, not in a limited number of acts, but in an unlimited number of scenes. In consequence, it would be exceedingly difficult to compute the precise number of days that are assumed to have elapsed between the first scene and the last of *Hamlet* or *As You Like It*, for example. The truth is that such a computation never occurred to the winging mind of Shakespeare. It was not at all necessary for him to work out a time-scheme of Hamlet's trip to England or to estimate the exact duration of Rosalind's wanderings in the Forest of Arden. The stage for which he built his dramas was incapable of keeping a strict account of either place or time.

The time-scheme of the drama became a little more restricted in the plays of Molière, and of his many imitators throughout the eighteenth century; but, even in this period, scarcely any account was taken of the time required for the actions of the leading characters off the stage. Throughout the history of the drama, the handling of the category of time has been inextricably intertangled with the handling of the category of place. In the eighteenth century, a room was represented by a back-drop and wings; and an actor left the room by walking through the walls. In such a play as *The Rivals*, a character walked bodily out of the story when he left the stage, and he did not again enter into the narrative until he was once more needed on the scene. What he had been doing in the meantime, and how many hours were required for this activity beyond the limits of the stage, were not accounted for in the subsequent spectacle of narrative. The play concerned itself solely with those events that happened to the eye within the limited compass of the two hours' traffic of the stage.

But the modern drama, with its precise insistence upon localization in place, assumes an equally precise insistence upon localization in time. Whenever an actor makes an exit from a modern box-set, the audience demands to know whether he is going into an adjacent room or quitting the house; and this demand requires an explanation of how he occupies himself throughout the period that intervenes before his reappearance on the scene. Thus, the physical conditions of the modern theatre impose upon the playwright a new unity of time by demanding an accounting of the actions of his leading characters not only on, but also off, the stage.

V

RHYTHM AND TEMPO

THERE is one phase of the dramatic art which has rarely been discussed by critics and is scarcely ever noticed by the average theatre-goer. Everybody knows that the drama is both a visual and an auditory art,—that, by virtue of its appeal to the eye, it offers many analogies to the art of painting, and that, by virtue of its appeal to the ear through its use of spoken words, it exhibits innumerable analogies to the art of literature. But comparatively few people have ever paused to realize that the drama is also a temporal art, owing much of its appeal to its manner of punctuating passages of time, and that, by virtue of this fact, it discloses an analogy to the art of music. The merit of many dramatic scenes is resident in the sheer rhythm of their presentation and the deft manipulation of this rhythm in the tempo of the acting.

The appeal of rhythm to the human sensibilities is the very basis of the arts of poetry and music. The periodical repetition of certain beats, unassisted by any more intelligible method of expression, may stimulate the listener to an eager apprehension of emotion. To prove this, it is only necessary to cite, for the purpose of experiment, two very well-known lines of poetry. The first line is—

> When the hounds of spring are on winter's traces

And the other line is—

> The long day wanes: the slow moon climbs: the deep

In each of these citations, I have purposely quoted only a single line, leaving the sense unfinished; for the experiment I am about to propose deals only with the rhythm of the lines and has no reference to their intelligible content. Let me now ask the reader

261

to repeat the first line to himself a hundred times, and, after an appreciable interval, to submit himself to a similar insistence from the second line. If his mind have any ear at all, the first experiment will induce a noticeable quickening of his pulses and the second experiment will retard his pulse-beats to a less than normal tempo. In the first case, his mind will be keyed up to the apprehension of dashing and alert emotions, and, in the second, it will be attuned to the reception of emotions that are somnolent and solemn.

The psychology of this experiment sits very near the center of the art of writing; but it may, perhaps, be illustrated more emphatically by the art of music. Every musical composer indicates not only the notes he wishes to be played but also the tempo in which he wants them to be rendered, knowing that the emotional message of his phrases may be altered utterly by a faulty retarding or acceleration of the rhythm that he has imagined. A familiar experiment is to play *Nearer, My God, to Thee* in rag-time, and thus to rob the melody of all its somber connotation. The opening bars of the *Moonlight Sonata* may be made ridiculous by playing them very rapidly, and *Anitra's Dance* may be robbed of all its gaiety by playing it very slowly: and these changes of appeal may be effected without the alteration of a single note.

The acted drama, since it is doomed to present a pattern of details in time, is subject to the same psychologic law which haunts these other temporal arts of poetry and music. Certain scenes can be properly effective only if they are played in very rapid tempo, and certain other passages can easily be ruined by an ill-advised acceleration of the acting. The consideration of this fact results in certain rules which must be followed by the playwright and the stage-director.

The true artist in either of these crafts senses these rules intuitively and abides by them subconsciously; and it is only when the rules of rhythm are violated that the observer becomes at all aware of the reality of their subsistence. A dramatic passage often requires a series of very subtle modulations in the rhythm of its presentation; and if it be enacted crudely, with invariable tempo, the observer will receive an impression of indefinite distress, like that which comes of hearing a Neapolitan song played solely with the feet upon a pianola.

Only the most obvious rules of rhythm for the drama may be

set down in uncompromising print, like the axioms of Euclid. For instance, it is obvious that most melodramas should be played very rapidly, in order to stimulate excitement and also to rob the audience of any opportunity to question the plausibility of the situations; and it is equally obvious, upon the other hand, that most tragic scenes should be enacted slowly, in order to give the audience time to accumulate a sense of the imminence of doom before the fateful lines are spoken. The majority of farces demand a very rapid rendering, and the acceleration of the acting needs to be increased in proportion as the farcical material treads closer on the heels of the ridiculous; but a comedy that depends for its effect on the subtle revelation of character through humorous dialogue must usually be played with frequent pauses, in order to give the audience time to develop thoughtful laughter. Such elementary principles as these may be formulated and set down as axioms; but, just as poetry and music attain their best effects by subtle variations in rhythm and modulations of tempo, so also the finest effects in the theatre are not infrequently achieved by momentary modifications of an expected time-scheme in the acting.

For the manipulation of such effects as these, the stage-director is finally responsible. This functionary has often been compared with the leader of an orchestra. He establishes the tempo in which a composition shall be rendered, and may often make or mar it by the mere direction of its rhythm. But the dominance of the stage-director does not relieve the playwright of responsibility in this regard. An orchestral composer who should hand a score to his conductor without any indication of the tempo of his leading passages would be deemed an inefficient artist; and any playwright who plans an act without establishing its rhythm in advance sets himself similarly in the class of incomplete composers. In the plotting of his business and in the writing of his lines, he should make it easy for his stage-director to arrange the rapidity or sluggishness of rhythm that is required to reinforce the emotional content of his scene. To ask his actors to sit still at a moment when the action should be hurried, to require them to speak in anapests while they are listening in fear to the tardy ticking of a clock,—these are errors which impose upon the stage-director a task which is unfortunately difficult.

This matter should be studied very carefully by all aspirants to the art of dramaturgy. A simple exercise may be suggested for the benefit of readers who desire ultimately to write plays or to direct them. Let them take a scene from *Hamlet* and another from *The Thunderbolt* and ask themselves precisely how rapidly or slowly these passages should be played in order to achieve their best effect upon the stage. Let them, if necessary, experiment with a metronome until they get the rhythm right. Subsequently, in attending the performances of successful current plays, these studious spectators will be better enabled to appreciate to what a great extent their appeal has been enhanced by a deft manipulation of the rhythm of their presentation.

VI

BUILDING A PLAY BACKWARD

AUTHOR'S NOTE.—The first section of the present chapter was originally published in THE BOOKMAN for February, 1914. It was this
article which suggested to Mr. Elmer Rice the pattern for his celebrated play, *On Trial*,—a fact which Mr. Rice graciously acknowledged
in the public press at the time when his play was produced. The second
section of the present chapter was written immediately after the popular triumph of *On Trial*. The third section was appended twenty-four
years later.

I

JOHN GALSWORTHY's novel, *The Dark Flower*—which is a great
work of art—tells three distinct love-stories, that happen to
the same hero at different periods of his career. In order to
avoid monotony, the author has employed a different chronological pattern for each of the three sections of his novel. In telling the first story, he begins at the beginning; in telling the second
story, he begins approximately at the middle; and in telling the
third story, he begins at the very end.

It is obvious that, so long as the novelist exhibits his events in
a pattern that reveals their logical relation, it is not at all necessary
that he should present them in chronological succession. In the
first chapter of *Pendennis*, the hero is seventeen years old; the
second chapter narrates the marriage of his parents, and his own
birth and boyhood; and at the outset of the third chapter, he is
only sixteen years of age. Stories may be told backward through
time as well as forward. Thackeray often begins a chapter with
an event that happened one day and ends it with an event that
happened several days before,—working his way backward from
effects to causes, instead of forward from causes to effects.

In reviewing any passage of our own experience, we are more
likely to think backward from the last event than forward from

265

the first. Retrogression in time is, therefore, a natural device of narrative; and it is not at all surprising to find it thoroughly established as a convention of the novel. What *is* surprising, on the other hand, is the fact that it has not yet been established as a convention of the drama.

I know of no play in which events have been exhibited in a pattern of reverted time. Of course, a present event is frequently employed as the exciting cause of a conversation which expounds some previous event; and, in such instances, the discovery of what has happened in the past is often more important to the audience than the observation of what is happening in the present. But, in these expository passages, the past events are merely talked about and never actually acted on the stage. In *Romance*, by Edward Sheldon, a prologue in the present is followed by a three-act play which narrates events that happened over forty years before; but, in the structure of the play itself, there is no retrogression in time. More interesting, from our present point of view, is the device of Sir Arthur Pinero in turning back the clock at the outset of the third act of *The Thunderbolt*. At the end of the second act, in the house of Thaddeus Mortimore, a servant arrives with a message from his brother James. The third act, in the house of James Mortimore, overlaps the second act in time; and an entire scene is acted out before the servant is instructed to set out with the message for Thaddeus. This simple expedient, which is used in nearly every novel, seemed exceedingly surprising in the drama; but there can be no question that, in *The Thunderbolt*, its employment was both useful and successful.

Might it not be interesting to go a step further and build an entire drama backward,—to construct a three-act play, for instance, in which the first act should happen in the autumn, the second act in the preceding summer, and the third act in the previous spring? Let us imagine a tragedy, for instance, in which, with no preliminary exposition, a murder or a suicide is acted out in the initial act. This would naturally awaken in the audience a desire to understand the motives which had culminated in the crime. Then, in the second act, we could exhibit the crucial event which had made the murder or the suicide inevitable. Again, the audience would be stimulated to think backward from effects to causes and to wonder what had brought this crucial event about. Lastly, in the third act, several previous events could be displayed,

which would finally clear up the mystery by expounding the initiation of the narrative.

Or, to invent an example in the mood of comedy, let us imagine
a first act which should exhibit the hopelessly unhappy home life
of a kindly and reasonable man who is married to a peevish and
unreasonable woman. The heroine is pretty, let us say, and there
are some seeds of poetry in her nature that flower every now and
then to momentary loveliness. But, like many people who are not
incapable of poetry, she abandons herself utterly to the emotion
of the moment; and whenever this emotion is not pleasant, she
makes life miserable for anybody who is near her. Because she is
pretty, she has always been spoiled. She is selfish, she is jealous,
she is vain; and whenever these ignoble motives are in any slight
degree assailed, she breaks out into a violent fit of temper. Just
now, in response to an insistent question, her husband has told her
that she looks better in pink than in blue. The heroine, whose
instinct is antagonistic, at once prefers blue; she does not see why
her husband, if he loves her—he *said* he loved her—should not
admit that she would look well in anything; and she proceeds to
kick the furniture. The husband seeks refuge in reading *The
Wind in the Willows*—whereupon she knocks the book out of
his hand. Very gently he remarks: "You didn't seem like this,
dear, before we were married." And on that backward-looking
line the curtain falls.

The second act shows them in their courtship, two years before.
The romance of falling in love has brought out all the lyric loveliness that is latent in the complex nature of the heroine. Her
prospective husband sees her at her best, and only at her best. Her
family could tell him that she is hard to live with; but—glad
enough to get her married—they refrain from doing so. Besides,
her brother is a gentleman. The hero is his friend: but what can
a decent fellow do in such a dilemma? The heroine seems lovable
indeed, when she graciously accepts a large bouquet of orchids,
and reads aloud by golden lamp-light the forlorn and lovely little
lyrics of Christina Rossetti. The hero proposes marriage: is accepted: and the curtain falls.—Would not this little comedy gain
greatly in ironic emphasis by being acted backward in time instead
of forward? The question, "What happened before?", is fully as
suspensive as the question, "What happens next?": and, in this
instance, it is by far the more important question of the two.

Though novels are frequently narrated in a pattern of reverted time, this proposal to build a play backward may seem so revolutionary that most technicians would dismiss it as impossible. But, why? The answer, of course, is obvious; but I am not at all sure that it is final. To follow a narrative forward, from cause to effect, requires a synthetic exercise of mind; and to follow it backward, from effect to cause, requires an analytic exercise. Of these two activities of mind, the analytic demands a greater alertness of intelligence, and a greater fixity of attention, than the synthetic. The collective mind of a helter-skelter theatre audience is less alert and less attentive than the individual mind of a cultivated reader. Furthermore, the reader of a novel, if his mind becomes muddled by the juggling of chronology, may always suspend his reading to turn back a dozen or a hundred pages and reread some finger-pointing passage whose significance he has forgotten; whereas the auditors of a play can never halt the performance to reinform themselves of some point that they have missed. Also, the theatre-going public abhors novelty, and never reads the program. These arguments—and many more—are so familiar that they need not be repeated in detail. Yet something may now be said upon the other side.

To students of the history of the drama, one of the most important phenomena of the last hundred years has been the very rapid development that has taken place, from decade to decade, in the intelligence of the theatre-going public. The average audience is at present more alert and more attentive than ever before in the history of the theatre. This point is evidenced by the fact that, throughout the last century, the technique of the prevailing type of drama has grown progressively less synthetic and more analytic. The prevailing pattern of the drama a century ago was the pattern that was worked out by Eugène Scribe for the so-called "well-made play." Scribe devoted his first act to a very thorough exposition, and only at the curtain-fall introduced an element of forward-looking action. Then, at the outset of the second act, he started his narrative in motion; and thereafter he followed it forward through time, to the climax and the close. He never asked his audience to think backward. He worked entirely from causes to effects, and centered his suspense in the obvious question, "What will happen next?"

Contrast this utterly synthetic pattern—a formula for putting

two and two together, instead of a formula for taking four apart—
with the intricately analytic pattern that was developed, forty
years later, by Henrik Ibsen. Ibsen caught his story very late in
its career, and revealed the antecedent incidents in little gleams
of backward-looking dialogue. His method has often been compared with that of Sophocles; but there is this essential difference,
—that, whereas the Athenian audience always knew the story in
advance and therefore did not need an exposition, Ibsen was required to expound a series of antecedent circumstances at the same
time that he was developing his catastrophe. For, instead of com-
pacting his exposition into the first act—according to the formula
of Scribe—he revealed it, little by little, throughout the progress
of the play. In the first act, he expounded only so much as the
audience needed to know in order to understand the second; in
this, in turn, he expounded such further antecedent incidents as
were necessary to an appreciation of the third act; and so on, to
the end of the play. In *Rosmersholm*, for instance, he was still
expounding in the very last moments of the final act.

This method requires the auditor to think backward, and therefore presupposes a more intelligent audience than the straightforward formula of Scribe. But, very recently, that masterly technician, Henry Bernstein, has gone a step further in forcing the audience to observe a story in retrospectory review. Instead of scattering his expository passages throughout the play, as Ibsen did,
M. Bernstein now compacts them into a single act; but, with a
startling overturning of the formula of Scribe, he exhibits this act
last instead of first,—setting it forth as an epilogue, instead of as
a prologue, to the action.

This new formula was first exemplified by M. Bernstein in
L'Assaut, which was acted in America under the title of *The Attack*. A noted politician who is running for office is accused of
having committed a crime many years before. Either he is innocent or he is guilty: and this dilemma is set before us in the first
act. The second act develops the presumption that he is innocent,
until his innocence is publicly established by process of law. This
is the climax of the play. Then, his innocence being now beyond
question, the hero confesses to the heroine that he was actually
guilty. This is the end of the second act. What remains to be
done? We naturally demand an explanation of the circumstances
which, so many years before, had led this admirable hero to com-

mit that reprehensible crime. In his third and last act, M. Bernstein expounds the facts at length and in detail. Now we know: and the play is over. This same formula is employed much more artfully in *The Secret*, a later and greater work, which is worthy of examination in detail.

Considered as a technical achievement, *The Secret* is perhaps the most wonderful of all the plays of Henry Bernstein. The work of this author is so well known in America that it is scarcely necessary to state that his plays are nothing more than *tours de force*. His plots are marvelously constructed, his characters are true to life, his dialogue is pithy and compact; and yet we always feel by instinct that he is not a great dramatist. The reason for this feeling is that he never heightens our interest in life or adds to our understanding of it. He lacks the God-given ability to make us care about his characters. We see them suffer, but we do not take them to our hearts and feel their sufferings as our own. His work is too objective, too abstract, to appeal to us as human. But, considered solely as a craftsman, he is the most ingenious artist in the drama at the present time.

In *The Secret*, M. Bernstein, for a full half of his play, makes us think [or, rather *allows* us to think] that his heroine is one sort of person; and then turns about, in the second half of the second act, and proves to us that she is a totally different sort of person. Amazed at the contradiction of the two opinions of her character which we have held successively, we find ourselves still groping for an explanation of this personal enigma. This explanation is afforded in the third and final act. Here again, as in *The Attack*, M. Bernstein has deferred his exposition till the end of the play, instead of giving it at the beginning. Thereby he has created what may be called an analytical suspense,—a suspense of asking not, "What happens next?", but, "Why did these things happen?" This is perhaps the nearest approach to building a play backward which has ever yet been made in the theatre of the world.

It will be noted also that M. Bernstein has brushed aside one of the most commonly accepted dogmas of the theatre,—the dogma that a dramatist must never keep a secret from his audience. The entire purpose of his pattern is to deceive his auditors for half the play, and then to use the other half to undeceive them. A considerable section of his second act runs parallel to the third act of *Othello*, with the heroine playing the part of Iago; but as yet we have seen no reason to suspect that she is not a generous and honest woman. It is as if Shakespeare, up to the middle of his third act, had allowed us to see Iago only as he appeared to the eyes of his general—"This fellow's of exceeding honesty,"—and had not allowed us to perceive the error until it became evident to Othello himself.

If this pattern had been proposed in advance to any jury of dramatic critics [including the present writer], it would have been rejected as unfeasible, because of the traditional belief that no audience will submit to the necessity of altering its entire conception of a character in the middle of a play. Yet M. Bernstein deliberately chose this pattern, in defiance of tradition; and his play has pleased the public, in both Paris and New York. Here, again, we encounter a practical evidence of the vanity of dogma, and an indication that no principle can ever be considered final in dramatic criticism.

But, at present, the most important point for us to notice is that M. Bernstein has turned the formula of Scribe completely upside down, and has chosen to end his drama at the point where Scribe would have begun it.

Shall the development of backward-looking narrative stop with M. Bernstein? If not, the only possible next step will be to act out events upon the stage in an order that reverses that in which they are presumed to have occurred. The actual action of *The Attack* and *The Secret* is straightforward in chronology; and it is only in his psychological effect upon the audience that M. Bernstein appears to build his plays backward. Regarding that next step, which now seems so revolutionary, the critic can only wonder if some very clever playwright will attempt it in the future.

There are certain stories which are seen most naturally if we follow them forward from causes to effects; but there are certain other stories which can be understood most truly only if we follow them backward from effects to causes. As a matter of experiment, it would be extremely interesting if some playwright should soon set before us a story of this type in the perspective of reverted time.

II

At the very outset of the autumn season of 1914, a great success was achieved by a youth of twenty-one whose name had never before been heard of in the theatre. Like Lord Byron, this new playwright awoke one morning to discover that he had grown famous overnight. His name—which is familiar now—is Elmer Rice; and the title of his play—which crowded the theatre every night for many months—is *On Trial*.

The most remarkable feature of the success of *On Trial* was that it was emphatically a success of art for art's sake. The piece has been accurately described by the author as "an experiment in dramatic technique"; and its instantaneous and huge success afforded a hitherto unprecedented indication that our public had grown sufficiently interested in the technique of the drama to welcome plays whose strongest bid for favor is their technical efficiency. Until this indication of a turning of the tide in favor of stagecraft for the sake of stagecraft, it had been generally agreed among observers of our current drama that popular success depended more on subject-matter than on technical dexterity.

But the subject-matter of *On Trial* is scarcely interesting in itself. The play has no theme; and the story that it tells is not sentimental or pretty or timely or even novel. A profligate induces an inexperienced young girl to spend a night with him at a road-house by promising to wed her on the morrow. The next morning the girl's father appears at the road-house, accompanied by a woman who is already married to the profligate. The villain runs away, and the girl is taken home by her father. Shortly afterward, her father dies; and some years later the girl meets and marries an honorable man. A daughter is born to them, and they develop a very happy home. It appears that the heroine was justified in concealing from her husband the misfortune that had befallen her before she met him. But the husband meets the profligate in the business world, is befriended by him, and even borrows money from him. This money he repays in cash; but the profligate takes advantage of the accidental renewal of acquaintance with the heroine to force her to yield to him again, under threat of allowing the past iniquity to be exposed. The husband, discovering the recent intrigue, seeks out the profligate and shoots him dead. A few moments before the shooting, the private secretary of the profligate has stolen from the latter's safe the cash that had just been paid him by the murderer; and it therefore appears to the police that robbery was the motive for the murder. The husband seizes on this circumstantial evidence to shield his wife and child from scandal. He confesses himself guilty of murder for the sake of robbery, and asks only to be sent to the electric chair. But the court insists on assigning counsel to defend him; and the defendant's lawyer, by calling the wronged wife to the stand, makes clear the real motive for the shooting. The private secretary of the dead man is also called as a witness; and when the defendant's counsel succeeds in forcing him to confess that it was he who had rifled the safe and that this robbery had had no connection with the murder, the jury agree at once in acquitting the defendant.

It will be noticed that this story is entirely traditional. At no moment does it exhibit any note of novelty. It is sound enough, indeed, to seem worthy of retelling; but no one can deny that it is trite. The characters concerned in the story are also true enough to life to warrant their revisiting the glimpses of the footlights; but they are neither original nor likable nor particularly interesting. Why should the public flock to the theatre to meet a man who leads a girl astray, or another man who shoots him dead? Why should the public still shed tears over a wronged wife, and a child who remains pathetically unaware of a scandal that has destroyed the happiness of her parents?

From questions such as these, it should become apparent that Mr. Rice was dealing with a story that by no means contained, within itself, the elements of sure success. Did he succeed, then, because of any trick of writing in his dialogue? The answer is, emphatically, no. The best that can be said of the writing of *On Trial* is that it is direct and simple and concise; but the dialogue is utterly devoid of literary charm and of that human richness which is akin to humor. Hundreds of plays which have been obviously better written have failed at once, in recent years, upon our stage. Why, then, did *On Trial* capture the public by assault?

The reason is that Mr. Rice utilized the novel device of building his story backward. This device was interesting in itself, because it had never been employed before on the American stage; and Mr. Rice's employment of it was made doubly interesting by the fact that he revealed, in this experiment, a technical efficiency that was truly astonishing in the first work of an author with no previous experience of the stage. Instead of inventing a story and then deciding how to tell it, this adventurous young playwright started out with an idea of how to tell a story in a novel way and then invented a story that would lend itself to this predetermined technical experiment.

We have observed already that the story of *On Trial* is rather commonplace; but Mr. Rice made it seem, in Browning's phrase, both "strange and new" by revealing it from the end to the beginning, instead of from the beginning to the end. Instead of starting out with motives and developing them to their ultimate expression in facts, he started out with the accomplished facts and then delved backward to reveal the motives which had instigated them.

In the first act of *On Trial* we see the murder committed on the stage. In the second act we see enacted an incident two hours before the murder which makes us aware of the exciting cause of the subsequent event that we have previously witnessed. But it is not until the third act, which reveals in action an event that happened thirteen years before, that we are permitted to discover and to comprehend the motives which ultimately culminated in the shooting that we saw in the initial act. By telling his story backward, from effect to cause, the author has added an element of theatrical suspense to a narrative which otherwise might have been dismissed by the public as an oft-repeated tale.

It must not be inferred from the success of Mr. Rice's experiment that there is, inherently, any greater virtue in building a play backward than in following the chronological sequence which has always heretofore been traditional in the drama. The choice of method must depend on the type of story that the playwright has to tell. It remains as true to-day as ever that the great majority of dramatic stories may be set forth most effectively if they are built up, synthetically, from causes to effects. It is only a particular type of narrative—and stories of this type will always remain in the minority—that can be set forth most effectively if they are analyzed from effects to causes. This statement must be emphasized, lest the public should be threatened with a rush of plays whose only claim to interest should be that they aim to illustrate the Biblical maxim that "the last shall be first and the first shall be last." The famous experiment of Columbus with the egg was bad for the egg: there are many objects in the universe that are not meant to stand on end.

III

It was not till nineteen years had passed since the advent of *On Trial* that the backward-building formula was used successfully upon the New York stage to set forth a serious drama in which the characters were emphatically more important than the plot. In the autumn of 1933, *Merrily We Roll Along*, by George S. Kaufman and Moss Hart, excited an unusual degree of public interest. The hero, a successful playwright celebrated for his clever cynicism, was introduced at the height of his career, surrounded by a group of worthless sycophants who wasted their days in mutual adulation; and the interest of the audience, disgusted by the spectacle of this *demi-monde* of art, was immediately focused in the question, "How did they get that way?" Thereafter, the play moved backward through time and showed the hero and his friends at several successive crises of their careers, in each of which they had sacrificed idealism and sincerity for the sake of self-advancement on the road to notoriety. The final scene exhibited the hero at the age of twenty-one delivering the valedictory address at his college commencement, flushed with youthful ideality and looking forward hopefully to a noble future. There could be no question that the dramatic irony of this impressive composition was increased immeasurably by the device of unfolding its development in a pattern of reverted time.

VII

THE POINT OF VIEW

THE PRESENT period of the drama is one that lends itself peculiarly to technical adventure. The rapid development in the physical efficiency of the theatre that has taken place in the last half century, and the simultaneous increase in the alertness and intelligence of the theatre-going public, have made it possible for playwrights to inaugurate a series of innovations that have broadened the boundaries of the technique of the drama. Traditional ideas, which formerly had stood for centuries, of what can be done in the theatre and (more particularly) what cannot be done, are now being altered every season, as adventurous playwrights press forward to the accomplishment of technical tasks which have never been attempted before.

In the previous chapter we had occasion to celebrate the successful transference to the service of the drama of a technical expedient which has long been customary in the novel—the expedient, namely, of constructing a story from effects to causes and revealing it in a pattern of reverted time. There are many other narrative devices which have long been used in the short-story and the novel, that might be transferred, with equal advantage, to the strategy of the contemporary drama. In past years, the critic has often been required to insist that the art of the novel is one thing and the art of the drama is another; but, under present-day conditions, he is also required to admit that the difference between the two crafts is by no means so decided as it used to be. For one thing, the gap between the novel and the drama has been bridged over by the motion picture play—an artistic product which is equally novelistic and dramatic; and, for another thing, the recent improvements in stage machinery, which have made it possible to shift a set in less than thirty seconds of absolute darkness and absolute quiet, have also made it possible for the playwright

276

to adopt a freer form of narrative than was imposed upon him thirty years ago. We may confidently expect that, in the next few years, the drama will avail itself more and more of narrative devices which, though thoroughly established in the novel, have hitherto been regarded as beyond the reach of stagecraft.

Students of the technique of the novel are aware that, ever since the outset of the eighteenth century, the novelist has been permitted to project his narrative from either of two totally different points of view, which may be called, for convenience, the internal and the external. He may reveal his story internally, as it appears to the mind of one or another of the actors who take part in it; or he may reveal it externally, as it would appear to a disinterested mind sitting aloof from all the characters and regarding them with what Mr. Alfred Noyes has greatly called "the splendor of the indifference of God." Heretofore, only the second of these points of view has been permitted to the dramatist. He has been obliged to set his characters equidistant from "the god-like spectator" (to quote William Archer's phrase), and has been required to reveal them through an atmosphere of inviolable objectivity.

Novelists like George Eliot have been accustomed to avail themselves of the privilege of vivisecting the brains of their characters and analyzing those most intimate thoughts and emotions that never translate themselves into speech or express themselves in action; but, since the renunciation (both for better and for worse) of the technical expedients of the soliloquy and the aside, the dramatist was for a long time denied this great advantage of entering the mind of any of his characters and forcing the audience, for the moment, to look at the entire play from this individual and personal point of view. One of the greatest services that have been rendered to the technique of the drama by that daring innovator, Mr. Eugene O'Neill, has arisen from his insistence, in *Strange Interlude*, on the elaborate employment of asides and soliloquies, for the purpose of carrying the action forward simultaneously along two parallel psychologic planes,—the conscious and the subconscious.

Recently, however, a few adventurous playwrights have discovered an even more effective means than any series of soliloquies and asides for shifting the audience, at any moment, from an external and objective point of view to a point of view that is internal and subjective. The second act of that beautiful and well-remembered play, *The Poor Little Rich Girl,* was exhibited from the point of view of a child whose mind is drifting under the influence of an opiate; and in a more elaborate play entitled *The Phantom Rival,* an entire act is devoted to the exhibition of events that happen only in the fancy of one of the leading characters.

The success of such experiments as these sets the dramatist once more on an equal footing with the novelist in the very important matter of being permitted to shift the point of view from which his story is to be observed. The full advantage of this technical innovation has not yet been reaped in the theatre; but a whole new field has been opened up to future playwrights. Would it not be interesting, for instance, to show a certain scene as it appeared from the point of view of one of the characters concerned, and subsequently to reënact the entire scene as it appeared from the very different point of view of another of the characters? This ironical device has already been employed in the novel, by such technical experimentalists as Arnold Bennett. Before long we may expect to see it successfully employed upon the stage.

The Phantom Rival was written by Ferenc Molnar, a Hungarian dramatist who has nearly always shown an adventurous originality in his technical attack. The American version was made by Leo Ditrichstein.

In the labor-saving first act of this play, the theme is outlined in a conversation between a writer and an actor, which takes place in a restaurant. The writer expounds a theory that most women treasure throughout their entire lives an idealized image of the man who has first awakened them to a consciousness of love, and that, even though they subsequently marry some one else, they continue, in the secret recesses of their minds, to compare their husband, to his disadvantage, with this phantom rival.

This explicit conversation is a sort of prologue to the play, in which neither the writer nor the actor is involved. The leading figure in the comedy is a woman married to a husband who is jealous not only of her present but also of her past. He discovers that before her marriage she had been interested in a certain Russian; and, though this Russian had returned to his native country seven years before, the husband now insists that his wife shall read to him the treasured letter which the lover of her youth had sent to her at parting. In this letter, the eager foreigner had told her that he would come back to her some day—as a great general, or a great statesman, or a great artist, or even, if the worst befell him, as a humble tramp who would lay the wreckage of his life beneath her feet. The husband sneers at this highfaluting letter, and thereby stimulates the imagination of his wife to rush to the rescue of his phantom rival.

She drifts into a day-dream, in which her mind, hovering between sleep and waking, bodies forth an image of her former lover in the successive guises of a great general, a great statesman, a great artist, and a humble tramp. These scenes are exhibited entirely from the heroine's point of view. She knows nothing of the actual conditions of any of the careers about which she is dreaming; and, naturally enough, her phantom lover appears to her as an utterly impossible sort of person, acting out heroical absurdities and talking all the while the stilted language of a Laura Jean Libbey novel.

In the third act we are recalled to actuality. The former lover of the heroine, returned from Russia, makes a business call upon her husband, and reveals himself to her as an utterly undistinguished and small-minded character. Comparing this trivial little person with the huge dreams she has had of him, the wife is forced to admit that her husband is the better man and to expel the phantom rival from the regions of her fancy.

VIII

SURPRISE IN THE DRAMA

IN RECENT years our native playwrights have devoted a great deal of attention to technical experiment. It might be argued that they would have fared better if they had thought more about life and less about the theatre; but, though they have discovered comparatively little to say, they have at least devised many means of saying things ingeniously. This is, perhaps, the necessary mark of a drama that is still so young as ours. Youth cares more for cleverness than it cares for the more sedentary quality of insight. When Mr. George M. Cohan is ninety years of age—and our theatre has grown hoary in the interval—he will have more to tell us about life, but he will no longer make a pattern so astonishingly dexterous as that of *Seven Keys to Baldpate*.

Not all of the adventurous experiments of our American playwrights have been so signally successful; but all of them are worthy of theoretical consideration. In the present chapter, it may be profitable to examine the concerted assault which has recently been made against the time-honored tradition of the theatre that a dramatist must never keep a secret from his audience.

Concerning this tradition, William Archer said in 1912, "So far as I can see, the strongest reason against keeping a secret is that, try as you may, you cannot do it. . . . From only one audience can a secret be really hidden, a considerable percentage of any subsequent audience being certain to know all about it in advance. The more striking and successful is the first-night effect of surprise, the more certainly and rapidly will the report of it circulate through all strata of the theatrical public." This statement, which seemed sound enough in theory, has failed to prove itself in practice; and the fact of the matter seems to be that the "theatrical public" is far less cohesive than Mr. Archer had assumed. News does not travel, either rapidly or readily, through all its very different strata. This fact was indicated by the career of Roi Cooper Megrue's surprise-play, *Under Cover*. Although the piece had previously run a year in Boston, the vast majority of those who saw it on the first night in New York were completely taken in by the dramatist's deception; and, even after the play had run for many months in the metropolis, and had been analyzed repeatedly in the press, it was still observable that the majority of those who came to see it were still ignorant of the precise nature of the trick that was to be played upon them. They came to the theatre with a vague notion that the plot would be surprising, but they did not know the story in advance.

Mr. Max Marcin, the author of a clever surprise-play, *Cheating Cheaters*, complained, after the first night, that it was unfair for the newspapers to print summaries of his plot, thereby revealing in advance to future audiences the nature of the trap the dramatist had set for them. This protest, perhaps, was justified in theory; but, in fact, the author had no reason for complaint. Even that minority of the theatre-going public who habitually read the first-night notices in the newspapers do not long recall specifically what is said in them. All that they carry away from the reading is a vague impression that the play was praised or damned: it is only the few people who do not pay for tickets to the theatre who read these notices more deeply and remember the details.

The reports of current plays that circulate by word of mouth among the ticket-buying public are nearly always very vague. A man will tell his friends that a certain piece is "a good show"; but rarely, if ever, would he be able to pass on in conversation a coherent statement of the plot. Though *Cheating Cheaters* was played to large audiences for many months, the big surprise of the plot remained a mystery to three-fourths of all the people who attended it. Those of us who go professionally to the theatre do not always realize how little the general public knows in advance about current plays with which we ourselves are thoroughly familiar.

Despite, then, what Archer said in 1912, it has been subsequently proved by several experiments that it is entirely possible to keep a secret in the theatre. But the question still remains whether it is worth while to do so. The success of a surprise-play proves nothing; for it does not prove that the same play would not have been equally successful if the surprise had been eliminated from the plot.

Consider *Under Cover*, for example. The hero was introduced to the audience as a smuggler, engaged in the perilous enterprise of sneaking a valuable necklace through the customs. For two acts he was pursued by customs-house officials; and, when ultimately captured, he bought them off with a bribe. Then, in the last moments of the play, the dramatist revealed the hidden fact that the hero was not a smuggler after all, but an official of the United States secret service engaged in tracking down corruption in the customs-house.

It cannot be denied that the suspense of the melodrama was increased by the retention of this secret till the final moment; but, on the other hand, several other elements of interest were sacrificed. For instance, the love-story was imperiled by the fact that the audience had to watch the heroine fall in love with a man who, by every evidence, appeared to be a criminal. Furthermore, the author had to tell lies to his audience in those passages in which the hero was left alone on the stage with his confederate; and telling lies, even in a melodrama, is a hazardous proceeding. The play was a great success; but what evidence is there to prove that it might not have been equally successful if the author had taken the audience into his confidence from the start and permitted the public to watch, from the standpoint of superior knowledge, the corrupt customs-house officials walking ignorantly into the trap which had been set for them? I do not state that this is so; but I do state that the only way to prove that it is not so would be to build the plot the other way and try it on the public.

Of course, the strongest argument against keeping a secret from the audience is that this procedure, in the admirable phrase of William Archer, "deprives the audience of that superior knowledge in which lies the irony of drama." The audience likes to know more about the people in a play than they know about themselves; for this superior knowledge places the spectators in the comfortable attitude of gods upon Olympus, looking down upon the destinies of men. It is not nearly so amusing to be fooled as it is to watch other people being fooled; and this would seem to be a fundamental fact of psychology. Against this fundamental fact, the success of a dozen or a hundred surprise-plays can scarcely be regarded as weighing down the balance. The audience, for instance, would feel much more sympathetic toward the heroine in *Under Cover* if, all the while that she was falling in love with a person who appeared to be a criminal, the audience knew that he was really an honest man.

But another argument against keeping a secret from the audience is that, in order to do so, it is nearly always necessary to tell deliberate lies to lead the audience astray. There is an instance of this in an interesting play by Mr. Jules Eckert Goodman, entitled *The Man Who Came Back*. This play leads us around the world and back again, following the fortunes of a prodigal son who has been cast adrift by his father. On the way, we meet another person drifting without anchor,—a certain Captain Trevelan. This British idler marries a girl whom he has run across in a cabaret in San Francisco; and, encountering the couple later on in Honolulu, we are shown at considerable length that their marriage has turned out unhappily. In the last act, we are told suddenly that Trevelan is not a British captain at all, but merely a New York detective who has been employed by the hero's father to travel round the world and keep watch upon the movements of his prodigal son. This statement comes, indeed, as a surprise; but nothing is ever said to explain away the wife that Trevelan has left behind in Honolulu. Was she also a detective, or did Trevelan really marry and desert her, for the purpose of preventing the audience from guessing his identity? The play as a whole is not imperiled by this jugglery, since the mysterious detective is merely an incidental figure in the plot; but we feel that the author has severely compromised himself for the sake of a single effect of sharp surprise in the course of his concluding act.

Another important point to be considered is that, when the appeal of a play is dependent mainly on surprise, the author is impeded from drawing characters consistently. It is impossible to draw the sort of person that the hero really is, and at the same time to persuade the audience, until the final revelation of the secret, that the hero is another sort of person altogether. Deception of this kind can, therefore, never be accomplished in a play that is sufficiently serious in subject-matter to demand reality in characterization. The pattern of surprise is available only for farces and for melodramas, in which the incidents are all that count and the characters are secondary. To deceive the audience successfully in high comedy or in tragedy would require a falsification that would consign the play to ruin. The public consciously will swallow lies only in regard to stories that do not seriously matter.

To sum the matter up, the sort of surprise which must be regarded absolutely as inacceptable in any play is the sort which depends for its success upon a clear negation of what has gone before. Nothing can be gained by the procedure of telling the public one thing for two hours and a half and then telling the public in two minutes that it has merely been deceived. Such jugglery is easy to encompass, and is sometimes entertaining in effect; but it leads away from that interpretation of the underlying truth of life which is the end of art.

IX

THE TROUBLESOME LAST ACT

HERE is an old saying in the theatre that hell is paved with good first acts; for many a play has started out with promise and failed to fulfil that promise in the end. It must not be supposed, however, that first acts are easy to construct. In fact, the very contrary is true; for the technical problem of laying out a well-ordered exposition is one of the most difficult for the playwright to attack. But, even if he falters in his handling of this problem, he may be carried safely by his subject-matter. If the project of his play is at all interesting, and particularly if it shows the trait of novelty, a barely adequate exposition of this project will attract the attention of the audience and hold it until time is called by the first curtain-fall.

In the subsequent acts, however, the attention of the audience is shifted from a consideration of the material itself to a consideration of what the playwright does with this material; and this is the reason why a faltering technique is more disastrous to a play in those acts which come subsequent to the exposition. A certain expectation has already been aroused; and the audience will be disappointed if this expectation is not satisfied with proper emphasis. To climb the ladder to a climax without ever missing footing on an upward step is a technical task that calls for nice discrimination. The climax itself is usually easy to achieve. It is the first thing that the author has imagined; it is, indeed, the *raison d'être* of his play; and the "big scene" so much admired by the public has seldom cost the playwright any trouble. But this climax is customarily succeeded by a last act that is troublesome indeed; and it is precisely at this point that the majority of plays are dashed upon the rocks of failure. It is harder to write a satisfactory last act than to write twenty good "big scenes" or ten adequately interesting acts of exposition. These figures have been gathered from observing many plays. The fact, then, is empirical: but wherein lies the explanation of the fact?

The main difficulty in laying out a satisfactory last act arises from the fact that it comes by custom after the climax of the play and is consequently doomed to deal with material inherently less dramatic than what has gone before. To state the matter in the simplest terms, it is more difficult for the playwright to conduct a falling than a rising action. Whatever follows a climax must appear an anti-climax; and the playwright, like the mountain-climber, is inclined to stumble on the downward trail.

Why not, then, obliterate this downward trail?,—why not build the action to its climax and then suddenly cut off any further consideration of the story? The negative answer to this question is based upon tradition; and it is therefore necessary that the origins of this tradition should briefly be examined.

In Greek tragedy the climax of the play was always followed by a period of falling action, in which the tragic tensity was lessened and the mood was softened to serenity. Nearly all the literary critics have assumed that the Greeks adopted this pattern in obedience to some esthetic theory; but to a critic of the drama it seems more sensible to suppose that this pattern was imposed upon them by the necessity of providing for an exodus of the chorus from the orchestra. The chorus could not march out while the three actors on the stage were still in the throes of the climax; and it could not remain in the orchestra after the play was over. Hence a period of falling action had to be provided as a sort of recessional for the supernumeraries.

The anti-climax at the close of Elizabethan tragedy may be similarly explained by reference to the physical peculiarities of the Elizabethan theatre. After Shakespeare had strewed the stage with bodies in the last act of *Hamlet,* he had to provide a period of diminished tensity during which the accumulated dead could be carried off the stage. The simple reason for this fact is that he had no curtain to ring down. Hence, in the original text, the long continuance of unimportant talk after the entrance of Fortinbras. Hence, also, in the original text of *Romeo and Juliet,* the interminable speech of Friar Laurence at the conclusion of the tragedy. This, obviously, was provided to afford sufficient time to carry off the bodies of Romeo and Juliet and Paris.

We are so accustomed to the proscenium curtain in the modern theatre that we are likely to forget that this revolutionary innovation was not introduced until the latter half of the seventeenth century. For more than two centuries it has been possible to drop the curtain and suddenly exclude from observation all the actors on the stage; but this fact has not as yet succeeded utterly in overturning a tradition of the drama which had been necessitated by the physical requirements of the preceding twenty centuries.

But, granted our proscenium curtain, is there any real reason why we should continue longer to follow the Greeks and the Elizabethans in their custom of carrying a play beyond its climax to an anti-climax? It is evident that Ibsen did not think so. Both in *A Doll's House* and in *Ghosts* he rang the final curtain down at the highest point of tensity, and left the most momentous question of the play still undecided.

The great example of Ibsen should make us bold to try to do away entirely with the period of falling action that characterized the close of Greek and Elizabethan tragedy. The best way to deal with the troublesome last act is not to write it at all. The insistence of this motive accounts, historically, for the fact that, late in the nineteenth century, the traditional five-act pattern was discarded for a four-act form, and that, early in the twentieth century, this four-act pattern has, in turn, been superseded in favor of a three-act form. These two progressive changes in the standard structure of the drama have been occasioned by a growing desire to do away with the troublesome last act.

The extreme of this treatment is exhibited in the famous close of *The Madras House*, by Mr. Granville Barker. The final curtain cuts off a conversation in mid-career; and the stage-direction reads, "She doesn't finish, for really there is no end to the subject." This piece was designed by Mr. Barker to illustrate the thesis that a play should have no end, since, in life itself, nothing is terminal and nothing is conclusive. The play, however, was an utter failure; and the disaster that attended its production seemed to prove that the public preferred the traditional pattern to Mr. Barker's unprecedented attempt to approximate the inconclusiveness of nature.

But this attempt to obliterate the troublesome last act might have been more hospitably welcomed if Mr. Barker had chosen to cut off his play at the moment of greatest interest and highest tensity. There seems to be no theoretic reason why the periodic structure developed for the short-story by Guy de Maupassant should not be successfully transferred to the service of the serious drama. It ought to be possible, by the exercise of sufficient ingenuity, to hold back the solution of a serious plot until the very last line of the last act. This feat was successfully accomplished by Augustus Thomas in one of the most skilful of his lighter plays, *Mrs. Leffingwell's Boots*.

In farce, however, the problem of the playwright is more difficult. A farce is customarily developed to its climax through a series of misunderstandings between the various characters. On the one hand, it appears impossible to close the play without clearing up these foregone misunderstandings by explaining them to all the characters involved; but, on the other hand, these eleventh-hour passages of explanation must deal necessarily with materials of which the audience has all the time been cognizant, and must, therefore, result in the falling-off of interest that attends the hearing of a twice-told tale. If some master could invent a method to do away entirely with the troublesome last act of farce, he would indeed confer a boon on future playwrights.

Nothing has been said thus far concerning that falsification in the last act of a play which is commonly assumed to be demanded by the public. In an absolute sense, any ending to a play is false to nature, since in life itself there can never be an utter termination to a series of events; and it has, therefore, frequently been argued that, to end a play, the dramatist is justified in cogging the dice of circumstance in favor of those characters with whom the audience has come to sympathize. This argument, apparently, holds good for comedy, since it is supported by the constant practice of such great dramatists as Molière and Shakespeare. But in proportion as a play becomes more serious, the audience will tend more and more to be disappointed by any ending that does not follow as a logical result from all the incidents that have preceded it. Shakespeare is allowed to falsify the end of *As You Like It;* but the audience would be deeply disappointed if Hamlet were permitted to live happily forever after the conclusion of the play.

There are certain plays, and not all of these by any means are tragedies, that—to use a phrase of Stevenson's—"begin to end badly"; and to give them arbitrarily a happy ending results merely in preventing the audience from enjoying the exercise of that contributory faculty which the late William James described as "the will to believe." Those managers, therefore, are misguided who persist in assuming that the public will prefer an illogical happy ending to an unhappy ending that has clearly been foreshadowed. Yet the recent history of the drama shows many instances of plays with two last acts—the one preferred for its logic by the author, and the other preferred for its optimism by the manager. Thus, *The Profligate* of Sir Arthur Pinero has two last acts. In the first version, the profligate takes poison; and in the second version he lives happily forever after. In a later farce by the same author, *Preserving Mr. Panmure,* one last act was provided for the production in London and a different last act was provided for the production in New York. When Henry Bernstein's *Israël* was produced in Paris, the hero committed suicide at the close of the play; but when the piece was subsequently produced in New York he merely married a girl in a picture hat. This change, suggested by the late Charles Frohman,—although it reduced the entire play to nonsense,—was accomplished with the consent and connivance of the author. Both *The Legend of Leonora*, by Sir James Barrie, and *The New Sin*, by Basil Macdonald Hastings, were produced in New York with troublesome last acts which did not exist at all when the two plays were first produced in London. It will be seen, therefore, that even authors of acknowledged eminence are not entirely immune from falsifying the concluding moments of their plays when pressure is brought to bear upon them by friendly and persuasive managers. To rescue comparatively unestablished playwrights from this insidious insistence, the only certain remedy will be the general adoption of a new dramatic pattern in which the troublesome last act will, by common consent, remain unwritten.

X

PROPORTION IN THE DRAMA

E VERY play is a dramatization of a story that covers a larger
canvas than the play itself. The dramatist must be familiar
not only with the comparatively few events that he exhibits on the stage, but also with the many other events
that happen off-stage during the course of the action, others still
that happen between the acts, and innumerable others that are
assumed to have happened before the play began. Considering his
story as a whole, the playwright must select his particular material
by deciding what to put into his play and what to leave out of it;
and any number of different plays may be made from the same
story by different selections from the material at hand.

Considering the entire story of *Hamlet*, for instance, it would
be possible to make an interesting play in which the climax should
be the seduction of Queen Gertrude by her handsome and un-
scrupulous brother-in-law, and the murder of the king by Claudius
should constitute the catastrophe. In this play, the young Prince
Hamlet, remaining ignorant of what was going on about him,
would play but a minor part and would be dramatically interesting only as a potential menace to the machinations of his plausible
but wicked uncle. Many other plays might be selected from the
entire drift of narrative from which Shakespeare derived the
specific dramatization that we know so well; and it is by no means
illogical to assume that the same great dramatist might have made
as great a tragedy of one of these innumerable other hypothetic
plays.

But after the dramatist has made a definite selection of events to
be exhibited, the nature of his play will still depend on the sense
of proportion with which he develops the materials selected. What
characters, what motives, what incidents shall he emphasize, and

what others shall he merely shadow forth in the dim limbo of his background? Suppose the dramatist of *Hamlet* to have decided to begin his play after the murder of the king and to end it with the retributive execution of the murderer. It would still be possible to project Claudius as the central and most interesting figure in the tragedy. He might be exhibited as a man self-tortured by the gnawing of remorse, harrowed by an ever-growing doubt of the security of his assumed position, wounded to the quick by the defection of his queen, and ultimately welcoming the stroke that cut the knot intrinsicate of all his tortures. In a dramatization so conceived, the young Prince Hamlet would once more be relegated to a minor role. A shift in the proportions of the narrative would alter the entire aspect of the tragedy.

Whenever we go to a play, we witness only one of a myriad possible dramatizations of the entire story that the playwright has imagined. If we are dissatisfied with the drama, this dissatisfaction may frequently be traced to a disagreement with the playwright concerning his selection of material. Often we wish that the author had begun his play either earlier or later in the general procession of events from which he chose his incidents; often we feel that much that we have seen might better have been assumed to happen off the stage, and that certain other incidents that happened off the stage would have thrilled us more if we had seen them. But even more frequently, we may trace our dissatisfaction to a disagreement with the playwright concerning the proportions of his narrative. We wished to see more of certain characters and less of others; we were keenly interested in certain motives which he only half developed, and bored by certain other motives which he insisted on developing in full. We cared more about Laertes than Polonius—let us say—and were disappointed because the garrulous old man was given much to say and do and his gallant son was given comparatively little.

When a play with an obviously interesting theme fails to hold the attention and to satisfy the interest, the fault may nearly always be ascribed to some error of proportion. Too much time has been devoted to secondary material, too little to material that at the moment seemed more worthy of attention. The serious plot of *Much Ado About Nothing*, for example, tends to bore the audience, because they have grown to care so much for Beatrice and

Benedick that they can no longer take any personal interest in what happens to Hero. When Edmond Rostand began the composition of *L'Aiglon*, he conceived Flambeau as the central figure of the drama. Later in the course of composition, the young Duc de Reichstadt ran away with the play; and *L'Aiglon* became, in consequence, a vehicle for Sarah Bernhardt instead of a vehicle for Constant Coquelin. Rostand was right in his ultimate perception that the weak son of a strong father would be more interesting to the public than a *vieux grognard à grandes moustaches;* and an obstinate effort to keep Flambeau in the center of the stage would have diminished the popularity of the play.

In handling any story, the dramatist is fairly free to select the incidents to be exhibited and to determine the proportions of the composition he has chosen; but there are always two exigencies that he cannot safely disregard. The first of these is covered by Sarcey's theory of the *scène à faire,*—or the "obligatory scene," as the phrase has been translated by William Archer. An obligatory scene is a scene that the public has been permitted to foresee and to desire from the progress of the action; and such a scene can never be omitted without a consequent dissatisfaction. The second exigency is that the dramatist must proportion his play in agreement with the instinctive desire of the audience. He must summarize what the public wishes to be summarized, and must detail what the public wishes to be detailed; and he must not, either deliberately or inadvertently, antagonize the instinctive desire that he has awakened. If the author has caused the public to care more about Shylock than about any other person in his play, it becomes, for example, a dramaturgic error to leave Shylock out of the last act. If the audience [as may be doubted, in this instance] really wants Charles Surface to make love to Maria, it becomes a dramaturgic error to omit any love-scene between the two. When *Ruy Blas* was first produced, the public was delighted with a minor character, the shiftless and rollicking Don César de Bazan. Thereupon, Dennery, with the permission of Hugo, made this character the central figure of a second melodrama, in which the public was permitted to see more of him.

There are certain characters that afflict the audience with disappointment whenever they leave the stage, and there are certain other characters that afflict the audience more deeply by remain-

ing on the stage and continuing to talk; and the distinction between the two types can seldom be determined before a play has
been "tried out," with the assistance of some sort of audience. To
fight against the popular desire in the matter of proportion is to
fight in vain.

XI

HIGH COMEDY IN AMERICA

───

N
O OTHER type of drama is so rarely written in America as
that intelligently entertaining type which is variously
known as High Comedy, or Comedy of Manners, or
Artificial Comedy. The purpose of High Comedy is to
satirize the social customs of the upper classes, to arraign with
wit the foibles of the aristocracy. It must conform to the requirement of comedy that the plot shall never stiffen into melodrama
nor slacken into farce, and it must attain the end of entertainment
less by emphasis of incident than by the nice analysis of character.
The medium of Artificial Comedy is conversation; it dallies with
the smart sayings of smart people; and the dialogue need not be
strictly natural, provided that it be continuously witty. The world
of High Comedy is a world in which what people say is immeasurably more important than what they do, or even what they are.
It is an airy and a careless world, more brilliant, more graceful,
more gay, more irresponsible than the world of actuality. The
people of High Comedy awaken thoughtful laughter; but they
do not touch the heart nor stir the soul. By that token they are
only partly real. They have merely heads, not hearts,—intelligence
and not emotion. They stimulate an intellect at play, without
stirring up the deeper sympathies. For this reason High Comedy
is more difficult to write than the sterner types of drama. It cannot strike below the belt, like melodrama, nor, like tragedy, attack the vital organs of compassion; it can only deliver light blows
upon the forehead; it must always hit above the eyes.

   In the genealogy of English drama, High Comedy can boast an
ancient and an honorable lineage. It was introduced in England
in 1664 by Sir George Etheredge, who imported it from France;
for, during that exile of all gentlemen to Paris which is known
in history as the Protectorate of Cromwell, Etheredge had studied

manners at the French court and the Comedy of Manners at the theatre of Molière. He was soon followed by that great quartet of gentlemanly wits, composed of Wycherley, Congreve, Vanburgh, and Farquhar, who carried English comedy to unexampled heights of brilliancy and irresponsibility. Unfortunately for their fame, the work of these masters was tinged with an utter recklessness of all morality, at which later generations have grown to look askance. Of this tendency—as Charles Lamb has defined it— "to take an airing beyond the diocese of the strict conscience," High Comedy was purged by Colley Cibber and Sir Richard Steele, who introduced, however, the infra-intellectual alloy of sentiment. Then came the richer period of the genial Goldsmith and the incomparable Sheridan, which gave us the greatest of all Comedies of Manners, *The School for Scandal*. Charles Lamb, who had seen this masterpiece performed by many of the members of the original company, lived long enough to pen the solemn sentence,—"The Artificial Comedy, or Comedy of Manners, is quite extinct on our stage." But even while this requiem was being written, the type was being kept alive in occasional comedies like the *London Assurance* of Dion Boucicault; and, late in the nineteenth century, it was brilliantly revivified by the clever and witty Oscar Wilde and the more humorous and human Henry Arthur Jones.

It is the privilege of American writers to share with their British cousins the common heritage of English literature, and most offshoots of the ancient stock have been successfully transplanted overseas; but there are certain of these offshoots which thus far have failed to flourish in America because we have had so little time, comparatively, to till our literary soil. Our native drama is already thoroughly alive in respect to melodrama and to farce; but it is not yet thoroughly alive in respect to High Comedy.

This fact, however, is not at all surprising; for High Comedy is the last of all dramatic types to be established in the art of any nation. It has frequently been said that it takes three generations to make a gentleman; but it takes more than three to develop a Comedy of Manners. Manners do not become a theme for satire until they have been crystallized into a code; and, to laugh politely, a playwright must have an aristocracy to laugh at. To all intents and purposes, the United States is still a country without an upper class; and the chaos of our social system precludes the possibility of social satire.

Before we can develop a Comedy of Manners in America, we must first develop an aristocracy to satirize. At present our few aristocrats are cosmopolitans; and, if they should be mirrored on the stage, our audience would think them un-American. For not only do we lack the subject-matter for High Comedy, but we also lack an audience that is educated to appreciate it. Compare the *clientèle* of the Criterion Theatre in London, under the management of the late Sir Charles Wyndham, with the *clientèle* of any of our theatres on Broadway. Our American audience is more heterogeneous, more democratic, and possibly more human; but it is certainly less cultivated, less refined. It is composed for the most part of the sort of people who are embarrassed by good breeding and who consider it an affectation to pronounce the English language properly. It is not surprising, therefore, that—as Mr. Walter Prichard Eaton has pithily remarked—most of our American comedies must be classed as Comedies of Bad Manners. We laugh uproariously at impoliteness on our stage, because we have not yet learned to laugh delicately at politeness. We are amused at the eccentricities of bad behavior, because we have not yet learned to be amused at the eccentricities of good behavior. We are still in the stage of learning how to laugh, because we are still in the stage of learning how to live.

There are very few ladies and gentlemen in the American drama, —there are none, for instance, in the very popular and thoroughly representative plays of Mr. George M. Cohan; but the primary reason is that there are very few ladies and gentlemen in the American audience, and the secondary reason is that there are very few ladies and gentlemen in American life. It would not be fair to blame our native dramatists for the dearth of High Comedy in America. Bronson Howard, in the first generation, and Clyde Fitch, in the second, strove earnestly to give us a native Comedy of Manners; but their successors in the present generation have, for the most part, given up the difficult endeavor. It is a thankless task to write about aristocrats for an audience that is unprepared to recognize them, and to search for subject-matter for a Comedy of Manners in a country that is still a little proud of the misfortune that it has no upper class.

XII

SATIRE ON THE AMERICAN STAGE

IT HAS frequently been pointed out that the ability to laugh is the only function that distinguishes mankind from all the lower animals. Furthermore, a man's degree of evolution may be measured by the sort of things at which he laughs most heartily. There are many different grades of refinement in the sense of humor,—so many that to codify them all would require the attention of a profound philosopher. I have never read the celebrated essay of M. Henri Bergson on the subject of laughter, and cannot tell—in consequence—whether or not he has covered the field: but this point, at least, is pertinent,—that it is possible to paraphrase an ancient proverb by saying, "Tell me what you laugh at, and I will tell you what you are." If any evidence were needed to confute the utterly unreasonable statement that "all men are created equal," it would be necessary merely to point out that all men do not laugh at the same order of ideas.

It is easy enough to laugh at physical eventualities. When a man's feet slip from under him and he falls "with a dull, sickening thud" on the fattest and least vulnerable part of his anatomy, no human observer of the incident can easily suppress a loud guffaw. The appeal of such material is perpetuated in the theatre by the proverbial slap-stick [which the greatest of all comic dramatists did not forbear to use in such farces as *Les Fourberies de Scapin*], and is kept alive forever by an endless race of amply-cushioned actresses like the late Marie Dressler.

A slightly higher degree of evolution is demanded before a man can learn to laugh at mental accidents. The French—in their reasoned catalogue of criticism—have registered a clear distinction between the *mot de situation* and the *mot de caractère*. To the common mind, it is obviously funny for any one to fall downstairs; but a greater degree of culture is required to realize the fact that some people may be funnier still if they merely walk downstairs and never fall at all. Of a certain small but very pompous citizen, some happy-minded commentator once remarked that he always seemed to strut while sitting down; and this phrase may be accepted as an illustration of what the French intend by a "quip of character."

But it is still comparatively easy to laugh at some one else; and civilization may be said to begin at the point when a man becomes capable of laughing also at himself. It is easy to be humorous; it is harder to sustain a sense of humor. It is easy to make fun, at the expense of the other fellow: it is harder to take fun, at the expense of oneself. Some of our greatest humorists have—by common account—been deficient in the receptive sense of humor. I scarcely knew Mark Twain,—although I met him half a dozen times and talked with him as a very young apprentice would naturally talk with an admitted master; but many of his friends have told me that this monumental humorist was incapable of seeing and accepting a joke against himself.

A slightly higher rung upon the ladder is attained when men begin to laugh at words, and at the jugglery of words, instead of laughing merely at situations or at people. Words are symbols of ideas; and only a civilized person can see the fun in an idea. When Oscar Wilde permitted one of his puppets to say, "I can resist anything except temptation," he carried laughter into the realm of the philosophical abstract.

A still higher realm is reached when the ideas that are laughed at are the very ideas that are held most seriously by the man that leads the laughing. This is the realm of satire,—which must consequently be regarded as the most loftily developed mood of humor. The satirist laughs not only at himself but also at those very thoughts which he regards as the light and leading of his life. A humorist can make a joke; a man endowed with the more subtle sense of humor can see and take a joke against himself; but a satirist can see and make a joke against his very God. Many things in life are holy; but to the satirist the gift of laughter is more sacred than any of the others.

The satirical mood may be illustrated easily by reference to Lord Byron's immense and teeming poem called *Don Juan*. Time after time, in the course of this composition, the poet winged his way aloft on a wind of lyric inspiration,—only to pause suddenly and laugh tremendously at the very incentive that had excited him to eloquence. When I was in my teens, I used to hate this poem, because of Byron's habit of laughing in his loftiest moments and blaspheming [as it seemed to me] against the dictates of his genius; but, in recent years, I have begun to appreciate [and almost to admire] his nimbleness of mind in presenting an august idea from antithetic points of view. Any man can see a subject from one side: but the mark of culture comes when a man is able to see a subject from several sides at once.

The satiric mood demands an extraordinary alertness of intelligence, not only on the part of the humorist, but also on the part of his audience. G. K. Chesterton, for instance, whose essential mood is one of deep religious reverence, has a disconcerting habit of laughing his way into the very presence of his God; and this habit is bewildering to minds that are less cultivated than his own.

Satire—which may be defined as an irresponsible and happy-hearted toying with ideas—can flourish only in those ages which acknowledge an obeisance to the high ideal of culture. Satire can be conceived and written only by gentlemen—like the Roman Horace, the French Boileau, the English Dryden, or the American Henry James. A man must be distinguished before he can afford to laugh in public against the very things he holds most holy. Also, he must feel assured of the existence of an agile-minded audience to appreciate the perilous gymnastics of his mind.

Our American theatre has long been regarded as uncivilized; but a certain sign of promise has been registered by its recent tentative incursions into the unprecedented realm of satire. If our native playwrights can afford to be satirical, a time has come at last when our American theatre may be accepted as a grown-up institution.

XIII

THE LAZINESS OF BERNARD SHAW

IN THE midst of his development, Mr. Bernard Shaw appears to have decided that there was such a thing as being too proud to write. Like many other men of slow beginnings who have suddenly achieved a huge success, he turned lazy at the very height of his career and ceased to take his own profession seriously. Mr. Shaw had waited long for recognition. Then, suddenly, by reason of the enterprise of Arnold Daly in this country and Mr. Granville Barker in England, he flashed forth unexpectedly as one of the most successful of contemporary dramatists. His success had been earned honestly by "hard study and long practice,"—to quote a phrase made almost classical by Sir Arthur Pinero; but this success had been so long deferred, and was ultimately launched so swiftly, that—temporarily, at least—it turned the head of Mr. Shaw. The author of such well-made plays as *Arms and the Man* and *Candida* and *You Never Can Tell* and *Man and Superman* decided—at the age of nearly fifty—that it was no longer necessary for him to undergo the manifest discomfort of making plays as well as he knew how to make them. He assumed that the critics would praise and the public would applaud anything that he might subsequently sign, whether it might happen to be good or happen to be bad. Betrayed by this assumption, he relaxed into a period in which he allowed himself the lazy luxury of writing down whatever chanced to occur to him,— without forethought, without selection, and without arrangement, —and adopted the audacious practice of calling the resultant mess a play. For this impudence, Mr. Shaw was promptly rebuked in London by the total failure of *Getting Married* and *Misalliance;* and he found himself so much discredited that, in order to recapture the good graces of the public, he was forced to write a carefully constructed comedy and to launch it without his name upon the program. *Fanny's First Play* succeeded, because of its inherent merits, before the London public had discovered that Mr. Shaw had written it. In New York, both *Getting Married* and *Misalliance* fared better than in London. Our public is less exacting than the public of the older capital; and we are more inclined toward the naïve assumption that anything that is signed with a big name must be a big work. We Americans are fond of bowing down to celebrated names. In illustration of this point, it is necessary only to call attention to the covers of our current magazines.

No other dramatist than Mr. Shaw would have been permitted —to state the matter in a vivid phrase of current slang—to "get away with" the lazy last act of *The Doctor's Dilemma* or the feeble and faltering construction of *Pygmalion*. As for *Getting Married* and *Misalliance*, their utter formlessness was actuated by the fact that they were easy to write. The author of a play so nearly great as *Candida* must have known as well as any other playwright or dramatic critic that these incoherent and protracted conversations were lacking in all of the essential merits of dramaturgic composition. He deliberately set them forth and—to quote another phrase of current slang—attempted cunningly to "put them over," because, at the moment, he despised the public that applauded him.

In this procedure, there is discernible what may be called an intimation of immorality. One of the highest and holiest of proverbs is the one which tells us that *noblesse oblige*. If the true artist may claim in any way to be superior to common men, it is only because his mental code calls for a stricter obedience to the dictates of a more exacting conscience. It is a point of morality for the true artist never to sign his name to any bit of work, however humble in intention, that he knows to be unworthy of the talents with which he finds himself endowed. An artist may be forgiven for a failing of his powers that may be caused by illness, temporary perturbation, senility, or any of a multitude of other causes that are clearly beyond his own control; but an artist should never be forgiven who, in the undisrupted plenitude of his ability, does work which he knows to be unworthy, for the simple reason that he deems it no longer necessary to exert himself in order to succeed.

Of all artistic tasks, there is none more difficult than the architectonic task of building a play; but, of all literary exercises, there
is none more easy than to pen an endless stream of incoherent
dialogue. For Mr. Shaw, the task of writing dialogue is even exceptionally easy, because he has a special gift for witty conversation. The dialogue of his indolent and sloppy pieces is fully as
amusing as that of his other and earlier plays which are worthy
of respect because of the dignity of their construction. But the
pity of it is that a man who had been capable of building *Candida*
should cease to be a master-builder, or, indeed, a builder at all;
and that this infidelity to a high vocation should be motivated by
both laziness and insincerity. *Noblesse oblige;* and Mr. Shaw
should have set a more inspiring example for younger playwrights
who, in later years, may be tempted also, by some sudden shower-
ing of wealth and fame, to deride the very public that has treated
them with courtesy and kindness.

As a propagandist, Mr. Shaw is never insincere: he believes his
own opinions, even at those many moments when they happen to
be wrong: but, as an artist, he is often insincere, and on this point
it is easy to convict him out of his own mouth. Consider, for
example, the impudent announcement which he printed as a
prefatory note to *Getting Married:*—"There is a point of some
technical interest to be noted in this play. The customary division
into acts and scenes has been disused, and a return made to unity
of time and place, as observed in the ancient Greek drama. . . .
I find in practice that the Greek form is inevitable when drama
reaches a certain point in poetic and intellectual elevation." This
statement, as applied to *Getting Married,* is not true: and—what is
more important—Mr. Shaw knows as well as any other critic that
it is not true. *Getting Married* is not Greek in form; and it never
reaches a point of either poetic or intellectual elevation. It is nothing but a witty conversation, without beginning, without middle,
without end, devoid of plot, devoid of climax, devoid of all those
other virtues of technique that were codified and analyzed by
Aristotle. The Greeks were mighty architects of plays; and *Getting
Married* no more resembles *Œdipus King* in structure than a diamond necklace resembles the Parthenon. Mr. Shaw is an educated
man. He must have studied at some time or other the *Electra* of
Sophocles, the *Trojan Woman* of Euripides, and the *Poetics* of

Aristotle: he cannot honestly plead ignorance of the principles and practice of the most strictly architectonic drama that the world has ever known: and, when he says that *Getting Married* is "classical" in form, he is talking with his tongue in his cheek. Not even Mr. Shaw can make a bad play look like a good play by writing a criticism of it which he knows to be a lie.

XIV

CRITICISM AND CREATION
IN THE DRAMA

I

B RANDER MATTHEWS, not so many years ago, in reviewing a book on *Types of Tragic Drama* by the Professor of English Literature in the University of Leeds, defined it as an essay in "undramatic criticism." The author of that academic volume had persistently regarded the drama as something written to be read, instead of regarding it as something devised to be presented by actors on a stage before an audience. His criticism, therefore, took no account of the conditions precedent to any valid exercise of the art that he was criticising.

The contemporary drama suffers more than that of any other period from the comments of "undramatic critics" who display no knowledge of the exigencies of the theatre. In the first place, the contemporary drama is more visual in its appeal than the drama of the past, and what it says emphatically to the eye can hardly be recorded adequately on the printed page. In the second place, the rapid evolution of the modern art of stage-direction has made the drama more and more, in recent years, unprintable. And, in the third place, the contemporary drama, with its full and free discussion of topics that are current in the public mind, requires—more than that of any other period—the immediate collaboration of a gathered audience. Such a drama can be judged with fairness only in the theatre, for which it was devised.

The fallacy of "undramatic criticism" of contemporary drama is a fallacy to which professors in our universities appear to be particularly prone. The reason is not far to seek. The prison-house of their profession confines them, for the most part, to little towns and little cities where no actual theatre, that is worthy of the name, exists. Condemned to see nothing of the current theatre,

304

they are driven back to the library, to cull their knowledge of the modern drama from the dubious records of the printed page. Thus, in the enforced and tragic solitude of Leeds or Oklahoma, they have been doomed to the opinion that Bernard Shaw, whose plays were almost sumptuously published, must be a greater dramatist than Sir James Barrie, who resisted for many years all illusory allurements to permit his best plays to be yanked and carted from the living theatre to find a sort of graveyard in the printed page.

In an interesting and well-written book about *The Modern Drama*, by Professor Ludwig Lewisohn of the Ohio State University, there is a chapter of fifty-three pages devoted to "The Renaissance of the English Drama." In this chapter, the author expresses the opinion that the work of Pinero and Jones is of no account whatever, because, writing drama, they chose to be dramatic, and, writing for the theatre, they chose to be theatrical. He prefers the plays of Galsworthy, Barker, and Shaw, because these plays are less theatrical and less dramatic. With this argument—despite its paradox—it is not at all impossible to sympathize. It is possible, for instance, to remember a sudden entry into the vestibule of the Laurentian Library in Florence, which induced an unexpected singing of the soul in praise of Michelangelo because, although an architect, he had dared for once to do a thing that was not architectural at all. But the reader loses faith in the leading of Professor Lewisohn when the discovery is ultimately made that, in this entire chapter of fifty-three pages, the name of J. M. Barrie has never once been mentioned.

In an equally interesting and still more monumental book on *Aspects of Modern Drama*, by Frank Wadleigh Chandler, Dean of the University of Cincinnati, no less than two hundred and eighty modern plays have been minutely analyzed. This book is supplemented by an exhaustive bibliography of the modern drama which covers fifty-six closely printed pages of small type. Yet nowhere, in the text or in the bibliography, is J. M. Barrie mentioned as a modern dramatist. In this scholarly and weighty treatise, the man who imagined *Peter Pan* is utterly ignored.

In another volume, called *The Changing Drama*, by Professor Archibald Henderson, of the University of North Carolina, an attempt has been made—according to the preface—"to deal with the contemporary drama, not as a kingdom subdivided between a dozen leading playwrights, but as a great movement, exhibiting the evolutional growth of the human spirit and the enlargement of the domain of esthetics." Yet, in this volume of three hundred and eleven pages, the name of J. M. Barrie never once appears.

Can it be that three scholars so well informed as Professor Lewisohn, Professor Chandler, and Professor Henderson never heard of J. M. Barrie? It may be that such masterpieces as *Alice Sit-by-the-Fire* or *What Every Woman Knows* or *A Kiss for Cinderella* had never been performed in Columbus, Ohio, Cincinnati, Ohio, or Chapel Hill, North Carolina: but is that any reason why a scholarly professor, condemned to live in the prison-house of one of these localities, should presume to write a comprehensive book about the modern drama without so much as mentioning the name of the best-beloved of modern British dramatists,—a man, moreover, who is famous in the world of letters and was made a baronet because of his services, through art, to humankind? These academic commentators should remember that their books may possibly be read by certain people who live in London and New York, and who have never missed a play of Barrie's, because his excellence has long been recognized by all dramatic critics, because every woman knows that he is the wisest of all recent dramatists, and because every child perceives that he is easily the most enjoyable.

In those books about the modern drama in which the name of Barrie is astoundingly ignored, the name of Bernard Shaw is invariably mentioned with ecstatic praise. Of all contemporary dramatists, Shaw is easily the favorite among the professors of "undramatic criticism." Before we read their books, we may always count upon them to consider *Candida* a greater play than *Iris*, and *You Never Can Tell* a better comedy than *The Liars*, and *Fanny's First Play* a subtler satire than *Alice Sit-by-the-Fire*. What can be the reason for this curious reaction of the "undramatic critics"?

Two answers to this interesting question suggest themselves to an investigating mind. The first answer is comparatively trivial; but it is not, by any means, too silly to demand consideration.

In all these academic books about the modern drama, the ranking of the recent British dramatists is proportioned directly in accordance to the pompousness with which their plays have been printed and bound and published to the reading world. This "undramatic criticism" of the current drama appears, upon investigation, to be based on nothing more than the setting-up of type.

When the early plays of Bernard Shaw were unsuccessful in the theatre [at a time when Pinero and Jones were being rewarded by their most remunerative triumphs] the disappointed dramatist decided to make an untraditional attack upon the reading public. He equipped his plays with elaborately literary stage-directions [the sort of stage-directions which, though interesting to the reader, are of no avail whatever to the actor]; he furnished them with lengthy prefaces, in many instances more interesting than the plays themselves; and he gathered them into volumes that were printed and bound up to look like books. These volumes, impressive in appearance and enlivening in content, were undeniably worth reading. They earned at once the right to be accepted as "literature"; and, among non-theatre-goers, they soon came to be regarded as the best contemporary contributions to "dramatic literature."

Meanwhile—among non-theatre-goers—the bigger and better plays of Jones and of Pinero were not accepted as "dramatic literature," because they happened only to be published in a form that made them look like plays instead of in a form that made them look like books. *The Second Mrs. Tanqueray* and *Mrs. Dane's Defence* were bound in paper covers and sold for twenty-five or fifty cents. The stage-directions were written technically for the actor, instead of being written more elaborately for the reader; and there were no prefaces whatever, to celebrate the greatness of the plays. No wonder, therefore, that the "undramatic critics" of the drama decided that the plays of Pinero and Jones were less important than the plays of Shaw! It was mainly a matter of the make-up of the printed page!

John Galsworthy and Granville Barker both followed the fashion set by Bernard Shaw, in publishing their plays. Barker's printed stage-directions are little novels in themselves. In consequence, Professor Ludwig Lewisohn considers Barker a greater dramatist than Pinero or Jones. No play of Granville Barker's has ever held the stage, in any city, for three successive weeks; yet Professor Lewisohn decides that *The Madras House* must be a greater play than *The Second Mrs. Tanqueray* [which has held the stage, throughout the English-speaking world, for more than forty years], because the published text of *The Madras House* looks like a book and the published text of *The Second Mrs. Tanqueray* does not.

Barrie, of course, receives no consideration whatsoever from these "undramatic critics," because his best plays, at the moment when their learned studies were conducted, had not as yet been printed. *Peter Pan*, which is acted every Christmas-tide in London before thousands and thousands of delighted spectators, had to be dismissed as negligible, for the accidental reason that a printed record of the lines had not been bound between cloth covers and offered to the reading public as a work of literature.

But we must turn attention now to a deeper, and a less facetious, explanation of the reason why the "undramatic critics" prefer the plays of Bernard Shaw to the plays of Sir James Barrie. They prefer the plays of Shaw because, to the academic and the non-theatric mind, these plays are much more easy to appreciate.

Shaw began life as a critic; and, ever since he took to writing plays, he has remained a critic. But Barrie began life as a creative artist; and, ever since he took to writing plays, he remained a creative artist. Among minds, the ancient maxim holds irrevocably— like to like. It may be safely said that no academic scholar is endowed with a creative mind; for any person so endowed would not permit himself to be an academic scholar. As Bernard Shaw himself has stated, "He who can, does: he who cannot, teaches." From academic scholars, therefore, we cannot logically look for a spontaneous appreciation of creative art: all we can expect is a critical appreciation of criticism.

The basic aims of criticism and creation are, of course, identical. The purpose of all art, whether critical or creative, is to reveal the reality that underlies the jumbled and inconsequential facts of actual experience. Art makes life more intelligible, by refusing to be interested in the accidental and fortuitous, and by focusing attention on the permanent and true. But this common aim of art is approached from two directions, diametrically different, by men whose minds are critical and by men whose minds are creative.

The critic makes life more intelligible by taking the elements of actuality apart; and the creator makes life more intelligible by putting the elements of reality together. In a precisely scientific sense, the work of the creator is constructive and the work of the critic is destructive. The critic analyzes life; the creator synthesizes it.

The difference between these diametric processes may perhaps be made more clear by a concrete scientific illustration. Suppose the truth to be investigated were the composition of the substance known as water. The critic would determine this truth by taking some water and dividing it up into two parts of hydrogen and one of oxygen; but the creator would establish the same truth by taking two parts of hydrogen and one of oxygen and manufacturing some water by putting them together.

That Bernard Shaw is the keenest-minded critic who has written for the modern stage, no commentator could be tempted to deny; but he is not a creative artist, in the sense that Barrie—for example —is a creative artist. Shaw takes the elements of life apart; but Barrie puts the elements of life together.

This proposition has been admirably stated by Professor Ludwig Lewisohn, who is one of Shaw's most ardent celebrators. In a notably clear-minded passage, Professor Lewisohn has said:—"This remarkable writer is not, in the stricter sense, a creative artist at all. The sharp contemporaneousness and vividness of his best settings deceives us. His plays are the theatre of the analytic intellect, not the drama of man. They are a criticism of life, not in the sense of Arnold, but in the plain and literal one. His place is with Lucian rather than with Molière."

The same commentator has clearly pointed out that Shaw is incapable of creating characters that may be imagined to live their own lives outside the limits of the plays in which they figure. Instead of launching a living person into the immortal world of the imagination, Shaw writes an analytic essay on his character and sends him forth upon the stage to speak it. In *Pygmalion*, for instance, when the cockney father of the heroine remarks that he is "one of the undeserving poor," we know at once that he is not; for no member of that human confraternity could possibly be capable of such a masterly self-criticism. When the greengrocer in *Getting Married* says, in describing his own wife, "She's a born wife and mother, ma'am: that's why my children ran away from home," we accept the witticism for all that it is worth; but we know, from that moment, that the greengrocer is not a greengrocer, but merely a mouthpiece for an essayist whose initials are G.B.S.

The method of Sir James Barrie is diametrically different, because it is utterly creative. In *What Every Woman Knows*, the humble but sagacious heroine has reconciled herself to the prospect of permitting her husband to elope with the more attractive Lady Sybil Lazenby; but suddenly she says to them, "You had better not go away till Saturday, for that's the day when the laundry comes home." In *A Kiss for Cinderella*, the Policeman sits down to write a love-letter for the first time in his life; and this is what he writes,—"There are thirty-four policemen sitting in this room, but I would rather have you, my dear." These people are alive. They do not have to tell us anything about themselves; and the author does not have to tell us anything about them.

No dramatist who lacks the primal gift of spontaneous and absolute creation—however brilliant be his talents as a critic—can finally be ranked among the greatest. For this reason, the plays of Bernard Shaw will ultimately be regarded as inferior to the plays of Barrie, and the best plays of Pinero and of Jones, and the few good plays of Galsworthy. All these other dramatists have brought us face to face with many characters whom we know to be alive; and Bernard Shaw has not.

In New York, throughout the early months of 1917, it was possible to see one night an excellent performance of *Getting Married* and to see the next night an excellent performance of *A Kiss for Cinderella*. Any open-minded person who afforded himself the luxury of this experience must have felt inclined to rush home to his library and throw the learned books of Professor Lewisohn, Professor Chandler, and Professor Henderson out of the window into the star-lit and unrestricted street. It must, in all fairness, be admitted that *Getting Married* shows Shaw very nearly at his worst and that *A Kiss for Cinderella* shows Barrie very nearly at his best; but the contrast, after all, is less a contrast of quality than a contrast of method. Barrie creates life, and Shaw discusses it; and the difference is just as keen as the difference between a woman who gives birth to a child and a woman who merely appears upon the platform and delivers a lecture on the subject of birth-control.

Externally—in what Hamlet would have called "their trappings and their suits"—*Getting Married* is a realistic play that apes the actual, and *A Kiss for Cinderella* is a romantic play that flies with freedom through the realm of fancy. But—considered in their ultimate significance—it is the realistic play that is the more fantastic, and it is the play of fancy that is finally more real than its competitor. We believe *A Kiss for Cinderella*, because we know, as Barrie knows, that nothing in life is true but what has been imagined; and we do not believe the text of *Getting Married*, because we know that people, in a crisis of their lives, are not ac-

customed to sit down calmly to discuss their motives in a mood
of critical intelligence.

Shaw attacks life with his intellect; Barrie caresses life with
his emotions. Shaw will always be admired most by scholars and
professors and "undramatic critics," who make their living by their
intellects and, in consequence, are prejudiced in favor of intelligence. But Barrie will always be admired most by women and
children and poets, who feel that the emotions are wiser than the
intellect, and who know—without discussion—that the greatest reason for the greatest things is incorporated always in the single,
mystic word,—"because . . ."

II

It would seem, in solemn justice, that no man should really
have a right to make so beautiful a play as *A Kiss for Cinderella*.
The undeniably accomplished fact is too discouraging to all the
rest of us, who would like to make good plays, if only our reach
did not exceed our grasp. The perfect fact, no less, is discouraging
to criticism; for, after enduring an evening of absolute enchantment, it seems very silly to sit down and try to write about it
without first borrowing or stealing the little Scotsman's magic pen.
It is only an ordinary fountain-pen,—or so it seems; but the little
Scotsman has been canny, and has fixed a lock upon it which pro-
hibits it from flowing for anybody else. And that is very much
too bad; for it is very difficult, with any other pen, to try to tell
the story of *A Kiss for Cinderella*.—

Her name was Miss Thing, and she was a little slavey in a London lodging-house, and her face did not amount to much, but she
had very small and very pretty feet. It must have been upon her
feet that God had kissed her, that day when she had come new-
born into the world; and doubtless that was one of God's very
busy days, when He had to hurry on. [Some days, God grows a
little absent-minded, because so many Emperors and Kings are
calling all-too-loudly on His name, and the Celestial Telephone is
kept jangling all day long by people who have got the wrong
number.] That is the only reason I can think of why Miss Thing
wasn't much to look upon above her ankles. But don't forget her
very small and very pretty feet; for otherwise the story might not
happen.

The room she liked to sweep out more than any other was a

queer place called a studio, which sat high up beneath the sky-light of the London lodging-house; for here lived Mr. Bodie. Bodie is a rather funny name; and Mr. Bodie was a rather funny man, for he painted pictures and told stories, and preferred to live, instead of working for his living. He lived with a life-sized plaster cast of the Venus of Melos, which he introduced to visitors as Mrs. Bodie, in token of the mystic fact that he was wedded to his art. The fun of sweeping out his place was this,—that all around the room were tacked up pictures that had been made, in playful moments, by other artists [Mr. Bodie would have called them his *confrères*],—Leonardo, and Gainsborough, and Reynolds, and the tender-hearted Greuze. Also, in odd moments, the little slavey could fish forth a tape-measure from a pocket in her skirt and compare the compass of her own waist with that of Mrs. Bodie's; and, if the dimensions seemed discouragingly different, she could always remember her own feet,—the little feet that God had kissed. Mrs. Bodie had no feet, to brag about.

It must have been because of her feet that Mr. Bodie first called her Cinderella and told her a very ancient story, of which she seemed to be predestined as the heroine. The little slavey listened, and believed; because a story that is told [by any man who is wedded to his art] is much more real than that other, rather tedious, story which is drifted to us, day by day, on the casual tide of actual experience. Art is more than life; for life is short, but art is long. It was to prove this to all unbelievers that story-telling was invented, long ago, before the world grew old.

Mr. Bodie never knew where the little slavey lived. She had told him merely that the words, "Céleste et Cie.," were printed in large letters on her door. One day he happened to look up this legend. It belonged to a famous shop in Bond Street. Was Miss Thing, in the leisure moments of the night, a glorified dressmaker to the upper classes? He did not know. What were the upper classes to a man who was married to Mrs. Bodie? All he actually knew about the little slavey was that she had a passion for collecting boards.

It was this passion that caused Miss Thing to be observed by an astute policeman. Collecting anything, in war time, is suspicious; and boards—what did she do with the boards? Clearly, she must be a German spy.

And that is why the policeman, one night, trailed the little slavey to a tiny hovel in a dark street, far away from the center of things, and found the words, "Céleste et Cie.," painted on the door. He donned a false beard, of fearsome and wonderful dimensions [for this policeman was a master of disguise], and entered the sorry hovel where the little slavey lived. He found her plying an active business, as tailor, as laundress, as lady-barber, and ever so many other things; for "Céleste" was nothing but a *nom de guerre* for a useful little woman, with a face of no account, who wanted to be serviceable and would do anything for anybody for a penny.

She did not want the pennies for herself. She needed them for something else. And that brings us to the mystery of the collected boards. All round the walls of the little place of business of "Céleste et Cie." were hung great boxes made of boards. What did they contain? The astute policeman desired very much to know, for the sake of the safety of the Empire. Forthwith, there popped up from each box a tiny curly head. These little girls, hung up in boxes on the wall, were orphans of the war. There was Gladys, whose father was serving in the British fleet, and Marie Thérèse, whose father had been killed in France, and Delphine, whose father had been massacred in Belgium; and there was yet another. "What is she?", inquired the astute policeman; and the foster-mother answered, "Swiss." But, when the policeman stuck his hand into the box, his hand was bitten. "Swiss, did you say?", inquired the policeman, for indeed he was very astute. "She was one of those left over," said Miss Thing, "and I had to take her in." This fourth child was, in very truth, only one of those left over. Her name was Gretchen. She had a habit of popping up her head and asking that God *strafe* this or that. But that was only her way. She couldn't help the blood that coursed throughout her tiny veins,— now, could she? Her foster-mother was one of those who understood.

The exceedingly astute policeman went away; for the mysterious collector of boards was evidently not a spy. And then the miracle began. If it were not for the miracle, this narrative would not amount to much; but there is always a miracle in every life, however humble, and that is the reason why stories are told. For a story is nothing more nor less than the testimony of a Tall Person who has seen a miracle to the shorter people who have seen it not.

Miss Thing had said so often to Gladys and Marie Thérèse and

Delphine and Gretchen that she herself was Cinderella that she had to promise them at last that the greatest of all balls would take place on a certain evening. The children expected it; and when children expect a miracle . . . oh, well, you know. So, after the astute policeman had gone away, Miss Thing went out into the street, and sat upon a little stone beside the door inscribed "Céleste et Cie.," and waited for the Fairy Godmother to come. She waited a long time; and then the miracle occurred, for the Fairy Godmother suddenly appeared to her.

What actually happened—if you care to know—was merely this:—the little slavey sat upon the stone until she was frozen and enfevered, and the policeman found her in the gutter and picked her up, and took her to a public hospital, where she lay in a delirium for days; and the policeman came to see her, and then, when she was getting well . . .

But all that really happened was what went on in a little chamber of Miss Thing's imagination, while her frozen and enfevered body was lying in the gutter. Nothing, in anybody's life, is real but what has been imagined. We are not what we actually are, but what we dream ourselves to be. "Men who look upon my outside," said Sir Thomas Browne, "perusing only my condition and fortunes, do err in my altitude"; and "he that understands not thus much hath not his introduction or first lesson, and is yet to begin the alphabet of man."

So the Fairy Godmother really appeared, and the famous ball took place, even as Miss Thing had promised to the children that it would. It was indeed a gorgeous ball; and the four little children, in their nighties, looked down upon it from a box [only, now, it should be printed Box] above the royal throne. First there came the King and Queen; and the King looked like a common laborer who used to collect boards for the little slavey, and the Queen looked like Mrs. Maloney (a patron of "Céleste et Cie."), and they both talked an 'orrid cockney, but they sat in patent rocking-chairs and resembled certain drawings in a book about a little girl called Alice. Then came a black person with a mighty axe, who was deferentially referred to as The Censor, and the Lord Mayor of London, and a mysterious and very influential person called Lord Times. And then there came the Prince himself, who was very handsome and exceedingly astute and easily inclined to boredom;

and his features were those of the policeman, and he spoke as one having authority.

The time arrived to choose a consort for the Prince; and many famous beauties were brought in, to be inspected by him. For this supreme occasion, the walls of Mr. Bodie's diggings were denuded. In they marched,—the Monna Lisa, and the Duchess of Devonshire, and the Lady with the Muff, and the Girl with the Broken Pitcher, and a Spanish dancer by the name of Carmencita. The Prince looked them over, and was bored. It is a princely habit to be bored. But then the pearly curtains parted, and down a wonderful great stairway Cinderella came. Her face was not so much to look upon, for it was only the face of Miss Thing, a slavey in a London lodging-house, and nobody had ever praised her face; but then there were her feet,—the little feet that God had kissed, that day when He was busy and had hurried on.

It was her feet that caught the eye of the Prince and rescued him from boredom; for his face was that of the policeman, and the policeman was exceedingly astute. One little fleeting look at her fabled and incomparable feet, and she was chosen; and then the fun began. A street-organ, mysteriously near though far away, began to play the old, old songs that are heard along the Old Kent Road, which lies [as many people say] on the wrong side of the river; and the children clapped their hands; and the whole court broke into a dance. Then somebody rolled in a push-cart, painted gold; and everybody snatched an ice-cream cone without being asked to pay a penny; and everything happened as it really ought to happen, until a Bishop appeared, looking marvelously like a stuffed bird on Mr. Bodie's mantelpiece, and married Cinderella to the Prince, and then . . . a great bell boomed forth, tolling twelve.

And that was the end of Cinderella's dream,—which was not all a dream, for what we really know is only what we have imagined. That is the message of this play; and if you do not understand it, by all means stay away and make room for the rest of us.

Several weeks elapse; and then we see the little slavey sitting up in bed in a hospital for convalescents. The policeman comes to call upon her every day. He thinks that he is only a policeman; but she knows—she really knows—that he is a Fairy Prince. She has made up her mind that he will make up his mind to ask her to marry him; and she wishes both to hinder him and help him in his laborious proposal. But, when at last he starts in to propose, she cuts him short. She would like to look back upon the luxury of having refused him before finally accepting him; and she makes him promise to ask her a second time if she should happen to refuse him now. He asks; and she refuses,—with that little hint of sniffiness for which a woman's nose was made. There is a pause. Then suddenly, from underneath the sheets, a tiny hand is shot out to grasp a hand more mighty than her own. "Ask me again," she says. . . .

And then we become aware of The Romantical Mind of a Policeman. She has thought of an engagement ring; but he has thought of something else, less usual and more romantical. He produces, from a mass of wrapping-paper, two little things of glass; and he fits them on her feet, and lo! they are slippers, and that is why her name is Cinderella for all time. "It is a kiss," remarks the romantical policeman [who is, in truth, a Fairy Prince]. And that is why the play is called *A Kiss for Cinderella.*

Now, this story, when recorded by a pen that has no magic in it, may sound as if it were a little mad; but, in reality it is not mad at all, but very, very real. Such things as this do happen every day, within the minds of the poor and the rejected of this world; and that is why the poor are not so poor, nor the rejected so despised, as we may think them; and that is, perhaps, the meaning of the saying that "the last shall be first,"—because they really are.

XV

DRAMATIC TALENT AND
THEATRICAL TALENT

Sir arthur pinero, in his lecture on *Robert Louis Stevenson: the Dramatist*, drew an interesting distinction between dramatic talent and theatrical talent. "What is dramatic talent?", he inquired. "Is it not the power to project characters, and to cause them to tell an interesting story through the medium of dialogue? This is *dramatic* talent; and dramatic talent, if I may so express it, is the raw material of *theatrical* talent. Dramatic, like poetic, talent is born, not made; if it is to achieve success on the stage it must be developed into theatrical talent by hard study, and generally by long practice. For theatrical talent consists in the power of making your characters, not only tell a story by means of dialogue, but tell it in such skilfully-devised form and order as shall, within the limits of an ordinary theatrical representation, give rise to the greatest possible amount of that peculiar kind of emotional effect, the production of which is the one great function of the theatre."

It was evidently the opinion of Pinero that dramatic talent is of little service in the theatre until it has been transmuted into theatrical talent; and, indeed, the history of the drama records the wreck of many noble reputations on the solid basis of this principle. There is, of course, the case of Stevenson himself. Concerning this, Pinero says, "No one can doubt that he had in him the ingredients of a dramatist," and again, "Dramatic talent Stevenson undoubtedly possessed in abundance"; but then he adds significantly, "And I am convinced that theatrical talent was well within his reach, *if only he had put himself to the pains of evolving it.*" But a greater instance is the case of Robert Browning. Browning was not merely, like so many of his eminent contemporaries, a reminiscent author writing beautiful anachronisms in imitation of

317

the great Elizabethan dramatists. He was born with a really great dramatic talent,—one of the very greatest in the history of English literature. But theatrical talent remained beyond his reach. He tried to write plays for Macready, but these plays were ineffective on the stage; and, after many futile efforts, he retreated from the theatre to the library.

Many men whose native endowment of dramatic talent was less remarkable than Browning's have succeeded in the theatre by the developed efficiency of sheer theatrical talent. There is, of course, the case of Scribe, who was—at least, from the commercial point of view—the most successful dramatist who ever lived. Scribe knew little, and cared less, about life; but he knew much, and cared more, about the theatre: and, in the matter of making an effective play, he could give both cards and spades to Browning.

On the other hand, there are a few instances—a very few—of men who have succeeded in the theatre by the sheer power of innate dramatic talent, without the assistance of hard study and long practice of the traffic of the stage. There is, of course, the case of Gerhart Hauptmann. When Hauptmann wrote *The Weavers*, at the early age of thirty, he had not yet progressed beyond the mere possession of the raw material of theatrical talent. This composition—the fourth in the chronological record of his works—was by no means skilfully-devised in form and order; but it is now acknowledged as his masterpiece, because of the overwhelming power of the artless and unimproved dramatic talent which it easily revealed.

It is, perhaps, a greater thing for an architect to dream a noble building than it is for a contractor to erect it. Pinero contends that it is only the finished edifice that counts, and that the architect is as impotent without the contractor as the contractor is impotent without the architect. Dramatic talent—which is born, not made— may be a greater thing than theatrical talent—which is made, not born. Pinero asserts that a great dramatist must be equipped with both. The great dramatist must have, like Hauptmann, "the power to project characters and to cause them to tell an interesting story through the medium of dialogue"; but he must also have, according to Pinero, the practiced power to "give rise to the greatest possible amount of that peculiar kind of emotional effect, the production of which is the one great function of the theatre." The best illustration, in this modern period, of the second half of this requirement is, of course, afforded by the finest plays of Pinero himself. Endowed with a dramatic talent of a high order, he also evolved a theatrical talent which—in the opinion of the present writer—is unsurpassed and, thus far, insurpassable.

Looking at them in the light of this distinction, it is still a little difficult to place the plays of John Galsworthy. There can be no doubt whatever that he possessed dramatic talent in abundance. He was certainly a great writer and probably a great man; and, in turning his attention to the drama, he was not merely—like Robert Louis Stevenson—a man of letters toying with the theatre. He saw many things in life that were dramatic—profoundly and tremendously dramatic—and these things he strove to render in the technical terms that were current in the theatre of his time. For this task he was endowed with many gifts. For instance, he had cultivated a careful sense of form, both in respect to structure and in respect to style; he had a keen sense of characterization; and, best of all, he came into the theatre, as many less considerable men come into a cathedral,—to watch and—in a lofty sense—to pray.

John Galsworthy, therefore, was not merely a man of letters playing a new game, of which he did not know, and scorned to learn, the rules. But a great question yet remains to be decided:— did he ever evolve a theatrical talent which was worthily concomitant with his innate dramatic talent?

No play of Galsworthy's ever made much money in the theatre. This consideration might seem merely sordid, were it not for the fact that the drama is a democratic art and that it is undeniably the duty of the dramatist to appeal to the many, not the few. On the other hand, John Galsworthy never wrote a play which was unworthy of serious attention. His best plays are not so good as *The Second Mrs. Tanqueray;* but his worst plays are not so bad as *A Wife Without a Smile.* Always, in his dramatic compositions, Galsworthy has had something to say; always, he has created living characters; always, he has told an interesting story through the medium of very interesting dialogue.

Why, then, did he fail to capture the great army of the theatre-going public? It was because he was not innately interested in the stage. John Galsworthy was a great man of letters; he was probably a great man; but he was not a great man of the theatre. Some of his plays are very effective,—for instance, *The Silver Box, Strife, Justice, The Pigeon,* and *Loyalties.* Some of them are ineffective,—for instance, *Joy*, *The Eldest Son*, and *The Mob*. Others, like *The Fugitive*, hover tantalizingly between the two extremes. Yet all these plays, in workmanship, are equally pains- taking. An ineffective play, like *Joy*, is just as well written, and nearly as well constructed, as an effective play, like *The Silver Box*. The difference, then, is not a difference in craftsmanship, but merely a difference in subject-matter. Pinero, the master-craftsman, could make a great play out of next to nothing, as he did in the instance of *The Thunderbolt;* but Galsworthy could make a great play only when he happened—as in the case of *Justice*—to hit upon a subject that was so inherently dramatic that it could carry itself without the aid of any notable exercise of theatrical talent.

No one can deny that the best plays of John Galsworthy are very good indeed; but the fact remains that, fine artist as he was, he cared much more about life than he cared about the theatre. This is the very thing that, in the vision of the leading literary critics, is said in praise of him; but, in the vision of the present writer, it is said a little—though only a little—in dispraise. Galsworthy seems never to have smelt the footlights. He had never been an actor, like Shakespeare and Molière; he had never been a stage-director, like Ibsen; he seemed never to have "counted the house," like Lope de Vega and the two great dramatists who bore successively the name of Alexandre Dumas. To actors, to stage-directors, to managers who "count the house," and to dramatic critics, John Galsworthy appeared always as a lofty man of letters who had not yet utterly become a fellow-laborer in the greatest of all the democratic institutions of the world.

Nobody would now deny the innate dramatic talent of John Galsworthy. Some few—including the present commentator—still deny that he ever developed a theatrical talent that was worthy of his native gift. Two or three reasons for this failing—if it be a failing—are evident, and even obvious. In the first place, Galsworthy considered life as God would look at it, instead of considering life as the average man would look at it. In this respect, he fulfilled the natural function of the novelist—to tell the individual what the public does not know—instead of fulfilling the natural function of the dramatist—to remind the public of what the public has unfalteringly known but seemed to have forgotten. Galsworthy never appeared to sit with his spectators in the theatre. He did not really understand and love his audience. Otherwise, he would have felt himself impelled to renounce the Olympian impartiality displayed in such a work as *Strife*, and would have descended to the arena, to fight and bleed for the humanly and naturally partisan. But John Galsworthy disdained to care about his public; and, only in a slightly less degree, he disdained to care about his actors. He asked them, every now and then, to refrain from doing things which would be exceedingly effective on the stage; and his only reason was that such things are seldom actually done in life itself. In other words, he rebelled against an evolvement of theatrical talent from a native and indubitable dramatic talent. He seemed, not infrequently, to smile a god-like smile and say, "This passage may not be theatrical; but, after all, it *is* dramatic. Life is bigger than the theatre; and, as the greatest of English novelists remarked, 'Life, some think, is worthy of the Muse.'"

It is quite evident that Galsworthy disagreed with the opinion of Pinero that "the one great function of the theatre" is "to produce the greatest possible amount of a certain peculiar kind of emotional effect." Given the subject-matter of *Justice*, for example, a theatrical craftsman like Pinero could easily have increased the amount of this emotional effect that is produced. When Galsworthy wrote this play, he was interested solely in his subject-matter and not at all in the technique of the theatre. The subject is inherently dramatic, and that is why the play is powerful; but the treatment of the subject is deliberately untheatrical.

Consider, for example, the unprecedented circumstance that the entire story of the play is told in the first act and the fourth, and that the narrative would still remain complete if the second and third acts were utterly omitted. In the first act we are shown all the motives and told all the circumstances of Falder's crime; he confesses his guilt; and, when he is arrested, his conviction is a foregone conclusion. The detailed report of his trial which is set before us in the second act is, in consequence, not technically necessary. Nothing whatsoever is told us in this trial which we did not know before; and the act is therefore empty of surprise. Furthermore, since the conviction of Falder has been certain from the first, the act is also empty of suspense.

When a self-confessed criminal has been convicted, he is naturally sent to jail; and consequently—from the point of view of craftsmanship alone—Mr. Galsworthy's third act adds nothing to the story. The narrative does not begin to move again until the fourth act, when Falder, having served his sentence, comes back to make his futile and pitiful attempt to begin life over again. For two entire acts—the second and the third—there has been no forward movement of the narrative. Here we have a pattern which Pinero would unquestionably have dismissed as offering an invitation to disaster; yet, curiously enough, these two acts, as Galsworthy has written them, are the most interesting of the four acts of the play.

The reason is that what we care about in *Justice* is not the story but the theme. The purpose of the author is not so much to interest us in what is done by Falder, nor even in what is done to Falder, as to interest us in a certain social fact. His sole desire is to force us to observe, with due consideration, the way in which that great machine without a soul, called Justice, habitually does its work. He makes us attend the trial because he wants to show us what an ordinary trial is like; and he makes us go to jail with Falder because he wants to show us what an ordinary jail is like.

As a further instance of Galsworthy's deliberate avoidance of "the greatest possible amount of emotional effect," consider the omission from his last act of what a craftsman like Pinero would certainly have seized upon as a *scène à faire*. Early in this act, before Falder reappears, we are told that the woman whom he loves, and for whom he stole the money, has been driven, by the economic necessity of supporting her children, to sell herself to her employer during the period of Falder's incarceration. As soon as we receive this information, we foresee a big scene between Ruth and Falder when Falder shall find out the tragic fact which we already know. Not only do we expect this scene, but we desire ardently to see it. Yet, when the moment comes in which the hero receives this revelation, the author at once removes both Ruth and Falder from the stage and shuts them up together in an adjoining room; and the big scene which we wished to see takes place on the other side of a closed door, while matters much less interesting are discussed before us on the stage. It is evident that Galsworthy deliberately made this choice, in order that we might remain more attentive to his theme than to the personal reactions of his hero and his heroine.

It has been said above that John Galsworthy disdained to care about his actors; and this point may be illustrated from the text of *Justice*. Consider Cokeson, for example, as an acting part. This character is naturally quaint and humorous; and he says many funny things, although he does not realize that they are funny. It is evident that the actor entrusted with this part could easily call forth many big laughs from the audience if he should play for comedy; yet all these big laughs would be what Mr. George M. Cohan calls "the wrong kind of laughs." They would disrupt the mood of the scene, and would distract attention from Falder or from Ruth. Hence, for the sake of the general effect, the actor playing Cokeson is required to suppress and kill the laughs which might easily be awakened by his lines. He is given funny things to say and is obliged to say them as if they were not funny. In consequence, this character, although extremely life-like, is extremely difficult to play. No such task, for instance, is imposed upon the actor by Pinero when he projects a humorous character, like Cayley Drummle, in the very midst of a tragic complication.

The few points which have already been adduced are sufficient to indicate that *Justice* can by no means be accepted as a consummate example of theatrical talent; but it should always be remembered that theatrical efficiency is the one thing that John Galsworthy made up his mind to get along without. It must be admitted, also, that he got along without it most surprisingly. So great was his dramatic talent that he seemed to achieve more by leaving life alone than he could possibly achieve by arranging life in accordance with a technical pattern, however dexterous theatrically.

It would have been easy, for example, to make the trial-scene in *Justice* more theatrical, by any of a multitude of means. For instance, Falder might have been innocent, and might have been convicted falsely by the piling up of apparently incriminating evidence. Or, if guilty, still the motive of his crime might easily have been made more sympathetic. Falder might, for instance, have stolen the money to save a dying mother from starvation, instead of to elope with a married woman. Or he might have been persecuted by his employer, or treated unfairly by the prosecuting attorney, or judged unjustly by the judge. One, at least, of these obvious aids to the production of "the greatest possible amount of emotional effect" would have been snatched at by almost any other playwright. Any other playwright, also, would have increased the suspense and the surprise of the trial-scene by cleverly deleting from the antecedent act the complete exposure of the case against the hero.

Again, in the third act, any other playwright would have augmented the "emotional effect" by making the warden a tyrant instead of a man who is obviously trying to be kind. The very purpose of the play is to attack the prison-system; yet Galsworthy is, if anything, more fair to the warden and the prison doctor than he is to Falder and the other convicts.

The author's theory, of course, must have been that life itself is so dramatic that it needs no artificial heightening to make it interesting in the theatre. Whether or not this theory shall work in practice depends, as has been said above, upon the subject-matter of the play. In *The Eldest Son,* for instance, the omission of the *scène à faire* from the last act sent the play to failure at a time when Stanley Houghton's discussion of the same theme in *Hindle Wakes* was carried to a great success by a thorough development of the very passage which Galsworthy had chosen to evade.

But *Justice,* in which the subject-matter is inherently dramatic, is undeniably a great play,—despite the fact, or possibly because of the fact, that the treatment of the subject is deliberately untheatrical. The piece appeals profoundly to the sentiment of social pity; and, since it is absolutely true and overwhelmingly sincere, it seems all the more dramatic because it is meticulously untheatrical.

XVI

THE LONG RUN IN THE THEATRE

W E HAVE become so accustomed to the long run in recent years that we are likely to forget that this factor in the conduct of the theatre was utterly unknown until the last half century. Euripides often wrote a play which was intended to be acted only once, and then contentedly went home and wrote another; yet many of his tragedies are likely to be remembered longer than *Abie's Irish Rose*. When Shakespeare first produced *Hamlet* at the Globe Theatre in 1602, we may be certain that he never expected it to be played so many as fifty times—not fifty times consecutively, but fifty times in all, before it was finally discarded and forgotten. Molière never even thought of running a single comedy throughout a season, however popular the comedy might be. In theatrical memoirs of the eighteenth century, we often read of a tragedy that took the town by storm and was acted for as many as ten consecutive nights, or of a comedy that proved itself so popular that it had to be repeated no less than twenty times during the course of the year. So recently as 1863, in our own country of America, Lester Wallack's *Rosedale*, which broke all preëxistent records for popularity, was acted only one hundred and twenty-five times during the first twelve months of its career. Yet nowadays, in New York, a play is commonly regarded as a failure unless it runs at once for at least a hundred consecutive performances.

The development of the long run in the last fifty years has been undoubtedly determined by the growth of modern cities to a population of more than a million; it seems, in consequence, a natural phenomenon; but our present familiarity with the long run should not lead us to neglect to ask whether a system which permits *Tobacco Road* to run consecutively for five years is really more salutary to the drama than the system which inspired the composition of such plays as *Othello*, *Le Misanthrope*, and *The School for Scandal*.

Nobody denies that the long run is a bad thing for the actors, except for the fact that they are thereby assured of continuous employment at a stated salary. It is a bad thing for the "star" performers, because any histrionic composition is likely to become perfunctory if it is repeated for more than a hundred consecutive exhibitions; but it is a much more devastating thing for the minor actors, who—condemned to spend a year in repeating inconsiderable "bits"—miss the needed opportunity for experience and training in a wide variety of parts.

From the financial point of view, the long run is a good thing for the author, since it permits him to make a fortune from a single play—a consummation that was never possible at any previous period in the history of the drama. Thomas Heywood, a successful Elizabethan playwright, was paid three pounds for his best play, *A Woman Killed with Kindness;* and, allowing for the increase in the purchasing power of money in the last three hundred years, this sum would now amount to about seventy-five dollars. On the other hand, the late Avery Hopwood amassed a fortune of a million dollars from the lengthy runs of half a dozen farces which are not likely to be remembered for three centuries.

But, though the theatre is now—as Robert Louis Stevenson remarked—a "gold-mine" for the author, the long run is disadvantageous to the dramatist from another—and perhaps a more important—point of view. Under our present system, the author is condemned to try for a long run, whether he wants to or not; for scarcely any manager is willing to produce a play that does not seem likely to run for at least a hundred nights. To seize an illustration from the analogous art of the novel, our present system in the theatre condemns our authors to emulate Harold Bell Wright or Gene Stratton-Porter, and forbids them absolutely to emulate George Meredith or Henry James.

Whether or not the long run is a good thing for the manager is a question more difficult to answer. Under our present system, the average manager produces four or five new plays in the course of a season. He hopes that one of these may run a year; and he expects, from the profits of this one production—whichever it may be—to liquidate the losses of the others, and thus to finish the year on the right side of the ledger. Any play which does not, almost immediately, show signs of settling down for an entire season's run is summarily discarded within a period of two weeks from the date of the original performance.

This system—to borrow an analogy from the game of roulette— is similar to the system of backing five successive single numbers and hoping that one of them may win, instead of playing more safely with a series of five even chances on the red and black. One of the most intelligent of our American theatrical managers said recently to the present writer, "Our theatre business is not a business at all; it is only a gamble." The main trouble with the business of our theatre at the present time is that it is utterly unbusinesslike.

There are two ways of embarking on a money-making enterprise. One way—the sound, commercial way—is to manufacture one hundred articles and to sell them at a profit of two dollars each. The other way—the dangerous and gambling way—is to manufacture one hundred articles, to sell one of them at a profit of four hundred dollars, and to sell the other ninety-nine at a loss of two dollars each. From the first of these hypothetical transactions, the business man will earn a profit of two hundred dollars; from the second, he will earn a profit of two hundred and two dollars; but everybody will agree that the first transaction is "business" and that the second is "only a gamble."

If our theatre business at the present day is "only a gamble," it is because our managers have made it so, by trying always for long runs. The main trouble with our commercial managers appears to be that they are not sufficiently commercial. They try, over and over again, to hit upon "the one best bet," instead of investing their money more conservatively.

Let us imagine for a moment that all the publishers in America, with two or three exceptions, should decide to-morrow never to print another book outside that field of fiction that is always expected to be "popular." Let us suppose, also, that each of our publishers should decide to issue five novels in the course of the next twelve months, in the hope that one of the five might achieve a sale of one hundred thousand copies; and let us imagine, further, that if any of the novels so issued should seem, within the first month of its career, to be unlikely to attain an ultimate sale of one hundred thousand copies, the publishers should determine to remove it summarily from circulation, destroy the plates, and burn the manuscript. Every author would protest at once that all the publishers had gone insane; and the reading public would clamor loudly against the discontinuance of all books of poetry, biography, history, criticism, scholarship, and science. Yet this hypothetical and almost unimaginable situation in the world of books is precisely the situation that confronts our dramatic authors at the present time in the world of plays. They must write a "best seller" or nothing: they must write a play that seems likely to run a year, or they must not write a play at all.

When every manuscript is judged by its likelihood to achieve a season's run, it follows that many great manuscripts must be rejected. Of such a piece as *The Weavers* of Gerhart Haüptmann, our gambling American managers said for twenty years, "It's a great play, of course; but there isn't a cent of money in it." What they meant, really, was that there wasn't a hundred thousand dollars in it; but the distinction remained unapparent to the gambling mind. When *The Weavers* was at last produced at an abandoned theatre in New York, it ran for more than two months, and it paid its way: but this sort of success has come to seem a sort of failure to the mind that is fixed forever on a season's run. Why bet at all—the gamblers seem to say—unless you have a chance of winning thirty-five for one? But anybody who has ever systematically played roulette will be likely to protest that "that way madness lies."

There are many great plays which might be produced for one month at a total cost of twenty thousand dollars—including all the necessary expenses both of the proprietor of the theatre and of the proprietor of the production—and which, during that period, would be certain to attract to the box-office at least twenty-two thousand dollars. A surplus of ten per cent. in a single month is considered a very good profit in any other business; but, in the gamble of the theatre, our managers persist in losing many times that sum in the hope of ultimately winning one hundred thousand dollars at a single cast.

What we really need is a system which will permit our managers to present a play for six weeks only, with the expectation of reaping a reasonable profit of not less than ten per cent. on each production, but with no intention of running any single play throughout an entire season. This sound and businesslike and sensible system has been adopted by the Theatre Guild; and it is reassuring to record that the productions which have been offered to the public by this organization have been registered among the most interesting enterprises of recent years.

XVII

THE ONE-ACT PLAY IN AMERICA

I

THE DEVELOPMENT of the drama is conditioned, more than that of any other art, by the economic principle of supply and demand. No considerable number of playwrights will devote their energies, in any period, to writing a type of play that is seldom or never called for in the theatre of that period. At the present time, for instance, it would be a waste of labor for an author to construct a play in two parts, of five acts each, to be played upon successive evenings, because, according to our present social custom, it would be almost impossible to persuade any audience to attend the same play two nights running; yet this form was frequently employed in the Elizabethan period (as in the case of Marlowe's *Tamburlaine the Great*) and again in the Restoration period (as in the case of Dryden's *Conquest of Granada*), and even so recently as 1873 it was used by Henrik Ibsen for his "world-historic drama" entitled *Emperor and Galilean*. What these playwrights were allowed to do, in other ages, by the custom of the theatre, our own authors are forbidden to attempt to-day.

But the main point to be observed is that the custom of the theatre is a variable thing, and that just as certain forms may be allowed to lapse from usage in any period, so also is it possible to call other forms into active exercise by the incentive of a general demand. The structure of the drama is determined mainly by the social habits of the theatre-going public. Such apparently minor matters as an alteration of the dinner-hour, for example, may necessitate a revolution in the dramaturgic methods of a nation. In its original form, *Hamlet* was written to be played at three P.M. and to continue until evening; but the piece is now too long to be exhibited in its entirety before an audience that dines late and prefers to go to the theatre after dinner. If Shakespeare were writing this tragedy to-day, he would feel impelled to tell his story in two hours, and he would probably feel forced to alter the superb opening of the drama in order to discount the inevitable interruption imposed upon contemporary playwrights by the discourtesy of tardy diners.

Thus far, the theatre-system in America has discouraged the composition of the one-act play, and the managers who regulate our theatres have steadfastly refused to be persuaded that this interesting type of drama would be welcomed by any considerable proportion of the theatre-going public. But the managers are by no means always right in their estimates of what the public does not want,—a fact that is indicated not infrequently when some adventurer among them achieves an emphatic success by a daring departure from established customs. The one-act play is so worthy in itself, as a medium of artistic expression, and the cultivation of this form would be so helpful to the cause of our dramatic art in general, that it is desirable that we should examine carefully the present attitude of the public and the managers, with a view of asking whether it would not be possible, without running counter to the present social customs of our public, to encourage the development of this special type of drama.

There are, generally speaking, only two ways in which the one-act play can be afforded a professional production. First, it may be presented as an adjunct to a longer play,—either as a curtain-raiser or as an after-piece. Or second, it is possible to make up a special evening's bill by presenting three or four one-act plays together.

Let us, first of all, examine the possibility of presenting one-act plays in conjunction with longer pieces. This possibility is habitually realized in London,—but with unsatisfactory results. In London, the normal dinner-hour of the aristocracy is eight o'clock; and it is therefore impossible to raise the curtain on the chief play of the evening until nine-thirty. But since the pit and gallery are unreserved, these sections of the house are filled before eight o'clock by people who have often stood in line for hours. Since it is necessary to entertain these humbler patrons until the hour when the aristocrats are ready to stroll into the stalls, it is a custom in the London theatres to put on a one-act play as a prelude to the main piece of the evening. But, in their choice of these curtain-raisers, the London managers seem influenced by a depressive sense that only the less important part of the audience will see them.

The custom of using curtain-raisers is not common in New York, for the reason that the dinner-hour is set sixty minutes earlier than in London, and that the entire audience is willing that the curtain should be rung up at half past eight—provided, of course, that everybody be allowed the boorish privilege of coming late. In practice, a successful British play which, in London, was begun at nine-thirty, is begun in New York at forty minutes after eight and is padded out with unnecessary intervals between the acts. By this process, the American manager makes the piece apparently fill the evening and spares himself the expense of preceding it with a curtain-raiser.

An habitual attendant at the New York theatres cannot avoid wondering at the meekness with which the public tolerates this padding. A play that has been announced for eight-thirty will actually be begun at eight-fifty; and, after every act, fifteen minutes will be wasted in an *entr'acte*. The manager is satisfied if he can contrive to defer the final curtain-fall until a few minutes before eleven; and he will subsequently state that there is no demand for one-act plays, because the public is unwilling to come to the theatre before eight-thirty and insists on being let out at eleven. He will tell you about the large proportion of the theatre-going public that has to catch suburban trains; but he will not listen while you count up the time that has deliberately been thrown away between the acts. Here again it must be evident that an opportunity is being wasted, and that the attitude of the managers cannot honestly be accepted as an indication of any real lack of interest, on the part of the public, in the production of one-act plays.

But let us turn now to the consideration of the second possibility. In many of the best theatres of Europe it is customary to present an evening's bill that is made up of three or four one-act plays; and there seems to be no logical reason why a similar experiment should not be successful in America. The example of the Grand Guignol in Paris has been, perhaps, too often cited. The policy of this little theatre is based upon the proposition that a shock, to the nerves or to the conscience, which would be unendurable if protracted through three acts, may safely be effected in the sudden, brief compass of a single act. Most of the plays exploited at the Grand Guignol have, therefore, been sensational.

The authors of these little dramas have combined to exhibit lurid glimpses of life in a Chamber of Horrors; but our loitering and huge and kindly life can really be considered no more as a chamber of horrors than as a vale of tears. The Grand Guignol has shut out from its range of vision the most enjoyable detail of human life,—for it has shut out joy.

In Germany, the one-act play is considered more seriously than in France. A typical instance is the evening's entertainment devised by Hermann Sudermann with the title *Morituri*. This bill consists of three distinct one-act plays which are related to each other only by the circumstance that, in each of them, the leading character is condemned to inevitable death within twenty-four hours and is so situated that he cannot possibly confide his doom to any of the other characters. Such an entertainment as this is eagerly received by the public of the German nations.

In the English-speaking countries, the only company which has committed itself to the policy of regularly presenting three short plays in a single evening is the company of Irish Players of the Abbey Theatre, Dublin. It is a significant fact that this company has repeated its success at home in its several appearances in London, and also in Boston, Chicago, and New York. Instead of offering a repertory of two or three four-act plays, this company presents a repertory of no less than forty brief compositions, in any of which its members are prepared to appear at an hour's notice. It is not difficult to estimate the opportunity that is afforded, by this policy, to the rising dramatists of Ireland. By this repertory system the young author is encouraged to try his hand at one-act plays and is enabled to achieve a reputation in his 'prentice years.

The benign and motherly patron of the Irish Players, Lady Gregory—perhaps in consequence of the demand effected by the policy of this very company—became one of the most accomplished artists in the one-act form in the English language. Her brief dramatic anecdotes rarely attain the tensity that is expected in a full-length play; but they are deeply human in sagacity and broadly generous in humor. They remind us a little of the one-act plays of Molière; and their unassailed success upon the American stage leads us to question if our managers have not been near-sighted in shying away from the production of such amiable compositions in the past.

The only point that may be advanced against a compound

theatre-bill of this sort is the point that is commonly brought forth by publishers to explain their hesitance in bringing out a volume of short-stories. It may be urged that it is difficult for an audience, in the brief space of two hours and a half, to shift its sympathy several times from one set of characters to another. This seems, indeed, to constitute a real objection to the compound bill. Especially when the successive plays are to be performed by the same company of actors, it is difficult for the auditors to forget the first piece in time to deliver themselves completely to the second. Yet this theoretical objection has not made itself apparent in the practice of the Irish Players; and where so much may be gained by the adoption of the European policy of the compound bill, it would seem captious to insist upon what, after all, must merely be a minor point.

II

It would seem, from the foregoing considerations, that the present prejudice in America against encouraging the composition of the one-act play is lacking in logical foundation. But we must now consider the more important question whether the one-act play, if properly encouraged, would prove itself worth while. To this question the only answer must be emphatically in the affirmative.

From the merely practical standpoint, the development of the one-act play is desirable, for two very different reasons. In the first place, a broad market for the one-act play would afford our rising authors a needed opportunity for the exercise of their preliminary efforts toward the ampler craft of dramaturgy. At present, our magazine system affords our future novelists an opportunity to test their talents in the cognate art of the short-story. The short-story, to be sure, is distinct from the novel not only in magnitude but also in method; but a training in the one type is the best of all exercises to fit a young author to adventure on the other. To prove this point, one need only cite the instances of Hawthorne and Daudet. But at present our incipient dramatists are afforded no opportunity to exercise their wings in swallow-flights; and this fact militates strongly against the general effectiveness of our dramatic art.

As much time is required to write a single four-act play as to write half a dozen one-act plays. In the case of a new author, his ambitious four-act play will probably be bad; but if he could spend the same time in working out six little dramas in a single act, it is probable that one of them at least might be worthy of production. Those who have at last succeeded in a difficult art are likely to forget the terrible necessity of encouragement to those who still are striving; but one success in six brief efforts must mean more to an aspirant than the failure of a single more ambitious effort. Hence, in order to encourage the authors of a younger generation, it is tremendously desirable that we should put in common practice the policy of producing one-act plays.

But, of course, it may be questioned whether or not it is the business of the manager to encourage the efforts of the rising generation. Looking at the matter merely from the financial standpoint, this question must be decided emphatically in the affirmative. It is true, at any time, in any art, that "the old order changeth, yielding place to new"; and, in the theatre, that manager is most sure of making money who can hitch his wagon to the rising star of an author of real promise. It would, therefore, be profitable for our managers to establish a training-school for the talents of potential dramatists; and the most efficient training-school would be a theatre devoted to the production of one-act plays.

In the second place, a more general composition of one-act plays would offer our amateur actors a more easy opportunity to exercise their talents. The production of the average drama of ordinary length requires an expenditure beyond the means of amateurs; but the majority of one-act plays may be produced at very small expense. Of course, the question may be asked why the guardians of our dramatic destiny should trouble their minds at all to consider the demands of amateurs; but the answer is very simple. From the professional standpoint, the advantage of amateur acting is that it fits the amateur performers for a more comprehensive enjoyment of the achievements of the professional theatre. The surest way to teach a boy or girl to appreciate the artistry of the sonnets of Rossetti is to encourage the student to write sonnets of his own. His efforts will probably be bad; but the mere exercise of his otherwise unrewarded attempts will prepare him the better to appreciate the achievement of the few great artists who have succeeded in the endeavor which has proved itself beyond his reach. To encourage amateur acting is to prepare an audience for the keen appreciation of the professional theatre; and any policy that meets the needs of amateurs should therefore be encouraged.

III

But apart from these immediate considerations, it must be maintained that the one-act play is admirable in itself, as a medium of art. It shows the same relation to the full-length play as the short-story shows to the novel. It makes a virtue of economy of means. It aims to produce a single dramatic effect with the greatest economy of means that is consistent with the utmost emphasis. The method of the one-act play at its best is similar to the method employed by Browning in his dramatic monologues. The author must suggest the entire history of a soul by seizing it at some crisis of its career and forcing the spectator to look upon it from an unexpected and suggestive point of view. A one-act play, in exhibiting the present, should imply the past and intimate the future. The author has no leisure for laborious exposition; but his mere projection of a single situation should sum up in itself the accumulated results of many antecedent causes. The piece should be inconclusive, and yet pregnant with conclusions. The playwright should open a momentary little vista upon life, and then—with a sort of wistful smile—should ring the curtain down. The one-act play, at its best, can no more serve as a single act of a longer drama than the short-story can serve as a single chapter of a novel. The form is complete, concise, and self-sustaining; and it requires an extraordinary focus of imagination.

In view of the technical difficulties of this artistic form, it might be questioned whether we are equipped with the necessary talent to achieve a literature of one-act plays, even if our managers could be persuaded to offer due encouragement to the composition of this type of drama; but to this question, once again, the only answer must be in the affirmative. It is undeniable that any of our established dramatists could write a one-act play if the policy of our theatres should encourage him to do so; and it is scarcely less deniable that acceptable one-act plays might be written, under the stimulus of due encouragement, by any of the large army of authors who now contribute meritorious short-stories to our American magazines. There can be no question that we possess the talent; all that remains requisite is a theatrical policy that shall call our latent talent into active exercise.

SEEN ON THE STAGE

1

THE FUNCTION OF DRAMATIC CRITICISM

I̶F I WERE asked to name the one thing that the drama in America stood most in need of at the present moment, I should say dramatic criticism. In order to cultivate the finest flower of any art, it is necessary to coördinate to a common end the complementary activities of the productive spirit and the critical spirit. The theatre in America is at present fairly healthy on the productive side. We have at least two native dramatists whose work is worthy of serious consideration; we have several native playwrights of real promise; we have many able actors; we have three or four fine stage-directors; and we have one or two managers who import the best plays of other nations, and make it possible for us to see them on our stage and to compare them with our own. But our dramatic movement is deficient on the critical side. We have at present no dramatic critic of the first rank, and we have only three or four writers who seem to be making any earnest effort to achieve the purpose of dramatic criticism. It is not that our newspapers and our magazines devote too little attention to the theatre; they devote, indeed, too much; but this attention is not critical in spirit. Nearly every newspaper in the country gives up many columns every week to comment, of some sort, upon the theatre; and several of our magazines conduct departments that are devoted to the stage. But the more we read the newspapers and the magazines, the more we shall perceive that the great majority of our professional commentators on the theatre are not, in the true sense, critics, and do not even aim to be. In fact, the one feature of their writing that strikes us most emphatically is the absence of any endeavor or desire to fulfil the function of dramatic criticism.

Concerning the function of criticism in general, there can be, I think, no question. It was stated once for all by Matthew Arnold, in one of those great phrases which, as soon as they are formulated, seem to have been graven forever upon granite. He defined criticism as "a disinterested endeavor to learn and propagate the best that is known and thought in the world, and thus to establish a current of fresh and true ideas." From this we may derive the definition of dramatic criticism as "a disinterested endeavor to learn and propagate the best that is known and thought in the theatre of the world." The critic incurs a double duty,—first, to learn, and secondly, to teach:—to study in general the theatre of the world, and in particular the theatre of his own place and time, in an unfaltering endeavor to discover what is best in the current drama; and then to teach the public what is best by making clear the reasons why. His ultimate responsibility is not to the creator but to the public. It is not his duty to teach Eugene O'Neill how to write plays (supposing that were possible!): it is his duty to teach the public how Mr. O'Neill *has* written them. But to do this, he must first have learned, and learned from the creative masters of the art.

The first mark of the true critic is, therefore, the eagerness to learn. Criticism requires, as a firm foundation, both a broad and general culture and a deep particular equipment for the work in hand. The critic must be cognizant of life; for the drama is a visioning of life, and how can he judge the counterfeit presentment unless he knows the zest and tang of the original? He must be familiar with the aims and methods of the other arts; for how else can he judge that complex product, a modern acted play, where all the arts do seem to set their seal? He must have studied thoroughly the drama of other times and lands; for by what standards, otherwise, can he appraise the merit of the drama now at hand? And all these studies should have furnished him material from which to derive inductively the principles to guide him in his judgment. These principles (which are empirical always, and never *a priori*) he should build into a body of belief; and this philosophy of the dramatic art he should expound, whenever necessary, to the public, and should illustrate, whenever possible, in each particular review.

So much for the necessity of culture. Let us turn now to that other necessity of a particular equipment for the work in hand. The art of the drama is a living thing, and like all living things is growing. As a consequence, the philosophy of the drama, in any period of criticism, can be regarded only as pragmatical. A principle will serve only so long as it will serve. A new invention (like electric-lighting, for example) may quickly revolutionize the making of plays and require a consonant revolution in the principles of judging them. The very next play to be produced may demand of the critic that he shall broaden, or materially alter, his body of belief: for—let us insist again—the purpose of criticism is never to announce dogmatically how plays shall be made (for that would be absurd), but always to explain how they *have* been made, and to elucidate the reasons why. The critic, therefore, can never rest upon his oars; he can never be certain that what he knows already has equipped him fully to appreciate the next important dramatist who may appear. Therefore, he should keep his mind forever fresh and open, to receive and to evaluate each new impression, with all its possibilities of principle. The dramatic critic must be a tireless theatre-goer. To be a theatre-goer is not considered, by most people, difficult; but to maintain a tireless and searching mind amid a making of many plays to which there seems to be no end requires a moral power which ranks only a little on the hither side of the heroic.

And there are other moral qualities without which a writer cannot serviceably fulfil the function of dramatic criticism, however broad his culture, however thorough his equipment. The first of these is sympathy; and this quality is rare. The critic must exercise an eager catholicity of taste. He must appreciate not only what he likes but also what he does not like, provided that there be any adequate reason why other people like it. In his tireless and impersonal searching for the best, he must equally evaluate whatever is good of its kind in any type of play. He should judge a given work in accordance with the endeavor of the author. He must find out what sort of effect the author intended to produce and then determine to what extent he has succeeded in producing that effect. Ibsen intended a certain effect in *Hedda Gabler;* and if that were a new play, it would not be at all fair for the critic to prejudge it adversely because that effect is totally different from the effect, for example, that Shakespeare intended in *As You Like It.* Though a man may write of Shakespeare with the eloquence of angels, he is still an inefficient critic unless he can both learn and teach the merits of Ibsen, who has made some stir in the theatre of the world with work of an entirely different order. The critic should have no prejudices. Although he may have suffered through ten successive bad plays by a certain author, he must always be ready to recognize the merit of that author's eleventh play if it should surprisingly surpass its predecessors. Authors sometimes grow up.

Since the endeavor of real criticism is to learn and propagate the best, it is evident that its function is not destructive but constructive; and this is another reason why the critic must be richly endowed with sympathy. There seems to be a prevalent impression that the business of the critic is mainly to make adverse remarks concerning plays that happen to be bad; and this impression—utterly fallacious as it is—is emphatically detrimental to the cause of criticism. It is not the proper function of dramatic criticism to waste good thought upon the subject of bad plays. Most bad plays would die a natural death if they were merely let alone; and the critic should ignore them. His duty is to discover what is good, to explain why it is good, and to do all in his power to make the good prevail. This is more than enough to keep him busy; and to ask him to explain why a bad play is bad is to impose a superfluous task upon his patience. From the point of view of the ideal of criticism, it is surely a mistake for our newspapers to devote an almost equal amount of space to the review of every new play, irrespective of the nature of its aim or the quality of its execution. When a bad play is produced, it would be better to review it in some such terms as these:—"Last evening a play called *Crime*, by John Smith, was produced at Brown's Theatre, with Mary Jones in the leading role. The audience seemed to like it (or seemed not to). There is nothing in it that requires critical consideration." Sometimes, of course, when a bad play has succeeded and is being patronized by the public in preference to several better plays, it may become the duty of the critic to prove that it is bad, in order, by this negative procedure, to help the better to prevail; but even this duty is of minor importance compared with some constructive task of criticism. Our magazine writers are granted this great advantage over our newspaper writers,—that they are permitted to ignore unworthy work; but they seem to be expected to devote more space to the consideration of plays that have succeeded than to plays that have failed. This latter editorial requirement leads them often into error. Any question of financial success or failure is impertinent to criticism. Criticism seeks the best; and for the critic it is more important to write at length about a good play that has failed in a night than about a poorer play that has crowded the theatre for an entire season.

But an even more important moral quality that is required of the critic is the delicate faculty of disinterestedness. He should always tell the truth as he sees it, for the sole and self-sufficient reason that that is how he sees the truth, and should remain impervious to any ulterior consideration. But it is very difficult to be disinterested. Our newspapers, for instance, seem to have a habit of judging certain plays according to what is called their "news value," instead of according to their quality as works of art.

The disinterested critic will not be influenced by that fetish of editors and publishers whose name is "what the public wants." If the public invariably and infallibly wanted the best that is known and thought, there would be no work for criticism to accomplish. And, in the pursuance of his labor to help the best art to prevail, the critic should never for a moment consider whether or not the public is likely to enjoy the things he has to say. He should never write for popularity; he should always be inconsiderate of himself; and this is, perhaps, the finest flower of disinterestedness.

The final mark of the true critic is the eagerness to teach. "Every great poet is a teacher," said Wordsworth, "I wish to be considered as a teacher or as nothing." Concerning this conception of the poet's function there may be some question; but I do not think that any one can doubt that every great critic is a teacher. What other word than this so aptly fits a writer whose endeavor is to "propagate the best that is known and thought"? It is the critic's privilege to teach the public what he himself has learned from his tireless study of the works of the creators. The theatre-going public is not tireless; it lacks, because it is a crowd, both culture and equipment; it is deficient in appreciation, in poise, in sanity, in judgment. It needs the service of the critic to estimate for it the value of its own experience. And the dramatist also needs the service of the critic to elucidate his message and explain his merits to a public that otherwise might miss the aim of his endeavor. The critic acts as a mediator between the artist and the multitude, explaining the one to the many, gathering the many to a fresh and true appreciation of the one.

This point,—that the critic must be considered as a teacher or as nothing,—seems to me to be, in any high view of the question, unassailable; and yet this is precisely the point that is missed in all but a very little of that vast volume of writing concerning the contemporary theatre which pours from the presses of our American newspapers and magazines. Most of our dramatic columns and departments seem to be edited with the idea that the function of the critic is not to teach, but to entertain, not to think, but merely (heaven knows why!) to be facetious. The critic of painting is not expected to be funny about Velasquez, but the critic of the drama seems to be expected to be funny about Ibsen. Of course there are times when the most effective way to teach a certain truth is by laughing very hard: consider, as an illustration, G. K. Chesterton's bracing habit of leading us to laugh our way into the very presence of his God. But there are also times for giving over laughter, and removing our hats decorously,—in the presence, say, of M. Maeterlinck.

The persevering triviality of the treatment of the drama in our press seems to be due to the fact that the majority of our American publishers have misconceived the sort of interest that our public has begun, latterly, to take in the dramatic art. Our drama is no longer a thing to joke about. Serious works by serious-minded playwrights are being set forth, with adequate acting and exemplary stage-direction, by serious-minded managers; and these works are being patronized by serious-minded people. Our publishers, for the most part, are a tremulous lot. They are beset forever with the fear—to use their own phrase—of "talking over people's heads." They do not dare to teach, for fear that nobody will listen. But the heads of those who read about the theatre in our various publications loom far higher than these publishers imagine; and the danger of talking over them is not nearly so considerable as that other danger—never thought about, apparently—of talking under them. The general reader—that genial gentleman who pays our printer's bills—does not read about the theatre unless he is interested in the theatre; and an interest in the theatre is in itself an indication of intelligence. Any person who cares at all about an art must be capable of caring earnestly about it; any intelligent person must be willing to think seriously concerning a subject that he cares about. Why, then, should we treat our theatre-going public as if it were incapable of thought, and eager only to look at pictures of pretty women and read facetious trivialities?

But not only is dramatic criticism wanted by the theatre-going public; it is also wanted—it is indeed desperately needed—by our best creative artists in the drama. The dramatist who has written a good play does not need to be told why it is good; but he *does* need that the public shall be told why it is good, by some one whose judgment the public has learned to respect. We are at present passing through a period of uneven merit in our theatre; and amid the multitudinous bewilderment of presentations, the average theatre-goer is left at a loss to know which plays to patronize. Hence the intervention of the critic is absolutely necessary, in order that the best plays may be assisted to prevail. Not until the function of dramatic criticism assumes among us the dignity and the authority which it has long exercised in Paris shall we be at all certain that the best plays will prevail and the poorest plays go under. And how, unless we can be fairly certain that the best plays will prevail, shall our promising dramatists be encouraged to stride forward boldly in their art,—to conquer new provinces of truth in the expectation of a new appreciation?

For, as Arnold said, it is one of the functions of criticism to prepare the way for new creative effort by establishing a current of fresh and true ideas. The drama, in particular, is an art that derives its inspiration from the attitude of the general and public mind. You cannot give a drama of ideas to an audience devoid of them; but to an audience that has been taught to think, you can give a drama that makes it think profoundly. The critic, by teaching the public to appreciate what is best in the plays it has already seen, may prepare it to appreciate what is best in the plays that our advancing dramatists will set before it ten and twenty years from now. Thus criticism not only follows but precedes creation. The critic is not only an expositor of the best that has been done; he is also a herald and annunciator of the best that is to be.

LIFE AND THE THEATRE

HE QUICKEST answer to the question, "What is the purpose
of art?", would come with the retort courteous, "What
is the purpose of life?"; for both aims are indeed identical,
since art is nothing else than the quintessence of life.
The purpose of life has been discussed ever since the human race
became articulate; and an adequate review of this discussion would
require a *résumé* of all the great religions of the world. Without
attempting to cover so colossal a subject in an unpretentious essay,
the present writer asks permission to offer an opinion concerning
what appear to him to be the noblest and the meanest answers to
this all-important question.

The most ignoble definition of the purpose of life was formulated, in fairly recent times, by the Puritans of England and the
Calvinists of Scotland. According to the concept of these dour,
sour, glowering religionists, this world is nothing but a vale of
tears, through which a man should slink whining, like a beaten
dog with his tail between his legs, in the hope of being caught up
subsequently into a nobler and a better life which shall offer to
him a renewal of those opportunities for positive appreciation
which, on principle, he had neglected throughout the pitiful and
wasted period of his sojourn upon earth. The Puritans and Calvinists warned their devotees against the lure of beauty, and
branded it as an ensnarement of the devil; and, by this token, they
are damned, if there is such a sentence as damnation in the supreme
court of everlasting law.

The noblest answer to the basic question, "What is the purpose
of life?", was asseverated by the noblest men who ever lived,—
those great Athenians who crowned this earth with their Acropolis,
two thousand and four hundred years ago. These men asserted that
our world should be regarded as a valley of soul-making,—a sort

of training-camp for infinite futurity, in which the individual should find an opportuntiy to indicate his worthiness to live, by accepting every offered chance to prove himself alive.

That lovely and lasting phrase, "the valley of soul-making," was not invented by the ancient Greeks: it was formulated by John Keats, who is their true apostle to all modern nations, and, because of that, the greatest poet of recent centuries. It was Keats, also, who was destined to remind a forgetful world that "Beauty is Truth, Truth Beauty," and that both of these ideals are identical with the ideal of Righteousness. There is one God, in three aspects:—Beauty, which appeals to the emotions; Truth, which appeals to the intellect; Righteousness, which appeals to the conscience. This is the Gospel according to John Keats: this is the Law and the Prophets.

If this world—according to the ancient Greeks—is to be regarded as a valley of soul-making, and if—according to the apostolic vision of John Keats—there is no basic difference between Beauty, Truth, and Righteousness, it becomes the duty of every transient visitor to this valley to develop, in the little time allotted to him, what Rudyard Kipling has described as "the makin's of a bloomin' soul," by keeping his spirit at all moments responsive and awake to every drifting evidence of what is True or Beautiful or Right.

If the purpose of life is to prove ourselves alive, in order to indicate our fitness for continuing to live in some hypothetical domain where second chances are accorded in the future, it behooves us to live as intensely and convincingly as possible throughout that fleeting period of three score years and ten which is allotted to us, on the average, in this immediate valley of soul-making.

It is only at infrequent intervals throughout our period of living that the best of us is able to feel himself to be alive. Sir Thomas Browne has penned an eloquent comment on this fact, in the concluding section of his famous *Letter to a Friend*, in which he says, —"And surely if we deduct all those days of our life which we might wish unlived, and which abate the comfort of those we now live; if we reckon up only those days which God hath accepted of our lives, a life of good years will hardly be a span long." There is also, in the record of eternal literature, a comparatively recent poem by John Masefield, called *Biography*, in which the poet, bemoaning the ironic chance that many inconsiderable days in his experience may be reduced by his biographer "to lists of dates and facts," celebrates with lyric eloquence the unrecorded dates of several magnificent impressions and expressions of the soul which would escape the merely secondary apperceptiveness of any scholarly investigator.

The purpose of life appears to be to live while yet we may—as the poet Tasso told us, in one of the most forlorn and lovely passages of lyric literature,—to seize every fleeting opportunity for feeling and asserting that we are alive, in order to indicate our fitness for continuing to live in some hypothetic future region, "beyond the loom of the last lone star through open darkness hurled." Immortality, in order to be won, should be deserved; and no man is worthy of eternal life unless he has accepted every chance for living that has been offered to him in his transitory progress throughout this difficult but dreamful valley of soul-making.

We feel ourselves to be alive only at those divided and ecstatic moments when we overwhelmingly become aware of the identity of Beauty, Truth, and Righteousness, and thereby undergo an instant flash of cosmic consciousness. It is evermore our purpose to repeat these moments. We desire ardently to prove ourselves to be alive. Many of us follow false allurements—drink or drugs, religion or the unspontaneous and manufactured fire of simulated love; but if such mortals fail in their pursuit, their failure should be written down to inexperience and not necessarily to conscious abnegation of a floating and far-off ideal. "Beauty is Truth, Truth Beauty"; and this axiom is so augustly sound that it is nobler to faint and fall in the pursuit of some *ignis fatuus* of truth or beauty than to slink through all experience reservedly, like a cringing cur with tail between the legs.

In the experience of the average man—whose acuteness of perception in the intellectual, emotional, or moral sphere is merely mediocre—the actuality of living offers only infrequent and wistful opportunities for life. For this reason, he is required to rely on art to present to him those opportunities for life that he has missed. Art extracts the quintessence of life, and serves it up freely to millions of men who, because of their own dullness, have not been able to extract it for themselves. Art offers, to the average man, the only royal road to an appreciation of all the wonders of this valley of soul-making, and affords him the only available opportunity to experience the sense of life vicariously.

This, then, is the excuse for art, and the answer to any theoretic question that seeks to probe its purpose:—the aim of art is to provide a sense of life for men who, in themselves, are not sufficiently alive to create art by their very living.

We may come now—as a corollary of this thesis—to consider the proper function of the theatre. The theatre exists—in theory—as an institution which promises to provide the ordinary man with a keen impression of life, in exchange for two dollars of money and two hours of time. The theatre promises the public a more instant and intense sensation of the miracle of life than is usually offered in a month of living. The average man has only a few years in which to live, in this valley of soul-making; and if he can save a day, a week, or possibly a month, by going to the theatre, he is more than willing to follow the allurement of this royal road. But in response to this fidelity, which can only be regarded as idealistic, the theatre incurs and is required to assume the duty of offering to the average man the promised taste of life.

There are two ways in which the theatre can furnish to the public a vicarious experience of life: first, by imitation, and, second, by suggestion. The first method is employed by the realists, and the second method is employed by the romantics. This is not a time to argue concerning the respective merits of these two contrasted methods: it is sufficient, in the present context, to state that neither method can succeed in practice unless it shall convince the public that the two hours required for the traffic of the stage have been spent more profitably in the theatre than they might have been spent elsewhere.

The average spectator—disappointed, for the moment, by his individual experience of living at large—attends the theatre in the hope of quickening his consciousness of life. He wants the play to happen not so much upon the stage as in himself. He goes to the theatre—quite literally—to enjoy himself:—that is to say,—his own contributive response of emotion and of thought. The play must happen *to him*; or else, by his judgment, the play must be dismissed as a failure. He is seeking an opportunity to live and to feel himself alive; and, if this opportunity is not accorded to him, he will warn his friends away from the production that he has attended.

For this reason, a realistic play that invites the quick response of recognition for facts that have been faithfully observed must carry out the letter of its contract; and a romantic play, which pretends, without reliance on admitted and accepted facts, to suggest some evident, irrefutable law of nature, must also convince the members of the audience that they have really witnessed vicariously a vision of life itself, as life is generally understood.

Nothing, in the theatre, can ever be successful unless it offers some vicarious experience of life. The best-made play will fail unless it affords some suggestion of life that is more potent than its emphasis on mechanism. The popularity of actresses and actors is measured by the extent of their ability to seem alive. This ability, in many cases, may result from training and experience; in many other cases, it may result more directly from that inexplicable power which is commonly described as "personality." Life is what the public seeks, in going to the theatre; and the appearance, or else the illusion, of life is what it welcomes and rewards in those who exert themselves behind the footlights.

III

PERSONAL GREATNESS ON THE STAGE

RALPH WALDO EMERSON once wrote a noble essay on the *Uses of Great Men;* but, in this disquisition, he neglected to discuss the simplest and the subtlest service that is rendered by great people to the ordinary public. "He is great," said Emerson, "who is what he is from nature, and who never reminds us of others"; and again, "Every one can do his best thing easiest": but the philosopher omitted the important point that any one who does his best thing easily, without reminding us of others, seems always more alive than the common herd of humankind.

Great men are more alive than others; and this is the token of their greatness. Furthermore, the liveliness—to call it so—that tingles in them is a central and creative source of energy that radiates an influence electrical through all of the environing ether. Nothing can be dark that sits unshadowed in the sun; and no human being can be dull when he comes into contact with a super-man. Of any personage who does supremely and superbly anything that ordinary people find it difficult to do, it may be said, in the Biblical phrase, that "a virtue goes out of him." Because he feels himself to be alive, he communicates unconsciously a sense of life to many other people who seemed dead before he walked among them.

Great men can never be mistaken or ignored. "By their works ye shall know them," if it be possible to watch them at their work, or to study—after many years or centuries—their easily accomplished products: but, otherwise, it is always possible to recognize them by their very presence. Something clutches at your throat and squeezes tears into your eyes. It is a recorded fact of history that one day, when Abraham Lincoln was gazing out of a window of the White House, he turned suddenly to Secretary Stanton and said, "There goes a man!" His eyes had been attracted by a casual pedestrian that he had never seen before. This man was Walt

Whitman,—the greatest American, with the single exception of Lincoln himself, that has ever yet been born.

The thing to be admired among men is greatness; and, wherever greatness undeniably exists, there is no time to quarrel about minor questions of degree or quality. Whoever can do any tiny thing, however trivial, more perfectly than any other person in the world is admitted, by this token, to the principality of greatness. Nearly forty years ago it was my privilege to meet a bootblack in Detroit whose name I never asked but whose eyes I shall never forget. My shoes were very shabby as I mounted his throne; for they had not been shined since I had left New York. He went to work upon them with a will: and, when he had finished, "Can they do that better in the east?", he asked, and, "No!", I answered. "That's because I put my soul into it," he said. This was an Italian boy, with a face like those that Ghirlandaio loved to paint, many centuries ago, in Florence; and he will never see this printed paragraph that celebrates his glory; but he made me feel alive, one little moment, nearly forty years ago; and I wish, now, that I knew his name.

Whatever sits in moonlight is lighted by the moon and silvered into poetry; and whoever comes into contact with a super-person is tingled, for the moment, into life. The recipient imagination leaps upon the back of Pegasus; for like calls out to like, and a great person unconsciously requires us to greet him sympathetically with a kindred greatness. We ascend to something better than our ordinary self when we encounter the greatest maker of poems or of pies that happens to be living in our world. These encounters add a cubit to our stature, and send us back to our customary tasks "eager to labor and eager to be happy."

The mystic force called "personality" is nothing but an aura that is worn by people who can do some single thing extremely well and with consummate grace. Personality is always charming and enlivening; and the application of its power is not at all dependent on the exercise of that particular proficiency in which the person who attracts us may excel. Great people are not called upon to prove their greatness. Sarah Bernhardt, at the age of six and seventy, could no longer slink about the stage with that agile grace, as of a panther, that some of us remember: in fact, because of her amputated leg, she could not walk at all. When the curtain rose, she was disclosed reclining on a couch or seated in a chair;

and only at the climax did she climb to her feet—with obvious assistance—and thereby send a shudder through the audience. But her triumph came early, at the very rising of the curtain, before she had made a movement, before she had uttered a single syllable with the shattered remnants of a voice that once was golden: for the audience immediately knew—without asking or waiting for any evidence—that this was one of the great women of the world. There were cheers and there were tears; for greatness is rare, and demands the sounding of sennets and the pouring of libations. Journeys are measured by mile-stones; and our journey through life is measured by those moments when we have been quickened into momentary greatness by contact with great people.

To be a great base-ball player is more impressive than to be a mediocre painter, a second-rate statesman, or an ordinary author. It is nobler to be able to beat the world at some plebeian task, like the sewing on of buttons, than to be an inefficient king or a defeated general. This the public always knows, without asking any questions; and nobody is certain or is worthy of applause unless he can do at least some little thing that he was born to do by nature, more perfectly than that thing can be done by any-body else. But such a person seems to be transfigured by the central and essential source of energy that lives within him; and this transfiguration easily includes whoever comes within the circle of its radiation. The service of great people to the public may be summed up in the saying that whoever looks upon or listens to them is always lifted, for the moment, out of mediocrity and re-quired to ascend to the height of the occasion.

On the evening of October 22, 1917, the Lexington Opera House—which is one of the largest theatres in New York—was crowded from the floor to the roof. Hundreds of people were standing up, and hundreds of other people had been turned away. This vast audience sat respectfully through a vaudeville program of five preliminary numbers. At last the orchestra struck up with a medley of familiar Scottish airs, and there came a quickened sense of something wonderful about to be.

And then the miracle occurred. A little stocky man in a red kilt came trotting on the stage, and turned the funniest of faces to the footlights; and the whole enormous auditorium exploded with volley after volley of applause and the high shrill shriek of cheers. It was a long, long time before this thunderous initial roar subsided; but, when he could be heard, the funny little red-faced man proceeded to sing a song, with the refrain, "I'm going to Marry 'Arry, on the Fifth of Jan-u-ary." There was no art in the words and very little in the music; but there was great art in the rendering. The audience shouted with laughter; and every laugh came precisely at the predetermined moment, with the full power of three thousand pairs of lungs behind it.

Then came other songs; and the stocky little man, who had made that whole vast theatreful of people laugh as one, soon made them weep as one, and ultimately made them sing as one. His third or fourth number was a new song, which nobody had ever heard before; but, when Harry Lauder came to the refrain, he heard it taken up and hummed by hundreds and hundreds of voices in the auditorium. Then he paused; and, with consummate tact, he deliberately rehearsed the audience in the proper handling of the chorus, so that, when he came again to the refrain, the very walls resounded with the singing of a thousand happy people. These people had come to enjoy the art of Harry Lauder; but the great man had given them a greater gift by teaching them to enjoy themselves.

Through all of this, the present writer retained sufficient critical intelligence to perceive the artist's mastery of rhythm and of tempo, his marvelous sense of the emphasis of pause, and his genius for taking immediate advantage of every unforeseen re-action of the audience. He never said or sang a word too little or too much; he never overworked a laugh nor allowed a tear to dry and be forgotten. But these are minor matters: for art, however brilliant, must take second place to life, and it was life itself that Harry Lauder flung full-fingered through the auditorium. When calls for encores came, it was, "Harry, sing us this!", and, "Harry, sing us that!", for he was only Harry now, and hundreds of people were shouting loud the titles of the songs that they desired.

There were many, many calls for "We Hoose Among the Heather," but Harry paused before he rendered it. "That's nae mair a song," he said, "it's a hymn now"; and then he told how he had sung it recently before fifteen thousand Scottish troopers at Arras. He sang it again in the Lexington Theatre; but it sounded now as if all Scotland had burst spontaneously into song.

And then the audience began to see the transfiguration of a great artist into a great man; for something had happened to the Harry

Lauder that we used to know; and it was this:—Death had touched him with its accolade, and bidden him rise up as a knight-errant in a stricken world, where now he lives the life of two.

Sir Harry went down to Camp Upton to entertain our soldiers. He told them of the flowers of France, and how they grew in full profusion right up to the line that the Huns had marked with desolation. He told them of his love for France,—the second home and foster-mother of all the artists of the world, who worship Beauty, Truth, and Righteousness. Then he paused, and added,— "I own a bit of France now: my boy is buried there. . . ."

IV

HERO-WORSHIP IN THE DRAMA

HERO-WORSHIP, as Carlyle has told us, is a fundamental instinct of the human mind; and this is particularly evident whenever people are gathered together in crowds. Nothing else so strongly stirs emotion in a multitude as the visible presence of a hero, whatever be the nature of his prowess. Line Fifth Avenue with congregated thousands; let General Pershing ride adown that human lane on horseback; and only the walking dead will be callous to resist that gulping in the throat which is the prelude to enthusiastic tears.

In the good old days of baseball, this phenomenon could often be observed at the Polo Grounds, when Christopher Mathewson was called upon in the ninth inning to save a game that hung tremulously in the balance. It was beautiful to see him as he strolled serenely to the centre of the diamond, apparently unconscious of the plaudits of the crowd. He was a great man in his own profession; and he had the dignity of greatness. He excelled all other pitchers; and this excellence was testified immediately to the eye by the unusual simplicity and ease of his bodily movements. His two arms swept superbly upward in an absolute curve that reminded the spectator of Græco-Roman statues of athletes in the Vatican; and that was all. He had perfect personal poise; he was never nervous, never flustered, never angry. Mathewson made himself a hero not merely by his prowess, but also by his personality. The multitude adored him. And, by awakening this adoration, he bestowed a benefit upon uncounted crowds; for nothing more effectually emancipates the average man from his dreary prison-cell of self than a wished-for opportunity to worship some big person who does something—it does not really matter what it is—much better than that same thing could be done by himself or by anybody else.

356

In view of this fact, it is hard to understand why the theatre should persistently neglect its easy opportunity to exhibit figures of heroical dimensions. Every audience is a crowd, and is subject to the incentives of crowd psychology. Design a set of Gothic buildings, suggestive of mediæval Orléans; throng the stage with supernumeraries; decree an entrance of Jeanne d'Arc, clad in silvery armor and seated high upon a snow-white horse; and the audience will cheer, and the most case-hardened of dramatic critics will have a hard time trying to hold back his tears. For this is drama. The drama began in the church,—an institution which exists for the purpose of stimulating a wished-for mood of worship in a gathered multitude, to the end that souls of men may be uplifted toward their ultimate salvation.

What is the use of fiction if it cannot show us imaginable people who, in one way or another, are bigger than ourselves? The opportunity of the theatre is immense; for it may unlock for us the ivory gates that give upon immensity. Is it, after all, worth while to pay five dollars for the privilege of seeing the heroine of a bedroom farce dive under a bed, when the same expenditure of time and money might procure the great experience of awakening within us that quick response to the heroic which is evermore instinctive in a gathered crowd?

> When the high heart we magnify,
>   And the sure vision celebrate,
> And worship greatness passing by,
>   Ourselves are great.

Because of the obtuseness of our American managers—for our managers are more to be blamed than our playwrights for the vacuity of our American drama—it remained for an English poet, John Drinkwater, to discover the simple fact that a great emotion could be evoked from the gathered public by exhibiting upon the stage a hero so generally known and so unanimously worshiped as Abraham Lincoln.

John Drinkwater has drawn a portrait of Lincoln that is faithful to the truth—if not, at all points, to the facts—of history. That is, very nearly, all that he has done; but it is enough. It is better to spend two hours in the imagined presence of one of the greatest heroes of all time than to spend a hundred evenings at the Winter Garden; and this the public knows.

Drinkwater's play is so extremely simple that either it is artless or else it is one of those rare works in which the highest sort of art succeeds in concealing itself. It exhibits six successive episodes in Lincoln's career. These episodes are not related logically to each other; but each of them shows the hero at some moment when he is required to make a decision that shall determine not only his own future, but also the future of his country. On past occasions, I have sometimes disagreed with the theory of William Archer that the element of crisis is the one most indispensable element of the drama; but, on this particular occasion, I am constrained to agree with Archer, because Drinkwater has undeniably succeeded in setting forth a satisfactory portrait of Lincoln by adopting the easy expedient of showing him at six successive turning-points in his career.

At a hasty glance, this play might be dismissed as a mere summary in dialogue of the high spots in Lord Charnwood's biography of Lincoln; but a closer study of the text reveals the fact that Drinkwater has written a piece that is surprisingly effective, not so much by reason of what he has done as by reason of what he has resisted the temptation to do. His drama is singularly beautiful in its reticence, and all the more impressive by reason of its shy and quiet dignity. It is so deliberately untheatrical that it could hardly have been composed by an author who was not a master of the theatre. John Drinkwater does not overstate the case for Lincoln; instead, he understates it, and thereby stimulates the audience to erect a huge, heroic statue of this man of many sorrows.

V

YOUTH AND AGE IN THE DRAMA

S OME years ago, when *The Boomerang*, by Winchell Smith and Victor Mapes, was settling down to its record-making run at the Belasco Theatre, the present writer happened to enjoy an interesting conversation with David Belasco concerning the career of that very slight but delicately modulated comedy. In discussing the basic reasons for the quite extraordinary popularity of this play, which he admitted to be fragile, Mr. Belasco said that the public flocked to see *The Boomerang* because it dealt with the emotions of young people, in terms that young people could easily appreciate. He then advanced the interesting theory that the average age of the theatre-going public is only twenty-two or twenty-three, and that, to attract a great deal of money to the box-office, it is necessary first of all to please the girl of twenty-two and the young gentleman whom she allures to take her to the play. If the young folks are satisfied, said Mr. Belasco, the success of any undertaking in the theatre is assured.

Whether or not this diagnosis of the case is justified from the standpoint of commercial calculation [and commercial calculation is a potent factor in dramatic art], it must be stated that the efforts of the dramatist would be extremely stultified if he should feel himself condemned to write forever for girls of twenty-two. There are many interesting and important things in life that an author cannot talk about to young girls, for the simple reason that young girls are not sufficiently experienced to understand them. The reach of the drama should be coextensive with the range of life; and any aspect of the life of man that may be made to seem interesting on the stage should be regarded as available for projection in a play. If a dramatist has created Romeo—whom any girl of twenty-two can understand—must he be forbidden, at some subsequent period of his own development, to create King Lear? Must the drama deal eternally with youth, and never at all with age?

These questions recall to vivid recollection a conversation with Sir Arthur Pinero which took place in London in the spring of 1910. Two of the very greatest plays of this great master of the dramaturgic art—*The Thunderbolt* and *Mid-Channel*—had recently received a rather scant appreciation from the London public. The present writer suggested that one reason for their lack of popularity was the fact that neither play contained a character that the average frequenters of the theatre could easily and naturally love. "You make them hate the Blundells, you make them hate the Mortimores; and they go away confirmed in the uncritical opinion that you have made them hate the play. They hate the play all the harder because the characters are so real that they cannot get away from them or get around them. You make your auditors uncomfortable by telling them the truth about certain men and women who are very like themselves. They do not like to listen to uncomfortable truths; they decide, therefore, that they do not like to hear you talk; and they tell their friends to stay away." By some such argument, the critic sought to draw an answer from the dramatist.

Sir Arthur's answer may be recorded most clearly in a paraphrase that is freely recomposed from materials that are registered in memory. It ran, in the main, as follows:—"It takes me a year to make a play,—six months to get acquainted with the characters, and six months to build the plot and write the dialogue. All that time, I have to seclude myself from the companionship of friends and live only with the imaginary people of my story. Why should I do this—at my age? I don't need money; I don't desire—if you will pardon me for saying so—to increase the reputation that I have. *Sweet Lavender* made my fortune; *The Second Mrs. Tanqueray* made my reputation: and for many years I have not needed to write plays. Why, then, should I go on? Only because the task is interesting. But it would not be interesting to me unless I were interested personally in the people of my plays. You say the public hates the Blundells and the Mortimores. I do not care. I love those twisted and exacerbated people, because—you see—they interest me. I think I must have what the critics call 'a perverted mind.' [It should be noted that the wise and brilliant playwright said this with a smile.] The only characters that seem to interest me nowadays are people whose lives have somehow gone awry. I like to wonder at the difference between the thing they are and the thing they might have been. That, to me, is the essence of the mystery of life,—the difference between a man as he is and the same man as God intended and desired him to be. But to see this, you must catch your man in the maturity of years. Young people —sweet young people in particular—no longer seem to interest me: I would rather spend my evenings at the Garrick Club than go down to the country and live six months with an imaginary company of people like Sweet Lavender. She was a nice girl; but, after the first hour, there was nothing more to know about her. I now prefer the Mortimores; for there is always something more to find out about people such as they are. You cannot exhaust them in an hour, or six months. Young people are pretty to look at, and theatre-goers like them, as they liked my little Lavender, so many years ago; but, now that I have lived a little longer, I prefer people with a past. A future—that is nothing but a dream: but a past—there you have a soil to delve in."

On the score of art alone—without regard to commerce—a great deal may be said in support of heroes and of heroines that are no longer young. A story of adventure or of love demands an atmosphere of youth; but there are many things in life more interesting to the adult mind than adolescent love or extravagant adventure. The greatest plays are plays of character; and character is nothing more nor less than the sum-total of experience. What a person is, at any moment, is merely a remembered record of all that he has been. To be alive, a person must have lived; and very few people have lived at all at twenty-two.

The greatest artists who have dealt with character have always preferred to depict people in the maturity of years instead of in the heyday of that superficial beauty which is nothing but a passing bloom upon the face of youth. Consider Rembrandt, for example—the most searching and most deeply penetrant of all the portrait-painters of the world. A Rembrandt portrait is a record of all that life has written on the face of the sitter; and the portrait becomes meaningful almost precisely in proportion to the age of the person whom the artist looked at. Like Velasquez, Rembrandt painted what he saw: but with this difference,—he had to have something to see. The disinterested Spaniard could depict the vacant faces of the royal family with absolute fidelity to fact and yet achieve a truimph of the artistry of painting; but Rembrandt, to be interested, had to have a sitter who had lived. If the all but perfect artist of the Netherlands can be regarded ever to have failed at all, he failed in the depiction of young girls. There was nothing in their faces for such a man to see. He was most successful in his portraits of old women and old men; for in these he was allowed to wonder—to quote once more the meaning of Pinero—at the difference between the thing they were and the thing they might have been. He depicted character as the sum-total of a lifetime of experience.

Another point to be considered is that young people, when imagined by the dramatist, must be depicted by young people on the stage. Hence a premium is set on youth and beauty among our actors and, more especially, our actresses. A young girl endowed by nature with a pretty face and fluffy hair is made a star, while many older and less lovely women who know more—much more—about the art of acting are relegated to the ranks. The greatest interpretative artist in the world, Madame Yvette Guilbert, once said in a public address that no woman could act well before she had attained the age of thirty-five. Twenty years of study of such technical details as those of diction and of gesture, and a maturity of personal experience, were absolutely necessary before an actress could be fitted to stand forth before the public as an interpreter of human nature. If this is true—and the solid fact must be accepted that Madame Guilbert herself at sixty was a finer and a greater artist than she had seemed even capable of becoming thirty years before—the premium that now is set upon the youthful charm of youthful actresses is seen to be a very shallow thing. What boots it, after all, to be a star at twenty-five, unless a woman can become, like Sarah Bernhardt, a central and essential sun at seventy?

Much, of course, might be said, conceivably, on either side. On the one hand, there is Keats, who died at twenty-five; and, on the other hand, there is Ibsen, who did not begin his greatest work till after he was fifty. Those whom the gods love die young or live long, as the chance may fall; and there is no mathematical solution of the mystery. But this much may be said with emphasis, in summing up:—that there is no valid reason why the dramatist should be denied the privilege of dealing with character at its maturity in terms that are intelligible to the adult mind. Youth may be served in the theatre; but old age is still of service, as a theme for the serener contemplation of a ripe intelligence.

VI

ACTING AND IMPERSONATION

IN A SUNDAY issue of the New York *Times*, Mr. John Corbin published an interesting essay on acting and impersonation. He pointed out the fact that the ablest impersonators seldom make good actors and that great actors seldom make more than passable impersonators. The reason for this fact is very simple. Imitation is the method of impersonation, but the method of acting is suggestion. Acting is an art; and the important thing about it is that essential something which the actor has to say, through the medium of all his stage disguises. Acting, like any other work of art, can be no greater nor less great than the man who makes it. Its purpose is to stimulate the imagination of the spectator into a quickened consciousness of life. The actor's subject-matter is himself; and, in a high sense, it is his duty always to act himself, regardless of the make-up and the costume that he may be wearing in his part. If he is a great man, it is to be assumed that he "contains multitudes," as Whitman said, or, in other words, that he is really many men. Consequently he can play himself in a score of different roles without incurring any danger of monotony. Thus Richard Mansfield was greater than any of his parts. His performances of different characters were very different, and he was noted for his range and versatility: yet he was always Richard Mansfield, and it was mainly for this latter reason that the public always went to see him.

The impersonator, on the other hand, confesses that he finds no subject-matter in himself and asks for admiration of the trappings and the suits of his disguises. His stock in trade is a special talent for exactness of imitation; and, whenever imitation is exact, there is no art. "*C'est imiter quelqu'un que planter des choux*," said Alfred de Musset; or, as Austin Dobson has translated it, in the refrain of the best of his ballades, "The man who plants cabbages imitates too."

An almost uncanny instance of exactness in imitation was afforded by the late Benjamin Chapin's impersonation of Lincoln, which was exhibited on the lecture-platform, on the legitimate stage, and, later on, in motion-pictures. Mr. Chapin was endowed by nature with a striking physical resemblance to the martyred president. His figure was almost precisely a replica of Lincoln's; and his face could easily be changed to Lincoln's by a very simple make-up. Furthermore, Mr. Chapin made a life-long study of the character and personality of the hero whose aspect was all but repeated in his own; and, by virtue of this study, he was able to depict the mutable expressions of Lincoln's living countenance. Yet Mr. Chapin did not even claim to be an actor; and, so far as the present writer is informed, he never appeared before the public in any other part.

Cissie Loftus, despite the exceeding cleverness of her imitations, never achieved a notable success as an actress in the legitimate drama. In fact, there is a legend in the theatre—which may or may not be true—that once, when she was being rehearsed by Augustin Daly in the part of one of Shakespeare's heroines, Mr. Daly suddenly stopped the rehearsal and said, "My dear Miss Loftus, won't you please imagine the performance of some actress in this part, and then give us an imitation of her?" Elsie Janis can imitate Bernhardt and Ethel Barrymore; but she cannot act like either of them. Even so supreme an impersonator as Albert Chevalier, a man without a peer in his own profession, looked like an ordinary stock-comedian when he acted a part in a regular play. On the other hand, so distinguished an actor as John Drew appeared in part after part without changing his mask or altering the cut and quality of his clothes, and yet contrived, by sheer suggestion, to create many living characterizations. Mr. Drew was always Mr. Drew; yet the people that he played were by no means the same people; and even an admiring public did not always recognize the exercise of art required in order that Mr. Drew might seem so easily himself in all his different parts.

The distinction made by Mr. Corbin should constantly be borne in mind in judging performances upon the stage. It explains, for instance, the reason for the fact that so many minor actors who make emphatic hits in what art called "character parts" never succeed in climbing up to the rank of leading players. It also explains the fact that a great artist like Yvette Guilbert can stand up in a corner of a room—without scenery, without make-up, without stage-costume, without any trick of lighting—and suggest, by sheer imaginative means, the very presence of any kind of woman, young or old, who ever lived in France. She does not have to smudge her face with coal in order to impersonate a scullery-maid, nor to wear a crown in order to impersonate a queen. I once saw Richard Mansfield, who was wearing a dinner-jacket at the time, change from Dr. Jekyll to Mr. Hyde in a chair of his own library, not more than half a dozen feet away from me. He had been asserting that the method of the true actor was to appeal to the imagination; and he performed this *tour de force* in order to convince me that he did not need the adventitious aid of lights and make-up, but could force me to imagine that I saw what he wanted me to see.

But, though Mr. Corbin's distinction is fundamentally sound, it must not be assumed that the art of acting and the craft of impersonation are never united in the same performance. A few great actors have also been remarkable impersonators, and have managed to combine the two methods of imitation and suggestion without any detriment to either. The most remarkable instance of this combination which has come within the range of the present writer's observation was the dual equipment of Sir Henry Irving. Irving was, first and foremost, a great actor; and that is only another way of saying that he was always Henry Irving. The personal aura of his keen imagination "informed"—in Aristotle's sense —every one of his creations. Yet Irving was also an astonishing impersonator. Anybody who has seen his Charles I, his Napoleon, his Dante, will remember how absolutely different they looked from each other and from Irving himself. Irving was actually a tallish, slender man; but any one who saw him only as Napoleon would have sworn that he was short and stout. The stoutness, of course, was easy to manage; but how did the actor cut a cubit from his stature? As Napoleon, he trotted rapidly around with quick and nimble feet, and his gestures were hinged from the elbow and the wrist. As Charles Stuart, his stride was long and slow, majestic and a little languorous, and his gestures were hinged from the shoulder. The face of Irving's Charles was copied from the numerous great portraits by Van Dyck; and the head of his

Dante was modeled from the bronze bust at Naples. But the craft of the impersonation did not end with this. Irving's Dante, as he walked, leaned forward and held his left shoulder a little higher than the other. These details, of course, were culled from the description by Boccaccio, who saw the Divine Poet with his own eyes when he himself was an observing little boy of nine.

Since the death of Sir Henry Irving, no other celebrated actor has also exhibited such clever achievements in impersonation as Mr. George Arliss. At the present time, Mr. Arliss is perhaps most noted for his impersonation of Disraeli; but he had already asserted his eminence in the finer art of acting long before he first put on the make-up of Lord Beaconsfield.

Mr. Arliss first came to this country in 1901 with Mrs. Patrick Campbell and made a keen impression with his performances of Cayley Drummle in *The Second Mrs. Tanqueray* and the Duke of St. Olpherts in *The Notorious Mrs. Ebbsmith*. He was equally at home in both parts, although the former had been created by Cyril Maude and the latter by so different an actor as Sir John Hare. For some years after this, Mr. Arliss appeared in a series of eccentric characters, in which the note of comedy was usually paramount. He was then persuaded by David Belasco to appear in several sinister and malevolent roles, such as that of the cynical hero of *The Devil* and that of the murderous prime minister in *The Darling of the Gods*.

Since Mr. Arliss, in these various disguises, contrived always to be somehow Mr. Arliss, we could have no surer proof that he is a gifted actor; for, off the stage, he is neither cynical nor eccentric. He is a man of keen intelligence, a scholar and a gentleman; and, in the habit of his mind, he is always simple, straightforward, and direct. He knows the art of acting not only subconsciously, but also consciously, with an intelligence that is not only creative but critical as well. He is one of the few actors I have ever known who have been able and willing to explain how bad they were in performances for which they had been highly praised. When Mr. Arliss was appearing as Judge Brack with Mrs. Fiske in *Hedda Gabler*, he told me that his performance was all wrong, despite the fact that it had been greeted with golden encomiums from every critic in New York. "Brack ought to shake things when he comes into a room," Mr. Arliss explained to me. "I can't do that; I am too slight and delicate; I have therefore been obliged to murder

Ibsen's character and substitute a totally different fabrication; anybody who does not see this does not understand the play."

Mr. Arliss's Disraeli was a masterly impersonation; but—and this is the important point that the writer has been trying to lead up to—his Alexander Hamilton was scarcely an impersonation at all. It was that far finer thing—a bit of imaginative acting. Mr. Arliss, with the assistance of a very simple make-up, actually looked like Disraeli. He did not look like Hamilton, and he did not try to do so; he attempted instead to make his spectators imagine that he looked like Hamilton. Mr. Arliss has neither the face nor the figure depicted in the Trumbull portrait; and he was actually twenty years older than Hamilton was at the period of the play. Yet the dominating note of this imaginative exhibition was the note of almost boyish youthfulness; and there was never a suggestion of the sinister or the eccentric. This impersonator of many "character parts" succeeded even more emphatically in acting a "straight part"; he re-created on the stage a great and ingratiating person who is honored in history as one of nature's noblemen, and he made this person every inch a hero.

VII

THE CAREER OF "CAMILLE"

T HE CAREER of *La Dame aux Camélias* is, in many ways, unique in the annals of the theatre. In the opinion of the best French critics [and the French are very careful in their criticism] this play has never been regarded as a masterpiece, nor was it rated very highly by the author himself; yet, though more than eighty years have now elapsed since the date when it was first produced in Paris, *La Dame aux Camélias* is still popular throughout the theatre of the world, and bids fair to be applauded a century from now, when the later and greater plays of the same writer have been relegated to the library.

Alexandre Dumas, *fils*, was born in 1824; and he was scarcely more than twenty-one when he wrote his first successful novel and called it *The Lady of the Camellias*. The material was drawn directly from his own immediate experience of that "demi-monde" of Paris to which he had been introduced by his prodigal and reckless father. As he said in later years, this youthful narrative was "the echo, or rather, the re-action, of a personal emotion." The book was immature, and sentimental, and immoral; but, in the turbulent days which anteceded the Revolution of 1848, it made a momentous impression on the reading public. The project of dramatization was suggested to the author; and he asked the advice of his famous father, who was perhaps the ablest playwright of the period. The elder Dumas reported to his son, regretfully, that it was impossible to turn the novel into a practicable play; and Alexandre Dumas, *père*, nearly always had the right idea in regard to questions of success or failure in the theatre.

Nevertheless, the youthful writer decided to waste a week or two in an attempt to dramatize his novel. He retired to the country, and wrote the play in eight successive days. Since the piece is in four acts, it will be noted that he allowed himself precisely two days for the composition of each act. It may be doubted if any other play which has held the stage for nearly a century has ever been written so quickly and so easily; but of course we must remember that the author was already familiar with his plot and with his characters before he sat down to write the dialogue of his play.

Yet, after the play had been completed, there was a doubt for many months that it would ever be produced. Although it had been dramatized from a successful novel, and although it was signed by the son of one of the most famous novelists and dramatists of France, it was rejected by nearly every theatre in Paris. After three years of hopeless wandering, the manuscript was ultimately accepted at the Vaudeville, only to be interdicted by the censorship. After new delays occasioned by political contentions, *La Dame aux Camélias* was finally produced in Paris, at the Vaudeville, on February 2, 1852. The author was, at that time, less than twenty-eight years old. The piece achieved an instantaneous success in France, and has since been added to the repertory of every other nation in the theatre-going world. Excepting *Cyrano de Bergerac*, it may be doubted if any other play composed since the initiation of the modern drama in 1830 has been so continuously popular in every country of the habitable globe.

In the opinion of those disinterested critics whose judgment is not conditioned by the verdict of the box-office, *La Dame aux Camélias* has always been regarded as inferior to many of its author's later plays, and especially to his admitted masterpiece, *Le Demi-Monde*. According to the judgment of the present commentor, Alexandre Dumas, *fils,* wrote, first and last, no less than half a dozen dramas which are more important, from the point of view of art, than this youthful effort that was struck off at white heat. The faults of *La Dame aux Camélias* are many and apparent. The view of life expressed is sentimental, immature, and in the main untrue. The thesis is immoral, because we are asked to sympathize with an erring woman by reason of the unrelated fact that she happens to be afflicted with tuberculosis. In the famous "big scene" between the heroine and the elder Duval, the old man is absolutely right; yet the sympathy of every spectator is immorally seduced against him, as if his justified position were preposterous and cruel. The pattern of the play is faulty, because it rises too quickly to its climax—or turning-point—at the end of the second act, and thereafter leads the public down a descending ladder to a lame and impotent conclusion. In the last act, the coughing heroine—like Charles II—is an unconscionable time a-dying. The writing of the dialogue is artificial and rhetorical. Indeed, this noted play exhibits many, many faults.

Why, then, has it held the stage for nearly a century? And why, if it is not a great drama, does *La Dame aux Camélias* still seem destined to enjoy a long life in the theatre? The obvious answer to this question leads us to explore an interesting by-path in the politics of the theatre. This celebrated piece is continually set before the public because every actress who seeks a reputation for the rendition of emotional roles desires, at some stage of her career, to play the part of Marguerite Gautier—or, as the heroine is called more commonly in this country, Camille. This part is popular with actresses for the same reason that the part of Hamlet is popular with actors. Both roles are utterly actor-proof; and anybody who appears in the title-part of either piece is almost certain to record a notable accretion to a growing reputation. No man has ever absolutely failed as Hamlet; and no woman has ever absolutely failed as Camille. On the other hand, an adequate performance of either of these celebrated parts offers a quick and easy means for adding one's name to a long and honorable list, and being ranked by future commentators among a great and famous company of predecessors.

Here, then, we have a drama which is kept alive because of the almost accidental fact that it contains a very easy and exceptionally celebrated part that every ambitious actress wants to play. *La Dame aux Camélias* is brought back to the theatre, decade after decade, not by reason of the permanent importance of the author, but by reason of the recurrent aspirations of an ever-growing group of emotional actresses.

VIII

LE THÉÂTRE DU VIEUX COLOMBIER

I

N THE now-forgotten period before the war, not even the most
civilized of nations escaped entirely that taint of decadence
which comes from long-protracted leisure and a consequent
excess of lassitude. In France, the flag of art had been nailed
to the mast for many centuries; but it began at last to droop, and
to seem a little sullied, when no vivifying wind had blown upon
it for more than forty years. Paris was becoming wearied of its
own distinction, as the citadel of "those who know." Even the
French theatre, which had led the world since 1830, was beginning to grow dull.

Something had gone wrong with France, and with the world
at large. The wreaths that decked the statue of Strasbourg in the
Place de la Concorde had almost begun to shrivel up and be forgotten; and then . . .

But we are talking now of the time before the war, and of the
condition of the French stage in a period of leisure and of lassitude. The theatres of Paris—unbelievable as it might seem—had
almost descended to the level of the tedious. There were two reasons for this sad condition,—two antithetic tendencies which account, together, for the dearth of living drama in the somnolent
and easy-going Paris of the light and laughing years before the
war.

In the first place, more than half the energy that was expended
in the French theatres of the time was devoted merely to a meaningless continuance of the traditions of the past; and, in the second
place, the only relief from this incubus of ponderous conven-
tionality was offered by a wild and whirling group of anarchists
and "lesser breeds without the Law." French art—to talk in terms
of politics—was languishing between a formal past of Louis
Quatorze and a formless future of the Bolsheviki,—between an

372

over-emphasized respect for Law and an exaggerated tendency to take a gambling chance on Lawlessness. Hence, those mixed and indigestible *Salons* of painting and of sculpture, which seemed bewildering at the passing moment, but which are easy enough to understand in retrospect to-day.

In that recent but now-superseded period, when the great art of the drama seemed destined either to die of old-age or to perish still-born in expectancy, an ambitious actor by the name of Jacques Copeau decided to establish a little, unpretentious theatre which should seek to light a vivid torch from the dying embers of the inspiration of the past. M. Copeau was neither a Reactionary nor an Anarchist: he was merely a lover of the maxim that Beauty is Truth, Truth Beauty: and he had a vivid feeling that there is nothing either new or old in that eternal region where Truth and Beauty join hands and dance together, to the music of melodies unheard.

M. Copeau assembled a little group of coöperative actors and founded a new theatre in Paris on October 22, 1913. This theatre took its title from that medieval street in the Quartier Latin, leading somewhat vaguely westward from the Place de Saint Sulpice, which might be called, in English, the Alley of the Ancient Dovecot. Between October 22, 1913, and May 31, 1914, more than three hundred performances of fourteen plays, both classical and modern, were exhibited, to ever-growing audiences, at Le Théâtre du Vieux Colombier. Among the many authors represented were Shakespeare, Molière, Thomas Heywood, Alfred de Musset, Dostoyevsky, Paul Claudel, and Henri Becque. Before the end of his first season, M. Copeau had received "golden encomiums" from Eleanora Duse, Igor Strawinsky, Claude Debussy, Henri Bergson, Paul Claudel, Émile Verhaeren, and many other leaders of the art-life of Europe. In the spring of 1914, M. Copeau was regarded, by the court of last resort, as the *régisseur* of one of the few theatres in the world which manifestly seemed alive.

The principles of Jacques Copeau were very simple. He was neither a Reactionary nor an Anarchist. He neither respected the past for the insufficient reason that it was the past nor revered the future for the insufficient reason that it was the future. He freed his mind at once from traditions and from fads, and devoted his attention to the lofty task of "drawing the Thing as he saw It for the God of Things as They Are." One theory he clung to, absolutely:—that the drama is essentially an art of authorship, and that the purpose of the theatre is to re-create and to project the mood and purpose of the dramatist. In adhering to this theory M. Copeau seceded not only from the immemorial tradition of the Comédie Française, which sets the actor higher than the author, but seceded also from the heresy of Gordon Craig, by which the actor is suppressed in order that the decorator may be almost deified. M. Copeau has little use for scenery or decoration. He does not believe, like Gordon Craig, that the drama is essentially a pattern of lines and lights and colors. Neither does he believe, like the late David Belasco, that the drama is a mere accumulated and assorted hodge-podge of properties and accessories. He believes that the *idea* of the dramatist is the only thing that counts, and that this idea may be rendered lovingly—without extraneous assistance—by an eager company of coöperative actors.

In the gospel of M. Copeau, "the play's the thing," and the purpose of the acting is to vivify and re-create the play. This gospel —simple as it seems—appeared exceptional in Paris in the year before the war; for, at that time, the reactionaries claimed that acting was the thing, and the anarchistic revolutionaries claimed that decoration was the thing. Between the shade of Talma and the shadow of Gordon Craig, the theatre was obfuscated by a twilight that was doubly deep. Then came M. Copeau, with his very simple *dictum:*—Molière wrote plays intended to be acted; Molière acted plays intended to be seen; therefore, the only purpose of the theatre is to convey, through the fluent medium of acting, the creative purpose of the author. Decoration, after all, is nothing more than decoration. The idea of the play is the only thing that is eternal.

With this formula, M. Copeau succeeded; and, before the advent of the month of May in 1914, Le Théâtre du Vieux Colombier was already known and celebrated throughout Europe. Shakespeare, Molière, and a dozen other dramatists were enjoying, once again, a vivid life in the Alley of the Ancient Dove-cot. Then fell the war. . . .

Most of the actors were immediately mobilized. The theatre ceased to be. For many months, it seemed that Art itself was being shelled and shattered by the Hun, together with that symbol of all that is, in art, most Christian and most sacred,—the church of Joan of Arc,—*la cathédrale de Rheims. Le patron du Vieux Colom-*

bier was—like Othello—a hero with an occupation gone. This artist of the stage—a man of more than military years—was suddenly divested of his theatre, or, in other words, his spiritual home. What was he to do? . . . The question was answered by the Minister of Fine Arts, who advised him to come to the United States, in order to deliver a series of *discours*.

In the now-forgotten days when this country still pretended to be "neutral" between Right and Wrong, many emissaries were sent over to our shores by the antithetic nations. The Germans and the Austrians sent over a small army of assassins, bomb-planters, artists in arson, and inciters to *sabotage*. The French sent over Jusserand, Brieux, and many other gentlemen instructed to do nothing and to say nothing, but to leave us quite religiously alone until we had had time to consult our own underlying conscience. Brieux, when he landed in New York in the fall of 1914, said to the reporters:—"I am coming as an emissary from the French Academy to the American Academy; I am coming from a free people who can think to a kindred free people who can think; and, so long as I enjoy your hospitality, I shall say no word about the war."

Jacques Copeau, when he first came to America in 1917, was similarly tactful. He talked to us of art and Molière, and said no word about the war. We know, now, that France was bleeding at the time; but this artist—sent over by his government—talked to us only about Truth and Beauty,—eternal matters, in the midst of many things succumbing momentarily to death. We welcomed Jacques Copeau,—because he wore the face of Dante, because he had the voice and the demeanor of one "having authority," because of any of a multitude of reasons that are trivial and real. We asked him, naturally, to remain among us; and this request was backed by a guaranteed subscription, collected in support of the occasion by Otto Kahn and some of his associates in the directorate of the Metropolitan Opera House.

In consequence of this support from a friendly nation overseas, the French Government was easily persuaded to encourage a transference of Le Théâtre du Vieux Colombier from Paris to New York. Such actors of the company originally chosen by M. Copeau as had not already been killed in action were demobilized, for the specific purpose of carrying the torch of art from Paris to New York; and a reconstituted theatre, wearing as a sort

of proud *panache* the name of Le Vieux Colombier, was sent overseas as an item of friendly and disinterested propaganda.

Meanwhile, Mr. Kahn and his associates had leased the old Garrick Theatre and caused the auditorium to be entirely rebuilt and
redecorated in conformity with the desires of M. Copeau. This
new edifice became as pleasing to the eye as any theatre-building
in America. The old top-gallery was discarded, the boxes were
removed from the proscenium to the rear of the auditorium, and
the gilt and tinsel of Broadway were replaced by the lath and
plaster of the sixteenth century. The interior became remarkable
for its simplicity and quietude of tone, and suggested a sense of
medieval innyards in Warwick or Beauvais.

The stage of the Vieux Colombier, as planned by Jacques
Copeau, more nearly resembles the stage of Shakespeare than the
stage of Molière. Before the curtain, there is of course an "apron"
devoid of footlights, which is accessible from either hand through
a couple of proscenium doors. Behind the curtain, the main stage
is spacious, free, and unencumbered. No scenery—in the realistic
sense—is ever used upon it; but sometimes the stage is developed
to two levels by the introduction of an elevated platform, about
five feet high, which is accessible by steps from every side; and
sometimes the acting-space is contracted with enclosing screens
or curtains and localized by the introduction of certain set-pieces
of "property." At the rear of the stage, there is a balcony, borne
aloft by columns, which may be used, when needed, as the "upper
room" of Shakespeare or, when not needed, may be curtained off
by an "arras" and employed merely as a decorative background.
This free and easy stage may be entered from any angle and from
a multitude of levels. As in the Globe Theatre on the Bankside,
the main purpose is to get the actor on and to allow him to deliver
the lines of the author. The lighting, of course, comes entirely
from overhead, like the natural sunlight of Shakespeare.

The "fluency" of this neo-Elizabethan stage [for "fluency," I
think, is the only word that is appropriate] was amply illustrated
at the opening performance, on November 27, 1917, when *Les
Fourberies de Scapin* was offered as the *pièce de résistance*. This
farce, though written so late as 1671, represented a return to the
earlier manner of Molière, inherited from the acrobatic antics of
the Italian *commedia dell' arte*. The scene is said to be a public
square in Naples; and Molière, no doubt, used the fixed set that

is summarized and still exemplified to students of the stage in the theatre of Palladio at Vicenza. But M. Copeau thinks rightly that the scene is really any public place accessible from all sides by actors unimpeded by an obligation to account for their exits and their entrances. He projects the piece upon two levels,—before, beside, beyond, and [more especially] atop, the portable platform with which he is enabled to adorn—as by a plinth of statuary—an otherwise empty and unfocussed stage.

M. Copeau's performance of Scapin may be described as a reminiscence and a revelation. It showed the acrobatic grace and rhythmic, keen agility that have been ascribed by history to Molière's own teacher,—that immortal Scaramouche who came from Italy to Paris to remind the modern world of the grandeur that was Rome. Plautus seemed alive again when this actor snaked and floated through his many *fourberies* and belabored the minds or bodies of his victims with literal or figurative slap-sticks. M. Copeau was ably aided by M. Louis Jouvet, who projected a memorable character-performance in the role of old *Géronte*. Jouvet's bewildered repetition of the famous line, *"Mais que diable allait-il faire dans cette galère?"*, is a thing to be remembered always and laid away in lavender, together with one's memories of the greater and the lesser Coquelin. The rest of the company was adequate to the occasion. M. Copeau has organized a group of players who have learned to speak and learned to act and learned a proper reverence for the authors who have written down the lines assigned to them.

As an induction to this inaugural performance of *Les Fourberies de Scapin*, M. Copeau composed an *Impromptu du Vieux Colombier*, which was modeled on the *Impromptu de Versailles*, and which repeated many of the most pertinent comments on the art of acting which were made, in 1663, by Molière himself. This playful skit served the purpose of introducing quite informally to the American public the associated actors of the company. One passage was especially noteworthy, because it summarized in a few words the attitude of those who came to us from France toward the cataclysm which, at that time, overwhelmed the world. A young actor, fresh from the trenches, M. Lucien Weber, said to the Director,—*"Il faut aussi nous laisser le temps, Patron, de nous ressaisir, d'écarter de nos yeux des images trop affreuses.— Moi, je suis de Rheims . . . ;"* and M. Copeau replied,—*"Ces images, mes amis, ne les écartez pas de vos yeux. Il faut qu'elles nous inspirent. Mais gardons-les secrètes. Nous n'exploiterons jamais des émotions sacrées. Nous ne parlerons pas de nos souffrances. Nous ne déploierons pas sur une scène de théâtre le drapeau des combats. Nous ne chanterons pas d'hymne guerrier. Nous ne ferons pas applaudir un acteur sous l'uniforme bleu. Celui qui représente ici la France, qui est l'ami de Ronsard, de Shakespeare et de tous nos vieux auteurs, nous a donné l'exemple de la délicatesse et de la dignité. Mais dans toutes nos actions, dans tous nos gestes, dans la moindre intonation du beau language qu'il nous est donné de parler, nous tâcherons d'être reconnus pour de véritables Français. . . ."*

IX

ALFRED DE MUSSET IN THE THEATRE

LFRED DE MUSSET once wrote a little poem in which he expressed a wish that, in due time, he might be buried beneath a weeping willow tree. I have forgotten the text of this poem; but I remember that it is inscribed upon the rather ugly monument that marks his grave in Père-Lachaise. Over this unpretentious tomb-stone there hangs—or used to hang—a lonely branch of willow,—the languid offshoot of a sapling planted by some pious hand. I remember being struck by the incongruity between the verses, carved in rock, and the sickly little tree that drooped forlornly over them.

This impression dates from forty years ago; for, at the age of seventeen, I renounced the youthful habit of visiting the graves of the great. [It must have been about that time that I read R.L.S. on *Old Mortality*.] But now the thought occurs to me that the sculptured verses may be taken as a symbol of the permanent fame of de Musset as a poet, and the struggling willow branch may be regarded as a symbol of his slender but still-growing reputation as a dramatist. Perhaps some later traveler can tell me if the simile may be developed even further. That nearly leafless sapling which made me smile, two scores of years ago, may now—for aught I know—be grown into a healthy and promising young tree. In that event, the fanciful comparison would be perfected; for the fame of de Musset as a playwright has steadily increased in recent years.

In the history of all the arts except the drama, the posthumous achievement of a noble reputation is not at all unusual. Many painters, many sculptors, neglected in their life-time and derided by their own contemporaries, have subsequently come to be regarded as men whose only failing was that they were doomed to work on earth before their time. So recent a painter as Jean François Millet lived in penury while he was making canvases that now are sold at auction for a hundred thousand dollars. The painter and the sculptor manufacture objects that are durable, and may appeal to the leisurely consideration of posterity. Their merit is finally evaluated by that small but perpetual minority composed of "those who know,"—a minority that may summon but a few votes in any single generation but that triumphs ultimately by an undisrupted repetition of its verdict throughout the tireless succession of the centuries.

The history of literature has been enriched by many similar instances of men who, scorned by their contemporaries, have been accepted as apostles by posterity. A notable example is afforded by the case of Keats. This man was absolutely honest; and when, upon his death-bed, he requested Joseph Severn to inscribe upon his tomb-stone the pathetic legend, "Here lies one whose name was writ in water," he believed exactly what he said. His poems had been appreciated only by the inner circle of his friends; even by this inner circle he had been regarded mainly as a promising disciple of Leigh Hunt; and to the general public he had merely been made known as a butt for the sarcastic and heavy-handed ridicule of Lockhart and Wilson. His short life seemed a failure, and he died a disappointed man. Yet now—only a little more than one hundred years after the publication of his faulty and faltering first volume—Keats is commonly regarded as one of the very greatest of all poets in the English language and one of the very few important apostles to the modern world.

It is only in the domain of the drama that these drastic reversals of an adverse contemporary verdict are so rare as to seem almost absolutely negligible. As a general rule [but rules, of course, are always open to exceptions] it may safely be asserted that a playwright who has failed to please his own contemporaries can scarcely hope to attract the patronage of posterity. The reason is, of course, that the drama is a democratic art. It succeeds or fails by a *plebiscite* of the immediate, untutored public, instead of by a vote delivered by the small but self-perpetuant minority composed of "those who know." A book may keep itself alive, if only a single printed copy chances to avoid the iniquity of sheer oblivion and happens, in some future century, to fall into the hands of an appreciative critic; but it is very difficult, at any time, to persuade a theatre-manager to reproduce a play that failed to interest the theatre-going public in the very year when it was first produced. The exercise of any art—as R.L.S. has told us—is nothing but the playing of a game; and the game of the dramatist is to interest the public of his time, assembled in the theatre of his time, in the predetermined antics of the actors of his time. The playwright—because of the conditions of his craft—is required to appeal to the immediate many, instead of the ultimate few; and his efforts to interest a helter-skelter audience must stand or fall by the democratic verdict of the public toward which he has directed his immediate appeal.

Such representative great dramatists as Sophocles, Shakespeare, Molière, and Ibsen succeeded amply in attracting the applause of their immediate contemporaries and thereby laid the basis for the favor that has been bestowed upon them by succeeding generations. Their plays are still produced by commercial-minded managers, because the fact has been established that there is a public willing to patronize them. On the other hand, there is nothing, in the general domain of art, more difficult to resurrect than a play that once has died in the presence of a gathered audience.

Volumes and volumes of testimony might easily be drawn upon to support the thesis that dramatic art cannot appeal to the verdict of posterity; but one exception to this reasonable rule of criticism is obtruded by the plays of Alfred de Musset. This author was regarded justly in his life-time as one of the supreme triumvirate that led the renascence of French poetry in the first half of the nineteenth century; but he received no recognition whatsoever as a writer for the stage. It is only since his death that de Musset has been at all respected as a dramatist.

His career, in relation to the theatre, is so exceptional that it calls for recapitulation. Alfred de Musset was born in Paris in 1810. His first play, *La Nuit Vénitienne*, was offered at the Odéon in 1830, the very year of Victor Hugo's epoch-making *Hernani*. It will be noted that de Musset was, at that time, less than twenty-one years old. This fledgeling effort was a failure; and the author, disgusted with the theatre, refused thereafter to write pieces for the stage. This petulant renunciation reminds us now of Dante's famous phrase, "the great refusal"; for there is no longer any doubt that de Musset, if he had chosen to take the theatre seriously, might easily have rivaled the popularity of Hugo with the contemporary public. He continued to compose in the dramatic form, because of a necessity of his nature; but, instead of offering his pieces for production, he printed them successively in the *Revue des Deux Mondes*. While Hugo was writing clap-trap melodramas, disguised as literature by the flowing garment of his gorgeous verse, de Musset was writing, in neat and nimble prose, fantastic comedies conceived in an unprecedented mood of witty and romantic playfulness. These pieces, as they appeared in print, were regarded by contemporary readers merely as vacationary exercises by a writer whose more serious medium was verse. The reading public tolerated these relaxations of a noble mind; but it never occurred to any critic that de Musset's printed comedies might possibly be actable. The author did not care. He hated *Hernani*, and despised the *Antony* of old Dumas; and he had a happy time composing little pieces for a theatre that existed only in his own imagination.

It was in 1833 that de Musset became involved in his famous affair with Georges Sand. Their trip to Italy took place in December of that year, and lasted till April, 1834, when de Musset returned to Paris. His final rupture with the famous female novelist took place in 1835. It was precisely at this period—and, for the most part, during the Italian tour—that de Musset wrote nearly all the comedies composed for the theatre of his dreams. Even as a closet-dramatist [if a critic of the living theatre can stoop to use that hated, self-defeating word], de Musset's work was finished for all time when he was scarcely twenty-six years old. It is only fair, in any posthumous appraisement, to remember that the comedies of Alfred de Musset were written not only for a non-existent theatre but written also by a young man in his early twenties.

The poet lived till 1857, when he was forty-seven years of age; and, before he died, the theatre of his time began to find him out. His one-act play, *Caprice*, was the first of all his comedies since *La Nuit Vénitienne* that was acted in his life-time. It was first presented, far away from France, in the French theatre of St. Petersburg; and its success was so striking that the piece was soon re-imported to Paris by Madame Allan. This was in November, 1847,—nearly fifteen years after *Caprice* had been composed. Within the next four seasons, the poet witnessed the production of half a dozen of his other plays in Paris; and, subsequent to his death, his career as a contributor to the current theatre was continued. *On ne Badine pas avec l'Amour*—which has remained in the repertory of the Comédie Française—was first produced in

1861. *Barberine*—which was acted in New York in 1918 by the company of Le Vieux Colombier—was not presented for the first time till 1882,—nearly half a century later than the period in which it was composed.

The biography of *Barberine* is unique in the history of the theatre. This piece was written, in his early twenties, by a man who had retired from the theatre before the date of his majority and was almost totally unknown to his contemporaries as a dramatist. It was acted for the first time fifty years after it was written and twenty-five years after the author had been laid away in his resting grave. Yet in 1918—when de Musset, to count the ticking of the clock exactly, was one hundred and eighteen years of age—*Barberine* pleased many English-speaking people in a city half the world away from Paris. To students of the theatre, the record of this fragile, unpretentious play is more remarkable, in many ways, than that of *Hamlet*. That sickly little willow-wand in Père-Lachaise need no longer weep and wither: a breeze is blowing from the west to cause its leaves to overturn their silver sides in a ripple of delighted laughter.

Barberine is delicately entertaining; and the appeal that it makes to the æsthetic sensibilities is representative of the appeal that is inherent in all the comedies composed by Alfred de Musset. Disdaining the theatre of his time, this poet understood more clearly than the celebrated author of the *Preface to "Cromwell"* the meaning and the method of the comedies of Shakespeare. Alone among all modern playwrights, he has recaptured and restored the magic atmosphere of the Forest of Arden,—an atmosphere which marries to identity the usually antithetic moods of loveliness and wit. He flutes a little melody upon a slender reed; but this music wakens echoes from an organ which resounds with the diapason of eternity.

The story of *Barberine* is suggestive of any of the hundred tales of Boccaccio, which date from a period when narrative was naïve and had not yet become self-conscious and sophisticated. Count Ulric is married to a perfect wife. A dashing, attractive, and self-conceited youth—Astolphe de Rosenberg—makes a bet with Ulric that he can seduce the latter's wife while her husband is away from home; and the laying of this wager is witnessed by the Queen of Hungary. The Baron Rosenberg goes to the castle of Count Ulric, secures admittance as a guest, and tries his arts against the Countess

Barberine; but he is unexpectedly repulsed by the clever Countess and locked up in a room to which both food and water are denied except upon condition that Rosenberg shall devote his entire time, without remission, to the woman's work of spinning. In this ridiculous predicament, the incarcerated Baron is discovered ultimately by Count Ulric and by the gracious Queen of Hungary.

This is a story of the sort that—according to our modern standards—may be described as a tale intended to be written in words of one syllable. But the author has embroidered it with many interesting corollaries and has told it with an art that is reminiscent of that sudden and surprising wisdom which comes occasionally from the mouths of babes. The whole play is so child-like, yet so utterly delightful, that it makes us fumble for a reason to explain the purpose of the manifest complexity of the majority of modern dramas.

Most of de Musset's plays provoke a similar response. Their merit is so simple and so obvious that it remained unrecognized for half a century. It was deemed impracticable to expect a gathered public to enjoy a sort of day-dream that a poet had narrated to himself in a mood of self-enjoyment. The tardy and almost accidental discovery of the fact that the fantastic comedies of Alfred de Musset are stageworthy, after all, is an incident unparalleled elsewhere in the whole history of dramatic literature.

X

THE MOOD OF MAETERLINCK

IN THE *Blue Bird* of Maurice Maeterlinck, the little boy who is the hero discovers the secret of seeing the souls of things, and wanders through the present, past, and future, seeing all things not as they actually seem to unillumined eyes but as they really are in their essential nature. This is the secret of M. Maeterlinck as a poet: he too, like Tyltyl, sees the souls of things. He removes veil after veil of the enveloping actual, to reveal at last the palpitant and vivid real.

When Robert Louis Stevenson was a very little boy, he drew a picture and showed it to his mother. "Mamma," said he, "I have drawed a man. Shall I draw his soul now?" This aspiration is fulfilled by M. Maeterlinck. He knows that nothing really matters in a man except his soul; and, in consequence, his characters are not people, but the souls of people. He knows that life, which—in the phrase of Shelley—is like a dome of many-colored glass, is merely a medium through which the human spirit catches glimpses now and then of the white radiance of eternity; and it is only with these glimpses that his fables are concerned. Reality is all he cares about; and he knows that actuality is merely an investiture which hides it from the eyes of those who cannot see. To enter the sanctuary of his mind is to withdraw from the sound and fury of the actual world into a vasty silence that seems evermore eloquent with echoes; it is to ascend to an absolute awareness of the identity of truth and beauty; it is to be reminded of all the beauty we have ever known and all the truth we seemed to have forgotten; it is to bathe in Dante's Eunoè,—the river of remembrance; it is to attain that mood in which happiness and sadness are as one,—the mood of Botticelli's *Primavera*, whereon whoever looks must smile through tears.

In this mood, emotions think and thoughts are feelings, and the mind is conscious of an utter clarity. This clarity is mirrored in the style of M. Maeterlinck. His speech seems less like speech than like a sentient and tingling silence. It is so simple that the ear feels tender toward it. His sayings are like little birds that flutter home to fold their wings within our hearts.

To interpret the plays of M. Maeterlinck upon the stage requires an art that is kindred to his own,—an art that is true and beautiful and clear and simple,—an art that can dispense with the actual and concern itself solely with the real. Such an art was displayed by the Washington Square Players in their memorable production of *Aglavaine and Sélysette.*

Aglavaine and Sélysette is the wisest and the loveliest of all the early plays of M. Maeterlinck,—the plays, that is to say, which preceded *Monna Vanna.* It expresses supremely the quintessence of an experience which occurs so frequently in actuality that it has been made the subject of innumerable plays by innumerable dramatists. One man loves two women, and is loved by both of them; furthermore, these women love each other: yet, though each of the three parties to this triangular relation is exalted by a holy and high affection for the other two, the situation is intolerable. Why should it be? . . . No poet yet has found the answer. As Aglavaine says to Sélysette, at the crisis of the play, "All three of us are making a sacrifice to something which has not even a name, and which nevertheless is much more strong than we are. . . . But is it not strange, Sélysette? I love you, I love Méléandre, Méléandre loves me, he loves you also, you love us both, and nevertheless we could not live happily, because the hour has not yet come when human beings can live in such a union." The hour has not yet come. . . . There are possibilities of spiritual intercourse so beautiful that the adventurous imagination knows they must be really true. "Such harmony is in immortal souls; but whilst this muddy vesture of decay doth grossly close it in, we cannot hear it."

Realism, which plays the sedulous ape to actuality, can merely imitate the trappings and the suits of an experience; but romance, which thrusts aside externals and plucks out the heart of a mystery, can communicate the wonder and the sting. Many realistic dramatists have told us all about this tragic triangle; but they have not told us what the tragedy was all about. They have told us everything except—everything. The advantage of the method of M.

Maeterlinck is that he shows us not so much the experience itself as the essence of the experience. We are asked to assume that Sélysette has the soul of a child and that Aglavaine is experienced and wise. It is because they are so different that Méléandre loves them both; and it is for this reason also that they love each other. Sélysette longs to grow up and to learn; and Aglavaine desires to mother her and teach her. Méléandre, hovering between the two, seeks eagerly to learn from Aglavaine the wisdom that he may in turn bestow on Sélysette. Yet all of this is told abstractly, as if this tremulous and thrilling equipoise were a thing too delicate to be expressed in the noisy terms of actuality. If a writer were to describe the Venus of Melos as a naked woman with no arms, he would express an apprehension of the facts but would inhibit an imagination of the truth.

There is scarcely any narrative in *Aglavaine and Sélysette;* and the five acts are almost totally devoid of action, in the usual theatric sense. What is shown is a delicately graded feeling of the successive states of the three souls that are involved in the experience. When it has become completely evident that the situation is intolerable, Aglavaine decides to go away. But the tender little Sélysette forestalls her. She casts herself from a tall tower; and, with her dying breath, she piteously begs both Aglavaine and Méléandre to believe that her sacrifice was merely an unpremeditated accident.

Any touch of actuality in the production would have marred the mood of essential reality in which the text had been conceived. Reality is abstract; and the illusion of reality can be suggested only by means that are illusory. The various backgrounds for the successive scenes were suggested, therefore, by different arrangements of gray-green curtains, hanging tall, and played upon by lights that differed in intensity and quality. No built and painted scenery was employed, except in the single setting at the top of the tower, when Sélysette was disclosed leaning from a lofty window with her long scarf blowing largely in the wind. There was one particularly lovely scene, imagined in the castle park, in which the interlacing tracery of trees was vividly suggested by an interplay of mottled lights and shadows on the tall folds of the gray-green curtains. This successful experiment in imaginative scenic setting deserves to be recorded as a very fine achievement of its kind.

THE SECRET OF "SALOMÉ"

THERE is a point of absolute intensity beyond which sensations that differ utterly in origin become indistinguishable from each other. This fact has been established by a familiar experiment in physiological psychology. Within ordinary limits, it is easy enough to feel the difference between heat and cold; but, if a man be blindfolded and if his back be pricked in quick succession with a red-hot needle and with a needle-point of ice, he will be unable to distinguish between the two impressions. Similarly, in the more exalted region of æsthetics, there is also a point of absolute intensity beyond which all emotions, regardless of their origin, produce upon the spirit an effect of beauty.

Oscar Wilde, in all his works, was a deliberate and conscious craftsman; and, in *Salomé*, he attempted the psychological experiment of producing an effect of beauty by intensifying an emotion that in itself is inconsistent with our ordinary notions of the beautiful. As a student and experimenter in the realm of theoretical æsthetics, Wilde was always singularly sane. He understood, of course, that the most revolting of all reactions is the response of the normal human being to the emotion of horror; but it occurred to him, also, that if horror were sufficiently augmented, it might cease to seem disgusting and might assume a virtue that is commonly accorded to many less intense emotions of another kind. In answer to this philosophical intention, the author set himself the task of composing a piece in which horror should be piled on horror's head until the finally accumulated monument should take the moonbeams as a thing serenely and superbly beautiful. This, according to my understanding, was the goal that Oscar Wilde was aiming at with *Salomé*.

Maeterlinck had proved already, with *La Mort de Tintagiles*, that the emotion of terror might be intensified to a point beyond which it would become indistinguishable from the more abstract emotion of the vaguely tragic. But terror is to horror as the soul is to the body; and it is far less difficult to raise to the nth power an abstract sense of fear than a concrete sense of physical repulsion. This latter task was attempted by Oscar Wilde in *Salomé*. Actuated by that careful niceness which always guided him in his æsthetical decisions, Wilde wrote the play in the French language and refused until his very death to translate it into English. [The current English version of the text was paraphrased from the original French by Lord Alfred Douglas.] The medium of the clearest-minded critics in the modern world was picked out as the only proper vehicle for this adventurous incursion into a domain of metaphysics that had scarcely ever been explored in English art.

This neat and simple language, selected by the Irish Oscar Wilde, was the same language that had been chosen previously, for the same æsthetic reasons, by the Belgian Maurice Maeterlinck; and, indeed, it is obvious enough that Wilde owed much to Maeterlinck in *Salomé*. In particular, he took over from his predecessor the expedient of repeating words and phrases, until this repetition should lull and drowse the auditor into a state of autohypnotism in which any pointed impression would register an effect that would be accepted as indefinitely beautiful. The danger of this expedient is, of course, that, if it fails, it is liable to throw the audience into titters of antithetic merriment, because the emotion of humor is scarcely distinguishable from the emotion of beauty when feeling has been lifted arbitrarily to a level that is unforeseen. Wilde, of course, was sufficiently a satirist to scent this danger; and this may be regarded as another reason why he chose to write his tragedy of *Salomé* in the language of Maeterlinck—a medium effectively immune from light-hearted and unsympathetic sallies of his fellow-countrymen. Also, he composed the play as a vehicle for Sarah Bernhardt and thus insured himself in advance against the danger of a hostile audience.

In foreseeing and in solving these minor incidental problems, Oscar Wilde was no less clever than in conquering his central difficulty of proving to the world the theoretical æsthetic proposition that the most repulsive sort of horror would seem beautiful if only it could be made to seem sufficiently intensified. Though *Salomé* was written nearly half a century ago, it must still be accepted and admired as a monument of dramaturgic craftsmanship.

XII

STEVENSON ON THE STAGE

I

ROBERT LOUIS STEVENSON was a man of many moods, and his attitude toward the question of composition for the theatre was subject to frequent oscillations; but the poles of his opinion may be pointed out by comparing two passages in his letters. At one time, he wrote to his father, "The theatre is a gold mine; and on that I must keep my eye!" Years later, he wrote from Vailima to Sir Sidney Colvin, "No, I will not write a play for Irving, nor for the devil. Can you not see that the work of *falsification* which a play demands is of all tasks the most ungrateful? And I have done it a long while—and nothing ever came of it." The first passage was penned in the high tide of his ambition as a playwright, and the second passage was written after this ambition had been quenched by disappointment.

Stevenson wrote four plays in collaboration with William Ernest Henley, and a fifth play in collaboration with Mrs. Stevenson. The last of these, *The Hanging Judge*, which was written at Bournemouth early in 1887, has never been acted, and was never printed, even privately, during the life-time of R.L.S. After her husband's death, Mrs. Stevenson printed a few copies and presented them to his intimate friends. I have seen a copy of this issue in the library of William Archer; but, in a very hasty reading, I failed to discover any noticeable merit in the play. In 1914, Edmund Gosse printed privately an edition of *The Hanging Judge* that was limited to thirty copies; but, so far as the general reader is concerned, the piece remains unpublished.

But the four plays which Stevenson produced in partnership with Henley are published in the works of R.L.S.; and all four of them, at one time or another, have been acted on the stage. *Deacon Brodie* was first produced at Pullan's Theatre of Varieties,

Bradford, on December 28, 1882. In March, 1883, a performance of the play took place at Her Majesty's Theatre, Aberdeen; and on the afternoon of July 2, 1884, it was introduced to the London public at the Prince's Theatre. *Admiral Guinea* was produced at an afternoon performance at the Avenue Theatre, in London, on November 29, 1897; and *Beau Austin* was produced at the Haymarket Theatre, in London, on November 3, 1890, with Mr. Beerbohm Tree [later Sir Herbert Tree] in the title part. I can find no record, in my notes, of the first performance of *Macaire;* but this piece, also, has been produced in public. Stevenson, however, never witnessed a performance of any of his plays, and was never even privileged to see a scene of his enacted in rehearsal.

The only one of these four plays which exhibited any indication of vitality in the theatre was the first, and perhaps the poorest, of them all,—*Deacon Brodie.* In 1887 this piece was presented in several cities in America,—the tour opening at Montreal on September 26; but its comparative success must be ascribed less to its own merits as a melodrama than to the very interesting acting of Edward John Henley, the brother of Stevenson's collaborator.

Deacon Brodie, which was elaborated from an early draft made by Stevenson himself, was completed by Stevenson and Henley in 1880, but was subsequently revised and rewritten. *Admiral Guinea, Beau Austin,* and *Macaire* were all composed in 1884 and 1885, during the period of Stevenson's residence at Bournemouth. His health, at that period, was at its very lowest ebb; most of his time was spent perforce in bed; and his main motive in embarking on the collaboration was merely to enliven the intervals of his lingering in the "land of counterpane" by a playful exercise of spirits in the company of a spirited and eager friend. There is ample evidence that Henley took their joint task much more seriously; but neither of the two collaborators had established a professional relation with the theatre.

As Stevenson looked back upon these plays, he clear-sightedly looked down upon them. In July, 1884, he wrote frankly to Sir Sidney Colvin,—"and anyhow the *Deacon* is damn bad"; and in March, 1887, he remonstrated with Henley, in the following terms, for sending copies of their joint plays to their literary friends:— "The reperusal of the *Admiral,* by the way, was a sore blow; eh, God, man, it is a low, black, dirty, blackguard, ragged piece; vomitable in many parts—simply vomitable. . . . *Macaire* is a piece

of job-work, hurriedly bockled; might have been worse, might
have been better; happy-go-lucky; act-it-or-let-it-rot piece of business. Not a thing, I think, to send in presentations."

II

These dictates of self-criticism—destructive as they are—have
been, in the main, accepted by posterity; for, even among ardent
Stevensonians, the plays of Stevenson and Henley have found very
few apologists. A fairly recent writer, Mr. Francis Watt, in his
interesting book entitled *R.L.S.*, has gravely stated [page 249]
that "the plays were too good to win a popular success"; but
this is an opinion that will be at once distrusted by any habitual
frequenter of the theatre. Plays do not fail because they are too
good: they fail because they are not good enough in the right
way.

The most illuminating criticism—in fact, the only finally authoritative criticism—of the plays of Stevenson and Henley is the
opinion of Sir Arthur Pinero, delivered in his lecture to the members of the Philosophical Institution of Edinburgh at the Music
Hall in Edinburgh on Tuesday, February 24, 1903. This lecture
—entitled *R. L. Stevenson: the Dramatist*—has been printed only
privately in England, because Sir Arthur entertained an ineradicable habit of reserving the limelight for his plays and keeping out
of it himself; but it has more recently been published in this country, in an edition limited to three hundred and thirty-three copies,
by the Dramatic Museum of Columbia University.

Since, however, this thoroughly authoritative paper is still unknown to the generality of readers, it may be profitable to summarize its most important points. The first of these is that "One
of the great rules—perhaps the only universal rule—of the drama
is that you cannot pour new wine into old skins. . . . The art
of the drama is not stationary but progressive. . . . Its conditions
are always changing, and . . . every dramatist whose ambition it
is to produce live plays is absolutely bound to study carefully, and
I may even add respectfully—at any rate not contemptuously—the
conditions that hold good for his own age and generation." The
second important point in Sir Arthur's statement that "*dramatic
talent*" is of service in the theatre only as "the raw material of
theatrical talent. . . . Dramatic, like poetic, talent is born, not
made; if it is to achieve success on the stage, it must be developed

into theatrical talent by hard study, and generally by long practice." Almost equally suggestive is Sir Arthur Pinero's distinction
between what he calls the "strategy" and the "tactics" of play-
making. He defines *strategy* as "the general laying out of a play"
and *tactics* as "the art of getting the characters on and off the stage,
of conveying information to the audience, and so forth." His
fourth important point is that fine speeches, and fine speeches
alone, will not carry a drama to success; for Sir Arthur makes a
clear distinction between "the absolute beauty of words, such
beauty as Ruskin or Pater or Newman might achieve in an eloquent
passage," and "the beauty of dramatic fitness to the character
and the situation."

III

In the light of these four principles, Sir Arthur Pinero examined
the plays of Stevenson and Henley; and, at each of the four points,
he found the plays defective. Stevenson's work in the drama was
anachronistic; and the models that he imitated not only were out-
worn but also were unworthy. Stevenson never took the trouble
to develop into theatrical talent the keen dramatic talent he was
born with. He never taught himself the tactics of modern play-
making, and did not even appreciate the good points in the strategy
of the melodramatists he chose to imitate. And, finally, Stevenson
never managed to unlearn the heresy that fine speeches, and fine
speeches alone, will carry a drama to success.

Sir Arthur's explanation of Stevenson's fourfold failure as a
dramatist was equally acute. He found that Stevenson failed to take
the drama seriously, that he worked at it "in a smiling, sportive,
half-contemptuous spirit," that he "played at being a playwright"
and "was fundamentally in error in regarding the drama as a matter of child's play." And, in a very interesting parallel, Sir Arthur
pointed out the close resemblance between Stevenson's own plays
and those typical examples of Skelt's Juvenile Drama that are celebrated with such a gusto of memorial eloquence in that delightful
essay in *Memories and Portraits* called *A Penny Plain and Two-
pence Coloured*. "Even to his dying day," Sir Arthur added, "he
continued to regard the actual theatre as only an enlarged form
of the toy theatres which had fascinated his childhood . . . he
considered his function as a dramatist very little more serious than
that child's-play with paint-box and pasteboard on which his memory dwelt so fondly."

This criticism of the plays of Stevenson and Henley, delivered by the finest dramaturgic craftsman of recent times, must be accepted as final; but a word or two should be appended in explanation of Stevenson's utter lack of preparation for the serious task of making plays. Owing mainly to the accident of birth—for Stevenson was born in a rigorous metropolis that refused to countenance the theatre—and owing also to the accident of his continuous ill-health, he grew up without ever going to the theatre; and his earliest impressions of the stage were confined, necessarily, to the repertory of the toy-theatre that he has celebrated with enthusiasm in the famous essay that Pinero has referred to. Stevenson's biographer, Mr. Graham Balfour, has stated [Volume I, page 161],—"although he had read (and written) plays from his early years, had reveled in the melodramas of the toy-theatre, and had acted with the Jenkins and in other private theatricals, I find no reference to his having visited a theatre before December, 1874." At this date, Stevenson was twenty-four years old; and it is not at all surprising that an author who first visited the theatre at the age of twenty-four should show himself deficient as a dramatist when he casually undertook the task of making plays in his early thirties.

In view of these facts, it seems only fair that Henley, more than Stevenson, should be called to account for the manifest anachronism of their plays; for Henley was a magazine-editor, and ought presumably to have kept himself in touch with the fashions of the theatre in his day. But it is possible, of course, that Henley was deterred from theatre-going by his bodily infirmity,—an infirmity much more painful and disastrous than that which kept Stevenson isolated in his bed at Bournemouth. At any rate, the one thing which the two collaborators never understood was the fact that the technique of the theatre had advanced beyond remembrance of the period of those transpontine melodramatists that they so blithely imitated.

IV

What Stevenson needed most of all was a different collaborator, —not a man of letters like Henley, but a man of the theatre like (for instance) Henry Arthur Jones, whose famous melodrama, *The Silver King*, had already been produced in 1882. He needed a professional assistant, to translate into terms of theatrical talent the keen dramatic talent he was born with. Many years after his death, a collaborator of this type was at last accorded to him, through the enterprise of Mr. Charles Hopkins, the director of the Punch and Judy Theatre in New York. *Treasure Island* was effectively dramatized by Mr. Jules Eckert Goodman,—a playwright whose sound theatrical talent had been developed to efficiency by hard study and by long practice. Mr. Goodman so successfully transferred the rapture and the thrill of *Treasure Island* to the stage that the delighted spectator came away from the performance with a feeling that could only be expressed by quoting Andrew Lang's ejaculation,—"This is the kind of stuff a fellow wants!"

The magnitude of Mr. Goodman's accomplishment can be appreciated only if we take into account the special difficulties of his task. Nearly all the critics who, from time to time, had been consulted concerning the possibility of making a successful play from *Treasure Island* had reported in the negative; and, among the many, the present writer is compelled to confess that he agreed with the majority. The special obstacles were three in number:— first, the utter lack of feminine interest in the story, which seemed to make the material dangerous for successful exploitation in the theatre; second, the apparent necessity of shifting the action rapidly from place to place, and of doing this at least a dozen times, without impeding the onrush of the action; and third, the particular requirement, in the case of a story known and loved by absolutely everybody, of clinging close to the original material and inventing nothing new.

But these three difficulties were swept away by Mr. Goodman. Despite the tradition of the theatre that the public cares much more for actresses than actors, the audience never seemed to notice the absence of any feminine interest in the narrative. Jim's mother is, of course, the only woman in the story, and she appears only inconspicuously, for a few moments in the first act; but the play succeeds so well without a heroine that a necessary inference is forced that love is not, by any means, the only subject that can capture the attention of the theatre-going crowd.

Mr. Goodman arranged the narrative in ten different chapters of time and nine distinct pigeon-holes of place; but the changes were so rapidly and easily effected on the stage of Charles Hopkins that the spectator was never released from the enthrallment of the story. The first act was, by far, the best, and this fact was a little unfortunate for the play; but the fault was Stevenson's, not Mr. Good-

man's. Stevenson began his story in a high tide of delighted composition; but, after drying up in the early paragraphs of the sixteenth chapter, he never entirely recaptured the zest of the initiation of his narrative. Mr. Goodman's first act, which is set, of
course, in the Admiral Benbow Inn, is quite as good as any first
act has a right to be; for if the theatre were often as enthralling
as this, no self-respecting person could ever find an evening off, to
sit at home and read *The Count of Monte Cristo.*

But Mr. Goodman's success is perhaps even more remarkable
in respect to the third difficulty that confronted him. He has made
a coherent play without inventing anything that was not set down
for him in the well-known and well-belovèd novel; and he has not
left out anything that even Andrew Lang would emphatically
miss. The great bother about dramatizing books for boys is, of
course, that every boy in the audience will at once become a critic
and will insist on having the story served to him—in Rudyard
Kipling's phrase—"just so." When the present writer first attended
the performance, a concentrated company of four boys sat in
back of him. There was a scene on the deck of the *Hispaniola,* dis-
closing the well-known apple-barrel "standing broached in the
waist." There were indications of impending mutiny, as the ragged
members of Flint's old crew muttered darkling in the corners of
the stage. Jim entered, strolling down the deck. "Get into the barrel," said one of the boys behind me. "Hurry up and get into the
barrel, before they see you: hurry up and hide, or how can you
overhear what they are going to say?" This comment convinced
the critic that the play was undeniably successful; but it also
seemed to point a finger at the greatest difficulty which the dramatist was overcoming.

v

The success of *Treasure Island* on the stage has called attention
to the fact that comparatively few of the tales of R.L.S. have enjoyed a similar transference to the theatre. The late T. Russell
Sullivan's dramatization of *Dr. Jekyll and Mr. Hyde* has heretofore
stood almost alone as an example of what may be done with the
Stevenson stories on the stage; and this play derived its public
popularity less from the inherent interest of the subject-matter
than from the very remarkable acting of Richard Mansfield. Mr.
Mansfield, who was accustomed to consider very highly his own
performance of Beau Brummell and to speak with an entirely be-

coming pride of his best achievements on the stage, told the present writer, not once but many times, that his performance of Jekyll and Hyde was little more than a matter of theatric mechanism, and expressed surprise at the continued favor of the public for the play. "It's nothing but clap-trap," said Mr. Mansfield, "yet they seem to like it as much as *Richard III*, in which I give a performance that is worth considering." The fact remains, however, that the play died with Mansfield's death; and that its continuous vitality for many years was due more to him than to Sullivan or Stevenson.

It may be interesting to record the fact that Stevenson never witnessed Richard Mansfield's performance in the dual role of his hero and his villain. At the first night in New York, in the Madison Square Theatre, on Monday evening, September 12, 1887, Stevenson's wife and mother saw the performance from Mr. Sullivan's box; but, on this occasion, the novelist himself was lying ill in Newport at the house of Mr. and Mrs. Charles Fairchild, and he never subsequently saw the play.

After Stevenson's death, Mr. Otis Skinner appeared in a dramatic version of *Prince Otto*,—made, if I remember rightly, by himself; but the piece was not successful. On April 22, 1917, the Morningside Players produced at the Comedy Theatre in New York an adequate dramatization of *Markheim*, by Zillah K. MacDonald. Mention must also be made of Mr. Granville Barker's dramatization of *The Wrong Box*, entitled *The Morris Dance*, which was disclosed at the Little Theatre in New York in February, 1917. This was a very vapid play; and it went down swiftly to a thoroughly deserved oblivion. I find among my notes no other records of plays made professionally from the tales of Stevenson, with the exception of a few scattered and unimportant one-act versions of various short-stories.

VI

It is a curious fact that the tales of Stevenson were, for the most part, left untouched throughout that period of the eighteen-nineties when there was a popular and insistent demand for dramatized novels,—the period when the indefatigable E. E. Rose used to dramatize three or four novels a year. The reason for this fact, however, will easily become apparent. It is true enough, as Sir Arthur Pinero has reported, that "dramatic talent Stevenson undoubtedly possessed in abundance." His tales are full of striking situations, in which the actors appear in postures which are vividly impressed forever on the eye of memory. But in two respects his novels, despite their emphasis upon the element of action and their vividness of visual appeal, have been singularly difficult to dramatize. In the first place, Stevenson usually neglected the interest of love and excluded women rigorously from his most exciting situations; and, in the second place, he was accustomed to allow his narratives to wander very freely in both space and time and to depend for his effect on a frequent change of setting. How, for instance, could one dramatize *The Wrecker*, which keeps the reader traveling over more than half the habitable globe?; and how could one dramatize *Kidnapped*, which leads the reader to a world in which there seem to be no women?

These objections, though they appear to explain the fact that very few playwrights have attempted to transfer the tales of Stevenson to the service of the theatre, afford no reason why they may not be successfully transferred to the service of the new and growing medium of motion pictures. *Treasure Island*, for example, has made a better motion picture than a play. It may sanely be conjectured that, if Stevenson were living still, he would probably devote his mind enthusiastically to the new craft of making motion pictures. In his *Gossip on Romance*, he said,—"The story, if it be a story, should repeat itself in a thousand colored pictures to the eye. . . . There is a vast deal in life . . . where the interest turns . . . not on the passionate slips and hesitations of the conscience, but on the problems of the body and of the practical intelligence, in clean, open-air adventure, the shock of arms or the diplomacy of life. With such material as this it is impossible to build a play, for the serious theatre exists solely on moral grounds, and is a standing proof of the dissemination of the human conscience. But it is possible to build, upon this ground, . . . the most lively, beautiful, and buoyant tales."

The Master of Ballantrae might be made into a good play, though the dramatist would experience considerable difficulty in projecting the last act; but this concluding passage would afford the very best material for the motion-picture craftsman. *Kidnapped*, also, could easily be shown in motion pictures, but could hardly be compressed into a play. Stevenson, in his stories, wrote mainly for the seeing eye; he was less concerned with character than with action and with setting; he exhibited events, harmoniously set in place and time, and he never disturbed the exhibition by psychological analysis. His literary style is perhaps his greatest glory; but, even if bereft of this, he would remain—to quote him once again— a master of "brute incident." While still alive, he failed in his efforts as a dramatist; but there seems to be no reason now why he should not enjoy a posthumous success as a master of the motion picture play.

XIII

UNDERSTANDING THE RUSSIANS

EW STATEMENTS are more silly than the usual assertion that human nature is the same the wide world over. The dog and the cat have different characters, though each of them is endowed with four legs and a tail; and we have lately learned that the psychology of the Germans is different from that of all the other races that walk upright on their rearward limbs. We shall never understand the Russians until we admit, in the first place, that human nature is not the same in Russia as it is in the United States. Rudyard Kipling told us, long ago, that the Russians may be regarded either as the most eastern of western peoples or as the most western of eastern peoples. At any rate, they are not wholly of the Occident, as we are. When the Englishman is in trouble, he conceals his feelings, talks lightly of trivial matters that have nothing to do with the occasion, and resolutely "carries on." When the American is in trouble, he makes a joke of his difficulties and curses laughingly in the latest slang. When the Frenchman is in trouble, he analyzes his own situation clearly, arrives at a reasonable judgment from the facts, and then waves his hand aloft in a graceful gesture and says merely, *"C'est la guerre!"* When the German is in trouble, he weeps sentimental tears and calls upon his tribal deity. But when the Russian is in trouble, he luxuriates in this abnormal situation, wallows nakedly in the pathetic, and indulges in a veritable orgy of self-pity. He loves himself the more because his lot is hard; he worries about his soul to an extent that western men will not permit themselves to worry; and his abject attitude of thanking God for chastisement remains quite incomprehensible to the occidental mind.

It is well for us to understand the Russians, because they are more numerous than we are, and are possibly predestined to play a larger part in the future drama of humanity. The quickest way to understand them is to study their literature, and to compare it with ours. The Russian writers easily excel our own in sheer immensity; but they cannot compete with our occidental artists in the matter of orderly arrangement. Here, at once, we sense a basic difference between two antithetic types of mind. The Russians exceed us in potentiality, in fruitfulness; but we exceed them in efficiency and in the scientific application of the practical. There is, here and now before us, no question of better or of worse; the immediate problem is to recognize and to define essential differences.

It may be doubted if Maxim Gorki's celebrated tragedy, *Night Lodging*, would be commercially successful if it were presented in New York for a regular run, for it is totally foreign to our American ideas of "entertainment." We are taken to a foul and filthy lodging-house, inhabited by the scum and dregs of Russian humanity,—a helter-skelter group of beggars, thieves, drunkards, prostitutes, murderers, and wastrels. We are made to witness their daily doings; we are made to overhear their momentary conversations; we are made to explore the darkest and most intimate recesses of their slimy souls. The first impression we receive is one of horror, —horror that such creatures should exist, and horror that any author with a manifest ability to wield a pen should permit his mind to brood so persistently on their existence. For *Night Lodging* is not true to life, as life is visioned by our occidental writers. Gorki's tragedy is sedulously faithful to facts; but its selection of facts from life is—to our minds—unfaithfully proportioned. There are seventeen people in this play. Suppose, now, that an enormous crowd of people should be gathered hugger-mugger in Trafalgar Square, the Place de la Concorde, Union Square, or the Lake Front in Chicago; and suppose, next, that somebody should hurl a bomb that should indiscriminately kill any seventeen people in this entire crowd. To the mind of such a man as Abraham Lincoln, it would be unimaginable that not one person in the seventeen should be worthy of respect, that not one person in the seventeen should have a single friend to love him and to lament the deep damnation of his taking off. The mind of Abraham Lincoln is the American mind. We believe in people. But Maxim Gorki is a Russian. God only knows what he believes in; for he does not believe in God, he does not believe in life, he does not believe in people.

No reasoned philosophy of life is apparent in this piece; but there is a single little clue that seems to open a tiny window on the author's mind. An old man—a sort of pilgrim—wanders into the play toward the close of the first act and wanders out of it again before the last act is arrived at. The other characters are intolerant of this aged wanderer; he has no friends; and yet—to a western audience—he seems comparatively likable. He is kind to people, without any reason to be kind; and he says one thing that is particularly worthy of remembrance. He asserts that human nature, even at its lowest, remains somehow human, and that none of us should ever dare to insult a human being by regarding him with pity. Pity, he tells us, is a base emotion, because it is born of egoism and is nearly related to contempt. "Judge not, that ye be not judged." This is a great saying. . . .

Yet, if we may not pity the helpless and the hopeless of this world, what can we do for them, and what shall we do about them? Maxim Gorki does not answer; for his lips are sealed. He is like a miner in the bowels of the earth, so blinded by the stinking darkness that envelops him that he forgets that, up above him, on the surface of the seas, many mariners are steering sleek and graceful ships by the shining of the everlasting stars.

Yet this gloomy and discomfortable Russian is endowed with an immensity of mind that puts our native dramatists to shame. He splashes at a ten-league canvas with brushes of comet's hair; and we westerners who yelp against him should perhaps regard ourselves as a pack of coddled little lap-dogs baying at the moon. The moon is cold and dead; but who are we to bark against it? We may conserve our dignity most gracefully by confessing that we do not understand the Russians.

To the occidental mind, *Night Lodging* is a formless play. It has no plot. It has no beginning, no middle, and no end. It never rises to a climax; yet every moment is unaccountably dramatic. It might go on forever, like a Chinese drama. The spectator may come late, and arrive at any moment; he may leave early, and forsake the theatre at any moment: any ten minutes of *Night Lodging* is essentially the same as any other, and as good as any other. The piece offers merely a sort of peep-hole upon Russian life, or so much of Russian life as Maxim Gorki has cared to contemplate; and this life is, in the main, a rather dreary thing that drifts along with no particular accentuation of excitement.

This is a totally different presentment from that shrewdly selected and meticulously patterned drama that we, in England and America, have inherited from France. But let us not surrender to the egoism of assuming that Maxim Gorki is not an artist; let us assert merely that Gorki is a Russian, and that our minds work differently. We build our plays more cleverly; but seldom or never do we achieve that absolute sincerity of sheer reporting which is evident in every line of Maxim Gorki's dialogue.

XIV

IBSEN ONCE AGAIN

ENRIK IBSEN died in 1906; and now, at last, he is beginning to be appreciated in this country from the disinterested point of view of sheer dramatic criticism. So long as he was still alive, his plays were studied not as plays, but under the different labels of "literature," "philosophy," or "sociology." The casual patrons of our theatre were told that they should see his dramas because of a sense of duty and not because of the incentive of enjoyment; and, in pursuance of this method, even so popular a piece as *A Doll's House* was heralded by many commentators as a sort of family funeral.

The reason for this *cul de sac*, which pocketed for many, many years the popularity of Ibsen as a purveyor of entertainment, is easily apparent. Our native knowledge of Ibsen was imported overseas from England; and it was in England that the misconception of this author as a "high-brow" first originated. Ibsen was "discovered" for the English public by William Archer and Edmund Gosse; but, when these two enlightened critics endeavored to deliver their discovery, they found themselves impeded by the medieval institution of the British censorship of plays. Because of this impediment, the very first performance of an Ibsen play in England—that epoch-making production of *Ghosts* which was shown in 1891 by J. T. Grein before the private audience of the Independent Theatre Society—was regarded by the general public as a thing tabooed and flung beyond the pale. In consequence of this condition, the comments called forth by this first performance of a play of Ibsen's in the English language were based upon contrasted theories of ethics instead of being based on theories of dramaturgic craftsmanship. The reviewers missed the point entirely.

Ibsen was criticized—in the England of the early eighteen-nineties—as a sociologist, a philosopher, a man of letters, a moralist, a propagandist,—in short, as everything except the one thing that he really was,—a practical and interesting playwright. His technique— as a professional dramatist—was not discussed, despite the repeated pleas of so appealing a dramatic critic as William Archer. Instead, his commentators—*pro* and *con*—contented themselves with throwing mud or throwing roses against his subject-matter,—which is, of course, the last thing to be considered by a genuine dramatic critic in analyzing any well-made play. Not what an author says, but how effectively he says it in the theatre, is the proper theme for analytic criticism; for, in the great art of the drama, the "message" of an author is superior to comment, and nothing offers invitation to the technical interpreter but the mere efficiency displayed, or missed, in the elocution of this "message" to the public.

Because of the incubus of the British censorship, an impression was spread abroad, throughout the eighteen-nineties, that Ibsen should be regarded as a philosophic thinker and a man of letters, instead of being judged as a playwright ambitious to receive the plaudits of the theatre-going public. From the effect of this misconceived impression, our casual American audience is only now beginning to recover. Our local public is now learning, tardily, to see that Ibsen was a playwright, first and last and all the time.

The truth of the matter now, at last, appears to be that Ibsen was a very great artist of the theatre, and was nothing else at all. Quite obviously—in the cold light of our later learning—he cannot be accepted seriously as a man of letters. He had no literary training; and he never acquired the advantage of a literary culture. In the decade of his 'teens, he did not go to school: in the decade of his twenties, he was not even registered as a regular student in the provincial University of Christiania. His entire education was not literary but theatrical. At the age of twenty-four, he went to Bergen as the general stage-manager of a stock-company in that isolated town; and, in this capacity, he worked a dozen hours every day throughout five successive years. His annual salary amounted, in round numbers, to three hundred dollars; and his apprenticeship may be understood most quickly if we face the fact that, throughout the formative period of his youth, he exerted all his energies, at a dollar a day, to the task of setting forth a new play every week with a stock-company localized before the public of a little city as secluded as Muncie, Indiana.

In these years of his apprenticeship, Ibsen had no time to read; and all that he could learn was acquired incidentally from his necessary business of presenting to the local Bergen public many French plays of the school of Scribe. His own first play of any prominence—*Lady Inger of Östrat*—was written in emulation of the current formula of Scribe; and this minor but inevitable incident is indicative of the important fact that Ibsen's education was derived not from the library but from the stage. Never at any time —in the midst of a perilous attempt to earn his living against agonizing odds—did Ibsen ever find the leisure to become a "man of letters." In his twenties and his thirties, he read a few plays of Schiller and a few plays of Shakespeare; and, at the same period, he seems to have become more familiar than he was willing later to admit with both parts of Goethe's *Faust;* but, to the end of his days, he remained distinctly—and this fact became with him a point of pride—a playwright who knew next to nothing of the history of literature. Though most Norwegians are accustomed, as a matter of course, to study many other languages, Ibsen never acquired an easy fluency in any foreign tongue but German. Late in his life, he said to one of his Boswells that he hated all the plays of Alexandre Dumas, *fils,* and added the unexpected comment,—"But, of course, I have never read them." The last remark was, presumably, more candid than the first: for Ibsen, in his later years, was genuinely proud of the fact that he had read little except the daily newspapers. When commentators pointed out that the patterned formula of *Ghosts* recalled the technique of Euripides, he would retort irately that he had never read Euripides.

It was not until the time of the Italian tour which Ibsen undertook in the middle of his thirties that he ever actually saw any of the major works of architecture, painting, or sculpture that are existent in the world. At this belated moment, he attempted—to employ a phrase that is current in the narrowly restricted world of professional baseball—a "delayed steal" of culture; and his experience ran parallel to that of our own Nathaniel Hawthorne, who also made a pilgrimage to Italy at a time of life too long deferred. Like Hawthorne, Ibsen appreciated the wrong paintings, admired the wrong statues, and waxed enthusiastic over the wrong works of architecture. While showing the sensitized impressibility of a responsive temperament, he betrayed also the effects of an early education that had been exceedingly defective. Even in responding to the appeals of such æsthetic regions as Rome, Sorrento, and Amalfi, Ibsen remained the stage-director of a stock-company in Muncie, instead of rising to the rarer atmosphere of a stimulated man of letters.

If Ibsen lacked culture in the realm of letters—and he frequently, when interviewed, insisted on the point that he was not well-read —it is even more obvious that he claimed no standing whatsoever as a sociologist or a philosopher. He regarded himself as a playwright, first and last and all the time,—that is to say, a craftsman whose task it was to interest the public by holding, as 'twere, a mirror up to nature in the actual, commercial theatre. His teacher was Eugène Scribe,—that exceedingly adroit technician who codified the formula of "the well-made play" [*"la pièce bien faite"*]; and the contemporary of whose exploits he was most justly jealous was Alexandre Dumas, *fils*,—who, like himself, attempted in his own way to improve and to perfect the formula of Scribe. Ibsen was not a philosopher; for he was ignorant of the accumulated records of philosophic literature. The author of *Brand* and *Peer Gynt* is not to be regarded as a scholarly poet; for he had never studied any other universally important poem except the first and second parts of Goethe's *Faust*. To sum the matter up, he should not be considered in any other light than as an honest craftsman of the theatre who endeavored—in accordance with that downright statement of the practical Pinero—"to give rise to the greatest possible amount of that peculiar kind of emotional effect, the production of which is the one great function of the theatre."

XV

EURIPIDES IN NEW YORK

T
WO THOUSAND three hundred and fifty years ago, the citizens of Athens, to the number of twenty thousand, assembled in the Theatre of Dionysus on the southern slope of the Acropolis, to witness the first performance of *The Trojan Women* of Euripides. On the twenty-ninth of May, 1915, seven thousand representative citizens of New York assembled in the beautiful new stadium designed by Arnold W. Brunner and presented to the city by the munificence of Adolph Lewisohn, to witness a performance of the same tragedy, rendered eloquently into English verse by Professor Gilbert Murray. The play had not grown ancient in this interval. It appeared not as a dead thing, of interest only to archæologists who delve amid the graves of long-departed glories, but as a live thing, speaking to the men and women of this modern world with a voice as living as the voice of God. Hundreds who had come to the dedication of the stadium merely because it marked a civic celebration of unusual significance, hundreds also who, knowing nothing of Euripides, had been attracted to this performance merely by a wide-eyed curiosity, were touched with pathos at the parting between Andromache and Astyanax and sat weeping through the ultimate lament of Hecuba over the dead body of the little murdered boy. The effect of these scenes on the assembled multitude sustained the verdict of the great dramatic critic, Aristotle, who called Euripides "the most tragic of the poets." But a deeper thrill than this response of recognition to the grandest tragic art that the world has ever known swept through and through the seven thousand citizens who sat in serried ranks, tier above tier, in the wide curve of the stadium; for a poet, dead for more than twenty centuries, seemed to be speaking with peculiar pertinence of the crisis which confronts the world to-day. The name, Ilion, went ringing through his verses;

408

but, as it echoed round the stadium, it seemed mystically to transmute itself into a kindred name, Louvain. This tragedy was written in a great crisis of human history. We stand to-day, once more, at such a crisis. Euripides is not only the most heartrending of all tragic writers; he is also one of the few authentic poets who have looked into the very mind of God and spoken to mankind with the ecstatic gift of prophecy. In *The Trojan Women*, he prophesied, two thousand three hundred and fifty years ago, the doom of military prowess in the ancient world; and now, with voice undimmed by all the intervening centuries, he is risen from the dead to prophesy the doom of military prowess in the world to-day.

To appreciate the peculiar timeliness of this immortal tragedy, we must inquire into the circumstances under which it was composed. During his dreamful and ambitious youth, Euripides had watched his well-belovèd Athens ascend to the highest pinnacle of culture that humanity has ever reached. Then, "drunk with sight of power," she deliberately resolved to embark upon the savage enterprise of conquering the world and imposing her own culture on unwilling peoples by force of arms. To this project the poet was opposed. He had served in the army for forty years, from the age of twenty to the age of sixty; he had fought for liberty, equality, fraternity, in hundreds of stirring combats, hand to hand; and, with all this vast experience behind him, he realized the vanity of war and longed at last for universal peace. But Athens was less wise; and, in his sixties, Euripides was doomed to witness the gradual giving-over of his city to a party hot for war and eager for dominion of the world.

In the year 416 B.C., the war-lords of Athens committed a great crime, the like of which was not repeated by any nation calling itself civilized until the year 1914 A.D. There was, in the Ægean Sea, a little island named Melos, which had steadfastly maintained neutrality through all the recent civil wars which had convulsed the mainland. Its inhabitants desired merely to be left alone; they imagined no military projects, and were contented to exist in peace on the products of their agriculture. But in this ill-omened year, the war-party that had seized control of Athens decided to annex this peaceful island. The Athenian envoys explained to the Melian senate that it suited their purpose that Melos should become subject to their empire. They announced their ultimatum in these words:—"We will not pretend—being sensible men and talking to sensible men—that the Melians have done us any wrong or that we have any lawful claim to Melos; but we do not wish any islands to remain independent—it is a bad example to the others. The power of Athens is practically irresistible: Melos is free to submit or be destroyed." The Melians replied that right was right and wrong was wrong; and that, rather than accept the principle that might was right, they would prefer "to go down scornful before many spears."

The Athenians crashed in, and had their way. They massacred the males of Melos, and sold the women and children into slavery. Then, elated with this easy victory, they prepared a gigantic naval expedition to subjugate a great, free people overseas,—the citizens of Sicily. It was precisely at this moment that Euripides, after several months of brooding, composed *The Trojan Women*. He was, at that time, sixty-nine years old. With an entire life-time of patriotic toil behind him, he perceived clearly that Athens had rashly started on the downward path; and he summoned all his powers to warn his well-belovèd city of the doom foretold to men who had unthinkingly assumed the burden of a crime so heavy as the crime of Melos. He chose for the subject of his tragedy the legendary fall of Troy,—a story which for centuries had been repeated as the greatest glory of the arms of Greece; but he told this old, heroic story in an utterly unprecedented way. Instead of lauding Menelaus and Agamemnon for the consummation of their ten years' campaign for conquest, he summed up the tangible results of this campaign from the unexpected point of view of the women of Troy—because the burden of any offensive war falls heaviest upon the women of the vanquished. The fall of Ilion—which, for a thousand years before Euripides, had been trumpeted by poets as a theme for celebration—was seen by this clear-visioned prophet— with the imminent example of weak Melos burning in his eyes—to be, instead, a theme for lamentation and for grim foreboding of a Nemesis to be.

For this prophetic poet had perceived that, in his own day, his own Athens had surrendered to the sin of Pride—a sin with which the gods made men insane before destroying them; and, in this poignant tragedy, he sought to show his fellow-citizens that the glamor of military conquest is nothing but a sham, and that, whenever a mighty wrong succeeds in trampling down a worthy right, the only real glory is the glory of the glimmering of truth for those who suffer nobly for the right, and die in misery with souls still undestroyed. Before twenty thousand citizens of Athens, this veteran of many wars was bold enough to champion the cause of stricken Melos, and to cry aloud,—in words that may be quoted from a kindred poet,—"That way madness lies!"

We know now that Athens failed to heed this prophet of the living God. Euripides was doomed to exile, and sent forth, in the winter of his years, to break bread with the barbarians of Macedonia, and, alone among their mountains, to write the *Bacchæ* and to die. Meanwhile, the expedition against Sicily set sail—and its sailing marked the doom of Athens. The Nemesis that lies in wait to punish those overweening mortals who surrender to the sin of Pride—the Greek word for which is *hubris*—overwhelmed, precisely as the poet had predicted, the greatest city of the ancient world. When Athens fell, the highest and noblest achievements of mankind fell crashing with her to oblivion. "Then I, and you, and all of us fell down,"—exactly as this prophet had foretold: and more than twenty centuries were destined to elapse before another nation dared to recommit the crime of Melos and to affront the anger of the gods.

Among the Greeks there was a fable that history would move in cycles and would repeat itself precisely in every thousand years. This fable was in the minds of many hundred citizens when, under the gray sky of the twenty-ninth of May, 1915, such words as these rang out from the voice of great Euripides:—

> How are ye blind,
> Ye treaders down of cities, ye that cast
> Temples to desolation, and lay waste
> Tombs, the untrodden sanctuaries where lie
> The ancient dead; yourselves so soon to die!

and again,

> Would ye be wise, ye Cities, fly from war!
> Yet if war come, there is a crown in death
> For her that striveth well and perisheth
> Unstained: to die in evil were the stain!

More than twenty centuries after Euripides was buried, there was dug up in the little isle of Melos an armless statue of the goddess Aphrodite which has become to millions of men and women of this modern age a living symbol of "the glory that was

Greece,"—the glory that was sacrificed when Athens set her culture at the service of efficient barbarism. Millions of people who are unaware that the fall of Athens must be dated from that rash moment when this city of all cities decided to violate the neutrality of a little island in the blue Ægean Sea, have bowed their heads in mere humility before that absolute expression of pure beauty—that utter culmination of all dreams of earth—which was rescued from this little island in some succeeding century. Even the Parthenon is now a shattered ruin, standing lonely on a sun-parched hill, to remind us wistfully of all that Athens used to be; but the armless, radiant wonder in the Louvre speaks more eloquently still of the vision of a man of Melos, whose island was made desolate before his birth by the armies of some utterly unnoted war-lord who rashly sought to trample down the world, and only accomplished for his country an everlasting shame.

The many thousand people of New York who witnessed this revival of *The Trojan Women* were all a-thrill with recent memories of Louvain and Malines, of Rheims and Ypres,—and of the *Lusitania*. This fact afforded a double meaning to the lines, which was analogous to that other double meaning which must have swept through the minds of the twenty thousand citizens of Athens who first listened to this tragic drama two thousand three hundred and thirty years before. The brooding skies seemed rent with prophecy; and, out of a vast silence, there seemed to come a voice, ancient of days and hoary with omniscience, that cried aloud, "Vengeance is mine, saith the Lord: I will repay!"

The translation of Professor Gilbert Murray is beyond all praise. There is, in the German language, a fitting symbol for this sort of work, which is incorporated in the word *Nachsingen*. Professor Murray does not merely repeat the meaning of Euripides: in a very literal sense, he "sings after" the great poet of the Greeks. He writes almost as well as Swinburne; and yet his writing is, at all points, faithful to his text. Consider, for example, such a passage as the following, in which Andromache, in *The Trojan Women*, is saying farewell to her little martyred boy:—

> Thou little thing
> That curlest in my arms, what sweet scents cling
> All round thy neck! Belovèd; can it be
> All nothing, that this bosom cradled thee

And fostered; all the weary nights, wherethrough
I watched upon thy sickness, till I grew
Wasted with watching? Kiss me. This one time;
Not ever again. Put up thine arms, and climb
About my neck: now, kiss me, lips to lips. . . .

In staging this tremendous play, Mr. Granville Barker ascended, at nearly every point, to the height of his great argument. His method of production revealed a tactful compromise between the expectation of the average modern audience and the expectation of the archæologist. He discarded the mask and the cothurnus; but he retained the formal evolutions of the chorus in the orchestra and the superior position of the three actors on the elevated stage. The stage itself—which was transportable from stadium to stadium—revealed a lofty wall, transpierced by the conventional three doors, and descended to the orchestra by the customary flights of steps. Upon this naked platform Mr. Barker contrived to recall a vivid reminiscence of all the pomps and glories of the ancient stage.

XVI

THE ATHENIAN DRAMA AND THE
AMERICAN AUDIENCE

EFORE the invention of printing, there were few books in the world; but all of these were worth reading. So long as every extra copy of a literary work had to be written out by hand on parchment, a certain care was exercised lest this lengthy labor should be wasted over words that were ephemeral. The Romans, Greeks, and Hebrews were human like ourselves, and liable to human error; they must have uttered, every day, the usual amount of trash, and this trash must have been passed about, from mouth to mouth, among the masses; but the ancients did not write it down. They allowed their trivial words to die,—unknell'd, uncoffin'd, and unknown; and they recorded in their libraries only those more memorable words that were luminous with intimations of immortality.

The library of Alexandria was burned; Herculaneum was buried beneath an overwhelming flood of lava; and comparatively little now remains to us of ancient literature. But what remains is not "ancient," in the narrow sense; and nearly all of it is really "literature,"—that is to say [in the noble phrase of Emerson] a record of "man thinking" and expressing his thoughts in unwitherable words. The invention of printing, and the enactment of that modern law which compels everybody, willy-nilly, to go to school and learn to read, has led to a widespread circulation of recorded utterances; but how many of these documents are "literature"? And those of us who ply the pen so busily in these days of rapid printing might profitably pause, every now and then, to ask ourselves whether we have ever written a single sentence that deserves to be engraved on granite and preserved from the erosion of innumerable future centuries. How much of our contemporary writ-

414

ing will be accepted finally as "literature," in the leisure of all time?

The ancients felt a more reverent respect for books and authors than we entertain to-day; but they had more reason for this feeling. They were not poisoned by a state of things that accords ten million readers every morning to the hirelings of Mr. William Randolph Hearst, and reduces John Milton to what—in the profane vocabulary of our friends, the French—is eloquently called "the name of a name." The ancients saw things in perspective and proportion. They never pretended—not even on the eve of a popular election—that "all men are created equal": they announced, instead, that certain men were nobler than their fellows and were worthy, by inherent right, of being listened to attentively. The Greeks gave prizes for literary prowess; and, when a man had won a public prize for authorship, he was erected to the aristocracy and considered as a leading citizen.

The ancients regarded their greatest authors as divine, and spread abroad the legend that these supermen had spoken to mankind with the authentic voice of God. The Hebrews accepted Isaiah not only as a poet but also as a prophet, and claimed that he wrote better than he knew. The Romans believed that Virgil was not merely a perfect artist, but also an unconscious mouthpiece for the Deity of deities; and, after the slow passage of a thousand years, the greatest composition of the greatest man that ever lived was immediately called, not by himself, but by his readers, *The Divine Comedy*. There was no real reason—on the other hand—why this title should not have been selected by Dante himself; since he has told us more than once, with the serenity of perfect confidence, that the things he had to say were suggested not by his own mind, but by the irresistible and overwhelming inspiration of all the things that are.

We are living now in an age of infidelity, when it is popular to laugh at high and far-off images of holy things; but we have no reason to dismiss as merely credulous the belief of our forefathers that their greatest poets were inspired from above. Without departing from the region of the intellect, it would be easy enough to prove that Dante is indeed, in a certain sense, "divine"; and there is also a reasonable motive for accepting several of the Hebrew writings, which have been gathered helter-skelter after many accidents of time into the canonical fold of the Old Testament, as authentic utterances of some power that is greater than ourselves.

The Romans held a "superstition"—to repeat a word that has grown current in our present period of cynicism—that Virgil was so wise that he had hidden away an answer to every imaginable human problem in some passage of his *Æneid;* and common men in need of guidance were advised to open his heroic poem blind-fold, to place a finger on an accidental passage, and to read this passage as a mystical, oracular response to their imaginative inquisition.

This pagan incantation is not yet out-moded. It is still possible to trust the ancient writers for an answer to our modern questionings. And, in these times of trouble, we may profitably turn to the tragic poets of the period of Pericles.

Why is it that any so-called "modern" play which is "revived" after an interval of only twenty or thirty years seems nearly always irretrievably "old-fashioned,"—while any adequate production of a play originally written in the age of Pericles appears always—in the phrase of Robert Browning—"strange and new"?

This question is not difficult to answer. The Greeks—in contemplating any subject for a work of art—sought only and sought always for inklings of eternity. By imagination, they removed their topics "out of space, out of time," and regarded them from the point of view of an absolute and undisrupted leisure. They sought, in any subject, not for transitory hintings of the here and now, but always and only for indications of the absolute and undeniable. By deliberate intention, they wrote "not of an age but for all time."

Another point to be recalled is that the tragic dramatists of ancient Athens were never tempted to pursue the *ignis fatuus* of novelty. No playwright—in those high and far-off days—was ever expected, or permitted, to invent a story. The Athenian dramatists dealt only with tales that had already been familiar to the public for a thousand years. Their function was—as artists—to extract a new and unexpected truth from the elucidation of an ancient fable, and not to catch the light attention of the public by the sudden flaunting of some flag of novelty. The augustness of Greek criticism may be measured by the fact that the *Medea* of Euripides took only a third prize in Athens in the year 431 B.C. It was probably too "modern" or too "revolutionary" to satisfy the honorable judges who accorded the first prize to Euphorion, the son of Æschylus.

If Margaret Anglin had accomplished nothing else, she would be entitled to a vote of gratitude for proving that there is a large and eager public in this country which is willing to pay money for the privilege of seeing the tragic dramas of the Greeks. For Miss Anglin's first performance in New York of the *Electra* of Sophocles, on the afternoon of February 6, 1918, the house was crowded to the roof; and it must be remembered that Carnegie Hall is capable of seating more than three thousand people. Miss Anglin was required, by a popular demand that was literally undeniable, to offer half a dozen repetitions of the *Electra* of Sophocles and the *Medea* of Euripides; and, for each of these matinée performances the gross receipts amounted, in round numbers, to six thousand dollars. There is always a great public for great art; and this Miss Anglin knows.

She has taught our public also that "Sophocles" and "Euripides" are not dead names, to be listed merely in card catalogues of dusty libraries, but living names of living playwrights, fitted to arouse the emotions of a public young and eager for sensation. Like all great artists, Miss Anglin is gifted, quite uncommonly, with common sense. She understands the simple point—which has escaped the notice of innumerable scholars and professors—that the Athenian public attended the drama not in answer to the call of duty but in answer to the call of pleasure. The aim of the theatre is not instruction; it is merely entertainment; and the most high-minded dramatist tries only to overwhelm the members of his audience with an awareness of "God being with them when they know it not." Euripides and Sophocles are not aloof and distant, like the "high-brows" of this present time; for, in their own day, they fraternized with common men and sought to entertain the inarticulate but none the less appreciative "gallery" that could neither read nor write.

In ancient Athens, the original production of a play was an event that is comparable, in contemporary terms, to the staging, in New York, of the opening game in a series to determine the World's Championship in professional baseball. In the year 431 B.C., the first prize for tragedy was accorded to Euphorion; the second to Sophocles; and the third to Euripides, for the composition of four plays, one of which was the *Medea*. When these prize-winning plays were acted, the whole town shut up shop and took a holiday, and sat upon the southern slope of the Acropolis to see what could be seen, and to enjoy whatever happened to be offered for enjoyment. These people—human like ourselves—did not congregate by thousands in pursuit of education: they assembled naturally in pursuit of entertainment. They went to the theatre to be interested and excited and enthralled; and—in that typical season which is numbered now by scholarly historians as the first year of the eighty-seventh Olympiad—Euphorion and Sophocles and Euripides earned the prizes they had won, by compelling the applause of a heterogeneous public which never numbered less than twenty thousand heads, for any one performance.

Miss Anglin, having seized the spirit of Greek tragedy, has decided that the thing to be pursued is not the interest of archæology but the interest of immediate theatrical appeal. She has handled the recorded texts of Euripides and Sophocles as if these ancient dramatists were contemporary and were standing at her elbow throughout the tentative period devoted to rehearsals. She has discarded the mask, and the cothurnus, and many other minor and mechanical conventions of the ancient drama; but she has preserved the wonder and the sting.

Miss Anglin's interpretations of Euripides and Sophocles were first disclosed in the summer of 1915, in the Greek Theatre at Berkeley, California. Rumors began immediately to drift eastward that she had "discovered" a couple of "young authors" who promised, in due time, to be "accepted" on Broadway.

The present writer, among others in the east, received letters, at the time, which told the tale. Miss Anglin had imagined, for the end of the *Electra*, a bit of "business" that was thoroughly in keeping with the high intention of the dramatist. Orestes, according to the orderly progression of the play, has entrapped Ægisthus, and challenged him to fight a duel for his life. The young avenger marches the elder murderer off stage, to the blood-bedewed halls of Agamemnon. From this heroic region, beyond the boundaries of the visible scene, there comes a noise of the clash of steel on steel and of the groans and grunts of supermen engaged in mortal combat. This sound is listened to by lone Electra, clad in dismal rags, who looms before the audience as a pillar of cloud, awaiting fearfully the outcome of the combat between the man who is her brother and the man who is her father's murderer. Off stage, there arises, in due time, a cry of agony, and then there comes a silence and a pause. Then, from out the portal of the house of Agamemnon, is hurled the sword of the vanquished. This token clatters, hurtling, down a stairway of enormous length. Electra shudders away from the symbol of defeat. Then, stealthily, she climbs down many steps, to examine it with anguished curiosity. With a wild cry, she catches up and flings the thing aloft: for she has recognized it as the sword of the hated murderer, Ægisthus. Then, at last, she dashes it beneath her feet, and tramples on it with a tardy sense of triumph. This point of high dramatic tensity concludes the play.

When Miss Anglin first presented the *Electra* of Sophocles in Berkeley, California, this final moment was received with utter silence. No hands were clapped together in the entire auditorium. A friend of mine was standing in the wings; and he told me—in a letter that was written at the time—that he heard Miss Anglin say aloud, "I've failed:—My God, I've failed!" Then, after an appreciable pause, there came a noise that sounded like the rushing of the tide at Mont Saint Michel. This noise was compounded of the cheering from ten thousand throats. Louder and louder grew the acclamation, until it seemed to shake the skies. Then, suddenly, the stage itself was assaulted by hundreds and hundreds of clamorous spectators. They swarmed about Miss Anglin and strove to touch her finger-tips. One old man, whose face was bathed in tears, tore his own hat into shreds and tossed the pieces high into the air. . . . That was what he wished to say in tribute to a dramatist who had been dead and buried for two dozen centuries.

XVII

A REMINISCENCE OF THE MIDDLE AGES

T
HE NEIGHBORHOOD PLAYHOUSE, at 466 Grand Street, New York, was the Mecca of many memorable pilgrimages throughout the dozen years when it was operated for the benefit of an undeserving public by the Misses Alice and Irene Lewisohn; but nothing that was ever shown at this theatre excelled in interest the presentation of *Guibour*, a French miracle play of the fourteenth century, which attracted overflowing audiences three nights a week throughout the months of January, February, and March, 1919. This play was first acted in the year 1352—precisely two hundred and fifty years before the initial performance of Shakespeare's *Hamlet*—by a confraternity called the Puys, which was partly ecclesiastical and partly literary in its character. It was planned as one of forty items in a cycle of religious plays, all celebrating in one way or another the miracles of the Madonna; and its content is indicated by the traditional sub-title, *Un Miracle de Notre Dame: Comment Elle Garda Une Femme d'Estre Arsée.*

The resurrection of this medieval drama was sponsored and directed by Yvette Guilbert, who also played the title part and thereby made her first appearance as an actress on the English-speaking stage. As an actress, Madame Guilbert, of course, is not so utterly incomparable as she is within the limits of her own unique and special art as a *diseuse*, and her ear for English is not by any means so fine as her ear for French; yet, despite the incidental handicaps to which she willingly submitted, she delivered a performance which was monumentally impressive. Representative artists of this calibre are not born more than once in a quarter of a century; and it is nearly so long as that since Modjeska died and Duse retired from the stage. In this performance, Madame Guilbert was supported by many able and enthusiastic amateurs, including the Misses Lewisohn, the versatile young artist, Rollo Peters, L. Rogers Lytton, and Margherita Sargent. No professional company could possibly have rendered this old drama with so many indubitable indications of a genuine love for the occasion.

The scenery and costumes for the production of *Guibour* were designed by Robert Edmond Jones; and, despite the current fame of this successful artist for the stage, it may be said with candor that he has never done anything more fine, in composition or in color, than his imaginative investiture of this relic of a by-gone age. The incidental music was gathered by Madame Guilbert from her ample library of medieval sources; and this music was beautifully rendered by choral singers trained by Edith Quaile. Especially impressive was the singing of Richards Hale, a young baritone endowed by nature with a gorgeous voice and equipped by study with a trained ability to use this great voice to the best advantage. The English version of the old French text was ably written by Anna Sprague MacDonald.

The presentation of *Guibour* was, in every respect, so satisfactory that the only matter which requires comment from the critical reviewer is the inherent importance of this rather artless composition, which was written down by some nameless and forgotten author—or syndicate of authors—more than half a thousand years ago.

In the first place, it may be stated that any veritable revelation of medieval art is greatly to be desired in this country at the present time. Alone among the mighty nations to which the predetermination of the future of the world has been allotted by the falling of the dice of destiny, our own country stands naked as a nation without a past. The ordinary citizens of England, France, or Italy, as they go about their daily business, walk beneath the shadow of many monuments of the middle ages, and are constantly reminded of the past by some gigantic relic like the cathedral of Canterbury, the cathedral of Amiens, the cathedral of Siena. In this country, we have inherited no cognate monuments of a world that used to be. Our most venerable buildings date merely from the seventeenth century; and most of these are being ruthlessly torn down in the interest of "progress." Ancestrally, we Americans, if we count our lineage from a common Adam, are just as old as the English, the French, or the Italians; but we are more in need of opportunities to recollect our ancient origin than our cousins overseas. In actuality, the modern world is too much with us; and it is difficult for us to trace back the tendrils of our best imaginings to the rich, dark soil of the world that used to be. To remind us vividly of the state of mind of our forefathers, we need a resurrection of the medieval drama more emphatically than an exhibition of this sort could possibly be needed by the contemporary public of Italy or France or England. *Guibour* was exceedingly important to the theatre-going public of New York, by virtue of the fact that it reminded the audience that there was a theatre-going public in the civic squares of France more than half a thousand years ago, and that the world was very much alive before the date of the discovery of America.

In studying any work of medieval origin, we should remember always that the art of the middle ages was calculated carefully to appeal to a public that was illiterate. Throughout the thousand years which extended from the triumph of Christianity over the Roman world, in the fourth century, to the beginnings of the Renaissance of ancient culture, in the fourteenth century, nine-tenths of all the people who were born and buried in Europe passed through life without ever learning to read or write. Literacy was reserved almost exclusively for the clergy; and, practically speaking, the only people who could read and write were dignitaries of the Church. This, of course, is the main historic reason for the absolute supremacy of the Church over the minds and hearts of the common people of the middle ages. Any ordinary citizen was required to believe what was told him by the priests, because he was cut off, by his lack of education, from the privilege of appealing, through any other medium than the Church, to the written records of the accumulated wisdom of mankind.

The Church, as the sole custodian of literary learning and the chosen teacher of the vast illiterate populace throughout a thousand years, rendered in the main a good account of its stewardship. The people could not read; the people had to be taught; therefore, it was necessary to teach them through the easily intelligible symbols of concrete art. Here we have the motive for that tremendous efflorescence of Gothic architecture which forces modern critics to their knees to pay obeisance to the middle ages. John Ruskin was happily inspired with a phrase when he called the greatest monument of Gothic architecture "the Bible of Amiens." It was indeed a Bible, a sacred book made up of many sermons writ in stone; and these sermons were so concrete, and therefore so intelligible to the unlettered mind, that it might actually be said that any one who ran might read them. All that the Church could tell about the past, the present, and the future, the miracle of life and the mystery of death, and that triune ideal of Beauty, Truth, and Righteousness—three in one and one in three—was trumpeted through solid stone to all the passing generations that were born and buried within the visible radius of this towering cathedral.

Although the drama, as an art, had been excluded from the world for more than a thousand years—and that is the main reason, the present scribe is fain to think, why the centuries in question have frequently been labeled by learned historians as "the dark ages"—the Church decided, in the twelfth century, to reinvent the drama, as the most effective medium through which the illiterate public might be convinced of the essential truth of many myths and legends that constituted what may be described most quickly as the "propaganda" of medieval Christianity. This newly reinvented drama immediately scored a popular success; and the enthusiasm of the public was so obvious that, when the daily overturning of the calendar had whispered its way into the fourteenth century, the Church and its affiliated organizations of representative men of letters were actively engaged, in nearly every European country, in pushing the drama as the most direct, and therefore the most effective, means of inculcating certain fundamental truths into the minds of an uneducated but eager and avid public.

To this enthusiastic season of the fourteenth century, *Guibour* belongs. Its characteristics as a work of art are similar to those of any representative example of medieval architecture. It is simple, homely, direct, concrete, and—fróm the point of view of the more sophisticated modern mind—naïve. This old play is surprisingly alive, because it reveals an almost astonishing intimacy with life as it was actually lived in that far century which brought it forth; but, at certain moments when it appears to appeal for a degree of credence that is difficult for the modern commentator to concede, we should remember that it was originally written for a public that had never read a book.

In Victor Hugo's monumental novel, *Notre Dame de Paris*, there is a famous passage in which a medieval priest, holding in one hand a copy of a newly printed book and sweeping the other hand in a gesture toward the vast cathedral, announces, *"Ceci tuera celà!"* The invention of printing was destined to supersede the function of medieval architecture. It is no longer necessary to erect Bibles in stone to edify a public that is fed with information by newspapers that issue eight or ten editions every day. Our modern laws, which impose a common-school education on every individual, without even consulting his desires, bequeath a greater potency upon the printed words of a propagandist than can ever be achieved by any such announcement of religious theory through the medium of lasting stone as has been imagined by the anachronistic projectors of the Cathedral of Saint John the Divine. The popular promulgation of the printed word has swiftly undermined the more specific and more concrete appeal of medieval art. *"Ceci tuera celà"*: "printing will kill architecture": this prediction has been justified by the event.

But any example of the drama of the middle ages should be judged by a contemporary critic not according to the theoretic terms of our modern printed literature but according to the terms of that more explicit medieval architecture which was designed to convey eternal messages to a running public unacquainted with the special craft of reading. Any such expression must be homely, and intimate, and quite unblushingly naïve. *Guibour* fulfils with ease these rather remarkable requirements. It is so simple in its thought that any child could understand it; it is so homely in its method that it reveals a memorable picture of the daily life of a French town in the middle ages; and it is so deliciously naïve in mood that it calls forth the sort of sympathetic smile with which we accompany the patting on the head of a lovely and appealing child.

One of the most delightful traits of the medieval public is that, being richly human, this public was quite illogically inconsistent in its moods. The one point about the great art of the Greeks which is impressed upon us most emphatically is that these supermen—and the world may nevermore be privileged to look upon their like again—could think only, and feel only, in one way at any predetermined moment. The Parthenon is absolutely holy: and no man may laugh irreverently when the moon is looking down upon it, under pain of being stricken dead by the drastic anger of the gods. But every Bible that was written in stone by the medieval builders exhibits many passages whereby the running observer is invited to laugh aloud at some emphatic abnegation of the sacred mood in which the edifice, considered as a whole, has been conceived. To the mind of the present commentator, no other habitual detail of medieval art is so impressive as the simple and almost childish sense of humor that is ascribed continually by all the artists of the middle ages to the God that they revere abjectly.

Guibour, which is a typical example of the religious drama of the fourteenth century, appears, at many points, naïve and funny to a modern audience. But the thing to be remembered by the commentative auditor is that this childishness of humor was not accidental but intended. The writers of the middle ages, who plied their pens for the benefit of those who could not read, were not endeavoring to set the gods of their imagination lofty above Olympus, but were trying rather to bring these gods within familiar converse with those citizens who wandered daily through the market-place.

The Virgin Mary, in *Guibour*, gives quick expression to a clearly appreciable sense of humor; and so do her attendant angels. This expression did not seem incongruous to the medieval mind. The reverent, unlettered people of the middle ages were wisely taught to laugh before they died, because death was fleeting but laughter was immortal. To the modern observer, trained by recent accidents to a more consistent singularity of atmosphere, this fine example of the medieval drama is perhaps most interesting by reason of its multiplicity of moods. It salutes us, with eternal laughter on its lips, as a thing that is not at all afraid to die.

XVIII

THE IRISH NATIONAL THEATRE

I

ART AND NATURE compete eternally with each other in the great task of making humanity aware of what is true and beautiful and good. They are the two teachers in this school-room of a world to which we are come—we know not whence—as scholars; and we have much to learn from both of them in the little time allotted before school is suddenly let out and we frolic forth—we know not whither. It would be difficult to judge decisively whether Art or Nature is the greater teacher. Nature has more to tell us, but Art is better skilled for utterance. Nature has so much to say that she has no patience for articulation. She thrills us with a vague awareness of multitudinous indecipherable messages; but she speaks to us in whispers and in thunders—elusive, indeterminate, discomforting. Art, with less to say, has more patience for the formulation of her messages; she speaks to us in a voice that has been deliberately trained, and her utterance is lucid and precise. She does not try, like Nature, to tell us everything at once. She selects, instead, some single definite and little truth to tell us at a time, and exerts herself to speak it clearly. We can never estimate precisely what it is that we have learned from Nature; but whenever Art has spoken to us, we know exactly what we have been told. Nature stirs and tortures us to a mazy apprehension of illimitables; but Art contents us with careful limitations and calms us with achieved lucidity.

But, in this compensatory universe, every advantage carries with it a concomitant disadvantage. The besetting danger to the usefulness of Art as a teacher of mankind lurks inherent in this very capacity for orderly articulation. Art is only human, after all, and is liable to the human sin of vanity. More and more, as Art advances in efficiency of utterance, she tends to take delight in listen-

ing to the sound of her own voice; she tends to value method more
dearly than material; she tends to forget that the thing to be said
is immeasurably more important than any gracefulness in saying
it. Thus artistry, as it advances toward perfection, destroys its
purpose and defeats itself.

Whenever artistry becomes too cleverly and nicely organized,
whenever Art succumbs to the vanity of self-consciousness, it is
necessary that seekers for the truth should forsake Art and return
to Nature. At such a time the really earnest scholar will throw
away his books and seek his reading in the running brooks. Humanity advances not along a straight line but along a circulating
spiral; it progresses through a series of revolutions and reversions;
and the motive of every progressive revolution is the recurrent
yearning to return to Nature. "Let us return to Nature! Let us
turn backward in order to move forward!"—this has been the
watchword of the revolutionists in every age when Art has grown
inefficient through efficiency. There is no other way than this to
cure the vanity of Art and make her useful once again.

We live at present in an age when the dramatic art has attained
a technical efficiency which has never been approached before in
the whole history of the theatre. Our best-made plays are better
made than those of any other period. Consider for a moment the
craftsmanship displayed in such a work as that ultimate monument
of intensive artistry, *The Thunderbolt*, of Sir Arthur Pinero.
There is no play of Shakespeare's that is so staggeringly admirable
in every last and least detail of technical adjustment. When
artistry has gone so far as this, there is nothing more for it to do.
Such accomplishment defeats itself, for it leaves the artist nothing further to accomplish. What is to be done when we are
brought to such a period? . . . There can be but one answer to
that question:—Let us return to Nature.

For it is evident that, though Art has taught our present playwrights more than she ever taught their predecessors, Nature has
taught them less. Our drama is too technical; our dramatists care
more for artistry than they care for life. The highest pleasure that
we may derive from the contemporary drama at its best is the
critical pleasure of following point by point the unfaltering development of a faultless pattern. But the theatre—as we know
from Sophocles and Shakespeare and Molière—is capable of afford-
ing a greater pleasure than this,—a pleasure less critical and more

creative. Our contemporary plays are masterly in method, but comparatively unimportant in material. It is a sign of their essential insignificance that they tell us truths that are not even beautiful; for it is only when truth has ascended to that level where—as in the vision of Keats—it becomes identical with beauty, that it is, in any real sense, worth the telling. Our drama deals mainly with the artificial emotions of super-civilized aristocrats who dwell in cities: it sets before us a Criticism of Society instead of the Romance of Man.

When we have dwelt for many months in a metropolis, and dressed for dinner every night, and exchanged small talk concerning trivialities, and grown exceedingly clever and witty and graceful and urbane, there comes a time for us to break away—it is the time when violets are peeping—to far places where people have no manners, where they talk from the heart instead of from the head, and where a wide earth is swept with winds all murmurous with whispers from the sea, and at night there is a sky of many stars.—The theatre has its seasons also; and when the drama has grown too clever and urbane, too artistic and too trivial, it is time to break away. For, somewhere, terrific seas are surging on forlorn coasts far away, and simple folk are making music to each other in imaginative speech. Let us then be riders to the sea, and wander till we meet a playboy, talking deep love in the shadow of a glen.

II

These general considerations must be held in mind as we turn our critical attention to the aims and achievements of the Irish National Theatre Society. This society was organized in 1901 by William Butler Yeats and Lady Augusta Gregory. The founders had two purposes in view:—first, to develop a drama that should be distinctly national, so that Ireland might have a voice in the concerted theatre of the world, and second, to reachieve a union between truth and beauty in the drama by effecting a return to nature, in both material and method. In practice, these two purposes soon proved themselves to be identical; for both the authors and the actors found that the surest method for accomplishing the first was to devote themselves enthusiastically to the second.

These Irish idealists at once rejected from their range of subject-matter all themes suggested by the life of cities and by the manners of what are called the upper classes,—first, because such material was not definitively Irish, and second, because it was not—in any deep sense—human. Facility of intercommunication has made every modern metropolis more cosmopolitan than national; and to seek the heart of any country it is now necessary to delve into aloof and rural districts. Furthermore, our modern civilization—which is largely artificial—has refined the higher classes of society to such a point that they now ignore, or cynically smile upon, those basic, impulsive, and primordial emotions that spring spontaneously from the heart of man.

The Irish authors decided also, from the outset, to revolt against that tyranny of merely technical achievement to which the international contemporary drama is subservient. This is an age of plot and stage-direction,—of emotion evidenced in action, of action elucidated to the eye by every deliberate aid to visual illusion. The Irish playwrights would have none of this. Not plot, but character, was what they chose to care about, since people are more real than incidents. They renounced the technical empery of plot, and rejected the tradition of the well-made play. If they could reveal character sufficiently in situation, they did not consider it a further duty to set it forth in action. They did not deem it necessary to rely on stage-direction to convince the eye, since they could revert to an earlier period of the development of the drama and rely on eloquence of writing to convince the ear. They chose to make a drama that is less visual and more auditory than that to which we have become commonly accustomed in the international theatre of to-day. They decided that the surest way to return to nature was to return to literature.

Actuated by these aims, the Irish playwrights found, in the peasant life of Ireland, innumerable subjects made to their hand. That life was at once definitively national and primordially human. By geographical position and by historical isolation, that emerald island floating in the far Atlantic has remained the utter outpost of European civilization. Only the larger cities have been annexed—in any real sense—to the British Empire; only the aristocracy is cosmopolitan. The peasants of the rural counties are not Saxon, but Celtic in ancestry and temperament; and the life of those aloof and desultory districts is not modern, but early medieval. The far, forgotten islands that are washed by the isolating western sea are populated with a peasantry who have escaped the long and gradual advance of time and who, defended from modernity, still play around the nursery of this grown-up and over-wearied world. Age has not withered them, nor custom staled. They love and hate and worship and blaspheme like little children, gloriously irresponsive to the calming and adult dictates of modern civilization, and panged with the terrible and thrilling growing-pains of the primeval human soul.

And, by a providential accident, these crude, uncultured people speak to each other with an easy eloquence that hovers only a little lower than the speech of angels. They have not yet, as we have, filed and simplified their speech to a workaday and placid prose. Their words have longer memories than ours, and float forth trailing clouds of glory. Their common speaking surges with a tidal chant, like that of the recurrent singing of the sea. When Wordsworth, leading his own lonely and much-ridiculed return to nature, sought to restrict the utterance of poetry to the daily speech of dalesmen, he lost his aim amid a diction inadequate to the occasion; and, for his greater sonnets, he found himself necessitated to revert to the language of the mental aristocracy. But the language of Lady Gregory and J. M. Synge is unfalteringly eloquent; and Synge, in his prefaces, and Lady Gregory, in her conversations, have both assured us that they have used no words in their writings that they have not heard falling naturally from the lips of Irish peasants incapable of reading or of signing their own names. Thus, in returning to nature, they discovered a well-spring ebullient with poetry. Faring forth to seek the true, they found the beautiful.

III

Such being the purposes of the founders of the Irish National Theatre Society, it was evident from the outset that they could not intrust the presentation of their plays to professional London actors trained to other aims. They therefore organized a company of their own, composed of young men and women engaged in various businesses in Dublin, who were eager to devote their leisure hours to the pleasant exercise of acting. This company, in origin, was *amateur*; and it was not till 1904, when it became established permanently at the Abbey Theatre, that it grew to be professional. In spirit, the Abbey Theatre Players, despite the passage of many years, are still *amateur*; and this is said, of course, in praise of them. It is still evident that they act for the love of acting. It would seem to be their motto that "no one shall work for money, and no one shall work for fame, but each for the joy of the working." Fame and money have been added unto them in recent years, for they have captured London and set successful siege to Boston and Chicago and New York; but it is apparent from their work that they are inspired still, as ever, with the joy of working. And this is the main reason why their artless artistry is charming; for there is nothing more enjoyable than joy.

Their acting is so different from ours, in aim, in spirit, and in method, that there can be no profit in arguing as to whether it is better or whether it is not so good. Their stage-direction is elementary and casual. They are sparing of gesticulation. They care far less than we do about making appealing pictures to the eye; and they care far more than we do about the delicate, alluring art of reading. They never move about the stage unnecessarily, in the fancied interest of visual variety; often, for long passages, they merely sit still, or stand about, and talk. But, with them the lines are all-important. Their plays are written eloquently; and they repeat this written eloquence with an affectionate regard for rhythm and the harmony of words.

Character, not action, is the dominant element in the Irish plays; and it is therefore not surprising that the Irish Players are inferior to our own in representing rapid and emphatic action, and superior in the deliberate and gradual portraiture of personality. All the Irish Players are what are called, in the slang of the theatre, character actors. But they draw their portraits mainly by the means of speech, and rely far less than we do on make-up and facial expression. With them, as with their authors, the drama has returned to literature.

IV

We may now examine a few of the most characteristic pieces in the repertory which the Abbey Theatre Players have presented, in recent seasons, in America; and, first of all, it will be pleasant to turn our attention to the one-act plays of Lady Gregory. In the sense of the word to which we have grown accustomed in the conventional theatre, these delightful little sketches are scarcely plays at all. It would be more precise to speak of them as anecdotes. The author sets forth two or three characters in a single situation, and draws them thoroughly in dialogue; she does not seem to care especially whether the incident which reveals the characters is active or passive; she does not work the situation up to any emphatic climax; but having opened a momentary little vista upon life, she smilingly remarks "That's all" and rings the curtain down. Her vision is both poetical and humorous; she enjoys the rare endowment of sagacity; and she writes with eloquence and ease.

Spreading the News is a good-natured satire of the extravagant growth of gossip among people whose imagination is stronger than their common sense. A farmer forgets his pitch-fork, on the outskirts of a fair; and a second farmer, finding it, hurries after to return it to him. A bystander remarks casually to a deaf old apple-woman that Bartley Fallon is running after Jack Smith with a pitch-fork. The apple-woman tells some one else that Fallon has attacked Smith with murderous intent. The story grows and grows as it passes from mouth to mouth, until an assembled crowd believe that Smith is slain and invent a number of plausible motives for the murder. The rumor reaches the ears of the police; and Fallon is arrested, protesting vainly against the embattled certainty of the accusing public. Then Smith strolls back, safe and sound, and finds it difficult to convince the crowd that he is not a ghost.

The Workhouse Ward is a deliciously sagacious bit of humorous characterization. Two old paupers are discovered lying in adjacent beds. They have been lifelong friends; but now, having nothing else to do, they spend their entire time in arguing and quarreling. To one of them there comes an opportunity to leave the workhouse and be cared for in a comfortable home; but he declines this opportunity because the offer is not extended also to his friend, the other pauper. Immediately afterward, the inseparable cronies fall once more to altercation, and beat each other eagerly over the head with pillows.

There is less humor and more sentiment in *The Rising of the Moon*. A constable is guarding a quay from which it is expected that a fleeing political prisoner will endeavor to escape to sea. There is a large reward upon the prisoner's head, and his apprehension would also mean promotion for the constable. An itinerant ballad-singer appears, sits back to back with the constable upon a barrel-head set lonely in the streaming of the moon, and sings him many songs which strum upon the chords of memory and remind him of his childhood and his home. Having tuned the constable to a proper key of sentiment, the ballad-singer confesses that he is the fleeing prisoner; and the constable, scarcely knowing why, connives at his escape.

In *The Gaol Gate* Lady Gregory has turned to tragedy and written in a somber mood. Outside the gate of Galway Gaol, the mother and the wife of a prisoner make lamentation, because he has, as they think, saved his own neck by betraying his companions. The Gate-keeper unwittingly contributes to this belief of theirs by telling them that the prisoner has died in hospital. He gives them the dead man's clothes; and over these they make a melancholy keening. But later they discover that the Gate-keeper has lied to them and that the prisoner has in reality been hanged. He had not sold his friends to purchase immunity for himself: he had died gloriously, after all. And now the two women lift their voices high in praise of him, chanting the grim glory of his doom.— This little tragedy is written in a very regular rhythm; and the keening of the women reminds the ear of the forlorn falling of many of the ancient Hebrew psalms and lamentations.

v

There is a poem of Walt Whitman's in the course of which he says,—"O what is it in me that makes me tremble so at voices?— Surely, whoever speaks to me in the right voice, him or her I shall follow, as the water follows the moon, silently, with fluid steps, anywhere around the globe."

The first thing to be said about the dead and deathless poet, John M. Synge, is that he spoke to the world in the right voice. He wrote with an incomparable eloquence. In the rolling glory of his sentences there is a rhythm as of waters following the moon. His words are immemorial and homely, ancestral, simple, quaint; they glow with gladness as they meet each other; and eagerly they glide along in rhythms, now lilting with laughter, now languorous with melancholy, making evermore sweet music to the ear.

But Synge is a great poet not only by virtue of his noble gift of style. He deeply felt the poetry, the pathos, the tragedy, the humor, of the incongruity between the littleness of human actuality and the immensity of human dreams. He writes of illusions and of disillusionments. Illusions are beautiful and funny; disillusionments are beautiful and sad. Life is at once pathetic and uproarious, being, as it is, a vanity of vanities: it is at once appalling and consolatory, being, as it also is, as glorious as imagining can make it. What would one have? . . . Life, with all its faults; life, with all its virtues; there is no greater gift than life. And now that Synge is dead, we may write of him, in Rudyard Kipling's words, "He liked it all!"

Synge's continual balancing of illusion against disillusionment—a weighing in which each is found wanting, and yet ennobled by a sad and smiling beauty all its own—is exhibited most clearly in his three-act parable entitled *The Well of the Saints*. It would seem that the lot of Martin and Mary Doul was most unfortunate; and yet it has its compensations. Both of them are blind; they are aged, bent, and ugly; and they gather up a bare subsistence by begging at the wayside. But each of them has a dream of the world and what it looks like to those with eyes to see; and, dreaming in the darkness, they have molded an imaginable scheme of things very nearly to their heart's desire. Each of them, for instance, believes the other to be young and lovely to the sight. They think the world unfalteringly fair, illumined by a light that never was on sea or land.

To them, contented thus in discontent, there comes a wandering friar who is able to work miracles. He anoints their eyes with holy water, and restores to them the dubious gift of sight. Martin seeks his wife among the young and glowing girls who have been gathered by the rumor of the miracle, and is startled at last to find his Mary ugly, bent, and old. Both of them find the visible world less lovely than they had imagined it to be; and they begin to long once more for the fairer vistas of the dream-illumined dark. Later on, their sight grows dim again. The miracle has been but temporary. The friar returns, to anoint their eyes once more; and he promises that this time the cure will be permanent. But Martin now prefers the visionary world of blindness, and dashes the holy water from the friar's hand.

There is a deeper poignancy in Synge's terrible and massive one-act tragedy entitled *Riders to the Sea*. Old Maurya is a mother of men; and it has been their calling to ride down to the sea with horses, to fare forth upon the sea in ships, and to be overwhelmed at last and tumbled shoreward by rolling desultory waves. Her husband, and her husband's father, and five of her strong sons, have succumbed successively to the besieging and insidious sea. Some of them have been borne home dripping in a sail-cloth; others have been dashed unburied on forsaken coasts. Michael has only recently been washed ashore in distant Donegal. And now Bartley, the last of Maurya's living men-folk, is about to ride down to the sea. She suffers a dim foreboding, and implores him not to go; but a man has his work to do, and Bartley rides away, mounted on a gray horse and leading a red pony by the halter. His mother walks across fields to intercept him by the way, so that she may give him the blessing that she had withheld when, manfully, he parted from her. But as he rides past, she sees a vision of the dead Michael riding on the red pony; and she comes home to lament the doom that is foretold. And as she is lamenting, the villagers carry to her something dripping in a sail-cloth,—the body of Bartley, the last of all her sons, whom the red pony has jolted into the aware and waiting sea. Maurya, confronted with the fact of ultimate and absolute bereavement, ceases to lament, and suc-cumbs to an appalled serenity of acquiescence. She has lost all; and thereby she has achieved a peace that passes understanding. And thus it is she speaks at the conclusion of the tragedy:— "They're all gone now, and there isn't anything more the sea can do to me. . . . It's a great rest I'll have now, and it's time surely. . . . No man at all can be living forever, and we must be satisfied."

In the Shadow of the Glen is a grimly comic revelation of the incongruity between life as it is lived and life as it is longed for. Nora Burke has lived unhappily with her gruff and aged husband, Dan, in a lonely cottage far away among the hills. Now Dan is lying dead in bed; and when a casual tramp appears, seeking food in that far cottage, Nora tells him of the thwarted longings of the years that she has wasted. A young herd-boy comes to woo her; but after he has spoken, the hated Dan sits up in bed and makes it known that his apparent death was but a sham. He orders Nora out of his house; and the timid herd-boy ranks himself expediently on the husband's side. Nora goes, indeed,—but not alone; for the irresponsible and roving tramp goes with her. There is something still to seek in the adventurous and hospitable world beyond the shadow of the glen.

But Synge's masterpiece is that uproarious and splendid comedy that is greatly named *The Playboy of the Western World*. It satirizes, with poetic sympathy, the danger that besets an airy, imaginative temperament, unballasted with culture, to lose itself in divagations of extravagant absurdity. The action passes among the whimsical and dreaming peasants on the coast of Mayo. A lonely lad with a queer, fantastic strain in his soul—an essential romantic launched amid a daily life that bewilders him with trivialities—having submitted for a long time to the tyranny of a hard-headed father who despises him, suddenly—in an impulsive moment—hits him heavily over the head and leaves him dying. He wanders, frightened and alone, for many days, and ultimately stumbles into the public-house of an isolated hamlet. Here, when he furtively tells that he has killed his father, he finds himself looked upon with an awe that soon warms to admiration. Unexpectedly—and for the first time in his life—he perceives himself regarded as a hero. This circumstance, of course, unleashes his unballasted imagination. He tells his tragic story again and yet again, embroidering the tale of persecution and revolt more and more as he repeats it, until he finds himself worshiped by all the women-folk for his spirit and his savagery. He falls in love with the daughter of the publican, who loves him in return because of his poetical and dauntless daring; and so strong is the stimulus of admiration that he wins with ease the various athletic contests that are competed in the hamlet on the morrow. But at the height of his wind-blown glory, his father enters, wounded but unkilled, with bandaged head and brandished stick, to order the boy about as in the meager years that were. The bubble of the playboy's fame is pricked; he is not a hero after all; and the simple-minded enthusiasts who had lauded him now laugh at him with scorn. This is more than he can stand. In tragical and disillusioned anguish, he once again attacks his father,—this time in the sight of all. But the very people who regarded his imagined parricide as an heroic act when they were merely told about it in romantic narrative now consider the playboy's immediate assault upon his father as a dirty deed. They noose him in a rope and are prepared to hang him; and he is saved only by the fact that his father has survived a second time. Now, "in the end of all," he has no friends; even the lass he loves has turned against him; and he is doomed to return home with his father, unappreciated in a lonely world. But he has had his little taste of glory; and he knows that henceforth he will rule his father, and "go romancing through a romping lifetime from this hour to the dawning of the judgment day."

But no summary can possibly suggest the imaginative richness of this comedy, its almost unexampled blend of poetry and humor, its rhythmic marshaling of fair and funny phrases, that echo in the ear like laughing music over waters. The man who wrote it was a great man, for verily he has spoken to us in the right voice; and when, in his noon of years, he died and went away, we "lost the only playboy of the western world."

XIX

TWO PLAYS BY ST. JOHN G. ERVINE

I F ART may fairly be defined as "life seen through a temperament," it follows that the flavor of a work of art must depend
less upon the sort of life that is looked at than upon the sort
of temperament through which it is observed. The mind of
the artist is more important than his subject-matter. This is particularly evident in the domain of painting. It did not matter
whether Rembrandt chose to paint a chine of beef or the face of
an old man; the result, in either instance, was a work of art, because it was sure to show the painter's incomparable eye for
chiaroscuro. In the theatre, the untutored members of the public
are likely to judge plays by their subject-matter,—to patronize one
piece because they like the story and to neglect another because
the narrative does not appeal to them; but, for the critical observer, there is matter of more interest in the way in which the
subject is handled by the dramatist. A block of stone is but a block
of stone: if it be hacked into a statue, its worth will depend on
what the artist does to it. One man might mold a better work of
art in butter than another man in beaten gold.

Life, the subject-matter of all art, is everywhere adjacent to us.
For the price of a ticket to the subway, we may read a hundred
stories in a hundred faces, all about us. Only, most of us don't
do it: we lack the seeing eye. The artist sees. He makes life interesting to the rest of us, by showing us a way of looking at it. The
life that he shows us may be commonplace; but his vision is not.
Velasquez might have painted a corrugated ash-can, with the
uttermost fidelity to fact; yet his picture would have been a thing
of beauty, and, in consequence, a joy forever. There are ways of
looking at the play of lights and shadows on an ash-can,—eternal
ways. "Life, like a dome of many-colored glass, stains the white
radiance of eternity"; but the mind of the artist is a prism with

the magic power to recompose the scattered colors of the spectrum into a clear and focussed beam of that eternal light that never was on sea or land.

There is very little in the plays of Mr. St. John Ervine to catch and capture the attention of those untutored theatre-goers who are avid for something novel or something sensational in subject-matter. Mr. Ervine deals with commonplace people—with people just as ordinary as the man who is crammed against you in a crowded hour of the subway, and whom you never see—and he contents himself with situations that are traditional. His dramas are, in subject-matter, as old as the hills: yet the aged and familiar hills of Cumberland were very beautiful when William Words-worth looked upon them. When Mr. Ervine writes a play, it is more than likely to be worth traveling many miles to see, for the simple reason that Mr. Ervine is endowed with a mind that is exceptionally fine. This mind is a sort of window through which we are permitted to look at life. A window is not at all an un-familiar object: but there are windows and other windows in this world, and that is the reason why Keats wrote his memorable phrase about "charmed magic casements opening. . . ."

In the facetious epilogue to *Fanny's First Play*, Mr. Shaw satirically put into the mouth of a dramatic critic, Flawner Bannel, the remark, "If it's by a good author, it's a good play, naturally. That stands to reason. Who is the author?" This remark was re-garded as uproariously funny by the anonymous writer of *Fanny's First Play* and by a diverted public that had solved the secret of this anonymity; yet there is a grain of serious truth in this amus-ing statement, after all. If a play is by a good author, it is more than likely to be a good play, "naturally,"—for authorship, to the discerning, counts more than subject-matter, and nearly every-thing depends upon the sort of mind through which the subject-matter passes in its transit from the archives which contain "the thirty-six dramatic situations," enumerated by the investigating Gozzi, to the attention of a gathered and receptive audience. A bad author might even impede the appeal of the subject-matter of *The Trojan Women*,—which, in the opinion of the present com-mentator, is the most pathetic play in all the world; whereas a good author may easily lift his treatment of an unpromising sub-ject to the level of enduring literature. In support of this argument, it is necessary only to compare what German scholars call the *Ur-Hamlet* with the revised *Hamlet* of William Shakespeare.

Mr. St. John Ervine is very welcome to our theatre, because of the simple fact that he is "a good author." It is a fine adventure to be permitted to look at some familiar character or some traditional situation through the window of his mind. We go to the theatre, not to hear what Mr. Ervine has to talk about, but to listen to Mr. Ervine and to enjoy his way of talking.

In *Jane Clegg*, the heroine, who is an ordinary woman, has wrestled for a long time with the not uncustomary problem of living amicably with a husband who is unworthy of her. Some years before the play begins, she had caught him in a flagrant case of infidelity; but, because of her economic dependence on her husband, and the crying need of her infant children for support, she had condoned this offense and had accepted the promise of her husband never to repeat it. Henry Clegg is a commercial traveler. Incidentally, he is a liar, a gambler, and a thief. His wife discovers these regretted facts successively, as the plot develops. She has recently inherited the sum of seven thousand pounds from a deceased uncle, and is now able to support—in case of need—not only herself but also her two children. When her husband gets into trouble, she is willing to help him out; and, to shield him from going to jail, she even consents to advance, out of her legacy, a considerable sum of money; but the soul of Jane Clegg rebels against the situation when she discovers ultimately that her husband, Henry, has been plunged into it by an ill-advised association with a "fancy woman." Henry Clegg has planned to run away to Canada, on stolen money, with his mistress. When Jane Clegg has discovered this, she does not try to compel her husband to remain at home. Instead, she opens wide the door, and forces him forth, to face a questionable future with the woman of his fancy.

The final scene of *Jane Clegg* is, of course, immediately reminiscent of that great colloquy which concluded *A Doll's House;* yet the dialogue, at many points, is even more poignantly intimate, and the episode is made by the genius of the author to appear both unfamiliar and engrossing. The antecedent action is entirely traditional; yet its progress is exalted far above the level of the commonplace by the uncustomary note of sheer sincerity in the author's attitude of mind. What he mainly cares about is characterization; and his characters are almost discomfortably real.

His careful depiction of Henry Clegg—an "absolute rotter," as the author calls him in the lines—is a masterpiece of sheer delineation; and all the other characters are drawn to the life.

John Ferguson, by the same author, is a great play, because it discusses a momentous theme through a medium of realistic utterance which, though apparently commonplace, reveals the virtue of utter intellectual integrity.

In common with many other great plays, *John Ferguson* deals anew with narrative materials that had already been worn threadbare in the theatre before the date of its composition. There is no surer way for any gifted author to win fame in the theatre than by repeating a familiar story and surprising the audience by telling the truth about it, in violation of traditional expectancy. In *John Ferguson*, we meet once more the ancient motive of the mortgage on the farm, the long-familiar heartache arising from the letter mailed too late, the conventional story of the maiden wronged and the murder of the villain who traduced her, and the subsequent juggling of credit for this murder between the weak man who, for moral reasons, ought to have committed it and the strong man who, for practical reasons, actually did the deed. The inspired half-wit who wanders in and out of the story, inciting better brains than his to action, is also a traditional figure in the drama. There is no element of novelty in this narrative nor in the handling of it; and there is nothing new nor unaccustomed in any of the characters that people the conventional pattern. Yet Mr. Ervine has portrayed these characters with an astonishing profundity of insight; and his story is set forth with such sincerity and fervor as to convince the auditor that it is absolutely true.

John Ferguson, considered solely on the basis of its subject-matter, might be dismissed as "old stuff," to use a rather vulgar phrase that is popularly current in the theatre; but this composition cannot rightly be regarded as "old stuff" when it is considered from the point of view of any commentator who is willing to delve beneath the subject-matter to the theme.

In one of the most memorable lines of modern poetry, Mr. Alfred Noyes has paid immortal tribute to "the splendor of the indifference of God"; and this magnificent indifference of an hypothetic Deity to the personal concerns of even His most faithful servants affords the basis for this tragedy by Mr. Ervine. Here is a problem of perennial importance,—a problem which, in fact, has evermore perturbed the foremost religious thinkers of mankind.

In harmony with the famous syllogism of Descartes—"I think: therefore, I am"—Matthew Arnold defined Deity as "the eternal not-ourselves." We are absolutely certain of our own existence; and we are reasonably certain, also, of the existence of another power—"not ourselves"—that dominates the universe. But Matthew Arnold added another phrase to his formula, and, by so doing, appended an uncertainty to a reasonable certainty. His full definition reads, "the eternal not-ourselves that makes for righteousness."

That Deity invariably "makes for righteousness," as righteousness is humanly conceived, is an assumption that cannot be proved by logic and appears to be controverted by experience. The late William James pointed out the difficulty of imagining a God that is less just than the great and noble men that have imagined Him; yet if there is a Supreme Mind that dominates the universe, this Deity may often be accused of dealing unjustly—or seeming to deal unjustly—with individual human beings. Virtue is not always rewarded, nor vice punished, in this world. The rain falls and the lightning strikes upon the good, the bad, and the indifferent. The noblest of mankind is hanged upon a cross, while villains prosper and leave fortunes to a church. Our own finite sense of justice would be more punctilious.

Great thinkers dream of Deity in the abstract,—as "the eternal not-ourselves"; but ordinary minds, accustomed to concreteness, require an image more tangible than that. They take their own most admirable attributes and imagine a Deity in which these attributes are raised to the nth power. Thus God is evermore created in the image of man. Primitive people worship idols with a human body; but this body is represented as larger than life,—more powerful, more terrible, more beautiful. In later stages of civilization, idol-worship is discarded and people progress from imagining a God with a human body to imagining a God with a human mind. This transition has been indicated in Dante's famous statement, "Thus, the Scriptures speak of God as having hands and feet, but mean far otherwise." But, though the tendency of this imaginary process points unerringly toward the ultimate abstract, the average mind—accustomed to concreteness, as birds to the air or fishes to the sea—is incapable of conceiving a Deific Mind that must be something other than a human mind, raised only to the nth power.

Thus God is spoken of as He or Him, and not as It; though the impersonal pronoun would be more logically applicable to "the eternal not-ourselves." The common concept of Deity is still—at the stage of thinking to which mankind in general has climbed—conveniently and irremediably anthropomorphic. God is still created in the image of man, and worshiped as a man raised, mentally, to the nth power. The wise Goethe stated that even the most sceptical must be required to admit that the human mind is necessarily anthropomorphic when confronted with the problem of imagining a God.

Thus, men in general have continued to speak of "the eternal not-ourselves" in human terms,—as God the Father, God the Mother, God the Brother, God the Friend. Yet, a moral problem of profound importance arises when this "not-ourselves" neglects to exercise toward human beings the beneficent functions of a parent, or a brother, or a friend. Either this neglect is real, or else it is merely apparent; but, in either case, it is disturbing to men whose faith has been founded on the normal concept of a God endowed with a basically human mind.

Our great religious dramatists, from a very early period, have seized upon this logical dilemma as their theme. Consider *The Book of Job*, for instance. Job is a blameness man, and a faithful servant of his God; yet this very God afflicts him in a manner that must appear incomprehensible to any finite mind. At the climax of *Prometheus Bound*, which was written by Æschylus, the most loftily religious of the tragic poets of ancient Athens, the hero—who represents mankind—though chained to a rock and doomed to endure the torture of vultures gnawing at his liver, talks back to Zeus—who represents "the eternal not-ourselves"—and says, "Although you are more powerful than I, I am more just than you!"

This defiance—so to speak—was flung in the face of God by suffering mankind two thousand and five hundred years ago; and it is not blasphemous to say that God has not yet justified His ways to man throughout the searching of all subsequent poetic literature. *John Ferguson* resembles *The Book of Job* in the basic fact that it exhibits in detail the progressive torture of a blameless man by an "eternal not-ourselves" that the hero himself believes to be not only just in judgment but also kindly in intention.

John Ferguson, a peasant of northern Ireland, is a faithful Christian of the Protestant persuasion. He believes in a personal God who is his Father and his Friend, and he serves this God with absolute fidelity. He strives to love his enemies; he deliberately does good to those who have deliberately done him harm; and, when smitten on the one cheek, he stoically turns the other to his adversaries. Yet the very Deity, or Destiny, in which he trusts—for the names applied to "the eternal not-ourselves" have differed in different centuries and lands—brings down his gray hairs with sorrow to the grave, accumulating horrors upon horror's head despite the innocence of his deserving. Truly, this Irish peasant might cry aloft with Greek Prometheus, "I am more just than that which tortures me." Instead, he bows his head in penitence and kisses the rod wherewith he is chastised.

John Ferguson, like Job of old, has led a blameness life; but, through an illness incident to his advancing years, he is no longer able to work his farm. His farm is mortgaged to Henry Witherow, —a hard man, who seeks an early opportunity to foreclose the mortgage. John Ferguson appeals to his brother, Andrew, in America, to send the necessary money to save the farm. Andrew sends the money; but carelessly forgets the mail-day. Therefore, the money-order arrives a fortnight too late to avert the terrible consequences that already have arisen from its non-delivery. When the belated letter comes, a maiden has been ruined, one man has been murdered, another has been jailed, and still another is stalking free with the guilt of murder on his conscience. Thereupon, the ruined girl cries out to her pious father, "God's late, da!":—and this seeming-blasphemous ejaculation is one of the most terrible and tragic lines in modern dramatic literature. Why should God be late, if God is both omniscient and all-powerful? . . . This is the abiding question that none of our prophets nor our poets has ever yet been able to answer to the satisfaction of the seeking soul. Preachers try to put us off with the assurance that God knows better about such little matters than we do, and that we should be satisfied with the assertion that "the eternal not-ourselves" works often through mysterious ways to "make for righteousness." But this answer sounds like something said to quiet children. It lacks the ring of that eternal truth "which moves the sun in heaven and the other stars."

John Ferguson, in form, is a realistic play; and it fulfils its realistic function by reporting faithfully the facts of life as they might have occurred to a typical peasant family in County Down in the period of the eighteen-eighties. But, in spirit, it is a poetic tragedy, whose basic theme is a thing to be considered "not of an age but for all time." There is nothing either new or old in the idea of a tragic struggle between a just man and an unjust God. This idea was formulated by the dreaming Hebrews of old time; it was illustrated by the ancient Greeks; and it has come down through the ages as the greatest question that has never yet been answered by religious thought.

Mr. Ervine, acknowledging his intellectual alliance with Æschylus and with the author of *The Book of Job,* has provided his drama with a chorus, in accordance with the ancient pattern. He has managed to do this, very cleverly, without disrupting the matter-of-fact appearance of his realistic composition. The play opens and closes with a reading from the English Bible, delivered as a matter of habit by the Bible-reading hero; and at each successive crisis of the action, this pious Irish peasant reaches naturally for his Bible and reads a verse or two aloud. The passages selected are chosen from the Psalms of David; and, æsthetically, they afford to the passage of the drama the same sort of philosophic and poetic commentary that was provided, in ancient days, by the choruses of Æschylus. The plot is carried out by ordinary people; but, every now and then, the Voice of God comments upon the plot through the medium of an ancient but eternal poet, —David, King of Israel.

XX

THE PLAYS OF LORD DUNSANY

I

IN 1914, a slender volume entitled *Five Plays*, by Lord Dunsany, was published unobtrusively in *The Modern Drama Series*, with an introduction by Mr. Edwin Björkman. Until that time, the name of Lord Dunsany had hardly been heard of in this country, although he had previously published, on the other side of the Atlantic, five volumes of imaginative prose,—*The Gods of Pegana* [1905], *Time and the Gods* [1906], *The Sword of Welleran* [1908], *A Dreamer's Tales* [1910], and *The Book of Wonder* [1912]. Since then, however, four of these five plays, and four other plays which have been written subsequently, have been afforded public presentations in this country; and, in the first week of December, 1916, it was possible to see no less than three of them professionally acted in New York.

This astonishing success in a country where the theatre still remains excessively commercialized is all the more remarkable because the author had never made the slightest effort to attain success in the commercial theatre. His first play, *The Glittering Gate*, was written in 1909 for the Abbey Theatre Players at the request of Mr. William Butler Yeats. His other plays have been written, at convenient intervals, to please no other person than himself. Lord Dunsany has never enjoyed, or suffered, any personal connection with the theatre of his day, either in London or in Dublin or in any other city. He has never asked a manager to produce a play of his. Yet all his plays have been acted; and, wherever they have been produced, they have been greeted with golden encomiums from the critics and the public. Without the slightest effort on his own part to exploit his wares, without even any knowledge of the eager interest that he had stirred up in America [for the man was very busy elsewhere in the world], Lord Dunsany, in the first week of December, 1916, was more talked about than any other playwright in commercialized New York. The moral of this simple fact is merely this:—that merit counts, and that it is better for a dramatist to retire to a far place and write a great play than to hang about Times Square and dramatize the views of all the current managers concerning "what the public wants." In the theatre, as in life itself, there is always room at the top; and, if a man can write so great a play as *The Gods of the Mountain* or *A Night at an Inn*, he need not even make an effort to secure a hearing. All the ears of the world will yearn instinctively in the direction of his eloquence until it shall burst forth by invitation and fill the theatre with a sound like thunder or the noise of seven seas.

Of this mysterious and mighty warrior, who broke into our commercial theatre by assault, without so much as marshaling his forces to win a fight in which so many other men have failed, very little news had come to us except such information as might have been gleaned from personal letters to half a dozen correspondents in this country. Mr. Björkman had summarized the entire career of this admired author in six sentences which may be quoted now:

Edward John Moreton Drax Plunkett, Lord Dunsany, is the eighteenth member of his family to bear the title which gives him a place in the Irish peerage. He was born in 1878 and received his education at Eton and Sandhurst. In 1899 he succeeded his father to the title and the family estate in Meath, Ireland. During the South African war he served at the front with the Coldstream Guards. He is passionately fond of outdoor life and often spends the whole day in the saddle before sitting down at his desk to write late at night. His work proves, however, that he is as fond of spiritual as of physical exercise, and that he is an inveterate traveler in those mysterious regions of the partly known or wholly unknown where the imagination alone can guide us.

To this somewhat meager chronicle a few facts may now be added. At the outbreak of the great war, Lord Dunsany was not sent immediately to the front with the expeditionary forces. Because of his experience under fire, he was retained in England to help in the gigantic task of training the raw recruits of Kitchener's army. Meanwhile, he wrote to two or three people in this country that, if he happened to emerge from the war alive, his first act, after peace had been reconquered, would be to visit the United States, for a physical and spiritual renovation.

Lord Dunsany was wounded in the Dublin riots; and, when heard from in 1916, he was waiting at Londonderry barracks to be released by the medical board and sent to the front in France. He seemed then to suffer from a premonition that he would not survive the war. In a letter to Mrs. Emma Garrett Boyd, a popular lecturer who had done a great deal to propagate the fame of Lord Dunsany in this country, he said:—"If I do not live to come to America, there is none who can tell you more about me nor with better understanding than my wife. I was wounded less than three weeks ago. The bullet has been extracted and I am healing up rapidly. I am also under orders for France as soon as I have recovered. Sometimes I think that no man is taken hence until he has done the work that he is here to do, and looking back on five battles and other escapes from death this theory seems almost plausible; but how can one hold it when one thinks of the deaths of Shelley and Keats?"

II

The definitive point should be considered at the very outset that all of the dramatic works of Lord Dunsany are one-act plays. The student should not be led astray by the unimportant fact that, in the published text of *The Gods of the Mountain*, the three successive scenes are headed by the captions, "The First Act," "The Second Act," and "The Third Act." Neither should the reader be deceived by the accident that the published text of *King Argimenes and the Unknown Warrior* is divided into two parts which are denominated "The First Act" and "The Second Act."

The purpose of a one-act play is to produce a single dramatic effect with the greatest economy of means that is consistent with the utmost emphasis; and, in all the compositions now before us, this purpose has been carefully maintained. Considered technically, *The Gods of the Mountain* is a one-act play in three successive scenes; and, in production, these scenes should be hurriedly disclosed upon the stage without any intermission. In *King Argimenes* also, the two scenes should be presented without any intermediary lapse of time, since they exhibit two projections of the same idea, —as if the dramatist should say, "Look here upon this picture, and on this!"

Lord Dunsany is as exclusively an artist in the one-act play as Edgar Allan Poe was an artist in the short-story. The strong point, with both of these technicians, is the intensity with which they are able to focus the imagination on a single definite and little project of the panorama of experience. Each of them is willing to sacrifice in range what he is able to gain in terrible intensity. Poe was not a novelist; and Lord Dunsany has still to prove that he can write successfully a three- or four-act play. Both men can seize a big idea and see it steadily; but this is a very different endeavor from seizing a great handful of experience and trying hard to see it whole.

"The Glittering Gate" [1909]

In *The Glittering Gate*, we are wafted to a Lonely Place, which shows the golden Gate of Heaven in a granite wall of great slabs that overhangs an abyss hung with stars. There are only two actors, Jim and Bill, both burglars, and both lately dead. Jim has been dead several months and has spent this time in opening innumerable beer-bottles which appear, as if by miracle, about him, and which turn out, one after another, to be empty. He has grown accustomed to the grim, sardonic Laughter of the Gods and has forgot the world. Bill joins him, freshly killed, remembering the yearnings of the life that used to be. Bill has brought along with him the "nut-cracker" that he had held in his hand at the moment when he was shot by a householder whose premises he had invaded. Bill endeavors to drill open with his "nut-cracker" the golden Gate of Heaven. Jim—the tired soul—is little interested, until the gold of the great gate begins to yield like cheese. Then both of these dead burglars give their minds up to imagining the glorious immensity of Heaven. Bill's mother will be there, and also a girl with yellow hair whom Jim remembers dimly behind a bar at Wimbledon. Slowly the great gate swings open, "revealing empty night and stars." Bill, "staggering and gazing into the revealed Nothing, in which far stars go wandering," says,—"Stars. Blooming great stars. There *ain't* no Heaven, Jim." A cruel and violent laughter is heard off-stage. As it grows louder and more sardonic, Jim replies,—"That's like them. That's very like them. Yes, they'd do that!" And, as the curtain falls, the laughter still howls on.

"King Argimenes and the Unknown Warrior" [1911]

King Argimenes and the Unknown Warrior is, perhaps, the least impressive of the plays of Lord Dunsany. King Argimenes has been conquered and enslaved by King Darniak; and we meet the hero suffering from hunger in the slave-fields of his conqueror. In passing, it may be interesting to note that the picture of hunger here presented was drawn from the author's memory of certain days in South Africa when Lord Dunsany and his soldiers sat hungry on the ground.

King Argimenes, digging in the earth, discovers the buried sword of some Unknown Warrior. The possession of this sword gives him courage to command. He slays, one by one, the six guards of the slave-fields, and arms with their weapons six of his fellow-slaves. Then he storms the armory of King Darniak and overturns the image of the God Illuriel. This play, which appears to be an allegory of the sense of power which is given to a man when he becomes possessed of the symbols of dominion, is effectively theatrical; but the outcome seems less inevitable than that of Lord Dunsany's other plays.

"The Gods of the Mountain" [1911]

We come now to consider the greatest, if not the most effective, play of Lord Dunsany, *The Gods of the Mountain*. This piece was first produced at the Haymarket Theatre in London. Mr. Austin Strong, who saw and remembered this impressive presentation, was the stage-director of the first important production in America, which was shown behind closed doors by the Amateur Comedy Club of New York City in the fall of 1915. This production in every respect was masterly; and all who saw it will remember the occasion with credit to Mr. Strong and to the many other members of the Amateur Comedy Club who helped him to achieve a great projection of a great play. The subsequent professional production by Mr. Stuart Walker, of the Portmanteau Theatre, was inferior to that of the Amateur Comedy Club, because the spacious grandeur of the play was inevitably dwarfed by the diminutive proportions of the Portmanteau stage. But even a second-rate production of this masterpiece is more impressive than a first-rate production of nearly any other play by any other modern author.

Three beggars are discovered, seated on the ground outside a city wall, lamenting that the days are bad for beggary. To them appears the super-beggar Agmar, from another city, accompanied by a faithful servant, Slag. Slag asserts that his master is a man of big ideas and that he has come to captivate the city by his

cunning. Agmar sends a thief into the town to steal green rai-
ment, and explains to the beggars that they will enter the city as
gods,—the seven gods that are carved from green stone in the
mountains of Marma. "They sit all seven of them against the hills.
They sit there motionless and travelers worship them. They are of
green jade. They sit cross-legged with their right elbows resting
on their left hands, the right forefinger pointing upward. We will
come into the city disguised, from the direction of Marma, and
will claim to be these gods. We must be seven as they are. And
when we sit we must sit cross-legged as they do, with the right
hand uplifted."

When the thief returns, with green garments, the other beggars
wish to put them on over their rags; but Agmar has a subtler plan.
They must not look like beggars disguised as gods; they must look
like gods disguised as beggars. He tears the green garments into
strips and makes each beggar don a shred beneath his rags so that
the green shall show through only casually. Thus arrayed, the
beggars enter the city of Kongros, and sit cross-legged in the
Metropolitan Hall, in the attitude of the gods of the mountain.

Agmar has caused a prophecy to be bruited abroad in the
market-place that the gods who are carven from green rock in
the mountain shall one day arise in Marma and come to Kongros
in the guise of men. Many citizens now gather in the Metropolitan
Hall and wonder if these seven are indeed the gods of Marma.
Agmar never actually tells them that his men are gods; but he
threatens them with dire penalties if they doubt revealed divinity.
A sacrifice of food and drink is brought, with due obeisance. The
other beggars eat hungrily; but Agmar refuses food and pours out
a precious bowl of Woldery Wine, as a libation, on the ground.
By this abstention he assures the citizens of his divinity; and the
seven beggars are enthroned as gods.

But still there are citizens who doubt; and these doubters send
two dromedary men to go to the mountains of Marma and see if
the carven gods have actually left their places on the mountain-
side. Agmar and his men are filled with fright when they learn
of this expedition; and they are all the more astounded when the
dromedary men return with the report that Agmar and his followers must be indeed the gods, since the ancient idols were no
longer to be seen in their mountain-seat at Marma. Then a frightened messenger appears, falls prostrate at the feet of the seven

beggars, and implores them not again to wander in the evening, as they walked the night before, on the edge of the desert, terrible in the gloaming, with hands stretched out and groping, feeling for the city. "Master," cries the messenger to Agmar, "we can bear to see you in the flesh like men, but when we see rock walking it is terrible, it is terrible. Rock should not walk. When children see it they do not understand. Rock should not walk in the evening."

When this cringing messenger has crept away, Ulf, the oldest of the beggars, cries aloud, "I have a fear, an old fear and a boding. We have done ill in the sight of the seven gods. Beggars we were and beggars we should have remained. We have given up our calling and come in sight of our doom. I will no longer let my fear be silent; it shall run about and cry; it shall go from me crying, like a dog from out of a doomed city; for my fear has seen calamity and has known an evil thing."

Then, off-stage, amid a horror of great silence, is heard the headlong heavy tramp of stony feet. The seven gods of Marma, carved of jade, stalk lumbering upon the stage. The leading Green Thing points a stony finger at each of the seven beggars, one by one. "As he does this, each beggar in his turn gathers himself back on to his throne and crosses his legs, his right arm goes stiffly upward with forefinger erect, and a staring look of horror comes into his eyes. In this attitude the beggars sit motionless, while a green light falls upon their faces."

The gods go out. The citizens return. They find the seven beggars turned to stone. "We have doubted them," they cry. "They have turned to stone because we have doubted them." Then, in a great and growing voice, there comes a chorus, "They were the true gods. They were the true gods." It is thus that big religions are begun. The faithful soul invents the faith it feeds on.

To this simple and straightforward narrative,—so terrible, so beautiful, so true, so absolutely self-sufficient,—many critics have applied the academic adjectives "symbolical" and "allegorical." With criticism of this sort, the author is exceedingly impatient. In a letter to Mrs. Emma Garrett Boyd, Lord Dunsany said:—"In case I shall not live to explain my work, I think the first thing to tell them [the American people] is that it does not need explanation. One does not need to explain a sunset, nor does one need to explain a work of art.

"Don't let them hunt for allegories. I may have written an allegory at some time, but if I have, it was a quite obvious one, and, as a general rule, I have nothing to do with allegories.

"What is an allegory? A man wants the streets to be swept better in his town or he wants his neighbors to have rather cleaner morals. He can't say so straight out because he might be had up for libel, so he says what he has to say, but he says it about some extinct king in Babylon, but he's thinking of his one-horse town all the time. Now, when I write of Babylon, there are people who cannot see that I write of it *for love of Babylon's ways*, and they think I'm thinking of London still and our beastly Parliament.

"Only I get further east than Babylon, even to kingdoms that seem to me to lie in the twilight beyond the East of the World. I want to write about men and women and the great forces that have been with them from the cradle up—forces that the centuries have neither aged nor weakened—not about people who are so interested in the latest mascot or motor that not enough remains when the trivial is sifted from them. . . .

"Take my *Gods of the Mountain*. Some beggars being hard up pretend to be gods. Then they get all they want. But Destiny, Nemesis, the Gods, punish them by turning them into the very idols that they desired to be.

"First of all there you have a very simple tale told dramatically, and along with that you have bound, without any deliberate attempt of mine—so far as I know—a truth, not true to London only or to New York or to one municipal party, but to the experience of man. That is the kind of way that man does get hit by destiny. But mind you, that is all unconscious though inevitable. I am not trying to teach anybody anything. I merely set out to make a good work of art from a simple theme, and God knows we want works of art in this age of corrugated iron. How many people hold the error that Shakespeare was of the school-room! Whereas he was of the playground, as all artists are."

"*The Golden Doom*" [*1912*]

In *The Golden Doom*, the playful aspiration of a little boy becomes inextricably intertangled with the destiny of a mighty monarch. The piece is set "outside the King's great door in Zericon, some while before the fall of Babylon":—and the reading of this simple stage-direction fills the ear with singing like that which

Ibsen's Hilda heard in those inspired moments when she hearkened to the music of harps in the air.

This little boy comes to beg the King of Zericon for a hoop to play with; and, in the absence of the monarch, he addresses his petition to the King's great door,—a sacred door, which it is death to touch. When the sentries are not looking, this unthinking boy scrawls upon the iron door a little doggerel poem that is running in his mind,—using as a pencil a nugget of gold which he has fished up from the river near at hand.

This golden legend on the iron door is subsequently found and regarded as a portent. The King's great prophets are summoned to interpret it. They read it as a doom from the stars. The King's pride has been too overweening, and he is marked for ruin. Therefore the King, to symbolize the sacrifice of all his pride, lays his crown and scepter humbly before the iron door and goes away bare-headed. The little boy comes back. His prayer to the King's door has apparently been answered. He regards the King's crown as a hoop, and the scepter as a stick to beat it with; and he frisks away, delighted with his toys. When the King returns, his sacrificial offerings have disappeared. "The gods have come," he says. "The stars are satisfied."

"The Lost Silk Hat" [1913]

The Lost Silk Hat has not as yet been acted in New York; but it has been produced by Mr. B. Iden Payne at the Gaiety Theatre in Manchester and by Mr. Sam Hume at the Arts and Crafts Theatre in Detroit. It is written in a lighter vein than the other plays of Lord Dunsany. Before a house in London, a young gentleman, "faultlessly dressed, but without a hat," is standing, in a most embarrassing predicament. He has just said farewell forever to the young lady in the house; but, in accomplishing his tragic exit, he has left his top-hat in the drawing-room, "half under the long sofa, at the far end." Being a conventional young man, he cannot confront with equanimity the prospect of wandering about the streets of London without a hat.

A laborer, a clerk, a poet, stroll successively along the street. The young gentleman implores each of these in turn to ring the bell and to invent some subterfuge for recovering his hat. The laborer and the clerk regard him as insane and go their ways; but the poet lingers long enough to talk the matter over with him.

The upshot of their conversation is that the young man eventually reënters the house, against the protests of the poet, who pleads that it would be much more fittingly romantic for the young man to go away to Africa and die; and that the young man, having been enticed once more within the dangerous precincts by the mere desire to recover his top-hat, nevermore returns from the toils of the young lady, to whom, once, in a dramatic moment, he had said farewell forever.

"*The Tents of the Arabs*" [*1915*]

The Tents of the Arabs was acted for the first time on any stage at the Arts and Crafts Theatre in Detroit, Michigan, on November 16, 1916, under the direction of Mr. Sam Hume.

The Tents of the Arabs is perhaps the least theatrical of Lord Dunsany's plays, but it is also the most lyrical in mood. It tells a very simple story of a camel-driver who wanted to be a king and a king who wanted to be a camel-driver, and how, because they had the luck to look sufficiently alike, they managed to change places in the world, so that each of them could be happy in the life of which the other had grown weary. There is no other mood more lyrical than that of longing—as Edgar Allan Poe pointed out in one of his acutest passages of philosophic criticism; and the longing of this fabled king who is weary of cities and desires evermore to wander over the illimitable desert is expressed by Lord Dunsany with incomparable eloquence. Thus, for instance, speaks the king: "O Thalanna, Thalanna, how I hate this city with its narrow, narrow ways, and evening after evening drunken men playing skabash in the scandalous gambling house of that old scoundrel Skarmi. O that I might marry the child of some un-kingly house that generation to generation had never known a city, and that we might ride from here down the long track through the desert, always we two alone, till we came to the tents of the Arabs. And the crown—some foolish, greedy man should be given it to his sorrow. And all this may not be, for a King is yet a King."

"*A Night at an Inn*" [*1916*]

On the night of April 22, 1916, three hundred people were gathered at the Neighborhood Playhouse, at 466 Grand Street, New York City, to attend the first performance on any stage any-where in the world of a new and theretofore unpublished play by

Lord Dunsany, entitled *A Night at an Inn*. The audience which
crowded the Neighborhood Playhouse on this particular evening
included less than half a dozen of those who, by professional connection, might have been expected to respond to the privilege of
the occasion. Yet, when this great play by a great man was presented by the local company of Grand Street, it reached out and
grabbed the casual auditors by the throat, and shook them, and
thrilled them, and reduced them to a mood of inarticulate lauda-
tion.

To those of us who were present on that memorable evening, it
appeared that *A Night at an Inn* was the most effective one-act
play that we had ever seen. In the colder light of after-thinking,
there seems to be no need to revise this judgment, except so far as
to admit a reasonable rivalry on the part of *The Gods of the
Mountain*, by the same author, and *Riders to the Sea*, by the dead
but deathless poet, John M. Synge. One of these three is, assuredly,
the greatest one-act play in the world; and the present writer will
not quarrel with the choice of any critic for a verdict of uttermost
supremacy among these three.

To tell in detail the story of *A Night at an Inn* would seem like
the betrayal of a trust. Basically, this one-act play is nothing more
than a melodrama of the "shilling-shocker" sort; but it is so ir-
radiated with imagination that the terrible theatric thrill of the
immediate performance is survived by a memory that serenely
satisfies the soul. The theme of *A Night at an Inn* is identical with
that of *The Gods of the Mountain;* but the later play is more
terribly immediate in the medium of its appeal. Though a romantic
work, it has a realistic setting; and the imaginative horror of the
narrative is brought so close to the audience that the action is accompanied by audible gasps and groans and a nervous gripping of
the arms of all the chairs. To write a more effective play than
this would seem, in fact, to be impossible. *A Night at an Inn*, indeed, might be accepted without discussion as an answer to the
academic questions, "What is a play?" and "What is, after all,
dramatic?"

"The Queen's Enemies" [1916]

The Queen's Enemies was first produced at the Neighborhood
Playhouse, in New York, on November 14, 1916. It shows the
author only at his second best; but the second best of such a man

is better than the very best of most of our contemporary dramatists.

The story is a little reminiscent of *The Cask of Amontillado*,
by Edgar Allan Poe,—an author whom Dunsany much resembles.
A little Queen of ancient Egypt is annoyed by the fact that she
has so many enemies. Therefore she invites them all to a banquet
in an underground temple that is sacred to the Nile. They come
—these mighty warriors—armed to the teeth, and accompanied by
their retainers. The little Queen of Egypt is unarmed, and is accompanied only by a weakling female slave. She invites her guests
to eat, to drink, and to be merry. The hostile warriors suspect the
food, and feed it first to their subjacent slaves. They suspect the
wine as well, and sedulously watch its effect upon their underlings.
But the little Queen disarms their fear of being poisoned by par-
taking eagerly and freely of the proffered food and drink. The
banquet begins to be successful. Light talk flows merrily around
the board. Meanwhile, the Queen of Egypt and her attendant
female slave edge their way gradually toward the only door. They
make this door, dash through it, slam and bar it. Then the little,
helpless Queen prays to the great god of the Nile. The river rises,
and pours through a grating in the wall of the underground temple.

In utter darkness, we hear the gurgles and gasps that mark the
drowning of the incarcerated enemies of the little Queen. Then a
sudden torch appears upon the outer stairs. The Queen ascends
serenely to the upper air. She has no enemies any more; and she
will sleep in peace.

"The Laughter of the Gods" [*1919*]

The Laughter of the Gods is not so august a composition as
The Gods of the Mountain nor so thrilling a fabric as *A Night
at an Inn;* but it emphasizes the same theme that was announced
in these antecedent compositions.

In the high and far-off times when Babylon was something
other than the echo of a name, there dwelt a king, called Karnos,
in the metropolitan city of Babul-el-Charnak, a teeming city
lauded by men of many nations as a wonder of the world. But
this king grew weary of cities, and moved himself, with all his
court, to a lonely palace in the jungle-seat of Thek, where wild
beasts might be hunted in the heat of the day, and where, at the
creeping on of twilight, a million orchids paled to purple beneath

a silvery sky. In his jungle-seat of Thek, the king was well contented, for the region cooled his thoughts, like the laying of soft hands upon a tired brow; but his courtiers grew restive, and desired to return to the teeming city of Babul-el-Charnak.

The ladies of the court were discontented because the single little street of Thek, which soon ended in the jungle, was devoid of shops in which to spend their money and their time; and they besought their husbands to persuade King Karnos to take them back to the metropolis; whither merchants were wont to bring their wares from all the corners of the world. But the king persisted in his weariness of cities, and announced that he would stay forever where the orchids paled to purple in the quiet twilight.

Therefore his councilors, being stimulated to a deed of daring by the stinging of their wives, conspired together and hatched a plot to scare the king away from his jungle-seat of Thek. They seized upon a Prophet of the Ancient Gods and commanded him to tell King Karnos that Thek was foredoomed to be destroyed three days from then, at sunset, with every living thing that still walked within its precincts. This prophecy, they argued, might be uttered with good conscience, since no reasonable man, in those advanced and scientific times, believed any longer in the Ancient Gods. But the Prophet still believed, and protested against this contemplated deed of blasphemy. His attitude was adamantine, until one of the appealing councilors revealed a knowledge of the fact that the Prophet had secretly taken unto himself a third wife, in defiance of the ancient law which limited to two the number of wives with whom Prophets were permitted to cohabit. Thereupon, the Prophet was constrained to obey the councilors, and to deliver to King Karnos the lying message of the Gods.

King Karnos listened sedately to this prophecy, and knew it for a lie, because it was not reasonable, and because, in those advanced and scientific times, none but priests and weakling women believed any longer in the Ancient Gods. Therefore the king decreed that, on the third day, at sunset, when the falling of the filtered sands of time should have proved the Prophet to be, in very fact, a liar, his head should be severed from his trunk by the royal executioner.

The Prophet was a large man, nurtured in religion; and what he feared, throughout the ticking of the hours still allotted to him before the execution of his doom, was not the awfulness of death itself, which is a customary and familiar thing, as when a wind arises and sweeps across a table crowded with innumerable lighted candles, but the greater awfulness of something unfamiliar,—some special visitation of the anger of the Ancient Gods against the first and only Prophet who had ever made them seem to lie, throughout immemorable centuries.

Time moved serenely till the coming on of sunset, on the third day after the announcement of the manufactured prophecy. The contented king looked out upon the jungle, and saw the sea of orchids pale to purple beneath the quiet touch of the twilight. The tortured Prophet waited for his death, until the sun dropped down behind the tangled trees, and King Karnos turned magnificently toward the royal executioner, and ordered, "Take away that man!" But then a rumble arose, quietly at first, like the sighing of the sea, and then more noisy, like the congregated roar and rattle of all the thunders of the world. This rumble was the rumor of the grim, sardonic Laughter of the Gods. The jungle-seat of Thek was overwhelmed and swallowed up; and every living thing that walked within its precincts was drenched and drowned beneath the heavy seas of absolute oblivion. The Ancient Gods—who cannot lie—had chosen to fulfil the prophecy which had been wished upon them, in a mood of fear and trembling, by one of their august apostles.

III

That these nine one-act plays of Lord Dunsany are great works, no reader or observer will readily deny. There remains only for the critic the cold task of pointing out the various influences that have contributed, more or less, to their creation. Lord Dunsany is one of the most original dramatists of modern times. In an age of realism, he has dared to blow a brazen trumpet in celebration of the ceaseless triumph of romance. In a period when the majority of minds have worked inductively, he has dared to think deductively. He has invented facts to illustrate a central truth, instead of imitating actuality in a faint and far-off effort to suggest the underlying essence of reality. He has imagined and realized a world "some while before the fall of Babylon" which is more meaningful in utter truth than the little world that is revealed to the observer of a Harlem flat or of a hired room in Houston Street at the present hour.

But no artist, however original, is entirely devoid of predecessors. Lord Dunsany has derived his inspiration from Sophocles, from Maeterlinck, from the English Bible, and from John M. Synge. From Sophocles he takes the theme that forever tantalizes and invites his genius. This theme is the inevitable overcoming of the sin of pride, or *hubris*, by the primal power of *ananke*, or necessity. Like the ancient Greeks, Dunsany loves to show the tragic failing of a hero who has set his wits against the power of the God that rules the gods. In his greatest plays, he projects upon the stage a conflict between a super-man and a sort of idealized abstraction that may conveniently be called a super-god. In this conflict, the eternal law inevitably conquers the temporal rebellion. In this reading of the evermore recurrent riddle of destiny, Lord Dunsany agrees with Æschylus, with Sophocles, and with Euripides. Though never Greek in subject-matter, he is nearly always Greek in theme; and, in the spirit of his plays, Lord Dunsany has reminded us, more than any other modern writer, of the sheer augustness of the tragic drama of the Greeks.

In method, however, the plays of Lord Dunsany are related clearly to the early plays of Maurice Maeterlinck. Like Maeterlinck, Dunsany has the faculty of saying one thing and meaning many others. In this sense—and this alone—his writings are "symbolical." Before studying his collected plays, it would be well to re-read the famous letter concerning *The Divine Comedy* which Dante addressed to Can Grande della Scala. Most of what Dunsany writes must be read in three or four ways; and this is also true of the earlier works of the poet laureate of Belgium.

But the prose style of Lord Dunsany was derived from a source no less familiar than the Jacobean translation of the Bible. Mr. Björkman has reported him as saying, "For years no style seemed to me natural but that of the Bible; and I feared I would never become a writer when I saw that other people did not use it." The indebtedness of Lord Dunsany to the prose style of the English translation of the Psalms of David may be indicated by the following quotation from *The Golden Doom:*—"Because if a doom from the stars fall suddenly upon a king it swallows up his people and all things round about him, and his palace walls and the walls of his city and citadel, and the apes come in from the woods and the large beasts from the desert, so that you would not say that a king had been there at all."

And sometimes, in sentences such as the foregoing, we hear a haunting echo of the voice of another Irish dramatist, untimely silenced,—the ever memorable poet, John M. Synge. Synge was richer than Dunsany in amplitude of outlook and variety of mood. But, like his only immediate successor in the theatre of the world, he saw life steadily more easily than he could see it whole. Lord Dunsany would cheerfully have died to write a masterpiece like *Riders to the Sea;* and Synge, who now is dead, would cheerfully have flung his hat into the air in recognition of such a masterpiece as *A Night at an Inn.* Both these men were natives of "John Bull's Other Island." The world of art owes much—oh, very, very much! —to this isolated outpost of European culture.

XXI

LORD DUNSANY: PERSONAL
IMPRESSIONS

———————————————————————————

O N A GUSTY night in October, 1919, an Irish peer—the
eighteenth baron of his line—stood in the rain in front
of a little theatre at 466 Grand Street, in the heart of
the Russian Jewish quarter of the great East Side of
New York City. He was easily distinguishable, because of his
extraordinary height and the hulking army overcoat which housed
him from the drizzle. Two or three hundred strangers—for the
most part, Jewish people of the neighborhood—grasped him by
the hand, patted him on the back, and asked him to scrawl his
name on the fly-leaves of many books which they produced from
pockets and presented proudly. The tall man was treated both
as the host and as the guest of an unusual occasion. Suddenly there
came a flash of lightning and a crash of thunder. "That must be
Klesh," said Lord Dunsany; "he has come a long way from India."

The Irish peer himself had come a long way from Dunsany
Castle and Messines Ridge, for the specific purpose of seeing a
couple of plays which he had never seen before—*The Queen's
Enemies* and *A Night at an Inn*—and finding out why so many
commentators had made so large a noise about them. I could not
be present at the Neighborhood Playhouse on this particular occasion; but I asked the author afterward to tell me how it felt to
see a full-fledged performance—with an audience and all—of a
couple of plays which he had sent overseas in manuscript. All the
other playwrights I have ever known have worried and worked
over their manuscripts, day after day, throughout the initial weeks
of rehearsals and the secondary weeks of "try outs," and have been
heartily sick of hearing their own lines repeated, long before the
date of a metropolitan first-night.

Dunsany answered that this unusual experience of his had

proved once more that you can't tell much about a play until you see it on the stage. *A Night at an Inn* exceeded his own expectations, and he was surprised to note the thrill which it communicated to the audience. "It's a very simple thing," he said,—"merely a story of some sailors who have stolen something and know that they are followed. Possibly it is effective because nearly everybody, at some time or other, has done something he was sorry for, has been afraid of retribution, and has felt the hot breath of a pursuing vengeance on the back of his neck." With *The Queen's Enemies*, on the other hand, the author was a little disappointed. "When I wrote these two pieces," he told me, "I thought that *The Queen* was a better play than *The Inn!* Now I know that *A Night at an Inn* is the more dramatic of the two."

"But don't mistake me," he continued, "*The Inn* is a more effective play than *The Queen*; but it isn't so fine an undertaking. Suppose that I should give a block of wood to a sculptor and ask him to carve it, and suppose that he should cut it very well; that is *A Night at an Inn*. Suppose, next, that I should give a tusk of ivory to the same sculptor and he should carve it not so well: that is *The Queen's Enemies*. It isn't so dramatic a play as *The Inn*; but it is intrinsically finer."

"Why do you think that?", I inquired.

"Because of the idea," the author answered. "The idea of *A Night at an Inn* is rather ordinary: that, I suppose, is the reason why it hits the audience so hard: and, as several critics, like yourself, have pointed out, it is an idea of the same sort that I had used before in *The Gods of the Mountain*. But I like the idea of *The Queen's Enemies*. I heard about an ancient queen of Egypt who invited all her enemies to a feast of reconciliation and suddenly drowned them. This meant nothing until I could imagine the motive for this extraordinary deed. Several months later, the motive occurred to me. The dear little queen had done this for the very simple reason that she didn't like to have any enemies: she wanted to be loved, not to be hated. The rest was easy; for the play was made when the motive was discovered."

"Do you always begin with a motive?", I asked.

"Not always," said Dunsany; "I begin with anything, or with next to nothing. Then, suddenly, I get started, and go through in a hurry. The main point is not to interrupt a mood. Writing is an easy thing when one is going strong and going fast; it becomes a

hard thing only when the onward rush is impeded. Most of my
short plays have been written in a sitting or two. The other day,"—
he said in December, 1919,—"I got an idea for a short play in St.
Louis. I began the composition on the train and finished it before
we arrived in Chicago. It's a little piece about a monk who grew
a halo. I hope that you will like it."

"How about *The Gods of the Mountain?*", I asked.

"I wrote that in three sessions," Lord Dunsany answered,—"two
afternoons between tea and dinner and another hour on the third
afternoon. *A Night at an Inn* was written between tea and dinner
in a single sitting. That was very easy. . . ."

"No trouble about the dialogue?", I suggested.

"Dialogue isn't difficult if you have been around with men a
lot, and listened to them. Somebody says something; the next man
doesn't quite agree, and unobtrusively suggests a reservation; the
third man says, 'No, not at all, the truth is . . .' And that is dialogue."

"But the writing?"

"Well, of course, there is such a thing as rhythm," Lord Dunsany answered.

"You agree with me, though, that the dramatic value of a play
stands quite apart from any literary merit it may or may not show
in the writing of its dialogue?"

"I do, indeed. Don't damn me as a 'literary' playwright. You
have read ten of my plays; but I have already written more than
twenty. The best of them are still unpublished. I am holding them
back, in the hope that people may be forced to see them before
they have a chance of reading them."

"That reminds me of Pinero," I replied. "Several years ago, Sir
Arthur started a friendly habit of sending me prompt-copies of
each of his new plays; but he made me promise never to read these
printed texts till after I had seen the plays in the theatre,—particularly if I should be called upon to write critical reviews of
them."

"I can understand that," said Lord Dunsany. "I misjudged *The
Queen* and *The Inn* until I saw them acted."

"If you write a play so quickly," I suggested, "I infer that the
whole thing must be planned out in your mind before you start
to write it. Among magazine men, I am known as a quick writer.
I publish more than half a hundred articles a year; and most of

them are turned out in a single night. But, before I sit down to write the first sentence, I have been thinking for three or four days, in the subway, between the acts, or when other people were talking to me. In the real sense, the task has more nearly consumed a week than a day. An impromptu speech takes only three or four minutes; but sometimes, with me,—if the occasion is important,— it spoils a day or two beforehand. I can't imagine anybody writing *The Gods of the Mountain* in a few hours, confined within three days, unless a long period of preparation—much of it subconscious, to be sure—had gone before."

"Sometimes," Lord Dunsany said, "I have thought the matter out, and know exactly what I am going to do; that was the case with *The Gods;* but at other times, I just get started and follow a mood as a hunter follows the hounds. I will give you an example, —*King Argimenes*. I saw a king in rags, digging up a bone, gnawing at it hungrily, and saying, 'This is a good bone.' I started the play with no idea whatever of its subsequent development. I merely wrote along, to find out what would happen."

"I have always thought so," I replied ungraciously. "You know, of course, that this is one of the few plays of yours that I don't especially admire. It seems to me inconsequential, and not built up to a climax."

"That must be because I didn't know the end when I started the beginning. . . . Of course, it is better to have things planned," the author added, "and not to trust entirely to the impulsion of a mood."

In recording this conversation, I have anteceded the chronological order of these haphazard personal impressions. As a matter of fact, the first time that I met Lord Dunsany was at a public dinner in his honor, at which I endeavored to do my duty as one of the speakers. It was a good occasion, of the customary sort. When we were coming away, I asked him if he were growing tired of publicity. "Publicity?", he countered quickly. "You don't call this public! You ought to have seen our trenches under Messines Ridge. That's the most public place I have ever been in. We were in a valley. The Germans were on a hill. They could see down to our boot-tops." He looked at me and asked, "How tall are you?" "Six feet one, or thereabouts." "I am six feet four. Our trenches were only six feet deep. I shall never fear 'publicity' again."

On a subsequent occasion, I asked Lord Dunsany to tell me something of his life in the army. "I was brought up to be a soldier," he replied. "I wasn't sent to Oxford or to Cambridge, but to Sandhurst. I went through the South African affair and the whole of the recent war. I have this to say about military preparation: it doesn't educate a man, it merely trains him. A trained man can do one single thing with almost mechanical perfection; but an educated man can do almost anything that he is called upon to do. I was merely trained. It is better to be educated. The college is a better place for this than the army."

At another time, I touched upon the point that Lord Dunsany had not yet enjoyed the dubious experience—so common to the rest of us—of peddling his plays from manager to manager. I told him that most of the American playwrights to whom I had presented him were required, by the nature of the game, to devote much more of their time to the practical task of "placing" their plays than to the more attractive task of writing them. Lord Dunsany answered: "That may be the reason why ten or a dozen of my best plays have not yet been acted. I have never had the time to peddle them. Ninety-seven per cent.—or thereabouts—of my actual life has been spent out of doors in the pursuit of various athletic activities,—such as following the hounds, playing cricket, hunting big game, or serving as a professional soldier. The remaining three per cent. has been spent in the writing of my tales and plays,—the records of my dreams. What time is left for peddling my literary wares? . . . I have recently written two or three plays, of full length, which treat of contemporary life in London. How does one sell these things in London or New York?"

This question surprised me, until I made the astonishing discovery that I had actually earned more money from a single "failure" in our commercial theatre than Lord Dunsany has earned from all of the "successes" in our little theatres that have made him famous. When *The Gods of the Mountain* was put into rehearsal at the Haymarket Theatre in London, he was offered ten pounds for the world-rights in perpetuity. This contract struck him as inequitable; and he requested that the world-rights should be limited to five years. This period has long ago elapsed; but the author received less than fifty dollars for the first five years of the actual existence of what is probably the greatest short play in the world.

It is gratifying to record that he has since developed, by experience, a business-sense that is more practical.

"Writing plays," he told me, "is the one thing I most dearly love; but I cannot talk of it at home, in County Meath. My aunt would be scandalized if she should hear that I have written plays; my neighbors would dismiss me as insane; everybody else would think me a fool; I had to come to your country to find a sympathetic audience."

I told him that Sir Arthur Pinero, after the comparative failure of *Mid-Channel* in London and the comparative success of the same piece in New York, had said to me jocosely: "If it were not for America, we couldn't keep alive." Lord Dunsany said, "Your public is surprisingly alert." Having been a lecturer myself, I answered adversely: "When people seem to like our speeches, and swarm around us to request us to sign books, we naturally think that they have brains." To this he answered, "That is not the point. In your country, I have met many people who are not ashamed to talk of art. In England, nowadays, the subject is laughed away from the carpet.

"When *The Gods of the Mountain* was first produced at the Haymarket Theatre, one rather snobbish critic said that the play was bad, for the mere reason that it had been written by a nobleman. He ordered me back to my ancestral castle, just as Keats was ordered back, a century ago, to his apothecary pots. Why should Keats have been despised, in a period of aristocracy? And why should I be despised, in a period of democracy? It isn't my fault that I try to write beautiful tales and effective plays.

"It is only in your country that my attempts have been appreciated. I have no fame in England. I have scarcely any ranking among the authors of my own country; you know many more of them than I do; but I am grateful to your nation for the incentive to carry on. Poets thrive upon appreciation; and I need the sort of encouragement that has been granted to me by your hospitable people."

"How about that division of your life," I asked, "three per cent. of which, according to your smiling statement, has been devoted to your writing, and the overwhelming remainder to athletics?" "I have found this out," said Lord Dunsany, "that you must not talk of art to the majority of men who follow active lives in the open air,—like cricketers, or huntsmen, or soldiers. On the other hand, I have found out that, among artists, you may extol without embarrassment the virtues of the athletes of the world. Why is it that the men of action are always afraid of the men of dreams, whereas the men of dreams are never afraid of the men of action? It must be because the dream is always stronger than the act. Jeanne d'Arc is evermore more potent to win a battle than a regiment of British soldiers. That is because this peasant girl of long ago has been made real by the imagination of millions of people. Nothing can, at any time, be realized but what has been imagined.

"I like the active life in the open; and, after four or five years in the war, I actually feel uncomfortable in a room with the windows closed; but the active life is very lonely. I can talk to a man of letters like yourself about cricketing or lion-hunting or soldiering, and you will be interested, because artists are interested in everything. But I cannot talk about my dreams to cricketers or soldiers or lion-hunters; they would think that something had gone wrong with me. I was very lonely in the trenches; and it has been a great pleasure for me to meet so many writers in America and to find that most of them are sportsmen as well."

"What do you think of the effect of the war upon the drama?", I inquired.

"Four years of hell and heroism have trampled down the immediate actual, and reminded us of the insistence of the perennial real. We have learned that idealism is the only absolute reality. The stricken world must reawaken; and the theatre should be resurrected with it. The time has passed away for such faithful but depressing records of the drabbest aspects of our current life as the *Night Lodging* of Maxim Gorki, an act of which I saw the other day. A moment has arrived for reminding the theatre-going public that such a thing as splendor is still to be discerned in the records of experience. Let us set before the public splendid images of beauty; for beauty is truth, despite the critic who tried to send Keats back to his apothecary pots."

"Keats died without knowing whether he would be famous or not," said I. "You are famous at forty. You have been luckier than Keats."

"Yes, I have been lucky," he replied, "thanks mainly to your country; but that is as it should be. I am not speaking personally; but, after all, I am a poet, and poets ought to be appreciated in their lifetime. In England, a poet has to die to be appreciated. Look at Rupert Brooke; they wouldn't read him while he lived. In England, I am merely a lord."

"Aren't you at all bored by being lionized in this country?"

"Not at all: I like it," he replied.

Lord Dunsany is a man who—whether you agree with him or not on any given point—is undeniably alive. He is excessively tall, loose-jointed, raw-boned, rather awkward, and encumbered with a large head and enormous hands and feet. He admits jocosely that, at home, he is generally regarded as the worst-dressed man in County Meath. He shambles along with a drooping posture, accentuated doubtless by his long and cramping experience in the trenches under Messines Ridge; but his mind is neither awkward nor drooping. He talks fluently and well; and his nature is so frank and simple that he is a very easy man to get acquainted with.

XXII

THE GRANDEUR OF ENGLISH PROSE

ROBERT LOUIS STEVENSON, in a letter written from Vailima, in December, 1893, to Henry James, stated that his two aims in fiction might be described as,—"First, war to the adjective; Second, death to the optic nerve." As a stylist, he regretted the growing tendency of the age to receive impressions through the eye alone. A public overfed on newspapers and magazines soon learns to skim them rapidly in search of subject-matter; and this faculty for gathering the content of a printed page with a single stroke of the eye is applied subsequently to the reading of books. Nothing could be more stultifying to an appreciation of either verse or prose than this pernicious practice; for verse and prose are auditory arts, not visual, and must be listened to, and even murmured with the lips, in order that their patterns may be appreciated. To the optic nerve alone, no remarkable appeal is made by such a sentence as De Quincey's, "Moonlight and the first timid tremblings of the dawn were by the time blending"; but if this phrase be read aloud, with loving intonation, a notable appeal will certainly be made to ears that have not forgotten how to hear.

Perhaps the most important function of Stuart Walker's well-remembered Portmanteau Theatre was to remind a rarely listening public of the historic grandeur of our English prose. The plays that he presented made patterns for the ear, and might be appreciated by the blind. This fact is now exceedingly unusual; because the entire tendency of the theatre, throughout the last half century, has been in the contrary direction. The contemporary drama has made a sort of fetich of the fact that it appeals primarily to the optic, instead of to the auditory, nerve. It was developed by Ibsen, and his many staunch successors, in a period of realism; and in the interests of realism our recent dramatists have exerted the most

470

punctilious literary tact in the effort to prevent themselves from writing any lines that might sound at all "literary" when spoken by the actors on the stage. Our contemporary drama, for the most part, is not written in verse nor even in prose; it is written, instead, in conversation: and the most successful playwrights of the present period are those who have mastered the difficult and tricky craft of writing lines that seem to catch and utter the casual drift of unpremeditated colloquy.

Even romantic and poetic dramatists, like Maurice Maeterlinck, have adopted the current habit of addressing themselves primarily to the eye instead of to the ear, and have grown to rely more largely upon the visible appeal of scenery and lighting than upon the audible appeal that might be made by the whispery and slippered footfall of soft syllables or the fanfare of a trumpet-blast of rhetoric. Truly, our plays in general have become again like little children,—in the proverbial sense that, when good, they should be seen and not be heard.

But Mr. Walker was fortunate in the discovery of a romantic and poetic dramatist who still dares to write in prose,—who still prefers to appeal to the listening ear, instead of twanging at the optic nerve, as the capeadors of Spain flaunt flaming cloaks to capture the attention of the charging bull. Since the passing of his fellow-countryman, John Millington Synge—who was endowed with the eloquence of angels—Lord Dunsany is almost the only dramatist who has appeared in the English-speaking theatre to remind the public of the grandeur of our ancient English prose. Even Barrie, who began life as a man of letters, preferred to write his dialogue in conversation; and even Bernard Shaw, for all his literary wit, has preferred to pretend that he was faithfully reporting the unpatterned speech of a generation that had never read aloud the exordium of Milton's *Areopagitica*.

The history of English prose, like the history of English blank verse, may be traced back to a great beginning along a single and undeviating line. Blank verse began in English in 1588, with the drums and tramplings of *Tamburlaine the Great*. The previous essays of Surrey and Sackville in this medium were really not important: it was Marlowe alone who molded for us our enduring mighty line. The new footfalls introduced successively by Shakespeare, Milton, Fletcher, Shirley, Cowper, Wordsworth, Tennyson, and Stephen Phillips, are merely variations from a standard norm. Wherever English verse is chanted and listened to among the far-flung millions that engirdle the revolving world, the accents of that aureoled and flame-haired youth, who was slain by a serving-man in 1593, at the early age of twenty-nine, are still predominant and overwhelming.

English prose, analogously, dates backward along a direct, undeviating line to the King James translation of the Bible,—which remains, for all time, the greatest monument of prose in any modern language. The nameless men who, actuated by no foresight of posthumous celebrity, built up, verse by verse and chapter after chapter, that amazing monument of literary art, plucked unconsciously the loftiest of laurel-wreaths and set it as a crown upon the brow of anonymity. Our earliest deliberate organists of English prose,—John Milton, Jeremy Taylor, and Sir Thomas Browne,—played merely the same tune that had already been orchestrated by these nameless predecessors; and it is not at all excessive to say that no man, since the outset of the seventeenth century, has ever learned to write great prose in English unless his ear had been trained from early childhood to appreciate the orchestral voluntaries of Sir Thomas Browne. De Quincey and Stevenson were brought up, according to their own confessions, on the *Religio Medici:* Ruskin and Rudyard Kipling, according to their own statements, were brought up on the English Bible: and no man, apparently, has ever yet attained a mastery of English prose whose ear, in early childhood, was not habitually trained to appreciate the slow dark march of measured and majestic syllables that was applauded in the high and far-off times of that curious and futile English king who patronized the arts and wrote a treatise on tobacco.

These remarks have been occasioned by Stuart Walker's production of *The Book of Job*, in the eloquent English version of the King James translators. This piece is probably the oldest dramaturgic composition still current in the theatre of the world; and its very antiquity is clearly worthy of reverence. It is constructed very simply and with unquestionable grandeur. From the modern point of view, it must be admitted, however, that the action is excessively subjective. Nothing seems to happen externally upon the stage, before the very eyes of the spectators; but everything happens, instead, within the souls of Job and his assembled collocutors. To the modern mind, this internal and analytic method of setting forth a great dramatic theme is less impressive than the synthetic external method which was employed by the reigning dramatists of ancient Greece. *The Book of Job*, despite its philosophical augustness, can never touch the modern heart so poignantly as *The Trojan Women* of Euripides.

But *The Book of Job*—in that historic English version which was sent to press, three centuries ago, by an anonymous committee of immortal men of letters that had been assembled by an arbitrary fiat of King James—was written with a grandeur of great prose that must remain forever unforgettable so long as men have ears for hearkening.

XXIII

THE LOVELINESS OF LITTLE THINGS

FOR THOSE who seek adventure among beautiful achievements, there is a special pleasure in contemplating the loveliness of little things. The tiny temple at Nîmes is not so great an edifice as the Cathedral of Amiens, but it is much more perfect and more fine. The mind is overawed by the tremendous seraphim of Tintoretto, cutting through chaos with strong, level flight; but the heart goes out with keener fondness to the little angels of Fra Angelico, that demurely set one tiny foot before the other on the pansied fields of Paradise. The vastest work of Byron is *Don Juan*, with its enormous incongruity of moods; but his loveliest work is the simple-mooded little lyric that begins, "She walks in beauty." Could any colossus of sculpture be so dainty or so delicate as the little bronze Narcissus of Naples, whose uplifted finger is eternally accompanied by a melody of unheard flutes? What is Shakespeare's finest and most perfect work? It is not *Hamlet* nor *Macbeth*; it is not even *Othello*; it is, I think, the tiny song beginning, "Take, oh, take those lips away." It is conceivable that any of his great plays might be improved by a hundred alterations in the lines; but to change a single syllable of that forlorn and lovely lyric would be like scratching the face of a little child.

It is one of the paradoxes of art that its very finest works are nearly always minor works. The pursuit of perfectness is incompatible with the ambition for amplitude, and a vast creation can seldom be completely fine. A cameo is a more perfect thing than a cathedral; and lovers of all that is most delicate in versification must turn to minor poets, like Catullus. The major poet can afford to be careless, but the minor poet is constrained to write perfectly if he is to write at all. With the major poet, mere art is a secondary concern; he may, indeed, be a great artist like Milton, or he may be a reckless and shoddy artist like Walt Whitman. But the minor poet loves art for the sake of art; he pursues perfection, and can rest content with nothing less faultless and less fine. Amid the drums and tramplings of all the great Elizabethan tragedies, there is no passage quite so perfect in pathetic delicacy as Austin Dobson's little lyric in dialogue entitled, *"Good night, Babette."*

Such exquisite minor works as this and all the others we have mentioned must be regarded as the little children of art. They awaken an affection that can never be inspired by those gigantic presences before which we bow our heads in awe. It is a great thing to strew roses in the triumphal path of Cæsar, but it is a sweeter thing to deck with daffodils the blown hair of some dancing little maid. In the autobiography of Benvenuto Cellini, we learn that the dearest heir of his invention was not the tall and agile Perseus that now takes the rain in Florence, but the precious little salt-cellar which now arrests the wanderer through many rooms in the vast museum of Vienna. In this minor work, the artist's medium was not bronze, but gold; he was not making a monument for multitudes to gape at, but was perfecting a tiny and a precious thing for the eyes of the enlightened few. In this regard, a minor work of art may be defined as a work of art designed for the minority.

In many modern languages, like French and German and Italian, the sweetest way of expressing endearment is through the use of a diminutive. "Mütterchen," in German, means not merely "little mother" but "dear little mother" as well; and when the younger Lippi was nicknamed Filipino, the name meant not so much "little Philip" as "the well-belovèd Philip." There is a famous passage in Dante's *Purgatory*, at the outset of the twenty-eighth canto, where the poet's keenness of affection for the perfect world is expressed by his appreciation of the little birds that sing on little branches in tree-tops swung lightly by a little breeze; and this succession of diminutives is like a reaching out of tiny fingers groping for the reader's hand.

Whoever has looked upon the sweetest painting in the world must know the love of little things. When you enter the tiny chapel of the Frari Church in Venice where the masterwork of Gian Bellini sits enshrined, you begin instinctively to walk in whispers. Your first impression is that of an ineffable serenity—a quiet that you must not interrupt. But this serenity arises partly from the fact that the Madonna is such a little lady, and that the winged musicians that stand listening beneath her throne are the youngest of the children of the angels. And her own child, despite his sturdiness of standing, seems such a little boy beside those dwarfed athletes that bulge their muscles in Raphael's cartoons. And the strips of landscape beyond the venerable saints open such enticing, tiny vistas of the earth. . . . Tintoretto may swoop roaring through immensity; but here is an artist whose heart was as a nest for all the sweet, winged wishes of the world. He reminds you of little children kneeling in the night and whispering "God bless . . ." to all the things that are.

Similarly, the devotees of the drama must always keep an open home within their hearts for the reception of the little children of this most adult of all the arts. There are certain plays that one would like to mention always with an Italian diminutive—with some such nickname as "Prunella," for example. There is no vastness and no grandeur in their structure—only an intimacy of little perfectnesses. One feels a bit afraid lest they might be seen by some one incapable of tenderness for tiny things. To this category must be assigned that exquisite dramatic poem of Alfred de Musset, *A Quoi Rêvent les Jeunes Filles;* and in this same context the reader must also be invited to consider such a fantasy as *Prunella*, by Mr. Laurence Housman and Mr. Granville Barker.

Prunella is a young maiden who lives immured in a little house and garden with three forbidding aunts, Prim, Privacy, and Prude. Along comes a company of strolling players, headed by Pierrot and Scaramel, who gain access to Prunella and awaken in her a longing to flee away into the mysterious and alluring world. Pierrot wins her love, and, aided by Scaramel and the others, abducts her from her prison-house at night. In the last act, after Pierrot has tired of her, she wanders home friendless and disenchanted. But Pierrot had learned [it is sweet to think he may have learned this little truth from Austin Dobson] that "love comes back to his vacant dwelling." His loneliness has taught him the value and the need of the old, old love that he knew of yore. Prunella once again becomes his Pierrette, and they look forward toward a life whose love is real.

This story is, in all essentials, the same story that was told in *Sister Beatrice;* but it lacks those overtones of eternity which Maeterlinck has imparted to his narrative. It was apparently the purpose of the authors of *Prunella* to emulate the pretty and witty art of such a piece as *Les Romanesques* of Edmond Rostand, but they lacked that brilliant exuberance of fancy which was demanded by their task. Every once in a while the authors permit us to regret that the piece could not have been written for them by Théodore de Banville or Austin Dobson. Several of Mr. Housman's lyric stanzas are delightful; but his handling of rhymed couplets is pedestrian, and the prose passages lack that illumination, as by a flock of fire-flies, that is desirable in a composition of this type.

XXIV

YVETTE GUILBERT—PREMIÈRE DISEUSE

THE STAGE is very empty; it is almost pitifully lonely. The back-drop [borrowed from some scenic storehouse] displays a conventional picture of a conventional French garden. There is no carpeting upon the bare boards of the platform. Forward, in one corner, a grand piano looks incongruously out of place; and at the instrument is seated a totally uninteresting man. The lights have been turned up, and a momentary hush has quenched the buzzing in the auditorium.

A woman enters through the wings, walks downward to the center of the stage; and at once the house is filled and thrilled with the sensation that this is one of the great women of the world. She is wearing a medieval costume—a robe to set you dreaming of the little church at Castelfranco and the magic carpet hung behind the head of the Virgin of Giorgione: but it is not the costume, but the woman wearing it, that has enchanted your attention. "She walks in beauty, like the night of cloudless climes and starry skies."

She has reached the center of the stage; she pauses and stands still; she is about to speak. A thousand ears instinctively yearn toward her. In a few sentences of finely chiseled French, she announces that she is going to render an old ballad of the people— a ballad of the fifteenth century—that tells the story of the birth of Christ. That is all; but, somehow, you have experienced already a drift of very great adventures. First, you have seen a woman walking greatly; and no other woman can do that, since Modjeska passed away. Next, you have seen a woman greatly standing still; and no other woman can do that, since *la* Duse, whom a nation called divine. Then, you have heard a woman speak; and you have been reminded of the goal of all your striving, ever since you were a little child and felt yourself first tortured by the imperious and yet elusive eloquence of words.

From the inconspicuous piano a few notes have been emitted;

and the great woman has begun to enunciate the words of the old ballad. The stage is not empty any longer; it will never be lonely any more. The silly old back-drop has faded quite away. The piano has become invisible. You are looking forth, in a wonderful clear night of stars, over the hushed housetops of the town of Bethlehem. From somewhere in the distance comes the high-pitched, thin, and drowsy call of the night-watchman droning forth the hour. You are back in the mysterious and dreaming East, where millions meditate upon the immanence of God—back in that year of years from which our time is dated. You see a heavy, weary woman toiling toward a tavern; you see her rebuffed rudely by a fat-pursed hostess; you share the timorous despair of her humble husband; you are relegated to the stable, and breathe the breath of cattle. There is a pause—a silence. Then, suddenly, there comes a chant as of a host of angels, trumpet-tongued, blaring forth the miracle of birth beneath the dancing of a million stars.

No play has ever made you conscious, with such keenness, of so much of human life; no music has ever given such wings to your imagination. You begin to wonder what has happened to you; you begin to realize that, in the drama of your own experience, the thrilling stage-direction has at last been written,—"Enter Art"! But, once again, the great woman pauses, and is silent, and stands still, and speaks. Next, she tells you, she will render an old-time ballad of the death of Christ. This ballad, in the sixteenth century, was chanted every Eastertide before the portals of all the great cathedrals of France. There is a silence, and a pause. "Including the Cathedral of Rheims," the artist adds: and you feel great tears welling up into your eyes.

Thence, forward through the centuries, she leads you through the history of France, projecting many ballads of the people, nearly all by nameless authors—some tragic, some poignantly pathetic, others charmingly alluring, others brightly gay. She changes her costume to suit the changes of the centuries; she alters her carriage, her gestures, the conduct of her voice, to suit the alterations of the moods that she imagines. But, every time, she seems to crowd the stage with many living people; and always she overwhelms the audience with the spirit of the piece that she is rendering.

You come away from her performance, swimming in a phosphorescent sea. For two hours you have worshiped in a temple where beauty is truth, truth beauty; and now you know that nothing else on earth is worth the knowing. You have been seeking, all your life, for Art; and at last you have met it face to face; and you are not afraid, but there is a terrible, sweet singing in your soul.

You have been reminded, in a single afternoon, of the great person that you meant to be when you were twenty-one; you have been enlisted, once again, in the little army of the good and faithful who labor evermore without discouragement to make the world more beautiful; you have been allured once more to such a love of the loveliness of language that you no longer hear the strident voices of the people in the street; you have been taught to imagine the possibilities of civilization; you have sold your soul to Art, and deemed the bargain generous.

There is no word in English for that medium of art of which Yvette Guilbert is the supreme and perfect master. It is not acting, it is not singing, it is not recitation; yet it combines the finest beauties of all three. It offers simultaneously an interpretation of literature and an interpretation of music; and it continually reminds you of what is loveliest in painting, in sculpture, and in dancing. The French call her a *diseuse*—that is to say, a woman who knows how to say things; and when we think how few people in the world this phrase could justly be applied to, we shall no longer wonder at the rarity of her performance.

The art of saying things, as exemplified by Madame Guilbert, has become, indeed, a synthesis of all the arts. Details have been selected from the methods of all the known media of expression and have been arranged in a perfectly concordant pattern. All the arts are merely so many different languages to give expression to the same essential entity; and this essential entity—which constitutes the soul of art—is rhythm. Painting, sculpture, and architecture make rhythmic patterns to the eye; music, poetry, and prose make rhythmic patterns to the ear. The art of Yvette Guilbert does both. By her bodily movements, her gestures, her facial expression, she makes patterns in space, to charm the eye; and by her enunciation of words and music, she makes patterns in time, to charm the ear. She has developed a universal language—a way of appealing simultaneously and with equal power to the deaf and to the blind.

The secret of her art is a mastery of rhythm—the quintessential element of all the arts that have ever been developed by mankind; and of this element her mastery is absolute. She is one of the great artists of the world—not only of our time but of all times. She belongs to that high company that is graced by Donatello, Gian Bellini at his best, Mozart, and Keats—the perfect masters of a finally perfected medium.

Her art, alas!, is not like theirs immortal, for the medium of her expression is the perishable temple of the human soul; but to us, who are privileged to see and hear her, the beauty that she bids to be appeals more poignantly because of the tragic sense that it is transient. It seems, indeed, an image of that "Joy, whose hand is ever at his lips, bidding adieu."

But Yvette Guilbert is not only a great artist, she is also a great woman; and this fact adds the final needed note to a performance that is necessarily so personal as hers. There are not so many really great people in the world that it can ever cease to be a privilege to come into their presence. She is a great woman, because—in Whitman's phrase—she "contains multitudes." She sits serene upon that height of civilization toward which uncounted generations have been toiling since the dawn of time; and, throned upon the summit, she "throws little glances down, smiling, and understands them with her eyes."

She is not only supreme in art; she is also supreme in personality. She seems to incorporate within herself the very essence of the nation that has engendered her. "Though fallen on evil days—on evil days though fallen, and evil tongues," a clear majority of living men still realize that there is such a thing as truth, and such a thing as beauty, and such a thing as right, and are ready to die for the idea that civilization is a better thing than barbarism. To all who are so minded, the most inspiring ideal that is tingling in the world to-day is the ideal of that beleaguered country that is holding firm the ramparts of the only world worth living in: that country of the neat and nimble speech, that country of sweet reason and unfathomable tenderness of heart, that country of liberty, equality, fraternity, that country which is the second home and foster-mother of all the artists of the world who meditate beneath the stars. All that this leader of the nations has to say seems summed up and expressed in the incomparable art of this incomparable woman. It is as if great France had blown a kiss to us across the seas.

DATE DUE

DATE DUE		
JUL. 1 2 1994		
JUL. 2 7 1994		
FEB 1 8		
DEC. 0 9 2002		
NOV 1 5 2006		
GAYLORD		PRINTED IN U.S.A.